Wilfred Cantwell Smith

THE MEANING AND END OF RELIGION

Foreword by

D1041706

Fortress Press ▪ Minneapolis

Smith –
idea list

THE MEANING AND END OF RELIGION

First Fortress Press Edition 1991

Library of Congress Cataloging-in-Publication Data

Smith, Wilfred Cantwell, 1916–
  The meaning and end of religion / Wilfred Cantwell Smith ;
foreword by John Hick.
    p. cm.
  Reprint. Originally published: New York : Macmillan,
c1962, 1963.
  Includes bibliographical references and index.
  ISBN 0-8006-2475-0
  1. Religion. 2. Religions. 3. Religion—Historiography.
4. Faith. I. Title.
BL48.S596 1991
200—dc20   90-44628
                                                                     CIP

The paper used in this publication meets the minimum requirements of American
National Standard for Information Sciences—Permanence of Paper for Printed
Library Materials, ANSI Z329.48-1984.   ∞™

Manufactured in the U.S.A.   AF 1-2475

95   94   93   92   91   1   2   3   4   5   6   7   8   9   10

equal –
To faith of other Men

Contents

Foreword

Wilfred Cantwell Smith's *The Meaning and End of Religion* has already become a modern classic of religious studies. Such a work should be continuously available, both to students and the general public, and its reissue now is to be warmly welcomed. Although I can add nothing whatever to the book itself, I am happy to have the privilege of pointing out its very great significance for some of our most lively current discussions and debates.

The originality of this book lies in the fact that it enables us to perceive the phenomena of religion in a new way. For Cantwell Smith makes us conscious of the intellectual spectacles, formed by our own culture, through which we have been seeing religious life; and he invites us to try the experiment of looking again without those spectacles. As recent work in the sociology of knowledge has emphasized, our ways of perceiving the world are profoundly affected by the concepts with which we select, group, and organize the multiplicity of events, assisting us to discern in them a coherent meaning which our language can express. And Cantwell Smith points out in this book that the grid through which human religious life is customarily seen today does not represent the only, or in his estimate the most fruitful, way of perceiving this area of reality.

The practical importance of Cantwell Smith's proposed conceptual and perceptual shift lies in the fact that it avoids a tangle of intractable problems created by the old way of thought and perception. The spectacles which we are invited to discard are those through which we see the religious life of humanity as divided into a number of theological and historical complexes called Christianity, Judaism, Islam, Hinduism, Buddhism, Sikhism, Zoroastrianism, Confucianism, Shintoism, Taoism, and so on. To anyone brought up in the Western intellectual tradition, and perceiving the religious world in this way, it seems obvious that to be religious means to belong to one or another of these mutually exclusive groups, each based on its own proprietary gospel or system of beliefs. And from this starting point the central question for the religious person is inevitably: which is the true, or the truest, religion?

It has been axiomatic to Christians that Christianity is the true religion, and that others are at best varyingly less true. But this axiom, given the initial perceptual grid, has generated inevitable perplexities in which the Christian theology of religions has become hopelessly entangled. If God is the God of all humanity, why is the true religion, the right approach to God, confined to a single strand of human history, so that it has been unavailable to the great majority of the thousands of millions of human beings who have lived and died from the earliest days until now? If God is the Creator and Father of all, can God have provided true religion only for a chosen minority? Why, within God's providence, has humanity's religious life taken the pluralistic form which history shows us?

Such questions are to some extent muted, but not answered, by current theological theories that devout people of "other faiths" may have implicit faith, or may be regarded as anonymous Christians, or may receive salvation in the "ordinary" way available within the world religions, as distinquished from the "extraordinary" way available in the church. Such theories function as palliatives rather than as solutions, because it is integral to them that they offer the devout non-Christian only an interim status until eventually, in this life or beyond, he or she fully encounters Christ and comes to wholehearted Christian discipleship. And so the original question recurs as to why the loving Father of all has treated some (those born in Christian lands) as first-class and others (born in non-Christian lands) as second-class children. It does not suffice to answer that the Bible declares this, for an analogous problem arises concerning the Bible itself. Does it contain God's definitive and exclusive word about the entire human race, past, present, and future? Or does it, rather, consist of the scriptures of one tradition among many, and moreover written at a time before the world ecumenical issue had emerged?

Cantwell Smith's researches have the effect of gradually dismantling this complex of problems. He shows with full historical evidence that the concept of religions, as contraposed ideological communities, is a modern invention which the West, during the last two hundred years or so, has exported to the rest of the world, leading men and women of faith everywhere to think of themselves as members of one exclusive salvation-offering society against others. He shows that the notion of a religion as a particular system of belief embodied in a bounded community was unknown (apart from early adumbrations which he notes at the beginning of the Christian era) prior to the modern period. Neither the classical Sanskrit of the Hindu and the Mahayana Buddhist scriptures, nor the Pali of the Theravada Buddhist writings, nor ancient Egyptian, nor classical Chinese, nor the Hebrew of the Jewish scriptures, nor the Greek of the New Testament, has a word for our modern concept of religion or religions. These literatures speak of such living matters as faith, obedience and disobedience, piety, worship, the truth, and the way, but not of religions as communally embodied systems of belief. Nor within the European tradition did the Latin word *religio* mean a religion in our modern sense. The title of St. Augustine's *De Vera Religione* should not be translated as "On the True Religion" (i.e., Christianity in contrast to other religions), but as "On True Religiousness" or "True Piety." It was still true a thousand years later, when Zwingli wrote his *De Vera et Falsa Religione*, that the subject was not Christianity as the true religion in contrast to false religions, but rather the true or false *religio*, i.e., "piety," of Christians. Again, Calvin's great work, *Christianae Religionis Institutio* is not properly translated as "The Institutes of the Christian Religion," but as "The Foundations" or perhaps "Structures of Christian Piety." It was later, after the red-hot volcanic experience and thought of the great reformers had cooled into the abstract theological disputes of the seventeenth century, that the notion of a religion as a system of doctrines was effectively formed. There was soon joined to this the thought of the human population which professes and preserves these doctrines, so that by the eighteenth century the understanding of "religions" as alternative systems of belief embodied in mutually exclusive ideological communities had become accepted. The nineteenth century added the historical dimension, perceiving the phenomena now called Islam, Hinduism, Christianity, Buddhism, etc., as complex organisms, each with its own long history, which nineteenth- and twentieth-century scholarship has traced and studied in ever increasing particularity. The full account of this development of the modern Western concept of religions is presented by Cantwell Smith with lucidity and learning, many additional fascinating details being found in the numerous and often lengthy notes at the end of the book. The history shows how something adjectival, the qualities of man's response and relationship to the divine, became congealed in Western thought and language into something substantival, the supposedly rival entities known as Christianity, Hinduism, and so on.

As part of this historical picture, Western Christians usually had to invent names for the religions from which they hoped to convert the other peoples of the world. "Hinduism" and "Buddhism," for example, are Western terms for the religious life of the people of India and for the way of those deeply influenced by the Buddha. Again, Western travelers were often baffled to find that in China a person might "belong" to three different religions at once: Confucianism, Buddhism, and Taoism. It only gradually dawned on them that the Chinese did not perceive these, through Western spectacles, as alternative religions, but as something more analogous to three interpenetrating fields of force within the continuous religious life of China.

The special case of Islam, constituting a partial exception to this thesis, and particularly intriguing to Cantwell Smith as a leading expert on Islam, is discussed at length in a special chapter.

Islam apart, Smith notes that religions have generally first been named and treated as distinct entities by opponents and in a spirit of combat. The evidence shows, however, that in the East people have not naturally applied the concept of a religion, with its own name, to their own faith, and that in the West the Christian tradition began to be treated in this way only with the rise of scepticism and unbelief in the modern period.

In contemporary scholarship the reification of religions is today less and less favored. The various streams of religious life and tradition turn out on detailed study to be too internally diverse, too richly various, and too subject to historical change to be characterized usefully in terms of some enduring essence. It is not adequate to the almost infinitely complex facts to think that there are in the world unitary entities called Christianity, Buddhism, Hinduism, Islam, etc. And so Cantwell Smith recommends that we now try to abandon this way of thinking and speaking.

Running alongside the development of named religions there has emerged the concept of religion as a general notion within which the particular religions are specific instances, and much thought and scholarship has gone into the attempt to define its essential nature. The difficulty is that this can be done in many different ways, among which the choice of definition is a matter of comparatively free decision. Some of the definitions proposed are in terms of belief systems, others in terms of social function, others again in terms of psychological effect, and yet others again in terms of ethical standpoints and life-styles. Consequently some of those definitions include Buddhism, Confucianism, and Taoism among the religions, while others exclude one or more of these. Some definitions regard Marxism and Maoism as religions, while others do not. Thus one can delimit an area and stipulate that this, and only this, is to be called religion; but the procedure is inevitably arbitrary, and Cantwell Smith contends that it would be more realistic and more profitable to abandon the assumption that religion is a "thing" with its inherent boundaries waiting to be mapped out. For there are not only no religions as contraposed socio-theological entities, but also no religion as a definable essence. But if we are not to think in those terms, how are we to grasp the multifarious facts of the religious universe of discourse?

Cantwell Smith's suggestion is that we should speak of two different realities, which he calls faith and the cumulative traditions, these being the inner and outer aspects of human religious life. What he calls faith (and although the word has both unhelpful and appropriate connotations, it is nevertheless very difficult to find a better) is an individual's, or many individuals', relationship with the divine Transcendent, whether the latter be known as personal or non-personal, as one or as many, as moral or as non-moral, as gracious or as demanding. Faith in this sense includes religious experience, the sense of the numinous, religious emotions of love and awe, hope and fear, the disposition to worship, and the commitment of the will to the service of the higher reality and value. All this is an immediate, inner, personal, living, and "existential" participation in an experienced relationship with the greater, perhaps infinitely greater, and mysterious reality which in English we call God.

In speaking of this inner life of faith as the human end of the relationship with God one is, of course, using religious language, with its presupposition of the reality of the supposed divine object of faith. Whether that presupposition is justified or delusory is the central problem concerning religion. Is faith a response to a genuine transcendent reality, or is it merely a modification of human consciousness, induced by our hopes and fears, perhaps compensating for our economic or political status or developed to give us courage before the final boundary of death? These are genuine and open questions, and they are not prejudiced by use of the word "faith." On the contrary it has the merit of identifying the radically problematic area within the total religious sphere, and of distinguishing it from the historical area which Cantwell Smith calls the cumulative traditions. Thus, his distinction should be equally acceptable and useful to atheistic, agnostic, and religious thinkers.

The cumulative traditions, as distinct from inner personal faith, are problem areas in the quite different ways in which history is always in varying degrees problematic. For the cumulative religious traditions come within the domain of the historian, to whom they are equally available, whether or not the historian be of any religious persuasion. They consist in the cultural frameworks in which the life of faith has been and is expressed, the institutions, customs and laws, creeds, teachings, and theological systems of a particular community. It is always within such a tradition that faith arises, although the tradition is itself in turn always subject to change—sometimes revolutionary, but usually very gradual—under the reciprocal influence of the life of faith.

There is an important point here about which I may differ from Cantwell Smith. I have listed creeds and theologies among the elements of the cumulative traditions, whereas he discusses them in his chapter on faith as its intellectual expressions. On the other hand, he also says that "Theology is part of the traditions, is part of this world" (p. 185). I would like at this point to draw upon the philosophical distinction between first-and second-order languages. First-order religious language, as we find it in prayer and prophecy and proclamation, in the confession of sin and the spontaneous utterances of love and joy, and awe in the presence of the Lord, is the expression of faith. The language of theology, on the other hand, is a second-order language which treats the first-order expressions of faith as data to be interpreted in systematic theories. I think that this is not far from Cantwell Smith's view, if indeed it differs from his at all.

One valuable consequence of Cantwell Smith's "exploding" of religion into the living faith of men and women and the cumulative traditions within which faith occurs, is to make it easier to see and accept the changing and diverse historical character of these traditions. Each distinguishable tradition has in fact undergone immense development through the centuries, and each is still developing in ways which are sometimes predictable but often quite unpredictable. The Christian tradition, for example, has produced an immense richness of differentiation in both time and space. Indeed, the state of the tradition into which Christians are born today in, say, New York might well be unrecognizable from the point of view of a Christian formed within the tradition of second-century Rome. And there are comparable contrasts between the Buddhist tradition in India in the century after Gautama's death and in, say, Japan today; or between the Hindu tradition before and after the writing of the *Bhagavad Gita;* or the Muslim tradition in Arabia at the time of the Prophet and in a West African Sufi community today; or between the Sikh tradition before and Gobind Singh—and so on.

Some of the main effects, then, of Cantwell Smith's experiment in re-conceptualization are: (1) to release us from the notion of the religions as contraposed socio-theological entities, and so from the unprofitable question, Which of these is the true religion? (2) to identify the religiously all-important, and at the same time philosophically problematic, area of inner personal faith and experience; (3) to free study of the cumulative traditions from monolithic illusions, thus allowing the rich detailed variety to show itself, not only between traditions but also within each tradition. The first two of these consequences further opens up vast issues concerning, for example, the relationship between faith and truth and the cultural traditions, some of which are treated by Cantwell Smith in his other books—particularly *Questions of Religious Truth* (1967), *Belief and History* (1977), *Faith and Belief* (1979), and *Towards a World Theology* (1981).

In his proposed shift of categories Cantwell Smith in effect consolidates the developments during several decades of scholarly study in the religious life of the various peoples of the world. He may well have been optimistic in hoping for an early reform of our terminology. Such changes can take a long time. The influence of this book and its central thesis is visible already in a number of diverse fields, whose often widely separated developments are seldom affected by one and the same work; this is perhaps especially the case among younger writers—philosophers of religion, historians of religion and of particular traditions, Christian and Jewish theologians, sociologists, anthropologists, and also modern thinkers of Asian communities of faith, Buddhist, Hindu, Muslim, and other. But even if we have to continue to speak of the various named religions and of religion in general, because these terms are so firmly embedded in the literature, no one who has been influenced by *The Meaning and End of Religion* can do so without an acute sense of the often profoundly misleading character of the language. And we may anticipate that in due course the changes now in process will become general, and that religious existence will be seen both in its inner life of faith and in the outer life of the various cumulative traditions.

JOHN HICK

CHAPTER ONE

Introduction

WHAT IS RELIGION? What is religious faith?

Such questions, asked either from the outside or from within, must nowadays be set in a wide context, and a rather exacting one. The modern student may look upon religion as something that other people do, or he may see and feel it as something in which also he himself is involved. In either case he approaches any attempt to understand it conscious not only of many traditional problems but also of new complications. Sensitive men have ever known that they are dealing here with a mystery. Some modern investigators have thought to strip the phenomena of any transcendent reference, to explain by explaining away. Yet their explanations, however persuasive each one might sound at first, have proven mutually discordant. They have left the sensitive still in the presence of an open element, unknown or undominated, but one that is surrounded now with a formidable range of new data bearing on the matter in an elaborate and perplexing way.

Many considerations, then, must be taken into account in any analysis that is to satisfy a serious modern inquirer. We may enumerate four or five as among the more weighty. First, of course, there is science. This impinges both in a general and in several particular ways. It is relevant in its broadest coverage, as signifying the growing body of knowledge about the empirical universe in all its sweep; as signifying further the method and mood of attaining that knowledge; as signifying also the practical mastery that it imparts. It is relevant also more specifically in so far as particular studies such as psychology, sociology, economic history, and also the *ad hoc* sciences of *Religionswissenschaft* have seemed to illuminate the ostensibly religious behaviour of man. Science radically modifies life intellectually and practically for all men, including those who would live it morally and spiritually; as well as modifying the scholar's understanding of its processes.

Secondly, there is the multiplicity of religious traditions. In addition to a myriad of lesser groups, there are on earth not one but at least four or five major religious communities each proclaiming a faith with a long and impressive, even brilliant, past and with the continuing creative allegiance of mighty civilizations. This is known in theory; the knowledge is today supplemented in practice by personal contact and widespread social intermingling. Any adequate interpretation of a Christian's faith, for instance, must make room for the fact that other intelligent, devout, and moral men, including perhaps his own friends, are Buddhists, Hindus, or Muslims.

Somewhat related to this consideration is the further fact of diversity within each tradition. Every faith appears in a variety of forms. Regarded from another angle, this may be seen as a problem of authority: the multiplicity of guidance with which modern man is faced religiously, which may approximate to an absence of guidance. It is no longer easy or even possible to have a religious faith without selecting its form.

Next may be noted the sheer fact of change. The world is in flux, and we know it. Like other aspects of human life, the religious aspect too is seen to be historical, evolving, in process. Any modern endeavour to clarify what religion is, must now include a question as to what at various stages of development religion has been. And if it does not venture on some speculation as to what it may become in the future, at least there is recognition that, like everything else that we know on earth, religion may be expected to continue to change.

Finally, we would mention the vitality of faith. The problems besetting a satisfactory understanding of religion are increasingly evident. Yet religion itself continues, and in many parts of the world appears perhaps to be resurgent. For a time some thought that the onslaught of science, comparative religion, uncertainty, and the rest—in a word, the onslaught of modernity—meant or would mean the gradual decline and disappearance of the religious tradition. This no longer seems obvious. The outside student in his attempt at explanation must reckon with the fact that, despite all 'debunking', men find in religion something outweighing the critics' charges. From within, the man of faith must strive to attain some exposition of that faith that will do justice to the values that, even in the modern world, are being made available to him.

Though this continuing or renewed vitality is general, it is also particular. One has not understood religion if one's interpretation is applicable to only one of its forms. On the other hand, neither has one understood religion if one's interpretation does justice only to some abstraction of religiousness in general but not to the fact that for most men of faith, loyalty and concern are not for any such abstraction but quite specifically and perhaps even exclusively for their own unique tradition—or even for one section within that. The Christian and the Muslim must be seen, certainly, in a world in which other men are Hindus, Buddhists, and Jews. Yet inter-religious and even intra-religious strife and disdain, and certainly difference, as well as any common characteristics that may be discovered, are significant and may be crucial. There is no *a priori* reason for holding that the unique may not be more significant, more true, than the common. The student must be careful lest he glibly decide before he starts that the differences between the various communities are either considerably

more or else considerably less important than the similarities—
thereby taking sides, in a facile and perhaps unconscious fashion,
on one of the most profound of religious issues. On this as on
other points, no analysis of religion is serviceable even for purposes of discussion if it is manifestly subordinate to one of the
great questions with which it should deal.

On these, then, and on other scores it has been easy for studies
of the religious quality of man's life and the religious aspect of his
history to fall short of adequacy. The philosopher of religion has
formulated interpretations that are at times penetrating and may
be brilliantly conceived; but to them the historian of religion
musters specific and stark exceptions. The historian of religion
has offered descriptions that may be meticulously accurate as to
detail; but in them the man of faith does not recognize the substance of that in which he is involved. The believer has propounded views that have the virtue of depth and genuineness;
but they are relevant or intelligible only to those within the same
or a similar tradition. The psychologist or sociologist has probed
the externals or the aberrations of faith; but has missed the heart
of the matter that has kept the externals living, or the norms from
which the abnormal, perhaps all too readily, deviates. The insider
knows something precious within the materials that he uses, but
cannot assimilate the external truths about those materials that
an observer has carefully ascertained and can convincingly document.

The rich panorama of man's religious life over the centuries
presents the observer with a bewildering variety of phenomena,
and the studies of those phenomena present him with a cacophony
of interpretation. Those who would understand, and those who
would intelligently participate, are confronted with a task of no
mean proportions.

ﮞﮞ
ii

Indeed, an argument can be made that the whole enterprise is inherently impossible or illegitimate. Any attempt to make a rational or scholarly study of religion, some have held, is foredoomed. Clearly I do not find these arguments convincing, or I would not write this book. Presumably those who take the trouble to read or even to glance at it are also not committed to a negative position of this kind. Nevertheless, although we may not find such views finally cogent, neither should we find them absurd. There is much to be said for approaching not merely with caution but with hesitation and even something akin to awe what some, with but careless rhetoric, have called 'this field of study'. In this case the analogy of a field can be misleading. No matter how extensive, how difficult to encompass, a field yet lies at our feet, to be surveyed and in the end dominated. The subject matter of our study, on the other hand, is not so abject or supine, not to be so paced upon by a would-be surveyor. It has been said that one must tread softly here, for one is treading on men's dreams. Furthermore, what we view in contemplating man's religion lies not only below us, stretching on and on without bounds, but around us and within us and above us. And not only does it lie, passively; here is something active, momentous, with its own initiative.

There are three main groups from whom comes a challenge to any scholarly inquiry into religion. First there are those who would disdain comparative or empirical study on the grounds that the elucidation of religion's meaning and nature, and an insight into its functioning and processes, is to be obtained only from a knowledge of Christianity—or of Islam, or whatever is one's own faith—as representing religion at its highest, or the only true religion. Such men would hold that to consider other religions as well, is to falsify and distort, rather than to enlarge one's understanding; that one gains in breadth by sacrificing both depth

5

and truth; that an understanding of roses is not enhanced by a study of rosettes.

As a criticism of the nonbeliever, this is not irrelevant. Even those who do not share such a conviction must treat it with respect. All should concede this much, that a person who has not seen the point of any one religion is not in the best position to generalize about the significance of them all.

Our answer to this point will develop only gradually, in the course of our argument. Part of it is that one need not accept the *either/or* dichotomy of those who thus contend that one should study Christianity (or, Islam; etc.) *rather than* religion in general. One may, and should, study both the Christian and the Islamic and the other individual traditions, so that ultimately one's interpretation may do justice not only to the insight or force or validity of one faith but at the same time to the facts of all.

It may also be objected that an understanding of Christianity is impossible except for those who have faith in it, that only a Muslim can understand Islam, and the like. This objection too must be taken very seriously. Again our answer will emerge only as we proceed. It will in part run along the lines of suggesting that the issue may be formulated differently, in a way that both sharpens the problem and makes possible a solution.

Secondly, a study of the world's religious life in its embracing variety can be decried also from quite another pole: not that it is beneath one's dignity, but that it is above one's competence. This argument would have it that in some degree all religions (and not only one's own) deal with what is holy, transcendent, infinite; and that therefore the attempt to subject them to rational analysis, empirical investigation, comparison, and human interpretation is not only impious but vain.

By accusations of irreverence modern man, particularly scientific man, is not much deterred: he will scrutinize all that is before him, sacrosanct or no. But before the other half of this charge he must, if honest, pause: that his scrutiny of holy things is vitiated by the inherent inappropriateness of the method to the material.

Religious men have charged that the objective study of religion leaves out the very part of religion that counts; it analyses the externals but misses the core of the matter, studying the only aspect of religious history that is available for study—namely, the mundane manifestations—but neglecting, or not understanding, or anyway unable to deal effectively with, the only part that essentially signifies. The student must be warned lest, from a study of the symbols, he come, perhaps with painstaking brilliance, to conclusions that are true but, so far as concerns the references of those symbols, irrelevant; or if he confuses the symbols with what is symbolized, then to conclusions that are absurd.

The irreverent, even insensitive, studies of certain scholars have done little to refute this. Such scholars might uncharitably be compared to flies crawling on the outside of a goldfish bowl, making accurate and complete observations on the fish inside, measuring their scales meticulously, and indeed contributing much to a knowledge of the subject, but never asking themselves, and never finding out, how it feels to be a goldfish.

A converse of this same argument may be advanced from the scientific side, in protest against an academic study of the world's religions. Objectors in this case also recognize, at least tacitly, the transcendence of the "spiritual"; their position is that that transcendence—or unbridledness—does not invalidate the conclusions so much as it disqualifies the undertaking *ab initio*. The religious may argue that the student of religion should have, in addition to objective accuracy and precise external knowledge about religious processes, also imaginative sympathy, appreciative understanding, and even experiential participation in them. The scientists, less concerned with whether he should have these, note that anyway he often does, sometimes all too generously; and may infer that thereby he forfeits a claim to a place in academic precincts, a claim to scholarliness in his studies.

It is urged, then, on the one hand that any scholarly study of religion is inherently inadequate, or on the other that any study of religion is inherently unscholarly. From whichever side it may come, the disturbing indictment is voiced that a study of religion from within an academic center threatens to undermine either the precious heritage of ultimates at the heart of the world's faiths, or the hard-won heritage of scholarship and science built up in recent centuries and now embodied in the tradition of the universities.

I stress these difficulties because, as I have said, I feel it important that one enter on this study with a due sense of trepidation. It is well that one should realize what one is attempting. Where only angels tread, he would be a fool to rush in; though perhaps the wise may preserve their dignity if, aware of their presumption, they enter cautiously.

· · ·
iii

For we must be humbled but not daunted by the dangers that the enterprise faces. Despite the pitfalls, today the task is not merely in the final analysis legitimate but immediately important and urgent. We need today more adequate understanding of religion, other people's as well as our own, than has been generally available if we are to meet at all adequately the human problems that press upon our modern world.

The two most fundamental questions confronting twentieth-century man, the one social, the other personal, both involve religion: how to turn our nascent world society into a world community, on a group level; and on a personal level, how to find meaning in modern life. To neither of these, of course, is the answer even primarily intellectual; and yet it is perhaps not fatuous to suggest that adequate answers will require *inter alia* an understanding of religion more clarified and effective than is now to hand.

On the latter, personal, question of meaning the traditional religions have answers in their traditional forms. Yet many a modern finds himself precluded from grasping those answers because, in their traditional form, he cannot comprehend them. Perhaps one might say, he cannot let himself be comprehended by or within them. On the former, community, question the answers have yet to be worked out. We have yet to learn our new task of living together as partners in a world of religious and cultural plurality. The technological and economic aspects of 'one world', of a humanity in process of global integration, are proceeding apace, or at least are receiving the attention of many of our best minds and most influential groups. The political aspects also are under active and constant consideration, even though success here is not so evident, except in the supremely important day-to-day staving off of disaster. The ideological and cultural question of human cohesion, on the other hand, has received less attention, and relatively little progress can be reported, even though in the long run it may prove crucial, and is already basic to much else. Unless men can learn to understand and to be loyal to each other across religious frontiers, unless we can build a world in which people profoundly of different faiths can live together and work together, then the prospects for our planet's future are not bright.

On the personal side as well, however, it is important also to place some stress. A world that has read Darwin, Marx, Fraser, and Freud; that has known the evil of Nazism, and of dropping two atomic bombs; that has seen the vistas from Mt. Palomar, and witnessed the opening of the space age—this world is open for a new understanding of religion that will enable it without subterfuge, hypocrisy, or anachronism to respond to a transcendent and concerned reality.

Some would agree that the world community must have some religious basis, conceding that a lasting and peaceful society cannot be built either by men without faith, or by men of clashing faiths unreconciled. They might go on to hold, however, that the only remedy is if their own one tradition prevail. They allow no possibility that diverse groups should come to effective mutual understanding and acceptance. No doubt to some, it would seem nice if all men were Roman Catholics, or Communists, or liberal universalists, or if all men would agree that religion does not really matter, or that it should be kept a private affair. Apart, however, from those that find such a vision inherently less appealing, many others will agree that for the moment its realization seems in any case hardly likely. And even the evangelist missionary must in the modern world learn to respect and to understand other men's faith which he wishes to see superseded. Neither religious conviction nor judicious observation can gainsay the need for a better understanding of religious faith, including faith that one does not hope to share.

Coexistence, if not a final truth of man's diversity, would seem at least an immediate necessity and, indeed, an immediate virtue.

The fact that men worship God in different ways, and apprehend God in different ways, the fact that even the most secular-minded of men live within societies based, *inter alia,* on men's worshipping and apprehending God in different ways, are facts, of course, of intellectual and spiritual significance, posing intellectual and spiritual problems that cry for attention. Yet that men worship and apprehend God at all, and that they do so in different ways, are facts also of economic and political and of agricultural and medical and industrial importance. Spending some time in the halls of the United Nations or in the coffeeshops of Lahore will convince one that the march of events has thrust upon all men, with immensity and urgence, the kind of problem with which the comparative study of religion attempts to deal.

Yet in insisting that comparative religion is concerned with problems that have practical immediate implications, even for nonreligious men, I am by no means endeavouring to sidestep the fact that the questions that it raises are primarily of intellectual and spiritual import. It is a religious problem, and I believe that religious people must face it. The man of faith can no longer get by by dismissing it with one of the traditional trite answers: namely, that all religions other than one's own may be ignored; or, that all religions are essentially the same; or, that all religions other than one's own are wrong. I will not take time here to dispose of these answers, merely commenting that none of them is able to stand up to simple observation—particularly the observation of a man who has members of other faiths as his friends.

I would even make bold to say that the future progress of one's own cherished faith even within one's own community, depends more largely than most of us have realized on the ability to solve the question of comparative religion. Unless a Christian can contrive intelligently and spiritually to be a Christian not merely in a Christian society or a secular society but in the world; unless a Muslim can be a Muslim in the world; unless a Buddhist can carve a satisfactory place for himself as a Buddhist in a world in which other intelligent, sensitive, educated men are Christians and Muslims—unless, I say, we can together solve the intellectual and spiritual questions posed by comparative religion, then I do not see how a man is to be a Christian or a Muslim or a Buddhist at all.

iv

The problem, then, is important. The difficulties, however, remain and are not exorcised by the worthiness or urgency of the endeavour. One must not allow the desirability of faith or the desperation of bleak alternatives to excuse one from recognizing and wrestling with the problems. Advance must be made, but we do well to remind ourselves that many brilliant and careful thinkers have set themselves the task of trying to define religion—both religious believers writing from within a given tradition, and outside observers or critics. Yet they have failed to satisfy each other, and none of their suggestions has commanded wide acceptance. It is perhaps not presumptuous to hold that no definition of religion so far proposed has proven compelling, no generalization has come anywhere near to adequacy.

My suggestion is that this in itself may throw some light on the kind of thing with which we are dealing.

Rather than hoping, perhaps presumptuously, to succeed with some *tour de force* where others, better equipped, have had but partial success, I would suggest that it would seem wise to try to learn from the limitations of their attempts. The situation until now may well indicate that the time has come when advance might be made by a quite new orientation, by considering more cautiously and comprehensively the quality of the special difficulties that pertain, by asking new kinds of question and looking for different sorts of result.

The present essay explores the possibility of clearing the ground for a quite new attack on the problems by revising the framework within which the questions are asked. Rather than addressing ourselves to the problem 'What is the nature of religion?', I suggest that an understanding of the variegated and evolving religious situation of mankind can proceed, and indeed perhaps can proceed only, if that question in that form be set aside or dropped, as inapt.

Similarly with any particular tradition: I will bring forward reasons for suggesting that a Christian can come to an adequate understanding of his faith, or a Muslim of his, and indeed, either of them to an understanding of each other's, only if he extricate himself from a concern as to the essence or nature of Christianity or Islam, only if he shift his attention away from questions such as 'What is true Christianity?', 'What is real Islam?' Both the Indologist and the Hindu are seriously distracted, if not misled, by the notion 'Hinduism'.

Neither religion in general nor any one of the religions, I will contend, is in itself an intelligible entity, a valid object of inquiry or of concern either for the scholar or for the man of faith.

At the very least, I would suggest that a radical reappraisal of our conceptualization may prove rewarding; that a rigorous re-examination of our presuppositions may be a clue to some of the understanding that we seek. It has often happened in the history of human knowledge that men's most dramatic advances have come when they have asked for less—or for what, at least for the moment, seemed less. By holding in suspense large questions that were proving recalcitrant, and learning to frame new and smaller ones more amenable to the data at hand, they have sometimes made partial advances along a line of inquiry that has seemed blocked, and even have sometimes found later that they had unwittingly turned the flank of the major obstacle that had seemed to stand in their way but that proved eventually to have been but the projection of their own misconceptions.

In the present instance, however, because the concern is religious, in abandoning these traditional questions one must learn to ask smaller questions but at the same time also larger ones. To look for 'religion' is to ask too much, and at the same time too little. Faith is concerned with something, or Someone, behind or beyond Christianity, or Buddhism. Scholarship must be satisfied with something less, but must make room for that out-reaching faith.

To do this, we are suggesting, scholarship must reformulate its own capacities and limitations, refraining more modestly from attempting to impose its limitations on faith, and recognizing more clearly to what its capacities are relevant. At the same time, faith must recapture its larger vision.

I hope that I have said enough to make it clear that in proposing to alter or abandon what have seemed the central questions of both scholarship and faith, I do not mean to evade the issues with which those questions were meant to deal. Diversion from matters of basic significance to minutiae would serve only petty purposes; possible advance in erudition at such a price would be exorbitantly bought. On the contrary, however, a readjustment of one's thinking is validated in so far as it enables one to cope with those very considerations that previously proved stubborn but important. It is the *engagé* participant, involved in the sustained endeavour to understand his own tradition (in my case, the Christian), and the serious student, involved in a sustained endeavour to understand one or more traditions other than his own (in my case, primarily the Islamic), that find themselves increasingly forced by the data before them to modify the presuppositions on which their basic questions were originally framed.

A new orientation is no improvement unless it is of service to the Christian or the Muslim apparently faced with the choice of either discovering, at least approximately, the true nature of Christianity or Islam and committing himself to it within the alarums and tumults of mid-twentieth-century life or else of abandoning it as an ideal. A new approach deserves to be taken seriously only if it is professionally helpful to the outside student at work on the academic problem of attempting to discover what Buddhism or Islam or Christianity really is—though also to the student who, as an outsider, yet has Buddhist or Muslim or Christian friends in a deep sense and is therefore personally involved in their ultimate but existential concern for the same question.

It is not through neglecting the issues with which such men are confronted but rather in closely wrestling with the problem posed, that one begins to see that the questions asked do not really mean what one has been brought up to suppose that they meant. One must then be willing to revise, but not to abandon, one's pursuit of understanding.

Even so, the sense of liberation that ensued on discovering finally how much more meaningful it is to ask a different type of question, would be counterbalanced by a reluctance to urge so radical a revision in the prevailing conceptions on such fundamental matters, did one not also discover on inquiry that the prevailing conceptions of our generation are of relatively recent origin, that only slowly and of late have our minds become prisoners to the kind of thinking that has proven itself inadequate to deal with the phenomena before us.

Let us therefore turn to examine historically the rise of some of the ideas that have come to dominate our fundamental thinking in this area.

CHAPTER TWO

'Religion' in the West

IT IS CUSTOMARY nowadays to hold that there is in human life and society something distinctive called 'religion'; and that this phenomenon is found on earth at present in a variety of minor forms, chiefly among outlying or eccentric peoples, and in a half-dozen or so major forms. Each of these major forms is also called 'a religion', and each one has a name: Christianity, Buddhism, Hinduism, and so on.

I suggest that we might investigate our custom here, scrutinizing our practice of giving religious names and indeed of calling them religions. So firmly fixed in our minds has this habit become that it will seem perhaps obstreperous or absurd to question it. Yet one may concede that there is value in pausing occasionally and examining ideas that we otherwise take for granted. Let us consider how and where this way of viewing human life arose, and how it has developed and how it has spread. Let us think about its implications, discovering if we can what is involved in thinking in this way. We may then be in a position to consider a question of whether or how far it is valid. In what ways does this analysis of human life clarify, and in what ways does it perhaps distort?

Retaining the historical treatment, we may rephrase the last question pragmatically. After surveying the route by which we have traveled to our present thinking on these matters, one may hope to be in a better position to see what the next constructive step in the continuing process may legitimately be. For with an historical perspective it will be seen that my proposals are not so radical or disruptive as they might appear. Rather than subverting a fixed position, they are offered as carrying forward a development. And if the new direction proposed seem at first an abrupt change, this is only in order to salvage the development from an impasse into which it has recently been sidetracked. What appears for the moment as a revolutionary reversal will be seen as rather a return to the long-range lines of classical advance.

The recent meeting of religious faith with rationalistic and then scientific inquiry, and the increasing meeting among diverse traditions of faith, have led to a temporary confusion of terms and beclouding of issues. These meetings have set our new problem but have first muddled our means of grappling with it. By seeing more clearly what has been happening to our thinking, we may be enabled to disentangle intellectually the various elements in the present situation, so that each may more easily move forward with renewed vitality.

Our method will begin with simply a verbal inquiry. For the way that we use words is a significant index of how we think. Also, more actively, it is a significant factor in determining how we think. To understand the world, and ourselves, it is helpful if we become critical of the terms and concepts that we are using. Further, to understand other people and other ages, it is requisite that we do not presume uncritically that their meanings for words are the same as ours. A mature history of ideas must rest on a careful scrutiny of new words, and also of new developments in meanings for old words. Once attained, it may further our realistic understanding of the world itself.

Three levels are here involved. First, there are the words that men use. Secondly, there are the concepts in their minds, of which these words are the more or less effective expression. Thirdly, there is the real world, of some aspects of which the concepts are the more or less adequate representation[1].

We must be alert lest, out of casualness or lack of historical perception, we fail to notice changes in word usage that may be quite significant, so that we read back into the past what are actually our innovations. We must be alert also lest we fail to grasp how the ideas behind even the same words vary, in subtle or profound ways, from thinker to thinker, from century to century, from community to community—so that we read into other people's minds ideas out of ours. Finally, and most exacting, we must be alert lest the concepts that either they or we have in our minds be taken as axiomatically valid, so that we read our ideas into the universe rather than vice versa.

In the next two chapters we shall consider the names of the individual religions, and the idea that each of these latter is in some sense an entity, deserving a name. Self-consciousness here is overdue.

At present, let us consider the word and the concept 'religion' itself.

The term is notoriously difficult to define. At least, there has been in recent decades a bewildering variety of definitions; and no one of them has commanded wide acceptance. In some cases of this sort, a repeated failure to agree, to reach any satisfying answer or even to make any discernible progress towards one, has turned out to mean that men have been asking a wrong question. In this instance one might argue that the sustained inability to clarify what the word 'religion' signifies, in itself suggests that the term ought to be dropped; that it is a distorted concept not really corresponding to anything definite or distinctive in the objective world. The phenomena that we call religious undoubtedly exist. Yet perhaps the notion that they constitute in themselves some distinctive entity is an unwarranted analysis.

It is not necessary, however, to be so hasty. The conclusion is too massive to rest on so delicate a foundation. An alternative suggestion could be that a failure to agree on definitions of religion may well stem from the quality of the material. For what a man thinks about religion is central to what he thinks about life and the universe as a whole. The meaning that one ascribes to the term is a key to the meaning that one finds in existence. To hope to reach any agreement, then, is perhaps to look for a consensus on ultimate questions of man, truth, and destiny. Social scientists and philosophers are naïve if they imagine that these questions can be answered easily, or that unanimity lies close within our reach.

Later I intend to propose a way of looking at religious phenomena that does not attempt to locate their essence, and that seems to me consequently serviceable perhaps for the questions that arise. However, we leave that aside for the moment. In the meantime I suggest that the inevitable particularism of any man's conception of 'religion' can in itself be turned to very profitable use. For what men think of 'religion', since they have begun to think about it, is as we have said highly illuminating as to their total orientation to life; it can become a major clue to their total thinking. If we can become self-conscious of our own limitations here, and aware of other peoples' particular attitudes, we shall have enlarged the horizon of our understanding.

First, we must note that what we call 'religion' is of much wider prevalence and of much longer standing than is the use of this term, or indeed of any other term, to designate it. In every[2] human community on earth today, there exists something that we, as sophisticated observers, may term religion, or a religion. And we are able to see it in each case as the latest development in a continuous tradition that goes back, we can now affirm, for at least one hundred thousand years[3]. Man is everywhere and has always been what we today call 'religious'. Yet there are today and have been in the past relatively few languages into which one can translate the word 'religion'—and particularly its plural, 'religions'—outside Western civilization. One is tempted, indeed, to ask whether there is a closely equivalent concept in any culture that has not been influenced by the modern West. I think that the answer to this is 'no', with the partial and highly interesting exception of Islam. And we shall later touch on the possibility that Islam has been an exception partly because of a link with Jewish-Christian developments at its rise.

This much at least is clear and is crucial: that men throughout history and throughout the world have been able to *be* religious without the assistance of a special term, without the intellectual analysis that the term implies. In fact, I have come to feel that, in some ways, it is probably easier to be religious without the concept; that the notion of religion can become an enemy to piety. One might almost say that the concern of the religious man is with God; the concern of the observer is with religion. This is too quippish; yet it is not absurd. For the religious man in less so-phisticated societies or of less mature piety one would have to substitute less absolute references than 'God' in this aphorism. Such a man is concerned with the divine as mediated—through the fetish, the ritual, the doctrines, or whatever. Again, in some traditions a less personal reference for the Absolute than 'God' would be required. In any case, it is not entirely foolish to suggest that the rise of the concept 'religion' is in some ways correlated with a decline in the practice of religion itself.

This is of course still too gross. Let us look at the matter more closely.

ii

The word is originally from the Latin *religio*, a term that even-tually was used in a great variety of senses, even by a single writer, without precision. In any case its pristine significance, continuing at least until Roman religious and other life came under the pow-erful and transforming influence of Greece, was much more re-stricted and specific than what it came to mean later. Modern scholars[4] are divided as to whether it first designated a power outside man obligating him to certain behaviour under pain of threatened awesome retribution, a kind of tabu, or the feeling in man vis-à-vis such powers[5] (or, indeed, whether the religious connotations are secondary developments from an originally secular word[6]). The difference between the former two can easily become blurred, since these powers, we as outsiders would hold, were conceived subjectively—though they were believed, or felt, to reside in some objective thing or practice. Thus that in which 'mana' was felt to dwell, and the person whose scrupulousness towards it was vivid, were each termed *religiosus*. There were *religiosae locae,* sacred places; and *viri religiosi,* reverent or devout persons careful in the conscientious fulfilment of the corollary prescriptions.

Over against the luxuriant and loose development of the meaning of the noun in later centuries, it is perhaps allowable to call attention here to the point that the Latin adjective had a considerably more stable history than did the substantive. This is perhaps because it is more legitimate, or at any rate more manageable, to think of these matters in terms of a quality of men's lives or a colouring of the world that they perceive, than in terms of some independent substance or entity. We shall consider later the notion that human history might prove more intelligible if we learned to think of religion and the religions as adjectives rather than as nouns—that is, as secondary to persons or things rather than as things in themselves.

To return: the early phrase *religio mihi est* is illuminating. To say that such-and-such a thing was *religio* for me meant that it was mightily incumbent upon me to do it (alternatively, not to do it: both are found, as is not unusual with 'mana', 'tabu', the holy, the sacred). Oaths, family proprieties, cultic observances and the like were each *religio* to a man; or, showing the ambivalence, one could equally say that to break a solemn oath is *religio,* that is, is tabu—as we might say, is sacrilegious.

Also the ritual ceremonies themselves were designated *religi-*

ones. Throughout Latin usage right to the end of its development, the sense of rite, the outward observance of a particular practice, is to be found. This is, perhaps, to be related to a Roman tendency to perceive what we would call the divine or the holy not so much, or not only, in the form of a figure or 'god' as in that of a series of standardized acts[7]. Whenever one meets the word in the later writers, the possibility must be borne in mind that this is what is meant. The *religio* of a specified god could then designate the traditional cultic pattern at his shrine.

This particular way of seeing and feeling the world has largely lapsed, and most of us today have become accustomed to a religious orientation that is quite different (whether we accept it or not). We therefore need considerable imagination to conceptualize the Roman situation wherein the cultic practice was in some significant ways more important, more holy, than the god. The word *religio,* referring to the ceremonies, consequently designated objectively what we tend to call the outward expression of a belief or attitude that for us is primarily directed elsewhere. Yet it accumulated the highly charged emotional connotation and subjective reference that we associate not primarily with the ritual but with the transcendent reality in whose name the ritual is observed.

By the first century B.C., Roman life had developed considerable sophistication; and under the impact of Greek thought, two important books were written significant for the development with which we are concerned. One was Lucretius's intense and stirring poem *De Rerum Natura* ('On the nature of things'), which welcomed scientific materialism as liberating man from the burden and terror of *religio*. The other was Cicero's *De Natura Deorum* ('On the nature of the gods'), which urbanely speculated not about religion itself but, as the title indicates, about what we would call the object of religion, the divine.

The important matter here one gets only incipiently. It does not come to fruition in Roman times, but is here adumbrated before lapsing again with the Augustan revival of the earlier Roman religious tradition and presently with the great sweep of the

Church. Yet though it remains but a suggestion, one does get something of that philosophic 'Enlightenment' in which the intellect stands aside from all religious behaviour and contemplates it as an outsider, reflective or critical.

There therefore emerges—but again, only incipiently—a new idea of religion, as a great objective something. It is thought of not as something that one does, or that one feels deeply about, or that impinges on one's will, exacting obedience or threatening disaster or offering reward or binding one into one's community, but for the first time as a theoretical entity of speculative interest, for conceptualization rather than decision—a generalization, abstracted, of something in which other people are involved.

In his long poem of over six thousand lines, Lucretius uses the word *religio* only eight times, and its plural six[8]; and in general he is perhaps more concerned, as his title indicates, to promote his vision of the world than to attack other people's. In some instances, here too the sense of religious practices, observances, is evident. In an arresting passage near the opening, however, which in some ways sets the tone for the whole poem, he virtually personifies *Religio* as a celestial being that glowers at mankind[9]. In this and perhaps three or four other places[10], the concept of religion as a Great Something is born.

One should note that the poet is attacking not actually the gods, whom he even invokes, but the way men have worshipped and feared them. Curiously, he calls these ways 'impious'[11], and in an impassioned, powerful passage[12] he portrays true piety not as the traditional rigmarole of Roman ritual but as an almost mystic quietude in nature.

Cicero, on the other hand, is concerned not with religion as a phenomenon but with the gods; and in so far as his work treats these from the standpoint of a human relation to them it is philosophers' ideas of the gods primarily, and not traditional religious practices, that are discussed. (Indeed, in the traditional religious practices of his society he is not much interested.) The term *religio* therefore occurs incidentally, although not infrequently. He presents the speakers in his imagined colloquium as using the word in more than one sense. That of the actual ritual is one, especially for the plural[13]; or perhaps more accurately (especially the singular), the performance of the ritual[14]. There is also, however, a distinctive tendency of his usage towards a personalism and subjectivism. Here *religio* is an attitude.

He has not only generalized but also very considerably softened the archaic meaning of *religio* as that awe that men felt in the presence of an uncanny and dreadful power of the unknown. Yet he preserves that orientation by thinking of it as a feeling, a quality of men's lives[15]. That *religio* is something within men's hearts is once directly indicated[16]. And in introducing what has remained ever since an important discrimination of 'religious' from 'superstitious' persons[17], he bases the distinction between the two on the attitude with which as worshippers they perform their observances[18].

Altogether, then, although it is incidental and indirect, Cicero's work contributed gently to the development of a notion of religion as a generic something in human life that is an attitude or practice of reverence and due diligence towards the gods. While Lucretius fortified the strand that used the term to refer to something 'out there' impinging on man, Cicero's designation was usually of something interior to persons.

iii

The next great development in the religious situation, reflected slowly and very partially in the development of an idea of religion, was a radical one. In the next few centuries something quite new in this realm emerged in the Mediterranean world, and eventually dominated it: namely, a systematic and organized community, which modernity looking back designates as the new religion of Christianity. It was new not only in content but in form. To use modern terms, this was a new kind of religion.

These were not the terms, however, in which those involved in the process at the time conceptualized what was happening. The idea that the Christian community introduced, a quite new notion covering a quite new phenomenon, was that of 'Church' (Greek and Latin, *ecclesia*), for the structured—and dynamic—community that was injected into the previously rather amorphous religious life of the Greco-Roman world. Men who previously had known (and a handful of whom had just begun to speculate a little about) a multitudinous congeries of religious practices relating mostly piecemeal to a diversity of gods, places, and occasions, now found themselves confronted or challenged by or living triumphantly within a new and large-scale order of systematized and coherent religious life.

Somewhat simultaneously other communities with new faith, formally comparable to the Christian or at least equally novel to the indigenous tradition, were being introduced from the Orient to the Roman world. We shall not examine their contribution to the development that we are tracing, merely noting that their presence confirmed the new and competitive situation that was beginning to obtain. The *either/or* quality of the novel situation was particularly important, introducing boundaries as a significant innovation.

As we have suggested, however, the concept of 'religion' did not altogether keep pace with the new evolution.

The Christian group, to verbalize the new life that they were experiencing and proclaiming, introduced in addition to *ecclesia* other elements of a new vocabulary. The most important was the new concept 'faith'[19]. In addition, however, they of course took over also a great many terms from the older religious life, which survive honourably until today: piety, reverence, devotion, divinity, ritual, chapel, to name a few from the Latin side. Among these was the word *religio*, which appears richly in Christian writing in Latin from the beginning.

Actually, until the fourth century it was used more than later. It would seem that there is perhaps a correlation between the

frequency of usage of this word and the historical situation of religious pluralism and rivalry, where there were many 'religions'
of which the Christian was one—a situation that had not been
known before in the Latin world and was not known again. By
the fifth century, when the Christian church had virtually elimi-
nated its rivals, the term was less actively in use, and in fact almost
disappeared. But in the meantime its meaning had evolved and
the word had become incorporated into the Christian tradition
from which modernity has inherited it, and we must therefore
observe what had happened.

All the early Fathers use the term[20]—in a variety of senses. As
we have seen, the word was already far from precise in its connotations. The new religious life of the Christians was distinguished from that relating to the traditional cultic observances of
the Roman world in many ways, not least in being far and away
more comprehensive. A distinguishing mark of the new faith was
that it ramified to every aspect of the believer's life, moral, social,
intellectual, as well as liturgical, in a way that was quite new. One
consequence was that the term *religio,* once the Christians adopted
it, quickly became more multi-faceted than ever, and took on
quite new depths. But it gained nothing in clarity.

The word continued to be used with its accustomed specific
references, particularly that to rites and observances[21]. This remained especially true of the plural, and is marked in the Christians' frequent use of it to designate the traditional practices of
the Greco-Roman cults which they condemned. In referring to
their own religious life, however, they developed the term more
richly. In this case too it served to specify the ritual practices, and
is even found in this sense in the plural. An innovating development from this, perhaps, was the use of *religio* to designate also
the structural organization of the Church, with its various ecclesiastical levels[22].

Yet alongside this form also, and one might say over against it,
the fact that the religious practices of the Church had unprece-
dentedly wide-ranging and profound implications for those who

used them, meant that the phrase *religio dei*, as signifying the worship of God, took on major new meaning. In addition, the writers can be seen carrying forward also the subjective sense: *religio* as the feeling on the part of the worshipper, his attitude to the Almighty and indeed to the universe as a whole. This included at times the old sense of awesome terror, now revived in a renewed vividness. Moreover, as in the new community men of faith found a new personal relationship to deity, *religio* became also the name of that relationship, the bond between God and man. Furthermore, in line with the new all-inclusiveness of this orientation, now and again one gets instances where the term seems to designate the whole complex of faith and practice indiscriminately, inner and outer, community system and personal piety. But this is incidental and rare.

There were in addition certain minor developments of a particular sort; such as, that from the fourth century *religio* is used 'as a title, addressed esp. to a bishop or other clergyman': 'your Holiness' or the like[23].

More interesting for our purposes are the tendencies that emerge from the new situation of religious pluralism. There was some recognition that however much the religious ways of those outside the Church might be 'astray'[24], yet a common human religiousness differentiates us from the brutes[25].

Much more pronounced, however, is the contrary emergence, of fateful consequence. In numerous instances, a meaning can be discerned that reflects the clash of religious systems and the new exclusivist situation—in which for the first time in this area the immensely significant notion was set forth that if it is right to worship God in one way then it is wrong to do so according to the alternative pattern of one's neighbours. This clear-cut choice superseding the previous unselfconscious coexistence of numerous patterns of worship and numerous objects of worship was for the Christian first not an intellectualist problem to be conceptualized but a dramatic existential one. To be a Christian meant to refuse to participate in the ceremonies of the traditional ritual, and often enough this meant to be put to death.

Martyrdom made it deep and clear that something new was abroad in the religious realm.

One of the first signs of this is the phrase *nostra religio* and its contrast *vestra religio, vestrae religiones*[26], from Arnobius. The contrast is expressed in more objective terms in *religio Dei* and *religio deorum*[27]. The second of each of these pairs should perhaps best be translated as 'your ritual practices', 'your way of worshipping', and 'the worship' or 'cult' 'of the gods'. *Nostra religio* I take as signifying 'our way of worshipping', as opposed to the way of worshipping of the pagans in which these writers refused to participate even as an outward formality. At times, however, it signified more than that. It would, I believe, be anachronistic to read into these phrases anything so inclusive as the modern 'our religion', 'their religion'—especially in the latter case: it was the purely ceremonial observance that was at stake. Nonetheless a significant step in the direction of such a concept had, evidently, been taken[28]. The new notion of boundaries is beginning to take shape: a *religio* of one set of people, clearly and radically distinct from the *religiones* of outsiders.

The next step, taken by Lactantius, is still more arresting. To express his conviction that the worship of God in the Christian Church's way is right, whereas observing the practices and ceremonies of the traditional cults is wicked, vain, and wrong, he introduces the terms *vera religio* and *falsa religio*. That 'one religion is true, others false' is a much more sophisticated and developed notion than can legitimately be read into these terms, unless I am seriously mistaken[29]; for one thing, the subsequent history of our concept bears this out, as we shall presently see. Nonetheless, words had been found for what ultimately became an immensely significant idea; and already in the fourth century the implications of the concept that had emerged, if not the concept itself, were major[30]. That worship can be true or false is a notion that may well give one pause; we shall be returning to it.

Of importance in these writings is a further point. Not only does their usage reflect the emergent discrimination of what a modern might call one religion from another, or at least one community and its faith and practices from another. It reflects also, in an imprecise way, a curious triangular involvement with philosophy (*sapientia*), which itself had by this time become for some people an alternative to the old religious tradition and its ways. What Lucretius and Cicero had begun to do did not, we earlier remarked, come to fruition: an intellectual critique of *religio* in general (which inevitably meant, at that time, of pagan *religio* in general) did not evolve far beyond incipience. Yet now the Christian attack on pagan *religio* found itself in some sort of alliance with this rationalism, over against the traditional cults. Into Lactantius's concept of the *falsa religio deorum*, the polytheists' false worship, went something of Cicero's and something of even Lucretius's ideas[31]. And on the positive side, *vera religio* he identifies with *vera sapientia*[32]. The notion of religion was becoming considerably more complex and more profound.

Early Western civilization was on the verge, at the time of Lactantius, of taking a decisive step in the formulation of an elaborate, comprehensive, philosophic concept of *religio*.

However, it did not take it. The matter was virtually dropped, to lie dormant for a thousand years.

Before leaving this, however, there are two men whose role in the whole development must be mentioned. The first is Jerome, for he introduced the term *religio* at a few places in his Latin translation of the Bible, fixing it therefore in the Western Christian tradition. He used it in the sense of a rite, rendering in the New Testament the Greek *thrēskeia*, 'religious observance', 'ritual practice', 'way of worshipping'[33], and in the Old Testament various terms for ordinance and ritual prescription[34].

Secondly, there is St. Augustine. He is the last writer before the Renascence to evince a significant interest in the concept. He took up one of the senses in which the term had come to be used, and that a highly important one. On it he wrote a book. This is the first time that a Christian writer had undertaken to explicate a notion of *religio*, rather than using the term somewhat incidentally. His is a careful and sustained exposition, and is therefore worth attention, the more so in that this particular wording regarding religion has for us in the modern period become crucial. St. Augustine entitled his work *De Vera Religione*. To understand what he meant by this is basic to our whole discussion.

Modern predispositions are betrayed in any impulse to translate the title as 'On the True Religion', and to suppose that the writer, since he is known to have been a Christian, would believe that the true religion is Christianity. In fact, this would be a misrendering. A closer translation would be 'On True Religion'; the idea is of the order of 'On Proper Piety', or 'On Genuine Worship'[35]. As the author himself comes close to saying, the book argues 'at great length and in many ways that *vera religio* means the worship of the one true God'[35a]; it hardly mentions 'Christianity'[36], and culminates in a warm, reverberating and sustained affirmation of a personal relation to that transcendent God 'from whom, through whom, and in whom are all things. To Him be glory for ever and ever. Amen'[37].

For this writer 'religion' is no system of observances or beliefs, nor an historical tradition, institutionalized or susceptible of outside observation. Rather it is a vivid and personal confrontation with the splendour and the love of God.

The Church, for him, exists in order to make this relationship possible[38].

He is Platonist, and is claiming that Christian faith is the true fulfilment of Plato[39]. His exposition endeavours to wean the reader's mind step by step from the good things of this world to the supreme good that lies behind them, who is God. He states flatly that the world consists only of good things[40], and discusses man's love of and therefore worship of things (the sun, stars, the world, fancies) . 'I say that there is no man who holds that there is nothing he ought to worship'[41]. Yet for him it is wrong to pursue the less good when one might pursue the better.

Man's problem is to rise from temporal good to eternal good, from bodily good to spiritual good, from the good of sense perception to that of intellectual perception, from lowest good to highest good[42]. All worship, he implies, is worship of something good; true worship is worship of the Best, namely God.

The culmination is mystic. For finally, *religio* is the bond[43] that unites us, let it not be to any creature but to the Creator Himself, nothing coming between our minds by which we know Him as Father, and the Truth, that is the inner light through which we know Him[44].

Thus is a concept of 'true' religion posited, suggesting for the first time on a serious scale[45] that there is an ideal, a perfect or essential relationship between man and God that ought to subsist. It is timeless: it 'existed of old and was never absent from the beginning of the human race until Christ came in the flesh. Then true religion which already existed began to be called Christian'[46]. He is not asserting 'my religion is the true one'—actually he admits that what he is talking of transcends his own apprehension of it[47]. He is arguing rather that man's true nature is fulfilled in a close personal *engagement* with the divine, and that Christ has made this possible.

Nonetheless, there is a new idea in this phrase 'true' religion; and one that helped to make possible the transition to the later institutionalized meaning. Because it is a Platonic form, even though it is intimately personal it is also universal and in some sense transferable; which perhaps enabled others later to think of it as a general community possession, eventually identifiable with an overt institutional phenomenon. This led at last to the concept that one religion (in a later sense) is true, others false— a major turning point in the history of man.

Radhakrishnan has remarked: 'The Jews first invented the myth that only one religion can be true'[48]. One sees what he means; but the analysis is not, I think, exact. What the Jews asserted is that only one God is real; which one may regard as just as reprehensible, but is not quite the same idea. Nor is Augustine introducing the idea; it is a much more complex error than the world was yet ready for. The concept of 'religion' had first to undergo more development. His predecessors had sown the seeds for it, by their sharp attack on what they considered the spurious religious traditions of their time (to which the word *religio* of course primarily applied). These seeds did not bear fruit, however, for over a thousand years; partly, perhaps, because of the victory of the Church and the disappearance of those alien traditions and of the conflict with them, partly also perhaps because of Augustine's Platonizing a personal glowing encounter with the Divine, even though it were one to which some later generations were not capable of rising.

iv

However that may be, after Augustine the word was little used. If the salient point about the early Fathers' use of *religio* is its rich diversity, the striking thing throughout the Catholic Middle Ages is how little current this particular term became. For the mediaeval Church the great word was always 'faith'. In this it was in tune with the New Testament—not only in terminology but in fundamental orientation. Faith is a dynamic response of the person to the living reality of God. So long as it is lively, the idea of religion is not very important[49].

The entire period, accordingly, need not detain us long. The one sense of the term *religio* that is found fairly steadily through the Middle Ages is a development from the meaning 'rite', namely the specialized designation of the monastic life as '*religio*'. This is cited from the fifth century[50]. Even the adjective was used to designate a member of one of the Orders: the 'religious' were distinguished from lay Christians. Similarly in the daughter languages: the first meaning of 'religion' in English, in the *Oxford Dictionary*, is 'a state of life bound by monastic vows'[51], testified by 1200 A.D. This is still seen in such Roman Catholic phrases as 'to enter religion'. The term also designated 'a particular monastic or religious order or rule'; in this sense a plural is attested about 1400, so that the various 'religions of England' are the various orders[52].

It is in this sense also that St. Thomas Aquinas chiefly uses the word[53]; though he touches on it briefly in its more general significance also. In his great *Summa Theologica* he devotes a few paragraphs to it (in the standard English translation, a dozen or so pages out of a total of twenty-some volumes[54]); discussing, for instance, whether it be one of the moral or the theological virtues. In any case, for him it is here an activity of the soul: it is the man of faith's prompting towards the due worship of God[55]. It is interesting, furthermore, that even so careful a thinker as Aquinas would at different times apply the term to at least three different things: the outward expression of faith[56]; the inner motivation towards worshipping God, and that worship itself[57]; and, à la Augustine (whom he cites), the bond that unites the soul with God[58]. Altogether, however, the concept does not play a big role in this thinking[59].

Nor in that of his era. It is nowadays customary to think of this period as the most 'religious' in the history of Christendom[60]. Despite this or because of it, throughout the whole Middle Ages no one, so far as I have been able to ascertain, ever wrote a book specifically on 'religion'[61].

And on the whole this concept would seem to have received little attention[62].

V

In the modern period, in contrast, it has as we know become a question of very major importance. This begins with the Renascence and expands with the Reformation, changes with the Enlightenment and develops in the nineteenth century. Let us, then, turn to these[63].

After a minor and obscure booklet of the same title[64], the new orientation begins with a brilliant and influential work of one of the major minds of the Italian Renaissance, Marsilio Ficino, the man who gave Europe its first full Latin translation of Plato (also of Plotinus) and whose chief original contribution was his humanist synthesis of a Christian Platonism. In 1474 he wrote *De Christiana Religione*[65]. This phrase, one is surprised to realize, was relatively new at the time [66]. It subsequently became common[67] and has remained so, but with a profound change of meaning.

There was certainly not in Ficino's mind when he wrote this what is normally conjured up today by the phrase 'the Christian Religion', if by this latter one understands any system of doctrines and practices, any institutional phenomenon or historical development, one of 'the religions' of the world. For these things he used other expressions. He saw that in different times and places men's ways of adoring God (*ritus adorationis*) are, with His permission, various. 'Perhaps indeed variety of this kind, divinely ordained, decorates the universe with a certain marvelous beauty'[68]. That to which Ficino gives the name *religio*, on the other hand, is universal to man; it is, indeed, the fundamental distinguishing human characteristic, innate, natural, and primary[69]. It is the divinely provided instinct that makes man man, by which he perceives and worships God[70].

If it is inherent in human nature, and stable ('all opinions of men, all their responses, all their customs, change—except *religio*'[71]: clearly, he is not thinking of externals!) , then it is difficult at first to understand what could be meant by using the adjective *Christiana* with it. If religiousness, as we might translate it, is a quality of human nature derived from God, can it be of different kinds? It was to tackle this problem that he wrote his book. The difficulty is solved when we remember that for Platonist thinkers the veritable form is ideal; the actual occurrences in human history in the lives of men and women are more or less inadequate, approximative, more or less *untrue* instances of that ideal[72]. *Religio* cannot be of different kinds. But it can be, and is, found in differing degrees of genuineness. It is better to worship God in any way, 'even ineptly', than out of haughtiness not to worship Him at all; so that all religion is to some degree good[73]. However,

God being what He is, namely the summit of all goodness, the truth of things, the light by which the mind operates, it follows that those worship Him best who sedulously revere Him in act, in goodness, in truthfulness of speech, in clarity of mind, in love. Such men, he proposes to show, whoever they may be, are worshipping God in the way that Christ has exemplified and taught[74]. This is what he means by *Christiana religio.*

(At the same time this is, equally, the way that philosophy essentially involves. Since *philosophia* is the love and pursuit of truth and wisdom, and since truth and wisdom are, precisely, God, it follows that true *philosophia* and true *religio* are identical[75]. Perhaps, in order to preserve his meaning against modern changed conceptions, we would have to translate this in some such awkward way as, 'genuine philosophicalness and genuine religiousness are ideally the same'.)

Further, if one reflects carefully on the term 'Christian' here, it will be seen that he is evidently using this adjective in the sense of 'pertaining to Christ'—a meaning that has since virtually lapsed. This word later came almost exclusively to mean, pertaining to Christians; or, to the institution of Christianity. The difference is not minor. Not only by *religio* did Ficino not mean what is today referred to in the phrase 'the Christian religion'; it would also be altogether meaningful to ask whether that to which today this latter phrase objectively refers is 'Christian' in Ficino's understanding of that term.

He had previously written a major work, *Theologia Platonica* (the title is arresting), setting forth to a rather unaccustomed Europe[76] his idea of a universal instinct in mankind to seek the good, which he argued is to seek the divine; an instinct to which he assigned the name *religio.* To translate into modern English the phrase that he in effect coined to entitle his smaller essay, namely *De Christiana Religione,* one would have to resort to some such cumbersome paraphrase as, 'On the Christ-Oriented Nature of Universal Human Religiousness, in its ideal form'.

The next books at which we should look come out of the Reformation.

34

Of the Reformers, Luther's great concept (and word[77]) is 'faith'. In this he was following the mediaeval Church, but he made it even more central—with his vigorous affirmation of 'justification by faith', that by faith alone man is saved. He seems not to have concerned himself with a concept of religion[78]. Even today there is among German theologians a tradition that is suspicious of it and even hostile[79]. And the German language is (with Dutch) perhaps the only one in Western Europe that has shown a certain reluctance to accept the term[80].

Zwingli and Calvin, on the other hand, adopted it, and indeed gave it wide currency, the latter in particular using it in the title of two of the most widely distributed books of his century. It behooves us to note, then, how they understood it.

In 1525 the Swiss Protestant leader Zwingli published *De Vera et Falsa Religione Commentarius*[81]. By this title he is not maintaining that Christianity is a true religion, other religions false. Neither he nor Calvin seems to use the term 'Christianity' at all. The opening sentence of Zwingli's work announces firmly that it will deal 'with the true and false *religio* of Christians'[82]. For him, *religio* is a relation between man and God. It is established when man comes to trust God who in His mercy reaches out toward him. False *religio,* or as he also calls it, false piety or superstition[83], is found therefore when anything is trusted as God other than He[84].

The whole point, we must remember, of the Reformers' position was that men should not put their faith in any external institution and treat what we might call the religious system, the Church, as divine.

For Zwingli, *false* religion is an oversanctification of popes, councils, church authorities, and the like[85]; a giving honour to the mundane organization through which the divine is mediated instead of to the divine itself. To use our modern terminology, one might almost represent Zwingli as introducing[86] the concept of 'false religion' precisely to characterize the tendency whereby men give their allegiance to religion rather than to God[87].

The major formulation of Reformation theology stems from

the work of John Calvin, first published in 1536 under the title *Christianae Religionis Institutio*[88]. This was subsequently revised and reissued in a great series of editions, enlarged and elaborated on the one hand, and abridged and rearranged in the form of a 'Catechism' on the other. Of the enlarged editions the seventh, final, one of 1559 was reissued another dozen times before the century was out; translations of this and of the catechism, many several times reprinted, appeared in French, Italian, Greek, English, Spanish, Dutch, German, etc.

In almost all these cases the phrase *Christiana religio* or its equivalent is preserved, sometimes in revealing forms. The phrase, and the catechism form, were taking up a practice that begins a little earlier[89] and becomes extremely popular; one of the major social movements of the sixteenth century appears to have been that of instruction by printed manuals in religious matters. Certainly for the Protestant world one consequence was that the term *religio*, and the phrase *Christiana religio*, in many languages relatively little used in 1500, were by 1600 entirely popularized and common. It would seem not unlikely that Calvin's use of the phrase as a title did as much as any other one factor to give it such currency.

We must still ask, however, what it meant.

I suggest that, beyond all reasonable question, there is serious misrepresentation in the translation 'Institutes of the Christian religion', first found in the nineteenth century[90]. For one thing, *institutio* meant 'instruction'[91], instituting, setting up, establishing, and in effect it is here followed by an objective genitive. Furthermore, *religio* is certainly not 'one of the religions'[92], an overt, institutional phenomenon nor an abstract system. It is rather, as with the other writers that we have observed, the sense of piety that prompts a man to worship. It is innate in everyman, and is the one characteristic that lifts man above the brutes[93]. It is an inner personal attitude.

The writers that we have considered, then, who were the leaders in this particular movement in the history of ideas, by *religio* referred to something personal, inner, and transcendentally oriented. Probably the nearest equivalent concept in modern English is that of piety[94]. It is significant that each of the three uses *religio* and *pietas* as at least correlative, and at times as equivalent[95]. Accordingly I would suggest that to the author and those who first read it the title of Zwingli's book meant, 'An essay[96] on genuine and spurious piety'; and Calvin's, something like 'Grounding in Christian piety'.

The validity of this is borne out by such facts as that when the latter was first translated into English, *Christiana religio* was rendered not as 'the Christian religion', an as yet unfamiliar concept to which we shall presently turn, but 'Christian religion'[97], which is very different. So strong have modern prejudices become that one is at first perhaps prone to treat the absence of the article as simply quaint, a curious sixteenth-century syntax; rather than recognizing that those involved were talking about something different.

The point may perhaps be illustrated from the language of another catechism roughly contemporary, published anonymously in London in Latin[98] and presently in English translation[99]. The latter gives 'Christian religion' without the article to render *pietas Christiana*. It uses 'religion' in such phrases as 'learne the truth of religion'; 'the only rule of true religion'; 'to furnish thy minds . . . with good opinions and true Religion'; 'Christian godlynesse and Religion'; 'Religion and true godlynesse'; 'of Religion . . . there are principally two partes, Obedience . . . and Faith'[100]. In these cases 'piety' could reasonably be substituted for 'religion'[101]; on the other hand, it would be impossible even today to insert an article before 'religion' without seriously changing the meaning[102].

vi

From the seventeenth century, however, Europeans and especially the leaders of their thought evolved new ways of looking at the world, new attitudes to the churches, new conceptions of truth. The new generations took over our term to designate now that in which they were increasingly interested, namely the intellectual construct, presently the various intellectual constructs, systematic and abstract, that were to be elaborated in the religious realm. They gave the name 'religion' to the system, first in general but increasingly to the system of ideas, in which men of faith were involved or with which men of potential faith were confronted.

Whether Ficino was or was not right in believing that each of us is endowed with an instinct or religious sense directing us towards beauty, truth, and justice, and beyond, towards God, in any case men in the pursuit of what they believed God to be or to enjoin have in fact 'always and everywhere'[103] elaborated great systems embodying and structuring their responses. Whether Zwingli was or was not right in believing that this religious sense is genuine only when it rightly perceives God's will and puts its faith in Him directly, rather than letting itself become involved with the historical tradition and ecclesiastical structure, in any case Christians were in fact, as the century increasingly showed, deeply and bitterly divided among themselves on what is true and what is false in this latter realm. Whether Calvin was or was not right in believing that this universal instinct is, because of the perversion of man, unable to construct anything but delirious illusions[104] except where God Himself, as He has done once, instructs us, in any case men's systems of worshipping and traditions of belief have in fact throughout the world been many and diverse.

Attention was increasingly turned away from these former questions to the latter matters. Thus began a long-range development, accumulating until today, of diversion of interest from man's personal sense of the holy to what we might call the observable product or historical deposit of its outworking.

The transition through the Enlightenment, however, did not go so far. Its concern, and its reference for the term 'religion', were not yet outward phenomena so much as abstract idea. We may observe the change in the application of our term from the dynamic of the heart to impersonal system; from singular to plural; and from a Platonic to a propositional conception of truth.

The matters set forth in Calvin's *magnum opus*—a pattern of doctrines, Church practices, interpretations of Scripture and of the Lord's Supper, etc.—are not themselves *religio*. They are, rather, things that he hoped would institute or induce in people or guide them to or instruct them in a personal, dynamic, and worshipful 'recognition'[105] of God to which he gave that name (*Christiana religio*). A century later men were calling by this name not that personal vision but the matters such as he set forth to lead to it: the system of beliefs and practices, considered as a system, irrespective of whether or not they elicited in the human heart a genuine fear of and love for God. The difference is momentous.

The system is called 'the' Christian religion. And since men have elaborated more than one system, instead of different kinds of *religio* (religiousness) one gets different religions, in the plural.

These can then be regarded as true or false in an intellectualist sense.

This radical transition can be illustrated from the extremely influential work of Hugo de Groot (Grotius) in the first half of the seventeenth century: *De Veritate Religionis Christianae*[107]. The transition is not yet complete: his position set forth under that title is about three-quarters of the way or more along a road leading from 'the genuineness of Christian religiousness' to 'the truth of the Christian religion'. Traces of the former orientation are to be found, viewing the Christian as one instance of a general (Platonic) type, but a surpassingly excellent instance, so that it is true religion. On the whole, however, he is concerned to show that it is *the* true religion, by proving that its precepts are statements of fact[108]. And where the earlier writers would have said that Christian religion *is,* he says that *the* Christian religion *teaches,* the worship of God with purity of mind and sincerity of moral behaviour[109].

This new conception, that 'religio' names a system of ideas, of beliefs, is in full vigour later in the century. This was so, for example, in (and as a result of) the writing of the influential Lord Herbert of Cherbury, who deliberately set himself the task of devising a method for coming to some assessment of whether or not a religion is true. Of interest to us here is not the content of his method but his presumption that the truth or otherwise of a religion is the truth or otherwise of its doctrines[110]. For the religion *is* the doctrine: that virtually is what the word now means.

This is the view of the Enlightenment, evinced not only in the religious realm but as a comprehensive world outlook which stressed an intellectualist and impersonal schematization of things. In pamphlet after pamphlet, treatise after treatise, decade after decade the notion was driven home that a religion is something that one believes or does not believe, something whose propositions are true or are not true, something whose *locus* is in the realm of the intelligible, is up for inspection before the speculative mind. This interpretation had by the mid-eighteenth century sunk deep into the European consciousness. A legacy of it is the tendency still today to ask, in explanation of 'the religion' of a people, What do they believe?—as though this were a basic, even *the* basic, question.

An altogether parallel development took place in philosophy; with the same transition from personal orientation to depersonalized intellectual systematization, and from ideal to logical conception of truth. In 1500 if one asked about a person, *ejusne philosophia vera est?* this would have meant, 'Is his love of wisdom genuine?' Came the Enlightenment, and it meant (and means), 'Is his philosophy true?'

'Natural religion', when it emerged as an idea[111] and was quickly popularized[112], signified beliefs—those about God, man, and the world that are supposedly common to mankind or attainable by his reason. The Deist movement generally was highly intellectualist in its outlook. However, its opponents also, though disagreeing as to the validity or content of its beliefs, unwittingly accepted the use of 'religion' to refer to beliefs. In the eighteenth century the argument was carried on, and to some extent has persisted since, in the terms in which it was posed prominently by Bishop Butler: natural religion and revealed religion[113]. Much attention was given to those matters to which the adjectives referred, while the noun slipped in rather unnoticed.

We must give very special weight to the concept 'revealed religion'. This was quite novel, and in fact is revolutionary. The concept of revelation had been standard in Christian thinking from New Testament times. Yet no one before the eighteenth century had ever supposed that what was revealed was a religion. We shall return to this immensely important point.

Butler explicitly, though no doubt inadvertently, writes, 'Christianity is a scheme'[114].

Striking in all this, and highly significant, is the great degree to which books on 'religion' in this sense are apologetic or polemic[115].

One may note another new and different meaning of our term arising out of the seventeenth-century practice of particularizing and reifying 'the religion of' a group other than those groups that we today regard as constituting the proper group of 'a religion', such as Jews and Christians. This practice never became so common and not nearly so influential as the latter one, which was later adopted as virtually ultimate[116]. Some of the usages, however, survive until today, others have virtually lapsed. One gets 'the religion of' a particular person: both from the outside, whether for[117] or against[118], and, more generally, from within—in a considerable series[119] of which the most famous, *Religio Medici,* shows that the exteriorization of the age did not triumph over personalism when one person only was involved[120]. One gets also 'the religion of the Dutch'[121], 'of the Church of England'[122]; one gets certain kinds of religion[123]; and one gets 'the Catholic'[124] and 'the Protestant religion'[125]. It is interesting to speculate what the situation might be today if perchance these usages of the word had become established instead of the one that has in fact dominated.

Roman Catholics, though apparently taking to the term much

less fully than Protestants[126], did use it somewhat in their anti-Protestant writings and other controversy[127], and occasionally still in the older sense of the monastic life[128]. On the whole, however, I have the impression that Catholics did not much share in the evolution that we have been considering. The word was not so important for them and did not become so intimate. I suggest as an almost probable generalization that the term has seldom meant for Catholics what it has meant for Protestants[129].

One way in which the Catholics differed proved extraordinarily fruitful. For it was they who introduced the plural, and the phrase 'the religions of the world'. In line perhaps with the third-fourth century Church Fathers' use of *religio* for practical observances, ritual, and with their own mediaeval meaning of monastic order, the term to them had a more concrete reference: the outward pattern of religious life[130]. Consequently, if they were to use the word at all, they were not shy to use a plural—even for the Christian scene[131]. They produced a book on 'the religions of the world' as early as 1508[132]. Protestants, with their concern with inner piety and personal faith, were not ready to take this step until they had exteriorized and reified their concept, which as we have just seen was only in the seventeenth century. Their first books of this kind are more than a century later than the other, though once they appeared they circulated very widely indeed[133], and it is from this point on that the usage becomes common.

This was an age of controversy and conflict in the religious realm, as well as an age of intellectualization in every realm. The intellectualizing of the concept 'religion' was part of the emerging claim of the mind to understand the universe and assert its domination; but it was part, also, of a response to the strident claims of many religious groups to refute each other. When one is setting forth one's own faith, one speaks of something deep, personal, and transcendentally oriented. If one uses the term 'religion' then, this is what one spontaneously means. If, on the other hand, one is rejecting what other people set forth—in and through which one does not oneself find or see any transcendent orientation, at

least no valid one—then one necessarily conceptualizes it in terms
of its outward manifestations, since these are all that is available.
One's own 'religion' may be piety and faith, obedience, worship,
and a vision of God. An alien 'religion' is a system of beliefs or
rituals, an abstract and impersonal pattern of observables.

A dialectic ensues, however. If one's own 'religion' is attacked,
by unbelievers who necessarily conceptualize it schematically, or
all religion is, by the indifferent, one tends to leap to the defence
of what is attacked, so that presently participants of a faith—especially those most involved in argument—are using the term in
the same externalist and theoretical sense as are their opponents.
Religion as a systematic entity, as it emerged in the seventeenth
and eighteenth centuries, is a concept of polemics and apologetics.

Two developments arise from this. One is the plural 'religions',
which is impossible so long as one is thinking of something in
men's hearts, such as piety, obedience, reverence, worship. (None
of these words has a plural.) The plural arises—it becomes standard from the mid-seventeenth century, and common from the
eighteenth—when one contemplates from the outside, and abstracts, depersonalizes, and reifies, the various systems of other
people of which one does not oneself see the meaning or appreciate the point, let alone accept the validity.

Secondly, there is another concept, of a generic 'religion' to
designate as an external entity the total system or sum of all systems of beliefs, or simply the generalization that they are there.
This is a concept primarily formulated and used by men who are
weary of the clash or suspicious of the whole enterprise.

That these processes actually took place can be observed and
documented in detail from a careful scrutiny of usage. If one ex-
amines verbal contexts closely, it is striking how regularly a new
usage is introduced first to name something that one wishes to
criticize. This is the case, for instance, with the use of the plural.
I find it not insignificant that the phrase 'religions of the world'
is first used in a treatise in which these are presented as such in
order to be refuted[134]. Moreover, the concept is applied only to

one's opponents' faith, not to one's own. The 'religions of the world' are contrasted first not with 'the Christian religion' but with 'Christian faith'. And the plural continues disparaging[135] if not rejective[136]. The case is similar also with 'natural religion'[137]. Again, the Catholics, who as we have remarked in general apparently took to the term 'religion' considerably less wholeheartedly than did Protestants[138], used it primarily in their anti-Protestant writing[139], and in the latter seventeenth and eighteenth centuries also in anti-deist and anti-irreligion apologetics[140].

Moreover, the generic abstraction 'religion' as an external something occurs at first only, and for long chiefly, in the recurrent phrase 'controversy about religion'[141].

If we may sum up this period, then, we may say that some Renascence humanists and then some Protestant Reformers adopted a concept religion to represent an inner piety; but that in the seventeenth and early eighteenth centuries this was largely superseded by a concept of schematic externalization that reflected, and served, the clash of conflicting religious parties, the emergence of a triumphant intellectualism, and the emerging new information from beyond the seas about the patterns of other men's religious life. These provided the foundations of the concept for the modern world.

vii

Yet three further developments, chiefly of the nineteenth century, were added before the concept was bequeathed to us. We shall touch on them briefly.

That the attention of leaders of thought in the Enlightenment, whatever their achievements rationally, had in the religious realm been diverted and even squandered on an increasingly arid intellectualism, could not fail to elicit finally a protest and recall on the part of the more devout. While the thinkers and the élite were evolving their new notions which came to dominate the intellectual life of the times, the common people were affected by them only partially, being open at the same time to the deeper piety of the tradition, with which the word 'religion' (except in Germany) continued to be associated for them in so far as it was presented, for instance, in the continuing catechisms[142]. Occasionally, too, a rather quiet voice would arise pleading in a more personal and by this time rather old-fashioned way for 'true religion' rather than 'contests about circumstantials'[143]. So far as corporate religious life is concerned, the movement of return to a re-emphasis on a richer and more personal and more moral attitude is to be seen in the work of the German pietists and of John Wesley. Our particular concept, however, we appropriately do not find these movements much employing.

For it, it is in nineteenth-century Germany that development is primarily to be traced. After adumbration by Kant[144], this is to be observed first in the work of Schleiermacher in forcing the intellectuals as such to modify their concept of 'religion'. He published just before the century began a work[145] addressed deliberately to those who conceptualized religion disparagingly. It would seem to be the first book ever written on religion as such—not on a particular kind or instance and not incidentally, but explicitly on religion itself as a generic something. He pleaded with his cultured readers to think of religion in terms of the heart rather than of beliefs or practice: 'I ask, therefore, that you turn from everything usually reckoned religion, and fix your regard on the inward emotions and dispositions'[146]. What is observed, what *appears*, is not to be thought of as religion but as an inadequate and particularized expression of it[147]. The plural, 'the positive religions', designates the particular forms in which religion, in its more proper sense, is manifested[148]. It has, he says, been a derogatory term for the intellectuals, and for him represents what is admittedly and necessarily corrupt[149]. Yet he retains it, and argues boldly that what it names is preferable to the abstraction called 'natural religion' just because this latter is a disembodied idea rather than a living, however perverted, actuality[150].

The result of Schleiermacher's influential work and of the whole romantic movement that it exemplified was, if not to shift the meaning of our term back to the inward and nonintellectual part of the religious life (the impact of the Enlightenment of Europe was, fortunately, too powerful and deep for its rationalism to be swept aside), at least to expand the concept 'religion' so that it has since, as an intellectual concept, included within its content the nonintellectual and the intellectual together. So far as 'the religions' is concerned, the content and significance that he insisted upon for that term were provided also, and more richly, by the general trend towards historicizing Europe's knowledge in this as in other fields. This trend began before Schleiermacher, and in many parts of Europe[151]; we mention it subsequently because it accumulated in scope and significance most strikingly in the nineteenth century. The static quality of the Enlightenment's rationalism was filled out with an increasing knowledge of, and presently sense of, history.

The concept 'the religions' accordingly came to mean not only in the Enlightenment sense the various systems of what people believed, and not only in the Catholic sense what they ritually practised, and not only in Schleiermacher's sense what they inwardly felt, but increasingly the historical development of all this over the long sweep of the centuries. During the nineteenth century information on this, which previously had at first trickled and then poured in more or less incidentally, chiefly from travelers, began to be systematically searched out, organized, and analysed, in academic seriousness. The process has continued until today, in almost overwhelming detail. For sheer quantity of fact, length of time span, diversity of form, recurrence of pattern, degree of developmental transmutation, mutual impingement, and the like, to no one before, say, 1850 and to almost no one before 1900 could 'the history of religions' (or '. . . of religion') possibly connote anything nearly so elaborate as an undergraduate student today knows that these mean.

However that may be, already in the nineteenth century the

historical quality of the material constituting the content of the idea of religion was being grappled with. The first philosopher to take history seriously was perhaps Hegel; certainly his powerful mind, comprehensive, brilliant, and no doubt misleading, was the first to wrestle with the problem of conceptualizing religion in flux. Apart from coining the phrase 'philosophy of religion'[152], he posited 'religion' as a *Begriff*, a self-subsisting transcendent idea that unfolds itself in dynamic expression in the course of ever-changing history—unfolds itself as 'positive religion' (in the singular) [153]. From now on, European (and presently world) thought entertains *religion* in the singular as a concept not of the humanities but of the social sciences.

Other thinkers had perhaps by the implication of their language come close to supposing rather incidentally something of the sort, but Hegel seems to have been the first to assert with clarity and massive vigour that religion as seen in society is something real in itself, a great entity with which man has to reckon, a something that precedes all its historical manifestations[154]. Though if formulated in these terms and ascribed explicitly to Hegel the idea would be consciously accepted by few, it has nonetheless in fact haunted Western thinking ever since.

This is seen particularly in the formulation presently set forth by one of his brilliant students, Ludwig Feuerbach, who in 1851 published a book called *The Essence of Religion*[155]. Ten years earlier he had published *The Essence of Christianity*[156]. The important point is not what he considered the essences to be, so much as the fact that he was suggesting that religion, and a religion, have an essence. Ever since the hunt has been on. The idea was widely accepted that religion is a something with a definite and fixed form, if only one could find it. This is the problem of the definition of religion, which occupied many good minds in the decades before and after 1900. Many were the books that set out in search of the nature of religion[157], or of Buddhism or whatever[158]; full of confidence that that nature is somehow there.

This is to carry the process of reification to its logical extreme:

endowing the concepts that an earlier generation has constructed (rather haphazardly, and dubiously, in this case) with a final and inherent validity, a cosmic legitimacy.

viii

The concepts 'religion' and 'religions' as we have inherited them today have been immensely enriched in content by the studies of the past century. This was effected in no inconsiderable part by the organizing of studies in this realm in the universities[159]. The observations on religious phenomena made by students of impinging disciplines, economic history, psychiatry, sociology, and others, have also been of quite major importance in modifying many people's conceptions of what is involved. A generation that has known the many modern critiques, analyses, and histories can hardly have the same impression of religious phenomena as its forebears.

However, the concepts themselves have not recently been either much criticized or, in form, modified. This is what I am proposing here, and our historical survey has been undertaken, as was said in introducing it, in order that we should be in a better position to consider this.

It is perhaps fair to summarize our survey by saying that we, as heirs to the somewhat chaotic developments, commonly employ the term religion in four quite distinct senses. It is important to discriminate these before we proceed. First, there is the sense of a personal piety. It is with this meaning that we are thinking today when we use such phrases as, 'He is more religious than he was ten years ago'; or if we remark that in every community, Christian, Hindu, and the rest, there are some men whose religion is harsh and narrow, others whose religion is warm and open. Secondly and thirdly, there is the usage that refers to an overt system, whether of beliefs, practices, values, or whatever. Such a system has an extension in time, some relation to an area, and is related to a particular community; and is specific. In this sense, the word has a plural and in English the singular has an article[160]. In each case, however, there are two contrasting meanings: one, of the system as an ideal, the other, of it as an empirical phenomenon, historical and sociological. Thus there are two Christianities: 'true Christianity' on the one hand, the ideal, which the theologian tries to formulate but which he knows transcends him; and, on the other hand, the Christianity of history, which the sociologist or other observer notes as a human, sometimes all too human, complex. Normally persons talk about other people's religions as they are, and about their own as it ought to be. (This is a basic reason why 'religion' in the plural has maintained from the beginning a different meaning from the singular.) Those without a faith of their own think of all 'religions' as observably practised. Hence insiders and outsiders use the same words while talking of different things.

Finally, there is 'religion' as a generic summation, 'religion in general'. Its meaning is inevitably derived in part, for anyone using it, from his sense of the other three. In so far as it is historical, it is as complex as all 'the religions' taken together. In so far as it is personal, it is as diverse as the men whose piety it synthesizes.

The first sense discriminates religion in a man's life from indifference (or rebellion). The second and third (possibly intermingled) discriminate one religion from another. The fourth discriminates religion from other aspects of human life, such as art or economics.

We have not defined religion in any of these senses. We have not said what it is that constitutes (or feigns) a personal piety; nor what it is that either characterizes or differentiates the religious systems that are found among men; nor what it is that has given human life and history their apparently transcendent dimension. Yet without definition one may insist that the word is used in four differing ways. And one may urge that no discussion—let alone, no definition—can be mature that is not self-conscious on this point.

My own suggestion is that the word, and the concepts, should be dropped—at least in all but the first, personalist, sense. This is on the grounds not merely that it would be helpful to do so; but, more strongly, that it is misleading to retain them. I suggest that the term 'religion' is confusing, unnecessary, and distorting —confusing and unnecessary especially in the first and fourth senses, distorting in the second and the third. I have become strongly convinced that the vitality of personal faith, on the one hand, and, on the other hand (quite separately), progress in understanding—even at the academic level—of the traditions of other people throughout history and throughout the world, are both seriously blocked by our attempt to conceptualize what is involved in each case in terms of (a) religion.

Before setting forth, in the second half of this book, the arguments elucidating so unusual a view, I would first turn our inquiry, in the next two chapters, to other cultures.

CHAPTER THREE

Other Cultures.
'The Religions'

THE CONCEPT 'RELIGION', then, in the West has evolved. Its evolution has included a long-range development that we may term a process of reification: mentally making religion into a thing, gradually coming to conceive it as an objective systematic entity. In this development one factor has been the rise into Western consciousness in relatively recently times of several so conceived entities, constituting a series: the religions of the world. This point has in our day become of dominating importance. Inquiry in this realm no longer concerns itself with only one tradition; our understanding of man's religious situation, our meanings for our words, take and must take into account the broader perspective that is nowadays ours.

In this matter, however, a double involvement can be studied. There is the process by which the available concepts have been modified by the new range of data. There is also the process by which the data have come to be understood (and perhaps misunderstood) within the limits of the concepts employed to handle them. Investigation in this realm will show, I believe, that conceptual evolution has some way yet to go before the form of our thinking will be adequate to its content, in our religiously plural world.

The question may be pursued along two avenues. First, one may ask whether or how other cultures have conceptualized those aspects of human life and society that the West has come, in the process that we have studied, to envisage as religion and the religions. Instructive similarities to and divergences from the Western pattern begin to appear, as we shall presently see; particularly in the matter of reification.

Secondly, one may move from the general concept 'religion' to the particularist conceptualization that, after reification has been accomplished, expresses itself in a series of names designating the several traditions individually. Here one may examine the historical process by which the West has come to formulate its notion of its own religious systems, most recently under the terms 'Christianity' and 'Judaism', and also its understanding of other peoples' systems, to which also it has recently given names, 'Hinduism', 'Buddhism' and the like. One may ask also how within those other traditions themselves the matter has proceeded. We may profitably inquire as to whether or how far there are parallels to the Western understanding; and whether or how far alternative interpretations of the data have been developed, and may perhaps help towards comprehension of them.

At a pre-reified level, for a concept of religion signifying that inner personal orientation for which there are a number of alternative or correlative words even in Western languages—piety, reverence, faith, and the like—it would seem that other cultures also have their designations. That some persons are 'religious', devout, God-fearing, is an observation that has been widely made throughout the world. Although I have not made a systematic investigation, I believe that parallels or rough counterparts to the adjective 'religious', as applied to persons, are to be found in a variety of cultures[1], and that among some of the more sophisticated of these a noun generalizing the adjective[1a] is also traditionally available.

When we move from considering this personal quality of life to thinking rather of an organized system, the conceptualization that envisages a series of entities in the world each of which is called a religion, then this unanimity of mankind vanishes. It would seem that few have shared this particular analysis of humanity's religious envolvement.

We may learn something from noting first the case of those, the large majority, who have not done so. In our next chapter we shall consider those that have, the few cultures where there are signs of a reifying concept—and shall find these linked not only with each other in a long-range historical evolution, so that here also reification has been a particular discernible process, but linked also at crucial points with the Western development.

Our first task, however, is largely that simply of reporting negatively on inquiries into several particular cultures. What emerges is that in almost every case careful observers are found to have noted the absence of any reificationist idea, though these observations have not been co-ordinated and an attempt made to discern an over-all significance.

ii

First, let us note the noncivilizational peoples of the world: those who in their small communities and with their nonliterary traditions have provided the source material for the many informative studies of what used to be called the primitive religions. Each community has what modern outsiders have tended to call its religious system[2]. Yet none, apparently, has traditionally had a name for that system. Nor have these groups a term for religion in general. The persons concerned will say, 'It is our custom to . . .', but they do not further postulate and name their complex of observances, or see it either as one of a series, or as one distinct segment of their life. They perform their rites, relate their myths, uphold their norms, and experience their emotions, without analytic reflection or linguistic generalization. Religion in any objectified sense has not been an idea in the minds of these groups.

Let us turn to more sophisticated cultures.

The opening sentence of the article on religious terms in the recent *Oxford Classical Dictionary* reads: 'No word in either Greek or Latin corresponds exactly to English "religion", "religious" '[3]. Of this categorical statement our own observation of how far the notion 'religion' has developed in two millennia of Western history will have helped us to appreciate the Roman side. On the Greek side, the lack of parallel is still more striking. Of the terms that the article does list and discuss, some in both languages come reasonably close to what we have called personal religion, in form if not in content. They deal with the same general area of life, even if they report it differently. The Latin term *pietas,* for instance, for all its highly particular overtones, is of the same order of ideas as the English derivative 'piety'; similarly, the various Greek words related to the root *seb-*[4]. What was missing in classical Greece is any concept for a religion as a systematic or historical entity—as discriminated either from another such entity, or from other areas of social life.

We have already seen of how much narrower significance was the Latin term *religio.* Even of this 'there was no adequate Greek equivalent', another scholar has observed[5]. Still a third writes: 'Strange as it may seem, Greek has no expression for the general idea conveyed by the word "religion" '[6]. The Greeks thought about the gods, about God; but they did not think about religion.

The result is similarly negative if we inquire of ancient Egypt. There was no word among the ancient Egyptians for our concept[7].

Moreover, their situation was such that there could not be. In describing that situation, modern scholars armed with the concept have come upon serious difficulties in their resolute attempts to apply it. Not only have they recognized that the Egyptians themselves never formulated what the modern observer is endeavouring to describe[8]. One student, in *his* attempt to formulate it, explicitly states what all writers in this field have come to emphasize: 'Religion in ancient Egypt was not a unit'[9]. Another scholar writes: 'The dividing-line which modern people strive [! —*sic*] to maintain between religious and social facts was unknown in ancient times, and more so in Egypt than anywhere else'[10]. This author goes on to argue that both institutionally and in personal feeling 'religion' was not separated off as a particular[11]. He then has to explain how it is that he in his modern treatment of Egyptian civilization will nonetheless devote a separate section to it (in addition to having touched on it under all his other headings). In effect he is saying what virtually all observers in such cases either say or imply: that 'religion' was not a distinct entity in the lives, or in the minds, of the people under consideration; yet since it is so in the minds of modern people, we in order to understand them must or may use (impose?) our conceptualizations and analyses in our interpretations[12].

Nonetheless, whereas Egyptologists used to speak readily of 'the religion of Egypt', some scholars, it seems, have themselves come to feel sufficiently awkward or hesitant in postulating such a thing that in the most recent studies a somewhat unwitting drift away from that phrasing can, in fact, be discerned[13].

Turning to ancient Iran, we find the flat assertion of one of the leading modern scholars: 'We do not find . . . any abstract idea "religion"—this word lacks all equivalent in the Iranian realm'[14]. The same situation would seem to apply to the ancient civilization of the Tigris-Euphrates valley[15].

A similar negative position will be found to obtain for the civilization of the Aztecs[16]; also for those of India, of China, and of Japan.

In classical India—again if we exclude personal religion, or religiousness—there is no word for our concept. In the threefold *trivarga* of mundane life, the realm of human behaviour is classified into those actions that one does for the sheer enjoyment of them (*kāma*), those that are means to some end (*artha*), and

those that are duties (*dharma*). The last of these, *dharma*, ranging in its reference from propriety to public law, from temple
ritual to caste obligations, and much more, has on occasion been
proffered by moderns as a term signifying systematic religion for
Hindus[17]. It does include a good deal of what the modern Western
student regards so, as normative ideal and as sociological pattern;
though it includes also a certain amount of matter that falls outside such a concept.

Yet it is at most one element in the Hindu affirmation. It omits
what are in some ways the most salient facets of Hindu faith. For
instance, it omits doctrine—such as the law of *karma,* which
makes *dharma* important. Furthermore, over and above *dharma,*
which relates to this world, another and indeed a crucial part of
what moderns mean by religion is to be found in each of the three
'Ways' of the *Trimārga,* which supplements and even supersedes
and in some ways contradicts the other. The Ways of intellect,
heart, and action-in-detachment (*jñāna-yoga, bhaktī-yoga, karma-
yoga*) are strikingly 'religious' avenues prescribed for the human
soul to break through from the bondage of the phenomenal world
(including *dharma*) to attain the counterpart of salvation, liberation (*moksha, muktī*). One might even argue that *mārga,* 'Way',
partly means 'religion', though one could not argue that it equals
it. And, in any case, it is ultimately more personal than systematic.
Furthermore, certainly neither it nor any other term conceptualizes institutional religion, either singular or plural. Nor was there
any term enabling an Indian to discriminate conceptually between the religious and the other aspects of his society's life.

It is not, of course, that this age was inhibited by lack of sophistication or self-consciousness. The classical Hindus developed
religious ideals and practices in richer profusion and subtler intellectual depth with more insistent emphasis and more refined
analysis earlier than any other people. They certainly did not lack
for technical terms, for names of gods, practices, principles, precepts, and much else. I suppose that the religious vocabulary of
classical Sanskrit is probably the subtlest and most elaborate that

man has ever devised. It is rather that, as we have seen with the ancient Egyptians and the mediaeval West, they were well able to be religious without reifying[18].

We are approaching here the heart of one part of my basic thesis in this essay, and to it we shall return. Put negatively for the moment, it recognizes that a religious understanding of the world does not necessarily imply that there is a generic religious truth or a religious system that can be formulated and externalized into an observable pattern theoretically abstractible from the persons who live it. This is to look for essences; to Platonize one's own faith and to Aristotelianize other peoples'.

For Buddhists, during the India phase of this community's development, this situation was not seriously different. The chief divergence is that for them *dharma (dhamma)* was transformed into something of much profounder, more cosmic import. This term named for them an ultimate cosmic pattern of behaviour, a transcendent moral law; the supreme 'ought'. To it, indeed, the Buddha pointed; and it became part of what modern students may call the Buddhists' religion[19]. Yet it is not equivalent to it. At its most austere, most rarefied, this is constituted of three simultaneous refuges[20], of which *dharma* is one, supplemented with the person of the Buddha and the organized community of his disciples. To equate *dharma* with religion, then, is to conceptualize Buddhism without the Buddha and without any Buddhists.

Both Hindus and Buddhists used terms conceptualizing teachings and norms, idealizing a systematic pattern of these in the case of divergent interpretations. Some of these terms approximate at certain points to one of the Enlightenment conceptions in the West of a religion, provided that one does not include anything less abstract or less intellectualist than an idealization of a group's belief, and also provided that one discriminates one sect from another, within what modernity would call the same religion, and not any one or all of these from the 'nonreligious' aspects of life[21]. The concept that these terms formulated, and the most reified concept that either Hindus or Buddhists classically attained, signifies what we might call the doctrinal position of a particular sect or community.

In the Buddhist case, as in the others that we have noted, I would again suggest that the absence of an entity-concept 'religion' does not indicate a failure of those concerned to formulate a designation for something with which they were confronted. Rather it represents, more faithfully than the newer Western concepts can do, the situation and the processes in which they were actually involved. Perhaps the most eloquent testimony to the inappropriateness of the new concept to that situation and those processes lies in the persistent problem of whether or not primitive Buddhism was a religion. The modern West has proven incapable of answering this question.

The early Buddhists and their neighbours, we may note, were incapable of asking it.

It may seem not overly bold to suggest a possible correlation between these two facts.

When the Buddhist missionary movement reached the Far East, it and the message and outlook that it was carrying and developing met and became a major participant in a quite different type of religious situation from that known in India. We shall look into that particular context presently when we consider the naming of individual traditions, of which conspicuously in China and Japan the Buddhist became one among others. In the meantime, we may content ourselves with noting the observation of a professor of Chinese at Oxford who had occasion to write some years ago: 'The Chinese, recognizing this deficiency [namely, that they had no word corresponding to the Western concept; their word usually so translated 'does not mean either religion or a church in our sense of those terms'] and feeling the need of a term meaning a religion, have recently adopted the term Tsung-Chiao from the Japanese, who had adapted it to suit their own need for a term to cover the Western idea of religion'[22].

This brings us to the important matter of present-day Western influence. In modern times, among most peoples of the earth the spread of Western ideas and attitudes and social patterns and the response to these seem to have led or to be leading among many other consequences to a development, at least at sophisticated levels, of a counterpart term and concept for 'religion'.

This is the case not only in Japan and China. For example, modern Hindi *dharam* is developing a meaning of the English term 'religion' that its classical Sanskrit counterpart did not have. Again, in modern Indonesia *agama,* from classical Sanskrit for 'text', has come to be used for the Western notion of a religion. There is even a contemporary move to conceptualize in the new phrase *agama Djawa* ('the religion of Java') the religious tradition of the Javanese, whose distinctive customs have in the past been practised but not dignified by being given conceptual status. Those who practised these ways had heretofore been considered Muslims of an 'unorthodox' sort. The introduction of the new concept raises quite new questions[23].

Let us turn, finally, to the source of the Western religious tradition, the Bible[24]. Classical Hebrew has no word signifying 'religion'. Except perhaps for a solitary Persian intrusion at the very end of its development[25], the Old Testament is innocent of this concept and this term. The phrase 'the fear of the Lord' (*yir'ath Yahweh*) is the closest approach in the sense of personal piety. Clearly it does not designate a system, sociological or ideological; and it cannot have a plural.

In the New Testament, the great word is *pistis,* 'faith', and its corresponding verb—a virtually new usage, reverberatingly affirmed[26]. The various forms of this root occur 602 times[27]. Other terms for reverence, awe, piety are also reasonably common[28]. In addition, St. Paul in passing uses once a term (*thrēskeia,* rite, ritual, observance) to designate apparently a religious community characterized by its normative ways and some would even say a religion as a systematic pattern[29]. The one other time that he uses the same word it is to denote a ritual observance of which he disapproves[30]. One does seem to catch a glimpse here in the former instance of that embryonic process, which we noted also in our

Latin survey, of the emergence in the eastern Mediterranean, at about this juncture, of the concept of an organized religious group ideal.

We shall return to such an emergence in our inquiry into the naming of individual religions, and again later in our Middle Eastern survey. For the moment, we may simply observe that there is no evidence in the New Testament that the early Christians were conscious of being involved in a new religion.

They, like Jesus himself, like the Hebrews before them, and like the Hindus, Buddhists, Far Easterners, ancient Egyptians, and others whom we have noted, simply did not think in such terms.

... iii

We turn next to the question of specific names for the individual 'religions'. Here the first point to remark is that we have grown quite accustomed to the absence of any such name in the majority of cases. We are happy enough in referring to 'the religion of the Greeks', 'Etruscan religion', 'the religion of the Trobriand Islanders', and so on without feeling embarrassed that there is no proper name.

For the major living religious traditions of the world, however, modernity has conferred names where they did not exist.

On inquiry, this proves to have been on the whole a process of the nineteenth century in the West.

To the special case of Islam (apparently the only religion in the world with a built-in name[31]) we shall give particular attention in our next chapter. With the Islamic movement the West had long had close and lively relations, and the naming can be traced back to the end of the sixteenth century—though it is presented under various forms, some of which now seem a trifle bizarre: 'Mahumetisme' (1597), 'Mahumetanism' (1612), 'Muhammedrie' (1613), 'Islamism' (1747), 'Musulmanisme' (1818)[32].

Gibbon wrote in 1788 that Muhammad called the faith that he

preached 'Islam'; otherwise this term is found in Europe only from last century[33].

The Manichees also the West had known about from even earlier; and although the mediaeval Church speaks of the people without, apparently, abstracting a system for them, a term 'Manichism' is developed in the seventeenth century also[34].

In other cases, I have not found any formulation of a named religion earlier than the nineteenth century: 'Boudhism' (1801), 'Hindooism' (1829), 'Taouism' (1839), 'Zoroasterianism' (1854), 'Confucianism' (1862), and so on[35]. These are stray references, in passing; there may have been earlier such occurrences that have escaped notice. In the more reliable and more significant matter, however, of book-titles, explicitly presenting these religious traditions to an inquiring Europe, these terms emerged into use still later. The earliest work on 'Buddhism' that I have found is 1828[36]; on 'Confucianism', 1877[37]; 'Taoism', 1879[38]; 'Shintoism', 1894[39].

Previously, reference in the West to these traditions had taken a different form. The development in the seventeenth century of the phrase 'the religion of' a given people, we have already observed; this later appears for new groups, such as 'the religion of the Japanese'. Earlier, from mediaeval times, one finds 'the sect of' or 'the heresy of' a people, as in the Islamic case which we shall be investigating below. Later, one finds such phrases as 'Chinese wisdom', 'the philosophy of the Hindus'; also (early nineteenth century) 'the religion of Buddha'. The mid-nineteenth-century change to a newly coined proper name followed somewhat after the trend towards reification in the concept 'religion' itself, which we have previously studied, and that towards a use of 'Christianity' and 'Judaism', which we shall investigate later in this chapter[40].

The development was not haphazard: a pattern can, on inquiry, be discerned. The transition to a specific name did not take place in any of those cases where a people's religious life remained integrated and coterminous with their social existence. Thus the West has never developed a name for the religion of the Incas, of the Samoans, of the Babylonians, and so on for a long list. In cases, however, where the religious tradition of one community developed historically to transcend the boundaries of the people among whom it first arose, so that on a considerable scale men of other communities became converts to that tradition, or in those where, on the other hand, religious practices were followed by markedly less than all the members of a given society, then a name did arise to distinguish 'the religion' from the social group. This process normally took the form of adding the Greek suffix '-ism' to a word used to designate the persons who are members of the religious community or followers of a given tradition.

iv

The process, although relatively recent in its rise, is already past its zenith, some indications would suggest. Modern careful writers are discernibly uneasy with the terms, if they retain them at all. The eleventh edition of the *Encyclopedia Britannica*, 1911, has an article SIKHISM, also an article SIKH which defines the latter in terms of the former; the most recent edition, 1958, has no entry SIKHISM, but discusses the various religious ideas and practices of this community under the heading SIKHS[41]. There is still an article CONFUCIANISM, but it opens with the words 'Confucianism, a misleading general term for . . .'[42]; one may guess that it will not be long before this heading is dropped or modified.

Clearly what has happened here, is that the editors have asked a scholar to write the article, they supplying the title out of the current concepts of their culture; the scholar may accede, yet is evidently hesitant about the terminology because in his greater knowledge of the subject matter he senses that it does not aptly fit. This is altogether typical of informed contemporary writing.

Earlier in this century, the professor of Chinese at Oxford whom we have quoted published a work bearing the title *The Three Religions of China*[43]. This phrasing formulated the then established Western approach. In 1950 his successor at Oxford and a collaborator were invited by the London publishers of a series on the world's religions to contribute a book 'on the religions of China'. They accepted in substance but demurred to the form. Their volume when published was deliberately entitled *Religion in China*. They explain in their preface that twenty-four years' residence in China followed by sixteen years' study and teaching at Oxford had led them to believe that 'the old convention of marking out this practice and belief as Confucianism and that as Taoism and the other as Buddhism . . . is misleading'[44].

If, then, the nineteenth-century rise of these terms in the West is to be understood in relation to the Western reificationist trend in general, the present-day incipient decline in their use is to be understood in relation to increasing familiarity with the actual situation that the terms were meant to describe. As knowledge continues to grow, one may reasonably expect these alien labels to be more and more abandoned[45].

v

Let us turn, therefore, to the Orient itself, to learn how these matters have been conceptually handled in the traditions concerned.

First, India. The term 'Hinduism' is, in my judgment, a particularly false conceptualization, one that is conspicuously incompatible with any adequate understanding of the religious outlook of Hindus. Even the term 'Hindu' was unknown to the classical Hindus[46]. 'Hinduism' as a concept certainly they did not have. And indeed one has only to reflect on the situation carefully to realize that it would necessarily have been quite meaningless to them.

A modern writer wishing to portray the religious life of the people of India in those centuries may construct or inherit such a term in order to inform his readers that he is studying this rather than the ancient Sumerians or the modern Eskimo community, and that his own abstracting interest is in what he and his modern readers call religion more than it is in economics[47]. Even so, for that early period modern students are hesitant to use the term, and it has in fact been now almost abandoned by scholars[48]. 'The religious life of ancient India' is perhaps the only valid way of designating what the modern has in mind. In any case, as soon as one considers the point, it is clear that the people involved could have had no use for a term or a concept 'Hindu' or 'Hinduism'. What could these conceivably have signified?

As we have previously observed, the classical Hindus were inhibited by no lack of sophistication or selfconsciousness. They thought about what we call religious questions profusely and with critical analysis. But they could not think of Hinduism because that is the name that we give as a totality to whatever it might be that they thought, or did, or thought worth doing.

The term 'Hindu' as a religious designation was developed by the Muslims after they had invaded the country in the second millennium A.D.[49]. For the Muslims it served to designate these aliens whom they conquered, and whose not being Muslim was of course now for the first time significant. It retained for some time its geographical reference: 'Indian', 'indigenous, local', virtually 'native'. And the indigenous groups themselves also began then to use the term, differentiating themselves and their traditional ways from these invading Muslim foreigners. It covered all such groups: those whom we now call Hindus, but also Jains, Buddhists, and all the others.

The arrival of the Muslims and their ideas was far from the first time that novel or discrepant views were being propounded or communities launched in India. The intellectual, theological, and religious ferment and variegated multiformity of the country had long been brisk. Many new patterns had arisen and many old ones had been criticized. Never before, however, had an organized, systematic, and exclusive community carrying (or being carried by) what was in theory an organized, systematic and exclusive idea arrived violently from the outside to reject all alternatives and to erect a great conceptual wall between those who did and those who did not belong[50]. A boundary between non-Muslims (followers of indigenous ways, 'Hindus') and Muslims was sharply drawn[51]. Yet on the other side the continuation of such boundaries so as to demarcate off a 'Hindu' community from other Indian groups was not clear[52].

Indeed, it is still not clear today. The census of India, 1941, gave up the attempt of previous British censuses (1931, 1921, and on back) to enumerate Hindus exactly. The census offices reported that they had been forced into a realization that the boundaries of Islam and Christianity were reasonably clear but that those of the Hindu community were not. They could draw a line discriminating Hindus from Christians and Muslims on the one side, but it was not possible to draw one discriminating them from animists on the other[53]. This on the practical, operational side is an unwitting empirical confirmation of my theoretical point, that the concept of a religious system, whether ideal or sociological, is here alien and invalid[54]. It is a Western (and Muslim) concept, which Westerners (and Muslims) have tried to impose upon their understanding of India; but it does not fit. There are Hindus, but there is no Hinduism[55].

Over against this point, one may recognize that historically the new term 'Hindu', after it was introduced into India by the Muslims, was presently followed both for Muslims and in a limited way for Hindus by certain new formulations one or two of which are nowadays on occasion rendered 'Hinduism'. Such a translation was perhaps rather more legitimate in the nineteenth century than in our day with our modern awareness of historical, institutional, and sociological dimensions. These are chiefly the phrases or compounds *Hindū mata, Hindū dharma,* basically 'Indian teaching, indigenous norms', the traditional ideals of the country. These designations are first found in rather recent centuries[56] and were relatively little used, but they did serve to discriminate from the Islamic importation all that system or those congeries of systems that locally existed.

My objection to the term 'Hinduism', of course, is not on the grounds that nothing exists. Obviously an enormous quantity of phenomena is to be found that this term covers. My point, and I think that this is the first step that one must take towards understanding something of the vision of Hindus, is that the mass of religious phenomena that we shelter under the umbrella of that term, is not a unity and does not aspire to be. It is not an entity in any theoretical sense, let alone any practical one.

'Islam' and 'Christianity', as we shall subsequently consider, are also in fact, in actual practice, internally diverse, and have been historically fluid. They, however, have included a tendency to wish not to be so; this is not how they conceptualize themselves. Many Christians and many Muslims have come to believe that there is one true Christianity and one true Islam. Hindus, on the other hand, have gloried in diversity. One of their basic and persistent affirmations has been that there are as many aspects of the truth as there are persons to perceive it.

Or, if some proclaimed a dogmatic exclusivism, insisting on their own version of the truth over against alternatives, it was always on a sectarian basis, one fraction of the total Hindu complex affirmed against other fractions—not of one transcending Hindu schema as a whole. Some Hindus have been tolerant of diversity, and indeed have made a principle of it; those who have not, have adhered to a particularist position that thereby segmented the Hindu tradition as a possible theoretic unity. In either case, 'Hinduism' has not been a feasible concept for them in any essentialist sense.

It is remarkable how many modern treatises on 'Hinduism' have as their opening sentence some such reflection as 'Hinduism is very difficult to define', and then proceed to try to define it[57]. This is to systematize and congeal the spontaneous; to insist on abstractions, a common core amidst the luxuriant welter of the faith of Hindus.

Instructive here is the case of Guru Nanak, the gentle and intense Indian mystic of the fifteenth-sixteenth century A.D. To call him 'the founder of Sikhism', as is often done[58], is surely to misconstrue both him and history. He was a devotee (*bhākta*) who, in spiritually passionate and directly personalist poetry and in a life of humane and humble service, preached sincerity and adoration and the overwhelming reality of God. He attacked religious formalism of all kinds. Several generations later his followers were religiously formalized, systematized; by organizers such as Arjan Dev and especially Gobind Singh. Out of this was born what we call 'followerism' (*Sikh* means 'disciple') . Gobind Singh organized what had by then become a movement, into a structured community, the Khalsa—counterpart of the Christian concept 'Church'; but by this time it was the eighteenth century[59].

To the explicitly indefinable[60] faith of the individual member of the movement, the term 'discipleship' (in Panjabī, *Sikhī*) was internally given, in the clearly Platonic sense of 'true discipleship'[61]. From this term, denoting the form though not the content of a transcendent personalist ideal, there has been gradually evolved a name for an abstract rather than transcendent ideal of the group rather than the persons, and finally the counterpart of the Western (outsiders') concept 'Sikhism' as the total complex of Sikh religious practices and rites, scriptures and doctrines, history and institutions.

We have here a recapitulation of a standard gradual process of reification: the preaching of a vision, the emergence of followers, the organization of a community, the positing of an intellectual ideal of that community, the definition of the actual pattern of its institutions. The last two steps seem to have been taken only in the nineteenth and twentieth centuries[62].

The Chinese also do not fit into a pattern of religious systems. We have already seen how the vigorous attempt to impose such a pattern on them from the outside is now beginning to be abandoned by Western scholars in the light of closer awareness of the situation itself in China. Western and Muslim students tend to be baffled when they first learn that a single Chinese may be and usually is a 'Confucian', a 'Buddhist', *and* a 'Taoist'. They cannot imagine how a person can 'belong to three different religions', as they put it, at the same time. The perplexity arises not from something confused or bizarre about China so much as from the conceptualization of religious systems, which is brought to bear but is evidently inappropriate.

Four Roman Catholic missionaries published in Paris in 1687 a Latin translation of three of the Chinese classics; and thereby introduced the term 'Confucius' to Europe[63]. From this there was developed in the nineteenth century the terms and concept 'Confucian'[64], 'Confucianist', as both adjective and noun describing persons.

For this there is no equivalent term in Chinese.

Nor are words for 'Buddhists', 'Taoists' found in that language.

The reason for this is fundamentally quite simple. The three schools of thought to which these notions relate do, certainly, exist in China, and have been cherished over the centuries. Around them, however, closed communities have not developed, parties with clear-cut boundaries and an *either/or* sense of adherents and outsiders. There is no overt procedure comparable to that by which a person 'becomes' a Christian or a Communist; no Church or Party to join, no sociologically identifiable or conceptually posited organization or group. Teachings are available, are cherished and are championed; but what a person does with those teachings is up to him. The teachings even have been systematized; but not the life to which, either ideally or socially, their application gives rise.

There was not 'a Buddhist religion', we have noted, in India; but there was a Buddhist community. In China there has come to be not even that; though here the Buddha has been more influential and significant, has been taken with more lavish seriousness, than anywhere else in the world. When Buddhist missionaries reached China and preached their views, many persons were interested, impressed, persuaded. They in turn have studied the message, lived it, transmitted it to others to delight in and explore. Many found in or through it a key to life's ultimate meaning. Yet the result was not an organization, but a tradition.

To ask a census-taker how many Chinese are Buddhist is rather like asking one how many Westerners are Aristotelian or pragmatist.

This sort of point is even more relevant to the teaching of which K'ung[65] has become the symbol. This is called *ju chiao,* which has sometimes been given as a Chinese equivalent for the Western notion 'Confucianism'. A more faithful, accurate translation, I suggest, would rather be simply 'the classical tradition' of China. *Ju* means scholar, representative of the class that has preserved and propagated this heritage; and *chiao* is 'instruction', 'teaching'.

Chiao has developed from being a generic or abstract noun to becoming a common, concrete one, referring to a particular tradition of learning—pretty much the English 'school of thought'—though the method of transmission is perhaps more formalized in the conception. This term was also used to designate other traditions, both for those growing up within China, such as *Tao Chiao* for the teaching about ultimate truth as Tao that developed luxuriantly around the inspiration of Lao Tse and others, and for traditions brought in from outside, such as *Fu Chiao* (also *Shih Chiao*) for the Buddhists' teachings and *Ming Chiao* for the Manichees'[66]. Three such traditions have stood out, and the phrase *San Chiao,* 'the three traditions', has been current. The translation of this into Western languages as 'the three religions', however, in the nineteenth century, gave rise to the serious misunderstanding that we have noted[67]. The critical difference between a religion and a transmitted tradition will be the subject of our sixth chapter.

For the moment, we may simply observe once again that the question 'Is Confucianism a religion?' is one that the West has never been able to answer, and China never able to ask.

If we turn to the term 'Taoism', we find this as probably the instance where an argument against the use of such a concept needs most strongly to be made, and where the ineptness is most conspicuous once one pauses to reflect. For surely if ever it has been true it was true for Lao Tse and Chuang Tse, who inspired this movement, that (not religion: they used no such word, but) a true apprehension of life is deeply personal. They preached that reality, Tao, is not a system, not a neat and ordered pattern as K'ung would have it, not a code of rules; but that it is a process, dynamic, vital, ebullient. If you catch it in any snare of words, in any net of logic, of morality, in any system, it dies. Life, they sang, is not a science but an art; and truth is a surging, inner force.

I would guess that these two poets turned in their graves when the freedom that they proclaimed for man was presented under a rubric as systematized pattern. No modern existentialist thinker has debunked essentialist rigidity with anything like their vigour and verve, their grace and wit, their pith and brilliance.

If Tao as they conceived it is at all a valid concept, then it follows that Taoism is a false one.

Turning to Japan, we find the term 'Shinto', which means 'the way of the gods' (or, 'of the spirits'). It has come to be thought of as a name of the national religious tradition, which goes back to before the days of the massive impingement on Japanese life from the sixth century A.D. of Buddhist and other cultural influences from China. On scrutiny, however, it turns out that the situation is not quite so simple.

The term itself does not go back so far. In those early days, what modernity has called the indigenous religion of Japan had no name. In fact, the word 'Shinto' is not itself Japanese. The modern Japanese equivalent (*kami no michi*) is a translation of this term, which comes from China. It was a phrase that the foreigners introduced, on their arrival in Japan, to designate the traditions of the natives and to discriminate these from their own cultural norms[68]. This compares with the Muslims' introduction of the concept 'Hindu' into India. Apparently it came into general use in Japan 'about the thirteenth century'[69].

Of the imported traditions, it is curious to note that the development in Japan of what for China has been called the Confucianist tradition has not been comparably conceptualized, although it has been historically of major permeative influence[70].

Actually an adequate descriptive history of the religious life of the Chinese people, if it were to be reasonably objective and balanced, would have to give as much attention to a fourth, altogether nonconceptualized, stream in China as to the usually recognized three, or as studies of Japan give to 'Shinto'—namely, the ancient indigenous folk-religion tradition of China[71]. For the great majority of the Chinese people, this has constituted at most times that around which their religious life and behaviour have in practice chiefly revolved. That this has not been given conceptual status in China, while its counterpart in Japan has, would perhaps seem primarily due to the fact that in China it was not, whereas in Japan its counterpart was, given literary acceptance by the small intellectual élite.

However this may be, 'Shinto' is still not rightly understood if it is thought of as the name of a religion. It means, as we have said, 'the way of the gods'[72]. In the nineteenth century, Europeans developed the interesting formulation 'Shintoism'[73]to designate 'the religion' of those who would honour this way and respond to it. They have since contracted this to 'Shinto' to refer not to the way of the gods but the way of men in Japan vis-à-vis those gods[74].

That way has not been a unified whole. There has been no systematic pattern, either in practice or in theory. 'Shinto' does not refer to an ideal; but at best to a congeries of disparate ideals and complex actualities.

And in the 1930's, a minor international issue grew out of the unanswerable question, 'Is Shinto a religion?' Until the nineteenth century, this question could not be framed in Japan. When it was raised by outsiders, the Japanese answered it 'no'[75].

vi

Finally, from abroad let us return to Western civilization itself, which has in modern times developed these terms for others; to see the evolving of names for the two religious systems that it has known, Judaism and Christianity. We have already noted that

THE MEANING AND END OF RELIGION

there is no word 'religion' in the Hebrew Old Testament. Neither is there a name for the particular religion of the Jews.

One can see the concept 'Judaism' arising, however, just at the end of the pre-Christian era; not in Hebrew but in Greek. (This in itself is not insignificant: the Greek *Weltanschauung* is *par excellence* a conceptualizing with nouns. Greek thought is pre-eminently reificationist-idealist.)

The Greek word *Iudaismos* occurs first in Second Maccabees[76] (first century B.C. or later), appropriately to designate that for which loyal Jews were fighting in their struggle against Hellenism. Even here, a more faithful translation of the original meaning of the passage would be that these men were fighting for their Jewishness[77], rather than 'for Judaism'. The impact of Greek ways upon the Jewish community was a threat, they felt, to the traditional character of their living. What began, however, as designating a quality of life, eventually came to refer to the formal pattern or outward system of observances in which that quality found expression. Thus the concept 'Judaism' was born[78].

This is perhaps the first time in human history that a religion has a name.

And like many another seminal idea, it arose out of that ferment engendered at the beginning of this era by the meeting of Middle-Eastern and Greek world outlooks[79].

The term is next found shortly after, again in the usage of a Greek-speaking Jew, this time one who has virtually left that community, having become Christian. St. Paul in the New Testament uses it twice of a way of living that he has since superseded[80]. Again, it is appropriate and revealing that the naming of a religious outlook should come out of a differentiation of two outlooks. One of the profound movements in which St. Paul was engaged was that by which 'Christianity' (we shall return to this term in a moment; it is not one that he used or had ever heard or imagined) was extricating itself from being simply one more Jewish sect and becoming an independent tradition or grouping, a separate 'religion' in its own right—a process of which today we

OTHER CULTURES. 'THE RELIGIONS'

take the results for granted, but which at the time was profoundly significant, and not easy.

'The disciples were called Christians first in Antioch'[81]. Soon after the religious community came into existence, we see here its members first being named. As is usual, the term was applied first by outsiders, who coined it. For a time it was resisted; the title was adopted by the community itself reluctantly and only gradually[82]. It is in the same city, early in the second century, that the use of a term that subsequently meant 'Christianity' is first recorded: in the writing of the city's bishop under sentence of martyrdom, Ignatius. He accepts being called 'Christian' as an ideal[83]; and speaks of *Christianismos* as that in accordance with which 'we should learn to live'. He contrasts it with the way people that we today should call Christians actually did behave[84]; and contrasts it also with *Iudaismos,* using the latter (also the corresponding verb) for Christians' 'living according to Jewish ways'[85]. That is, he speaks of the *Iudaismos* of Christians. In effect, he is saying that their being Christian should take precedence over their being Jewish, over their Jewishness; or, more actively, that their living Christianly should take precedence over their living Jewishly. Both *Iudaismos* and *Christianismos* are for him personal qualities, not institutions.

The verbal quality of *Iudaismos* might in Christian usage become weak, so that the word could come presently to mean a system of Jewish norms rather than the fact of living in accordance with them or the quality of one's life that this involved. The same transition, however, could and did come only much later for *Christianismos,* since much of the point of the new 'good news' was that faith freed a man from norms. What was proclaimed was explicitly not a system, but a person, and life 'in' that person. It was the *imitatio Christi,* living in Christ and in a Christ-like way, to which Ignatius gave the new name[86].

This Greek term was subsequently adopted into Latin, as 'Christianismus'[87]. From the third century an original Latin term, 'Christianitas', is also introduced[88]. (Both survive in, for in-

THE MEANING AND END OF RELIGION

stance, modern French: *le Christianisme, la Chrétienté*. In fact most Western languages have a pair of terms.) Neither was widely used, however, by any means. The latter especially occurs through the Middle Ages occasionally, chiefly in the sense of the people constituting the Christian community, or Christendom[89]; less often in its original sense of a verbal noun ('becoming Christian', 'being Christian') ; occasionally as an abstract idea. St. Thomas Aquinas was able to produce his vast output—a shelffull of books —while hardly speaking of Christendom, and so far as I have been able to ascertain virtually without mentioning 'Christianity'[90]. Certainly no one throughout the Middle Ages ever wrote a book on this topic.

The standard mediaeval phrase for what Christians today would call 'Christianity' was *fides Christiana* ('Christian faith'). The difference is subtle, but profound. As with the rest of mankind, so in Christendom an age of faith is not an age of reification.

It is only well after the Reformation that the term 'Christianity' becomes current, and only during the Enlightenment that it becomes standard. Even so, all through the eighteenth century and even beyond it refers to an ideal, first transcendent, then intellectual. Only within the last century or so has the meaning of an historical phenomenon come into use.

In the first printed book-title in which I have found the word 'Christianity', it means 'Christendom'[91]. In the mid-sixteenth century it begins to appear in a few of the catechisms[92], including some versions of Calvin's[93], as equivalent to 'Christian doctrine'[94], 'teaching about Christ'[95]. It is also found in the ill-fated work of Servetus, both book and author perishing[96]. But throughout the sixteenth century it remains comparatively rare.

In the seventeenth century the word comes to be used in two senses. The first is a pietistic one, more or less equivalent to 'Christ-like-ness' or 'Christian living', almost as in St. Ignatius. Thus Johann Arndt inspired the later Pietist movement in Germany with a book that protested against rigid formalism and doctrinalism in the Church, calling instead for an inner personalizing of Christ in one's heart. To this latter he gave the name *das wahre Christentum*. What he had in mind by this novel phrase may perhaps be rendered 'true Christianness'; or better, 'on being truly Christian'[97]. The sense of 'Christlikeness' seems striking in an English work later in the century entitled *The Reasons of the Christian Religion: The first part, of Godliness. . . . The second part, of Christianity,* though actually here the transition to our second meaning has begun[98]. In the eighteenth century the first meaning persists, designating a quality of Christian living[99]. But it had become rather rare.

The other meaning, which develops with the Enlightenment, is systematic (ideal), and increasingly intellectualist. More and more this word, which had had only a meager history, came now to be used as the name of a system of beliefs. 'The truth' (or, truths) 'of Christianity' became a stock phrase[100]. Whether 'Christianity' is or is not true, is or is not reasonable, became at this period brisk questions. This is well shown in such influential works as John Locke's *The Reasonableness of Christianity*[101], just before the eighteenth century. Our interest here is not so much in why he thought or how successfully he argued that it was reasonable, as in reflecting on what it was that he thought reasonable; and on what it was that Tindal, a generation later, believed to be 'as old as the creation'[102].

Again it is possible to observe how those who disagreed, at any rate on the intellectual plane, acceded to the terms of the argument as postulated. Thus a 1691 title proclaims 'Christianity a Doctrine of the Cross'[103], where the first three words are unwittingly as important as the last three. They are certainly as revealing, and a good deal more novel. And the first of the spate of pamphlets and books ensuing on Tindal's highly provocative affirmation accepted his phraseology, and to some extent perhaps even the form if not the content of his conceptualizations[104]. This was true also of many of the succeeding writers.

In the discussion above in our preceding chapter on the concept 'religion', we observed that during the early centuries of the modern era that term came into use and gradually was shifted in meaning from a personal to a systematic reference. The term 'Christianity' on the whole began the process, on a considerable scale, later; made the transition more quickly; and presently outpaced the other. By the nineteenth century it had substantially superseded 'the Christian religion' as a phrase. We have seen that in that century also, although chiefly in the latter half or last quarter of it, terms such as 'Hinduism', 'Confucianism', 'Buddhism', and the like were replacing the earlier 'the sect of the Banians', 'Chinese wisdom', 'the religion of Buddha'[105]. These processes can be not only observed but studied, measured, and formulated.

Thus in the Christian case, if one takes a readymade selection of something over six hundred titles of printed books in which the terms 'Christian faith', 'Christian religion', and 'Christianity' occur, or their equivalents in other European languages, and arranges their relative frequency by century, one gets the distribution that is illustrated on our next page[106].

A closely parallel result is secured if one measures other indices. Thus if one abstracts from the above set those titles that are in English and that include the word 'religion', and if one arranges these by relative frequency of the use or absence of the article, one gets the same movement from the personal idea of 'Christian religion' to the impersonal and finally institutionalized concept 'the Christian religion'[107]. This result is confirmed by taking a different set of data and observing the same transition[108].

Here, then, is a process of institutionalization, of conceptual reification. Concepts, terminology, and attention shift from personal orientation to an ideal, then to an abstraction, finally to an institution.

By the end of the eighteenth century the term 'Christianity' had come to be used primarily and almost without question as the name of a systematized 'religion'.

Reification in the West

Percentage Distribution
in Modern Times

of

"Christian Faith"
"Christian Religion"
"Christianity"

in 639 book titles ar-
ranged according to
century.

	15TH CENT.	16TH CENT.	17TH CENT.	18TH CENT.	19TH CENT.	20TH CENT. TO 1950	
	100%	47.5%	8.1%	1.3%	8.2%	5.7%	Faith
		42.5%	67.7%	31.9%	15.6%	9.4%	Religion
		10.0%	24.2%	66.8%	76.2%	84.9%	Christianity

vii

Development was not finished, however, by any means. As with the term 'religion' also, so with their individual names. The nineteenth century and the first half of the twentieth effected the radical and momentous shift from ideal to mundane actuality, from a theoretical system of doctrine to a sociological entity, an historical phenomenon. When the Enlightenment debated whether Christianity is 'reasonable', it was calling reasonable something quite different from what men were referring to under the name 'Christianity' in a phrase such as Karl Kautsky's, when he calls it 'one of the most gigantic phenomena in human history . . .', 'a movement of impoverished . . . proletarians'[109]. This author, no believer, is thinking of Christianity not as an intellectual system but as a social phenomenon. In the usage of his age, even at times among believers, 'Christianity' had become the name of an overt, observable institution, with a geographical location or distribution, a temporal evolution, a massive involvement in social, economic, military, linguistic, and other human complications. The word now designated something with a history, with the overtones and undertones of something with a history, from sheer fluidity and change on the one hand to the ramifications of human waywardness and sinfulness and creativity on the other. Out of the sky on to the chaos of earth, from essence to existence.

The objective quality was even more pronounced in the case of the names of the Oriental traditions. There was not even a lingering memory of a time when 'Buddhism', for instance, had meant 'Buddha-like-ness' or the quality or act of a personal fulfilment in self-commitment. 'Buddhism', in English as in other Western languages, was more or less from the start the name of an historical development, an evolving complex of observable beliefs, practices, institutions, data. In the nature of the case, it could not refer but to observables. It and the others began, no doubt, with an emphasis on doctrines. Yet even this was inevitably an intellectual construct, an abstract idea rather than a transcendent ideal. (The difference is monumental.) It designated not what Buddhists ought to believe, but what Buddhists have believed[110]. And this presently was supplemented by further accounts of what they have done and been.

An enormous weight of evidence began to accumulate, both through the general increase in education, communication, and the widening of horizons, and through the specific work done by the concentrated scholarship of 'historians of religion'; evidence that radically transformed the sophisticated awareness not, perhaps, of what religion is, but certainly of what religion has been, and so of each particular religion. It requires a powerful act of imagination to transport oneself back a hundred or more years in order to realize how inescapably different must be what either a European or a Buddhist could possibly have understood by the term 'Christianity' or 'Buddhism' then from what we must conceive by them now, historically[111]. The meaning of the term has inevitably changed radically.

Yet of course the question still remains whether the historical meaning of these terms is, let us not say the 'real' one, but the most illuminating.

Indeed, in this religious realm there is a significant question as to whether we have at all adequately understood even what history we know. Information about the historical activity of a community, even detailed acquaintance with its rituals, formulations, and institutions, have not necessarily been accompanied with a sympathetic insight into what these have meant to men and women whose faith they have expressed. We have learned more about 'the religions', but this has made us perhaps less, rather than more, aware of what it is that we have tried to mean by 'religion'.

CHAPTER FOUR

The Special Case of Islam

SO FAR we have not dealt with the Islamic situation. This particular case has been reserved for separate treatment because it is both unusual and intricate. It is in some ways different from the others, and in some ways similar. On both scores it is illuminating.

We may take the differences first, since they lie closer to the surface. The first observation is that of all the world's religious traditions the Islamic would seem to be the one with a built-in name. The word 'Islam' occurs in the Qur'an itself[1], and Muslims are insistent on using this term to designate the system of their faith. In contrast to what has happened with other religious communities, as we have partly seen[2], this is not a name devised by outsiders, those inside resisting or ignoring or finally accepting. On the contrary, it is they who proclaim it, and teach it to others. Indeed, Muslims are zealous in their campaign to persuade the rest of the world to abandon other spontaneous names for their 'religion' (such as 'Muhammadanism') in favour of this proper one, which they proudly bear.

This name for their religious system, moreover, has the sanction

80

not only of the Muslims and their tradition but, they aver, of God Himself. God is presented as announcing: 'This day I have perfected your religion for you, and completed my favour unto you; and have chosen for you as a religion *Islam*'[3]. Again, it is written: 'Verily, *the* Religion in the eyes of God is Islam'[4]. Such verses, which we will later carefully reconsider, are basic for many a Muslim. The assurance of divine approval could hardly be more squarely based, more explicit.

Secondly, we may note a further point, which the Qur'an verses just cited also illustrate. This is that the Arabic language has, and has had since the appearance of Islam and indeed from shortly before[5], a term and concept that seem to be quite closely equivalent to the Western 'religion'. Indeed this word—namely, *dīn*—is used in all the various senses of its Western counterpart. It carries the sense of personal religion: the classical dictionaries give *warac*, 'piety' as an equivalent, a word that never has a systematic or a community meaning and that cannot have a plural. It carries also, however, the sense of a particular religious system, one 'religion' as distinct from another. In this sense it has a plural (*adyān*). This plural is not in the Qur'an, but is traditional. Furthermore, the word in its systematic sense can be used both ideally and objectively, of one's own religion and of other people's, the true religion and false ones.

In fact, it may be used of these both at once. Muslims quote classical verses from the earliest period that affirm that 'the religion of Muhammad [is] the best of the religions of mankind'[6]. I have previously suggested that such a conception is remarkable, especially for an early period. In Latin, as we have observed, a plural *religiones* was common, but it referred to rites and observances, and the plural was regularly used with one specific God. The Christian Latin writers used the plural to refer to what might today be called in the singular the pagan religion (or, cults) of the Greco-Roman world; they also use the singular, and sometimes the plural, for their own Christian rites or worship[7]. I have not, however, come across any instance where a Christian writer of that period uses a plural to designate his own and the outsiders' religious systems collectively and simultaneously. That 'Christianity is one of the religions of the world' is a concept that, as we shall see in our next chapter, is still resisted. No early Church Father, so far as I have discovered, can conceptualize his situation in this way. To do so involves a notion that there exists a series of phenomena of essentially the same kind. Of them one may be affirmed to be the best, as in the Arabic verse just cited; but it is the best of its kind, not something *sui generis*[8].

To return to the Arab singular, *dīn*. We may note that this is used, finally, of religion as a generic universal, in both senses: as generalizing personal religiousness or human piety at large, and as generalizing the various systematic religions as ideological or sociological structures[9].

The Muslim world, then, is definitely and explicitly conscious of something that it calls, and is persuaded that it ought to call, a religion, as one among others but in its own case one given as such by God. Further, it is emphatic in naming that religion 'Islam', holding that God Himself has so named it.

Lest there be any doubt that it is systematic religion that is so named, we may note the practice of Muslim use of the word *niẓām*, 'system', in connection with 'Islam'. This is conspicuously prevalent in Urdu[10] but is affirmed also by religious leaders in the Arab world[11].

The West's adoption of the term 'Islam' to name the religion of the Muslims is a process still going on. It began only recently. For, on more careful examination, it turns out that in this case also outsiders did invent a name for the system and applied it; those within did resist. The difference is that their resistance is proving now successful. The West became aware of the religious communities of India and China and their traditions only in relatively modern times, through Western exploring: whereas with the Islamic it came into immediate contact, and conflict, from the beginning. Europe has throughout been aware of what it now calls Islam. For long, however, it was not aware of and certainly did not use this name. And to be quite accurate, since conceptions are relevant to perceptions, one should say rather that Europe was aware of the Muslim community. To a very limited degree and rather hazily, distortedly, it was aware also of some of its ways and notions.

In the Middle Ages, the common European practice was to refer to the sect or heresy of the Saracens[12]. After the Renascence and Reformation, when the term *religio* was coming into currency for these purposes, one finds the phrase 'the religion of the Saracens' and by now, also, '. . . of the Tartars and Turks'[13]. More impersonally, substituting an adjective for a noun that names the people, one gets 'Mohammedan religion' and the like in the Enlightenment[14]. As we noted earlier, the systematic term 'Mahumetisme' is found in English in 1597, 'Muhammedrie' in 1613; two centuries earlier than comparable names for any other Eastern system[15]. 'Islam' is first used in English, curiously, for 'Muslim': 'the Islams, that is, Catholike or right-believing Musulmans' (1613)[16]; this persisted into the nineteenth century: 'Thou art . . . an Islam in thy creed' (1814)[17].

Various other names for the adherents of this community, chiefly varieties of either 'Muhammadan', the Western term, or 'Muslim', the internal one, appear fairly early in the modern period[18].

In the eighteenth century, a term 'Islamism' was introduced[19], and is still used in modern French[20]. We shall later recognize by inference that there is some validity in this, even though it seem awkward to us now.

In the nineteenth century and into the twentieth, the chief term in English was 'Muhammadanism' (in a cheerful variety of spellings) , as the established subject entry for library catalogues, encyclopedia articles, book titles, and the like. At the present time, chiefly since World War II, this is giving way in Europe and America to 'Islam'[21]. The transition is being pushed partly by Muslims themselves, partly by Westerners who have lived among them, and not least by orientalists. The argument for it turns basically and simply on the point that this is the proper name used by the Muslims themselves. Its use by outsiders, therefore, is urged as both more courteous and more correct[22].

The Islamic tradition, then, we would suggest, seems to be unique in this matter of having its own name. If our whole argument has any validity, one must suppose that this may not be insignificant. We may well then ask the question, *Why?* Wherefore is it an exception to the general rule? What is involved in the fact that this particular religious community differs from all the others on this point?

The matter, I believe, is indeed significant. I suggest that there are two fundamental considerations to be brought to bear on it.

The primary observation is perhaps a retort: Why not? In the comparative study of mankind's religious history, certainly one of the first considerations must be to recognize and to take seriously the fact that the various religious traditions *are* different. They are different not only in detail but in basic orientation. Each is unique. Each is an exception on some quite fundamental matters to any generalizations that one might make about the others. Christians at times have devoted a good deal of vigour to insisting that, or to asking whether, Christianity is unique. Of course it is unique; every religious tradition is unique. Each is unique in some quite special way. One of the first illusions that must be dropped in such comparative study is that of imagining that all the traditions are of a given form, are varieties on a single theme. One must come to recognize—and it is not always easy—that not merely do they propound differing answers but rather that often they are asking different questions.

Islam, it could be argued, may well in fact be characterized by a rather unique insistence upon itself as a coherent and closed system, a sociologically and legally and even politically organized entity in the mundane world and an ideologically organized entity as an ideal. This could be seen as true in ways deeper and more patterned than pertain to the self-consciousness of any other religious group—true particularly of standard orthoprax Islam, with its dominating concept of law (*sharī'ah*)[23]. If so, it would be one of the matters to which the Sufi mystics' emphasis through the centuries could be seen as an alternative or supplement—if not in protest against it, at least as an attesting to a less impersonalist, less formal concept of Islam.

This much, at least, is clear, or can be fairly readily shown: that the various religious traditions of the world do in fact differ among themselves in the degree to which each presents itself as an organized and systematized entity. If this be so, then one of them may well be, must be, the most entity-like. One could suggest that Islam, it so happens, is that one.

To anyone who knows India it is evident that both Christian and Islamic ideals are much more coherent and consolidated matters than the religious orientation of Hindu India can readily appreciate. Again, the 'three religions' of China are, as we have noted, less distinct, less mutually exclusive, are more amorphous, than Muslims or the West can usually appreciate. One may suggest that the Islamic tradition is even more 'morphous', if one might use such a term, than is the Christian. If it be true that the forms of the religious life of the world differ, it may be taken as simply a datum of observation that Islam is more reified than any other of the world's great living faiths.

Our second consideration is of another order. It is historical. If the Islamic tradition appears both to its adherents and to some outsiders to be more reified than others, one may ask how this has come about. On inquiry, it turns out that, like everything else on earth, there is an historical process by which this situation came to be what it is. Actually, I discern three historical processes. The Islamic world over the centuries proves to have been subject to the pressures of three processes of reification.

An examination of these not only helps to explain and clarify the peculiarity that we have noted, but also reveals that this is not nearly so deep-rooted nor so essential as at first might appear. Historically, it turns out that the Muslims are different from the rest of us not enigmatically, but have been involved rather, though as is to be expected in their own particular way, in the same kinds of development as has mankind at large. Indeed it turns out that the particularities of their rather special reificationist trends are related to the particularities of their specific involvement in the totality of world history. What makes the Muslims specifically different from other groups is the very fact that makes them generically the same as other groups; namely, that they are persons living *sub specie aeternitatis* in concrete and particular historical situations.

The first process of reification that has impinged on Islamic development is a very long-range one. To apprehend it one must go far back in Middle Eastern history, and bring to awareness trends that are less generally known than their major consequences warrant. Our exploration of these will prove rewarding for the light that they throw not only on the Islamic tradition, elucidating the context in which this arose, but also on the world religious situation. For as we shall see, pre-Islamic developments in the Middle East set a context for the religious history of much of the world. They elucidate in part the emergence of a differentiation of man's major religious traditions. A recognition of this would seem, indeed, to make incipiently possible a unified view of man's religious history on a world scale.

The Islamic is historically the youngest of the world's major religious traditions[24]. It was proclaimed by Muhammad and accepted by its early adherents in a world in which religious communities in our systematic sense, organized as independent entities, were already in evidence. Jewish and Christian self-consciousness had become accepted facts, and the existence of their groups had become part of the accepted outlook of the area. Formal conceptualization among these groups, we have seen, was not yet as much developed as it was later to become. Yet the innovation was well established of a demarcated religious grouping, separating off those of a common religious loyalty from others among whom they lived. We saw that when it was launched in the Mediterranean world the Church was a novel kind of religious form. Its missionary zeal, its openness to individuals from all varieties of traditional background and from all places, on the one hand, and its sharp metaphysical rejection, on the other hand, of those who did not join, instituted a new phenomenon in society. At about the same time, the Roman Empire forcibly ejected the Jews from their homeland yet they continued to subsist as a widely scattered yet religiously integrated community bound only by the system of their faith. This too was a novel phenomenon. The independent religious community had been born.

And it had been noted.

By Muhammad's time not only had these developments begun to impinge a little on Arabia, fairly significantly on its more alert and sensitive minds. Also, they had sunk deeply in the mentality of those more urban areas such as in Egypt and Syria where the formative centuries of the new Muslim community's history were to be centered. In addition, there had been further and more elaborate evolution in this realm both of life and of thought, further east. Not only Judaeo-Christian developments but those of other traditions, other communities as well were important in the areas into which the Muslims from Arabia carried their new message and in which they constructed its early elaborations. Indeed, in some eddies of these new eastern developments a few levels even of Arabian life can be seen to have become involved, already in Muhammad's day.

To inquire into this whole development takes us into a cultural tradition, centered chiefly in Iran and the Tigris-Euphrates valley, that for many centuries had been religiously and intellectually effervescent. Its role in the general stream of man's religious history is greatly more formative than has usually been recognized, far outside its own borders. We must accordingly look at it for a moment a little closely.

ii

In Middle Eastern religious and cultural history one may go back almost as far as one likes. We here must go back from Muhammad somewhat over a thousand years to the origin of an immensely creative Iranian movement, an origin rightly or wrongly symbolized in the enigmatic but powerful figure of Zarathushtra[25]. Stirred by a new apprehension of God, of man, and of the world, he preached to whoever would listen a new and dynamic vision. He saw the world as a mighty and absolute conflict between good and evil. He saw man as a free moral agent, whose life is given cosmic significance by his active participation in this conflict, and who therein stands in direct relation to God, who is one, great, and transcendent and yet is involved with him, and who cares.

Zarathushtra did not preach 'a religion'. The only religious traditions and practices that he knew he attacked, with an ardour born of his vivid faith. (He did preach faith[26].) The God that he had come to know, and the resonant imperatives that demanded and got his absolute commitment, were against these.

He did not 'found' 'a religion'. Yet, his inspiration was by no means lost. The ideas that he launched, by which he conceptualized his faith, and more especially the moral fervour that he communicated, and not least his way of looking at the world, which was the form in which that fervour was given analytic meaning, these things deeply moved many in his day and later, and were cherished in memory.

In the streams and crosscurrents that ensued in that part of the world, arose a number of notions and attitudes that have been consequential in the subsequent history of mankind.

Those who use the concept 'the religions of the world' usually regard as one of these that to which since the late nineteenth century they have given the name Zoroastrianism[27]. This is seen as being held today by a numerically small community existing chiefly in India. It is no derogation to that group to say that this is, in fact, an oversimplification. The creativity in the religious realm of the Persians and their immediate neighbours in the millennium or so from Zarathushtra to the later Sasani Empire (roughly, a half-dozen centuries before and after Christ) is represented in the modern world on a vastly wider scale than such an analysis suggests.

To put the matter another way, these people participated in

the total religious history of mankind, to which all of us belong, much more creatively than can be understood in terms of the Parsis, or of now obscure or dead 'religions' such as the Mandaean and the Manichee. For in addition to initiating a tradition that became self-conscious in such groups, this milieu has played a basic part in the development of both the content and perhaps especially the form of traditions that have more luxuriantly survived and grown into dominant communities—particularly the Jewish, the Christian, the Islamic, and in our day the Marxist movement. To a list of such items as cosmic conflict-dualism (rehabilitated by Marx[28]), Heaven-and-Hell, the Devil, angelology, and in part messianism[29], it may be that the very phenomenon of an organized religious community and the concept of systematic religion should be added, as contributions related to this tradition.

In addition to the historical problem, herein is posed a nice locus of the theoretical issues raised by our whole investigation. For one might write an important history of the development until today of Zarathushtrian (better, Zarathushtrian-cum-Manichee, or pre-Islamic Persian) religiousness among men. Yet this development is not simply in the form of an organized entity or conceptualized system[30]. It is real. It has played and still plays today an immense part in world history[31]. Yet it is not an ism.

The development was certainly neither immediate nor precise. Influences were neither exclusively onesided nor clear. The very word 'influence' is somewhat prejudicial: to speak of the influence of one group, one tradition, and especially of one 'religion' on another already implies that the two are in some sense separate in the very affirmation that they are not. A statement has often been made that, for instance, in the centuries just before and just after the beginning of the Christian era the religion of the Hebrews was influenced by, or absorbed, elements of Persian and Mesopotamian origin. The facts might more adequately be expressed by one's saying rather that the development of the religious life of one particular group of people[32] within this area can be understood not simply in itself but only if seen within the context of the wider area, in whose history, including religious history, it was a participant. (We shall in a later chapter return to consider how this sort of process can best be conceptually analysed—in our judgment, in personalist terms.)

Something similar can be said of the rise of the Christian Church. In our inquiry into the Latin concept *religio* we noted that the emerging Church represented a new type of phenomenon in the Mediterranean world; new in many ways, one of which was its *either/or* emphasis. It was not unique in this: there were other movements of comparable form emerging at that time and in that part of the world. We did not then ask, however, whence this quality arose, this new conception of a religious community. The question is complex, in both its historical and its theological aspects. On the former, suffice it to say that among the factors apparently involved were ideas current in the Jewish community and its environment after its members had become participants in the wider flux of the then Middle Eastern world. These included concepts such as personal immortality and salvation, a Day of Judgment, and much else; and particularly relevant to our present considerations, included a way of looking at the world that sees mankind as divided (metaphysically) into two great opposing groups. The sheep and the goats, the saved and the damned, a voluntary membership organization (to which one either does or does not belong)—these are fundamental ideas. In their historical emergence Persian conflict-dualism as a cosmic postulate had played a part[33].

The evolution of these concepts, however, continued. Moreover, it continued in ways that were not altogether parallel in the West and in the Middle East. In the West the growth of the Church was finally triumphant, not only over indigenous religious traditions of a different kind but also over other comparable new systematized intrusions from Persia such as the cult of Mithra. And we have previously traced briefly the development by which, over a long number of centuries and in interaction with many other factors such as the rise of rationalism, out of the fact and idea of the systematized community eventually arose a concept of 'religion' as a systematic entity.

Further east the development, as might be expected, was somewhat different.

Religiously, the salient differences are that the Christian Church developed in the eastern region in an environment in which other patterns of religious life of a somewhat comparable kind were to be found in active development, and were not superseded. In particular, a Buddhist community was being established from India, especially in Bactria; and more tellingly, vigorous Mesopotamian-Persian traditions were being carried forward in ebullient and continuing creativity, not without major Hellenistic influence.

The only things that the Church met in the West of comparable force to these or to itself were the philosophic tradition of the Greeks and the state organization of the Romans. These it did not supersede. With these two and their successors, Christian relations were and have continued to be immensely intricate. We content ourselves with this observation: that the upshot in the West has been a bipartite or plural society, with what it now calls religion as one element, and alongside of it elements from these other sources. In the Middle East there emerged rather (and the difference is radical) a pluralism of 'religions'. (Into this type of situation, and globally, the West has moved or is moving only in modern times.)

Western civilization accordingly has been composed of two traditions, one from Greece and Rome, one from Palestine. These have developed together, sometimes at peace, sometimes in conflict, often interpenetrating. But they have never fused. This has had many consequences[34]. One relevant here is that those aspects of human life stemming in the West from the former, have not been included in the Western concept 'religion'[35].

In our survey of the Western developments we did not point this out, let alone emphasize it, since it has been so profoundly accepted in Western thinking as to seem self-evident or 'natural'.

That religion and philosophy are distinct things; that religion and not merely the state but a whole realm of social life under a heading of 'secular' are distinct things; these are for most Westerners rather presuppositions than beliefs. It would be more realistic, however, to recognize this as a local development, of paramount but specific significance.

The differentiation between a secular social sphere and a sphere of religion is not quite shared by the Islamic world, which does have a concept 'religion' (*dīn*). Obviously neither this distinction nor that between philosophy and religion could be held by that majority of mankind that has lived without the latter concept. One may recognize that both distinctions are irrelevant to and may even be misleading for any understanding of many such cultures. For example, a differentiation between religion and philosophy is palpably out of place for the history of India. And a dichotomy between religious and other social life is inept for an analysis of many societies, including not only most present-day 'little traditions' but also, as we have already seen, for such major civilizations as that of ancient Egypt[36].

⋯
iii

To return to the Middle East. It is certainly not our purpose to try to follow the multitudinous developments that were going on when a Christian Church began its spread there. These included some awareness of India and its teachings. They included the evolution of a tradition from Zarathushtra, and from other Iranian sources. They included the inebriating welter of ideals, practices, experiences, fears, aspirations, phantasies, insights, changes, contradictions, and consolidations that some moderns like to sum up in a few syllables in the word 'Gnosticism'. They included a group of 'Baptists'. And so on. All this would take us too far afield.

We may look for a moment, however, at the catalytic figure of Mani (216–277 A.D.) .

Some of my remarks in the preceding chapter would suggest perhaps that no great religious leader of the world seems to have gone about deliberately establishing a religion. This may be unfair to Mani, since its validity would largely rest on not counting him 'great'. Genius he certainly was, brilliantly perceptive and displaying both a creative imagination and a major capacity for constructive organization. Some will esteem him more highly than I find myself ultimately able to do, and certainly many millions of people for a thousand years from Europe and Africa to China were devoted members, and several were inspired members, of the Manichee 'Church'[37] that he launched. If one withheld from him a rank of true religious greatness, if one failed to see him as in a group with such commanding figures as Zarathushtra[38] and the Buddha, both of whom he claimed to supersede, or those that he did not know such as K'ung and Guru Nanak, it would be precisely because he appears to have been basically concerned more with religion than with either God or man.

Let us examine this.

Mani was a cosmopolitan. The milieu in which he grew up was a crossroads of culture and religious life, in some ways a center of the world. He saw the mighty Sasani empire established in Persia, which was to last for four centuries, and he was a friend of the emperor. In addition to his immediate language, the Semitic lingua franca of the Middle East at that time—Aramaic—he was at home in Greek and in Persian; and he traveled in India. Thus he was heir to the significant cultures of his day. His mind was fascinated by the clash of great religious traditions that he saw, of great religious communities in competition; and, over against these as individual and limited, he dreamed of a universal system that would embrace all mankind.

In fact, he not only dreamed; he produced it. He called it 'Justice'[39]. Outsiders have come to call it Manichaeanism[40].

Until recently, modern knowledge of his community and its ideals was limited to what could be gleaned about them from accounts of their adversaries. In recent decades, however, exciting finds of documents of the group itself, including Mani's own writings, are transforming our understanding[41]. They are still in process of being deciphered, published, and interpreted, by a handful of scholars; so that any assessment is necessarily tentative. And since virtually all the documents are translations[42], one is still a little short of precision as to Mani's own thought. However, a very great deal of progress certainly has been made.

We are interested here not in the content of Mani's religious scheme so much as in its form, which is highly illuminating and perhaps crucial. We have already stressed that he found himself and his followers confronted by something quite novel: a plurality of independent, missionary, competitive religious traditions. In his writings for perhaps the first time in human history a plural for a concept 'religion' or 'religious community' is found[43]. Furthermore, he used this concept in the construction of his new system. It is not without significance that he is the first and perhaps only major religious teacher who is presented as explicitly calling a system that he proffered 'mine', as well as calling it a religion[44].

When Amos, a farm labourer, inveighed against social injustice as he discerned it in Bethel, he did not speak in his own name, but rather in that of Yahweh, his God. Moreover, he had no inkling that he was composing a section of what would later become a scripture called the Bible. The poetic utterances to which he was inspired took a memorable form and were remembered— by a community that, cherishing them and other comparable pronouncements, formed them later into a corpus and then formulated a concept 'scripture'. Similarly St. Paul in writing letters to the congregations of disciples in Rome and other centers had no idea that he was helping to construct a 'New Testament'. Gautama the Buddha and Zarathushtra and others similarly had a quality of personal life and they lived it, had something to say and they said it; by subsequent generations cherishing a memory of these men and of their declarations both they and their preserved teachings were honoured by being given a special status.

Furthermore, these men had spoken not to any demarcated group but to whoever would listen. Subsequently those who had listened began to find themselves a demarcated group, differentiated from others in their society who had not responded—and later, particularly in a crossroads situation such as the Middle East, differentiated from others who were responding to some other teacher[45]. The Christian movement in particular was self-consciously and systematically organized; not so tightly knit and so coherent here as in the West, but with an impetus in this direction. And there were several other somewhat comparable groups, as we have noted.

None of them perhaps had yet completed the transition process to a self-conceptualized definable entity. But with one exception they were all moving in that direction. (The one major exception to this generalization is the Greek philosophic tradition. Its ideas were a highly important factor in the total development, but they never emerged into a systematic, organized -ism carried by an exclusivist membership community[46].)

This is the situation into which Mani came. The traditions of the Jews, the Christians, the Zarathushtrians, the Buddhists, had originated from a certain content and were developing gradually a form. Mani discerned the form[47], appropriated it, and set about to fill such a form with new content.

Others had spoken what eventually became or was becoming scriptures. Mani began with the concept 'scripture', and wrote books to fill this role. He is perhaps the first person in human history ever to have written a scripture consciously. Others' personal sense of God's[48] presence or guidance was so vivid that they felt themselves to be, or came to be regarded by their followers as having been, especially sent by God. Mani took this concept as a concept and claimed to be the greatest of them, 'the seal of the prophets'[49]. He is the first person in human history ever to have consciously played the role of a world prophet[50]. To others, or to their later memories, so many followers were attracted that organizations formed. Mani set up an administrative organization, to systematize a religious community. He was the first person in human history ever to do this and to know what he was doing[51].

One must not be disparaging. He was brilliantly successful, and it worked—for a thousand years. The content that he cast into his new conceptualized form was considerable.

This is something quite new in the history of mankind. Form previously could not precede content, since the form itself was only now evolving. Yet even after it had become available, there is still perhaps a question as to whether it could make a satisfactory starting point. This turns perhaps on whether one believes that ultimate truth can be adequately expressed in a mundane form. Neither Zarathushtra, the Buddha, nor Jesus, the three 'prophets' whom Mani claimed to supersede, had thought so. Mani was right in discerning that the religious systems stemming from these historically, fell short of perfection. Was he right also in feeling that what was needed was a better system?

We have paused for some while on Mani, even though one cannot be sure that in this conceptualizatiton of religious forms he was as original as our analysis would suggest. In any case he is important; for if not original, he is illustrative. How many others in his milieu had began to see the world in somewhat the same light as he, only were less effective in dealing with it, is not altogether clear. Certainly he was not out of step with the general trend of his time and place; and while it would seem that he formulated what others were only vaguely feeling, and at which they mostly arrived only later, in any case he is significant for our purposes because he typifies the direction in which the entire current of his culture was moving.

As we have seen, the situation was immensely complex and fluid[52]. There is some evidence that Mani's systematizations contributed to the crystallizing of other traditions.

The Iranian tradition, from Zarathushtra and earlier, at about this time reorganized itself into greatly more systematic form than previously. Some scholars believe, though the point is debated, that this was done in a kind of reaction to Mani's activities; even that the drawing up of the Avestan Canon as a written document is to be so traced[53]. One of the high-ranking Irani priesthood, called Kartir, a younger contemporary of Mani, has recently come to light, who was busily engaged in turning his tradition into a more systematically organized corporation; and it was he who succeeded in having Mani put to death[54]. Other groups or movements also were beginning to coalesce and to congeal into new entities[55].

The emergence of a Manichee community, then, may be seen as a stimulating factor in, or just as a symptom of, a wider tendency. In any case, the fact is that the centuries from the second to the sixth or seventh in the Aramaic- and Persian-speaking world are a time of the increasing systematization, crystallization[56], and definition of what previously had been a more chaotic welter of unorganized movements and what gradually became a situation of boundaried and self-conscious religious plurality[57].

However crucial may have been the part played in the process by Mani personally, one can observe a process towards the crystallization in fact and the conceptualization in theory of religious systems (in the plural) as independent intelligible entities. We have seen a comparable process in the West, developing chiefly more than a thousand years later. We have seen also that nothing comparable developed on this scale in India and China, until modern times. Indeed it is this Middle Eastern evolution that allows the whole religious history of mankind, on this matter, to be seen in one conspectus.

For the conceptualization 'a religion', 'the religions of the world' and so on, for all men today other than Muslims, we considered in our earlier chapters the tradition that clusters about the term *religio:* first in the West and then in modern times, as we saw, impinging on the entire world. We may now add that the Muslim situation culminates another tradition, which is in some ways comparable, and at some points related. This Middle Eastern tradition is older than the Western one, and indeed would seem originally to underlie it. At the very least, one may say that the two have a common origin; and although the two branches of the stream have at times in the past two and a half thousand years run separately, they have at other times interlaced with each other if not actually reunited.

This evolution, then, has been almost crucial not only in connection with Muslim thought, but in the realm of metaphysical orientation for half mankind. The development, I would make bold to suggest, has in fact been one of the most profound and significant in the entire sweep of the history of ideas.

iv

The chief verbal and conceptual vehicle for the Middle East branch of this development has been varieties of the term *dēn, dīn*. That is, the processes with which we are concerned may in large part be formulated in terms of the history of the meanings of this word, the evolution of what persons in this area designated or conceived when they used or heard it[58]. As we have already partly seen, eventually this international term served through Arabic for a complex concept somewhat corresponding to the Western concept 'religion'. Yet as with the latter, we may observe in part how it came to do so.

One must remember, of course, that part of what such a term meant in any particular case must have turned on the personal quality of the person using it, the vitality of his own faith and the perceptivity with which he responded to externals and could see beyond them, the degree to which he was primarily an individualist or alternatively felt the community aspect of religious rites; and so on. Again, it is inherent and inevitable that a phrase such as *dēn-i mazdayasna*[59] designating the *dēn* relating to Mazdāh (Ahura Mazda: 'the wise Lord') should mean different things to those who worshipped God under that name and those who did not. Similar considerations apply to 'Christian religion', *dīn al-Islām*, etc., and we shall consider the point more carefully in a later chapter; but we may recall here that these problems are involved. Nevertheless, as with the Western tradition, we may find that contexts do to some degree limit the range of possibilities and provide a clue as to usage[60].

The historical development is made more difficult for modern scholars to reconstruct, but for the people concerned was made greatly easier to happen, by the fact that in the various languages of the area (and particularly in the two separate language families, Semitic and Indo-European), words of quite similar sound or even identical sound were already available designating one or other of elements that subsequently were comprised in the complex concept *dēn, dīn*.

The single most important original element in the evolution was the Persian *daēnā*. This was used by Zarathushtra and appears in the Avesta. Although its etymology is not altogether clear[61], there is no question but that it begins by designating something inner and personal: it is part of a man's psychology, and seems to be that by which he perceives and responds to religious truth or to God or to moral imperatives. It in effect postulates and designates a religious faculty in man. Although the concept was particularized in characteristic ways, yet of the various senses of the Western term 'religion' it undoubtedly comes closest to that of personal religion, and approximates more significantly to personal 'faith'. Like everything else of this kind in Avestan thought, it is hypostasized and personified; and it became an important myth that each man would meet his own *daēnā* after death, in the form of a charming young maiden or a ghastly old hag, or anything in between, depending upon the quality of his personal religious life during his earthly career[62].

A development from this, of major consequence for our purposes, was a generic *daēnā*, where again there is both an earthly and a heavenly figure, the latter personifying 'Faith' as a divine being (god), the earthly typifying the community of the faithful.

Over the centuries—illustrating once again perhaps the general tendency that we have noted in this field, towards gradual externalization—this latter sense becomes increasingly common, and perhaps predominant though it never ousts the personal quality. The two survive side by side; as in the Western case, probably without much self-consciousness. In the course of the centuries the word became *dēn* (modern Persian *dīn*), and designated a religious community, and/or its characteristic system[63], as well as continuing to express the notion of inner faith[64]. In the period that we have been particularly considering, from the rise of the Christian Church to the rise of Islam, when various religious communities and the conceptual systems with which they were associated were crystallizing in this area as we have seen, this is the term used to designate them.

In this development two important processes are observable. For one thing, the word in this sense begins to have a plural. We have seen this used by Mani[65], and remarked that it is perhaps the first time in history that a concept of 'religions' is introduced[66]. Secondly, the idea spreads geographically. One finds gradually a similar development in other languages of the Middle East.

In Jewish Aramaic, it was another, earlier, loanword from Persia, *dāth,* previously meaning 'law', that began to do duty for the new concept[67]; and this is the word that has become the term for systematic religion in modern Hebrew[68]. On the other hand, in several cases the Persian term *dēn* itself was apparently taken over in the new sense by groups speaking other languages. This was so not only in the case of those related to Persian, such as Parthian and Sogdian. It occurred also with some groups that, in this cosmopolitanism, rubbed shoulders with the Persians although they spoke languages less closely related—for instance, Armenian—or not related at all, such as those from the Semitic family, where it became acclimatized as *dīn.* From Mani's time, if not before, this word in this sense is found in Christian Aramaic, that is Syriac[69], and eventually, as we have remarked, also in Arabic.

It had become indeed a fully international term.

The matter is complicated, however. For in some of the Semitic languages, a word of virtually this same form had been in use for millennia, meaning law (*droit, Recht*) or system of law (*loi, Gesetz*)[70]. And in other cases as well the word had previous indigenous significance, which in some instances was at least in part contributed also to the international complex.

With the intermingling of peoples, languages, and concepts, we are hardly surprised to find, then, a transition at the end of which *dēn, dīn* signifies in some cases religious community, organized and definite, and in some cases systematic religion: the abstract pattern of beliefs and practices characterizing a particular tradition or group. By the sixth or seventh century A.D. this seems true of virtually all the languages of the Middle East where the phenomenon of these religious organizations was found (though a plural is not yet found in all of them).

In each case, of course, our word had also the local meanings already pertaining to it in that particular tradition. There seems to be none of the area's languages in which a term roughly of the form *dīn* or *dēn* had not already existed. The process that we are observing could perhaps then better be described by saying that, during the centuries under study, each people in the Middle East, in so far as the new phenomenon of independent systematic religious organizations came within the purview of its perceptual and conceptual awareness, generally used their local term *dīn,* or something of the sort, to designate it.

This was true of the Arabs. For them it was particularly easy, since their word *dīn* was already used for concepts sufficiently neighbouring for the innovation to be rather gentle.

The word *dīn* in seventh-century Arabia had, in fact, many meanings, which may be classed in three principal groups according to three distinct sources. There was the new concept, as part of the impingement on Arabia at that time of new ideas, movements, and sophistications from the surrounding cultures: namely, the concept of systematic religion. This was new, of course, not only in the sense that the idea was only beginning to be found in Arabs' minds. It was new more inevitably in that in the traditional life of these Arabs there had previously been nothing in practice to which such an idea could have referred. Arabian life had had facets that modern scholars, as with the Aztecs or ancient Egyptians, may dub and indeed have dubbed 'the religion of' the pre-Islamic Arabs. But the customs and orientations to which the modern student gives that name had not been organized or systematized or reified either sociologically or conceptually in the area itself by their participants. It was only as new religious communities with new ideas of religious life and loyalty began from outside to filter down into Arabia that the Arabs began to see alternative ways of being religious and hence began for the first time to see also their own ways as something conceptually identifiable, though still not consolidated.

Secondly, there was a verbal noun meaning 'judging, passing judgment, passing sentence'; and along with this, 'judgment, verdict'. This is found also in the Qur'an, for instance in the expression 'day of judgment' (*yawm al-dīn*) [71]. This represents an ancient Semitic root that we have noted[72].

Finally, there was the indigenous Arabic meaning: as the verbal noun of a verb 'to conduct oneself, to behave, to observe certain practices, to follow traditional usage, to conform'; and subsequently thence as an abstract noun 'conformity, propriety, obedience', and also 'usages, customs, standard behaviour'. There was no plural (as there may not be, for a verbal or abstract noun)[73].

The Arabs, then, in the seventh century A.D. were on the periphery of a cosmopolitan world religiously very much alive. They had their own background of peninsular culture, their own language which expressed this. In addition, at least some Hijaz Arabs were incipient participants in the new thought-world of their more sophisticated neighbours, as is evinced by their adopting some of the new internationally current religious and other terms expressing the new concepts and designating the new phenomena that had been developing in the wider Middle East. Equally important for our purposes are, outside of Arabia, the older centers of that Middle Eastern culture into which the Arabs presently moved once the new Islamic faith had fired them, and in which their new Muslim religious community itself developed. Here the old populations, heirs of three thousand years of civilizations, learned Arabic as a new language in addition to their old ones, entered or observed the new Islamic movement, and helped or saw it gradually formulate its new self-expressions.

v

With this awareness, then, of historical and linguistic context, we are ready at long last to return to the question of the rise of Islam, and to our question of how to understand its apparent divergence in form from man's other major religious traditions. Do the reificationist trends of the Middle East that we have discerned help to clarify this?

For the Muslim, the argument becomes delicate here, since the issue raises questions of the relation between revelation and history—between the timeless truth that God discloses and the concrete, limited situation at a particular time and place in which the revelation takes place. This is in a sense one aspect of the issue of our entire study. The delicacy at this particular point for Muslims lies specifically in the fact that, since we are discussing the history of ideas and the terms used to express them, we touch upon the relation between religious truth and religious language. This involves a characteristic and profound article of faith with Muslims[74].

The seriousness of this matter is evinced in the traditional Islamic refusal that the Qur'an be translated. This is reasonable in so far as words that God has chosen are not to be thought interchangeable with those that are human constructs. We have been assuming throughout our study that words used in particular historical situations may be treated as expressive of ideas in men's minds, and that these ideas may not be final characterizations of the universe in which we live. Phrased theologically, we take seriously the possibility that the terms that men use may not necessarily formulate concepts in the mind of God. A plea for a critical reappraisal of concepts presupposes that we may be the victims, and may become the masters, of human ratiocination.

The Muslim, of course, is as ready as is anyone to admit that human conceptions may fall short of perfection, and even of adequacy[75]. But the *terms* in which he conceptualizes the world are given to him in the Qur'an.

For him these terms do stand for concepts in the mind of God. They are ultimately valid and permanent. It would be intolerably arrogant for him to think of criticizing or improving upon them, and fatuous for him to think of rejecting this gift.

He does, however, have an acknowledged problem in ascertaining, so far as he is able, what these terms may mean. The Muslim and the rest of us, therefore, join company again at this point, especially in so far as one may give one's attention to the problem of what meaning the words of the Arabic language had for the Arabs of the time and place in which the Qur'an is presented as having been revealed. The need to ascertain this has been a standing demand of Muslims themselves, as requisite for Qur'an understanding. To it, modern students add the historical question of how these words came to have those meanings.

For the meanings of words, like everything else in the life of the pre-Islamic Arabs, were of course the product of an historical evolution up to that time. And they were the result of various influences, including some from outside their traditional environment. Men's concepts change, and these men's were changing, partly under the impact of new ideas, partly under the impact of new experiences, new things that they saw.

Furthermore, the convinced Muslim and the outside observer may join forces also in endeavouring to ascertain what, whether rightly or wrongly, particular persons at particular times have in fact understood given words to mean. Apart from the question as to what a term or text properly and truly signifies, what it ought to mean, there is the mundane question of what it actually has meant in the minds of actual men. This, both he and the historian may agree, has varied. It is also empirically ascertainable. The true meaning of a given passage may be transcendentally given, but the actual meaning to particular persons has been historically conditioned, and may be historically elucidated. The historian may help the theologian, perhaps, if the latter would like to put it thus, to understand why men have misunderstood.

One need not assert, therefore, what a Muslim would inevitably and vigorously reject, that the text of the Qur'an was influenced by Manichee ideas or that the essential form of Islam is to be understood in terms of Persian concepts of religion. Yet one may proffer the suggestion that some Middle Easterners in the early days of the Muslim community, when they heard the Qur'an or thought about Islam, were influenced in their understanding of the one or conception of the other by such pre-Islamic pressures.

This much, at least, would seem clear: that a few sophisticates and cosmopolitans among the Hijazi Arabs who first heard a new faith being preached by Muhammad and first saw the movement that gathered round him and his message, and many among the subsequently Arabic-speaking groups in the cities of Syria and especially Iraq and Iran who received the new teachings into their society or their hearts, were presumably mentally somewhat prepared to perceive as such a new religious system.

In this light, the significance is more apparent of the fact that we earlier stressed: that by the seventh century A.D. the Christian and the Jewish religious traditions were not only facts but had become defined and self-conscious communities and to a significant degree were also explicit, systematic ideas. This was true in general, and was beginning to be true also in Arabia[76]. That is, they were facts and ideas in the light of which the Islamic message was preached and was received. Further, in the wider Middle East in which that message was presently elaborated, there were still other religious traditions known and communities organized, and ideas of them were still more systematic.

A Muslim might phrase this differently; by saying, for instance, that this was the particular time and place that God chose for His final proclamation to mankind. In the Arabic environment in which the Prophet delivered his message, two organized religious communities of the new type were already conspicuous, the Christian and the Jewish; and the new community and its faith, while actually different in form and in substance, yet patently appeared a member of the same general species. Again a Muslim might formulate the proposition in different words, but the facts are not in dispute: it is sound Islamic doctrine that the Jewish, Christian, and Islamic as historical systems are variations on a single theme[77].

With this historical overview, also, one may perhaps understand that, in a way that is not true of any other great religious leader of the world except Mani, Muhammad to some seems self-consciously and deliberately to have set about establishing a religious system. He might be said to have believed himself called upon by God to do just that. In a sense one could characterize him as, after Mani, the only 'founder of a religion' who knew what he was doing. Muslims themselves regard God as the founder of their religion in its ideal sense, but Muhammad (under God's guidance) as manifestly the founder of it as a sociological system and historical phenomenon, and withal as executing that assignment in a very clearheaded and careful way.

We have already observed that it is hazy thinking to speak of Guru Nanak as 'the founder of Sikhism', or Lao Tse and Chuang Tse of a Taoist religion; the same applies in some degree to K'ung, to Gautama the Buddha, to Moses, and to Jesus. It is both theoretically and historically of moment that these men were concerned with communities; yet they did not preach abstract or consolidated systems. One cannot imagine Plato talking of 'Platonism'—he was talking about the universe. Jesus was not interested in Christianity, but in God and man. He could not have conceptualized 'Christianity'. Muhammad, on the other hand, seems to some observers and to some Muslims to have known what he was about when he talked of Islam.

One finds him taking steps, at first incidentally rather like other religious leaders, but later in a careful and calculated way, to organize a community socially, legally, and politically, as the expression of a religious idea. This has had, we believe, large consequences. The *Sangha* is important to Buddhists, certainly; and the Church to Christians—important religiously. Moreover, men like Durkheim[78] have drawn attention vividly to the intimate tie between the religious and the sociological universally. Nevertheless the role of the *ummah*, the Islamic community, in Muslim life is distinctive and crucial[79]. And I have argued elsewhere that

Muslims find more religious significance in their community's history than is true of any other religious group[80]. It would appear that here is something fundamental to the uniqueness of the Islamic among the religious orientations of the world. It would appear also that this may be related to the uniquely deliberate implementation of a sociological-system concept of religion by the Prophet.

Germane to all this is a further point on which we have had occasion to touch more than once: that a religious system appears as a system, an intelligible entity susceptible of objective conceptualization, primarily to someone on the outside. In the light of this, an historian may find it illuminating to observe that the Islamic seems to be the only religious movement in the world[81] that arose historically not primarily out of a reform of the indigenous religious tradition of the people to whom it was presented. It arose rather among, and was preached to (a Muslim might say, God revealed it among) a people for whom it was the reform of outsiders' religious traditions.

What non-Muslims call the Jewish-Christian[82] impact on Islam, but what to those within is postulated rather as a transcendent connection[83], has often been studied. We may quote some words of a scholar very decidedly a non-Muslim, but among nonbelievers one of the most careful students of the externals of the Qur'an:

"From the fact that Muḥammad was an Arab, brought up in the midst of Arabian paganism and practising its rites himself until well on into manhood, one would naturally have expected to find that Islam had its roots deep down in this old Arabian paganism. It comes, therefore, as no little surprise, to find how little of the religious life of this Arabian paganism is reflected in the pages of the Qur'ān. . . . Even a cursory reading of the book makes it plain that Muḥammad drew his inspiration not from the religious life and experiences of his own land and his own people, but from the great monotheistic religions which were pressing down into Arabia in his day"[84].

The phrasing here is very much that of an outsider; the passage will be offensive to Muslims[85]. Yet it expresses how an outside historian views something that to them is in fact obvious anyway, namely that the Prophet's message was delivered to the Arabs as a reformulation not primarily of their own, idolatrous, religious tradition but of the tradition of Christians and Jews, which in Muslim eyes needed reforming. In an historian's eyes it is the adaptation to its people of a reform of outsiders' traditions.

The gulf that separates how the same facts appear to a Muslim and to an outside observer, to those who are and to those who are not *engagés* in a tradition, is itself of major significance, and is relevant to the course of our whole argument. The concept of a religious system is inherently different for those who stand outside.

For our immediate purposes, this point is relevant for what the word *dīn*[86] might mean to those Arabs who were not Christians and Jews. Here would seem a second factor in the potentially reificationist conceptualizing of Islam by those among whom its message was proclaimed. First, as we have seen, of all the major religious communities of the world today the Islamic is the only one that has come into historical existence this side chronologically of that period in human history when schematized religious systems had evolved, and in that part of the world where the process of systematizing them was developing. Secondly, we have seen that the practice of naming a religion and conceptualizing it systematically is appropriate primarily for outsiders, for those for whom it is not a medium of faith; and the Islamic is the only religious movement in the world that was launched by a reformer and accepted by a people standing outside the tradition (in this case the two traditions) being reformed[87].

vi

This, then, is the first of the long-range processes of reification that, so far as an historian can see, would help to explain how it happened that 'the Islamic religion' came to be a named entity. I suggested that there were yet two others. This first was an external force, an evolution in the Middle East chronologically prior to the emergence of the Muslim community and operating upon it from the outside as an historical pressure acting to mould the new tradition into a pre-established form. The second process, to which we may now turn, has been rather an internal development, by which Muslims themselves have tended over the centuries to reify their own concept of their faith. It need not detain us long.

A discrimination between the two may not be pressed far. For the second tendency whereby the Muslims have themselves systematized and rigidified their faith was doubtless facilitated by centuries-old patterns in their milieu. Even more important, it has gained force and come to full fruition only since the end of the nineteenth century under the new influence of Europe and in reaction to massive Western pressures, the third process. Considering it under a separate heading is nonetheless somewhat useful for analysis. This is so partly because to appreciate this internal evolution one must recognize what mighty forces within the Islamic community were originally at work against reification. One discovers that also in the Islamic case as in others the emergence of a conceptualized and named entity has, despite appearances to the contrary, been in significant part a gradual and rather late aberration.

The religio-historical situation in the Middle East in the latter part of the first millennium A.D. was such, we have seen, that in the minds of some who heard them the words *islām* and *dīn* could conjure up the idea of Islam as a reified entity, one religion among others. Yet on inquiry it becomes evident that this was by no means the only, and indeed not even the primary, interpretation.

To assert that a different reading is possible is not merely to propound a logical point but to record an historical observation. As with other religious traditions, given symbols have in fact meant different things to different people. Interpretations have varied, from person to person, from century to century, from village to city. Islamic religious symbolism being preeminently verbal, the observer must simply record that words have had different meanings for various members of the community. The matter is

not primarily a linguistic one, but a question rather of fundamental orientation, raising the deepest issues of faith and destiny.
To say that another interpretation is possible of the words of the
Qur'an and the general preaching of Muhammad is to observe
that historically these have indeed been understood in another
way by persons to whom they and the universe and God and destiny and duty could and did appear in quite a different light.

Once examined, this other, nonreifying (or pre-reifying) interpretation is found to be more in conformity with the traditional
usage of the Arabic language, and to be that of persons more sen-
sitively religious, less superficial in their response, less liable to
an outsider's mundane view and more perceptive of transcendent
overtones. Further, such evidence as is available indicates that
these persons were in early Islamic times in preponderating majority, at least among leaders; and that over the course of the centuries there has been a demonstrable drift from the personalist,
vivid, and open sort of interpretation towards the other, the closed
and reified view that today is common.

We remarked earlier that certain interpretations of Qur'an
terms and passages, though historically they may actually have
been held, may yet be regarded by the theologian as misunder-
standings. And he may bring to bear powerful linguistic and other
arguments to support his judgement. On inquiry it proves that
such a protest applies with particular force to an impersonalist,
entity-like interpretation of the term *dīn* that takes it as a Persian
loanword in the sense of 'a religion', and takes the term *islām* as
its systematic name. The original meaning of these words in traditional peninsular Arabic, and the early acceptation of them in
Muslim conviction, was something much more vibrant, searching,
and transporting.

If we look carefully at the Qur'an, we find, first of all, that the
term *islām* there is relatively much less used than are other related
but more dynamic and personal terms; and secondly, that when
it is used it can be, and on many grounds almost must be, interpreted not as the name of a religious system but as the designation
of a decisive personal act.

First of all, the fundamental fact is that in the Qur'an the word 'God' appears 2,697 times; the word *islām,* eight times[88]. (In a good deal of modern Muslim writing this ratio is perhaps, roughly, reversed.)

Secondly, in this scripture, and in classical Muslim religious literature later, even for the manward side of the relationship the great term and concept is 'faith'. (One is reminded also therefore of the New Testament, and of classical and mediaeval Christian writing.) While the word *islām* occurs in the Qur'an, as we have said, eight times in all, *īmān* ('faith') is found 45 times. Similarly the latter's correlative *mu'min* ('man of faith, faithful') in its various forms is more than five times[89] as frequent as *Muslim*[90]. Still more striking, in the case of the verbs from which all these are derived, that referring to 'faith' occurs more than two dozen times more often than the other[91].

Moreover, the verbs not only precede the nouns structurally and logically, but outnumber them also in Qur'an usage. *Islām* is a verbal noun, occurring about a third as often as its foundation verb *aslama* ('to submit, to surrender oneself wholly, to give oneself in total commitment'). This term is found in various inflectional forms 72 times in all, among which 22 are strictly verbal (that is, direct, active, personal), 42 are participial (as personalist adjective or noun), while only eight are the gerundial or generic form.

The Qur'an is concerned, and presents God as being concerned, with something that persons do, and with the persons who do it, rather than with an abstract entity.

Īmān ('faith') is a verbal noun also. And it too is found in this gerundial form much more often, certainly, than *islām,* yet less than a tenth as often as in its own more unambiguously verbal, operational instances[92]. We may perhaps stress, too, that it signified something that is much more closely rendered by 'faith' than by 'belief'[93]. 'Belief', as we shall later consider, is a derived and can be an exceedingly watered down and inoperative matter, compared with the richness and warmth and the *engagement* of 'faith'. Faith is an active quality, one that commits the person and by which he is caught up into a dynamic relationship with his Maker and his fellows. It is the ability to see the transcendent, and to respond to it; to hear God's voice, and to act accordingly. That we are not exaggerating either the profundity or the activism, becomes clear if, on the one hand, one reads the chapters on *īmān* of the classical theologians[94], and, on the other, if one notes the actual behaviour of the Muslim community who in their early creative history set forth to remake the world.

The message was a message of faith, and the men who adopted it were men of faith, deep, ardent, and effective. Faith in what? In a God who commands. As I have affirmed elsewhere[95], for the Muslim the eternal word of God is an imperative; and this word came down among men and reverberated in their very hearing. God was speaking to them: and their part was to heed, to obey. The word *aslama* means to accept this imperative, to choose to recognize it as binding on oneself. Similarly, *kafara*[96] (the verb from which *kāfir,* sometimes rendered 'infidel', comes) means not to disbelieve, but rather *to reject:* it too is active, *engagé.* We see the pattern in such a phrase as 'They rejected what they knew [to be true]'[97]. What the Qur'an presents is a great drama of decision: God has spoken His command, and men thereupon are divided, or, rather, divide themselves, into two groups—those who accept and those who spurn; those who obey, and those who rebel.

'*Islām*' is obedience or commitment, the willingness to take on oneself the responsibility of living henceforth according to God's proclaimed purpose; and submission, the recognition not in theory but in overpowering act of one's littleness and worthlessness before the awe and majesty of God. It is a verbal noun: the name of an action, not of an institution; of a personal decision, not a social system.

Its verbal quality is in some cases inescapable: 'They refused, after they had accepted' (after their acceptance, after their *islām*)[98]. It is personal: the Qur'an speaks also of *islāmukum*[98a]: your *islām,* your personal commitment to heed God's voice.

If we turn, also, to the classical verses that in modern times have been used as proof-texts for reification, these too yield a universal and prophetic, a dynamic and personal, summons, rather than systematized and impersonal statement. What in modern times has become 'Verily *the* religion in the eyes of God is *Islam*'[99] originally meant (was taken to mean; for instance, by the most respected and authoritative of the early commentators, al-Tabari[100]) rather that to conduct oneself duly before God is to accept His commands; the proper way to worship Him is to obey Him—or, simply, true religion (*not* 'the true religion') is obeisance. To many when it was first proclaimed and for some centuries after, this verse was saying what any man must say whose faith is vivid and whose orientation is moralist. Far from being primarily sectarian, it is, curiously, virtually identical even to the wording with the statement or definition given in the *Catholic Encyclopaedia*: 'Religion . . . means the voluntary subjection of oneself to God'[101].

Similarly other verses in which this term occurs: 'If anyone opts for anything other than self-surrender as a norm, it shall not be accepted from him'[102]; or, again, the ability to respond to God is itself a grace from God[103].

There are even passages where the exclusivism of boundaries of religious communities is attacked, in the name of a direct and uninstitutionalized moralist piety[104].

Vivid and dynamic—and personal: these are the qualities of the term *islām* in the Qur'an[105]. What was proclaimed was a challenge, not a religion[106].

Not being myself within the Islamic community, I am of course in no position to suggest that this sort of interpretation of the Qur'an is the right or transcendent one. What one can affirm is that it is a perfectly possible reading, that it is in fact closer to the straightforward and simple meanings of the Arabic words, especially if considered before their complication by Persian and other foreign influences, and historically that this in fact was the interpretation given to these passages by many, if not most, of the leaders of Muslim religious thought in the early centuries[107].

Our point is illuminated if one considers the question in relation to the two languages Arabic and English—roughly, the languages of participants and observers, believers and nonbelievers, respectively. If I say in English, as I may readily do, 'I am not a Muslim', everyone who knows English can understand what I mean and the point seems perfectly straightforward. Curiously, however, it is impossible to translate this sentence into Arabic.

I cannot say, *Lastu bi-muslimin*—for that would mean I do not submit to God, which of course is not true and would be certainly obstreperous and indeed blasphemous. For a reverent person it is a quite absurd combination of words. I am a submitter (in Arabic, *muslim*) in accord with the truest apprehension as to what God's will is of which I am capable. I am not a Muslim with a capital M in the technical English sense of belonging to the institutionalized Islamic community system, partly by accident of birth and partly because the chief tradition of those who are members of that community system and I differ as to how best one knows what God's will is; but we do not disagree in our acceptance, our *islām*, of such commands as we do apprehend[108].

Again, if we return to the *Catholic Encyclopaedia*, let one attempt to translate into Arabic the article cited above. One comes up with the arresting observation that a Roman Catholic priest and scholar in an authorized church publication is apparently affirming that the true religion is Islam. This seems ridiculous; and indeed is ridiculous unless one recognizes that in such an Arabic sentence the word *islām* would be referring not to a religious system that has developed historically with that institutional name, but to the personal relationship of faith that unites a free moral agent to his Creator.

When the situation between two different languages becomes as odd as this, one may reasonably guess that something has happened to the ideas that one is trying to express.

That 'something has happened' the historian, indeed, can document. On investigation it turns out that over the centuries a very gradual closing in of the reificationist view can be detected. It begins, as one might expect, with secular writers in the community, but gradually extends to some, though until the end of the nine-teenth century by no means most, of the more religious writers as well[109].

One index that can be set up is that showing the relative fre-quency of 'faith' and *islām*, the one being the personalist and activ-ist term and the other gradually more systematized and externalist. We have already seen that in the Qur'an the ratio between these is over five to one in favour of *īmān*. In Arabic book titles until the end of the nineteenth century, *islām* slightly outnumbers 'faith' in a ratio of three to two. In modern times this ratio jumps to thirteen to one[110]. This gives the graph on the following page, which compares interestingly with what we found for 'faith' and 'Christianity' in our last chapter[111].

vii

Since the latter part of the nineteenth century, there has de-monstrably been a sudden and almost complete shift among vocal Muslims to a use of the term Islam to name a religion. We opened our chapter with illustrations of and comments on the resulting situation. We now are in a position, however, to modify our un-derstanding of this by recognizing it as true today, but as having become true historically and in large measure even recently.

On scrutiny it appears that the almost universal Muslim use of the term *islām* in a reified sense in modern times is a direct consequence of apologetics[112]. As we saw above in our second chapter[113], the impulse to defend what is attacked would seem a powerful force toward reifying. This process has clearly been at work in the Islamic case, as in the European; only, more relent-lessly. Once this factor was added to the internal secular tenden-cies towards institutionalizing, these seem to have become virtually irresistible.

The modern situation, then, is strictly modern. We noted above that the term *niẓām*, 'system', is commonplace in the twentieth

Reification in Islam

Percentage Distribution

of

"Islam" and "Īmān"
(Faith)

in the Qur'ān and in Arabic
book titles as listed in C.
Brockelmann, "Geschichte
der arabischen Litteratur,"
rearranged chronologically.

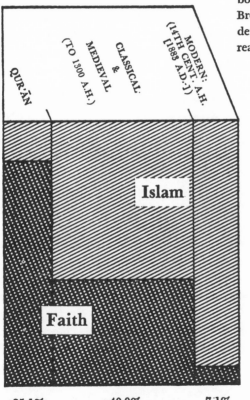

QUR'ĀN

CLASSICAL & MEDIEVAL (TO 1300 A.H.)

MODERN: (14TH CENT. A.H. [1883 A.D.-]))

Islam

Faith

| 85.1% | 40.0% | 7.1% | Faith |
| 14.9% | 60.0% | 92.9% | Islam |

century in relation to Islam. This term, however, does not occur in the Qur'an, nor indeed does any word from this root; and there is some reason for wondering whether any Muslim ever used this concept religiously before modern times[114]. The explicit notion that life should be or can be ordered according to a system, even an ideal one, and that it is the business of Islam to provide such a system[115], seems to be a modern idea (and perhaps a rather questionable one) [116].

At the present time, then, the word *islām* is used in three distinct senses, referring to three related yet different things. First, there remains the verbal noun of which we have been speaking: the self-commitment of an individual Muslim. This is his own personal submission to God, the act of dedication wherein he as a specific and live person in his concrete situation is deliberately and numinously related to a transcendent divine reality which he recognizes and to a cosmic imperative which he accepts. It is immediate and existential. It involves a decision, private and inalienable. His personal submittingness—if we may use such a term —is of course quite distinct from any other person's.

Secondly and thirdly there are the empirical actuality and the Platonic ideal of a total Islamic system as an institutionalized entity. This is a generalized pattern, of 'the religion' in the one case as tangible reality, a mundane phenomenon historical and sociological, and in the other case as it ideally is at its conceivable best.

Of these three there can be no question but that the first is chronologically and logically the first, however dominant the second and third may have seemed to become in the twentieth century. Their dominance can be traced to historical factors, which are important and which we have tried to uncover. Yet they must not be allowed to obscure the first, on which they rest. Our conclusion is that the Islamic has been in some ways from the first the most reified of all man's living religious movements, that it has at its birth and throughout been subject to massive reifying pressures; and yet that like all the others it began (was proclaimed in the Qur'an) as a ringing personal summons to men and women to have faith in God and to commit themselves whole-heartedly to His commands, and that the institutions and con-ceptualized system of what is now called Islam have been the result of that faith and commitment. We suggest that that result has come into historical existence and into conceptual thought more gradually and indeed in its modern form much more re-cently than is usually recognized.

The Islamic instance, then, does not after all disprove, as it at first seemed calculated to do, our general interpretation of reli-gious reification as a mundane process—by which men come to substitute, for a vivid personal faith in direct commerce with transcendence, a human and limited conceptualization. Rather, it illustrates this in an unusually intricate and yet revealing way.

Smith's argument to this point —

↓

his understanding of religion at its most basic = the thing held in common?

CHAPTER FIVE

Is the Concept
Adequate?

IF WE LOOK at the development of mankind's religious life in some sort of total historical perspective, then, we recognize that an understanding of it may involve new terms of understanding. As the content of our human awareness grows in this realm in modern times, so also the forms of our awareness are undergoing, and should undergo, evolution. In particular, my argument so far has been devoted to bring into consciousness the fact that a use of the concept religion, the religions, and the specific named religions, has been one part of the whole process, and a particular, limited, and not necessarily final part.

Mankind has been religious now for a very long time, and in many different ways. For most of that time, and in many of those ways, it has been so with other conceptual orientations. Yet one idea that has been produced in one part of its world development, namely the notion of a systematic religious entity, conceptually identifiable and characterizing a distinct community, has been of special interest to us in this present inquiry and of special influ-ence lately throughout the world.

It would seem from our survey that this way of looking at man's religious life can be traced back to origins in the Middle East somewhere around about the beginning of the Christian era; that it was developed by several local groups there, such as the Manichees, and then was taken up by the later Muslim community and carried widely by its expansion; that it was injected into the stream of Western civilization through the Jewish and Christian traditions and of late has been developed there strongly; that it has been conveyed into India twice, once at the beginning of the second millennium A.D. by Muslims and once towards the end of that millennium by the West; and that in recent times it has under Western expansion percolated to some extent throughout the world.

We have noted, however, that even where it has been received its conceptualization has been neglected or resisted, has almost always been ambiguous, and has developed, if at all, only slowly and only under special external circumstances. In recent Western history and in recent Islamic history, for special historical reasons in each case, it has become rather firmly entrenched, though in a rather unwitting way. There is a *malaise,* however, wherever it is used, the more scholarly or the more devout the user the greater being that *malaise.* In its contemporary form there would seem little question but that the concept of a religion is recent, Western-and-Islamic, and unstable.

This much, at least, would seem evident: that humanity is now reaching a stage of awareness in the religious realm where it may, and its leaders of thought perhaps must, decide whether or not in the future to use the concepts 'religion' and 'the religions' as fundamental elements for understanding. This awareness is now historical, in immense sweep. It is also conceptual, as self-awareness. To this latter one may perhaps hope that the present inquiry may in a small way contribute. Thinkers in other parts of the world have to choose whether they will adopt, and in the West and in the Islamic world whether they will prolong, the framework of thought, the presupposition of analysis, that these terms represent.

My present plea and hope are that at least the choice will be made consciously and deliberately.

In the present chapter my purpose is to investigate the validity and helpfulness of the concepts religion and the religions. My own view has come to be that they are not only unnecessary (which has become perhaps manifest from our historical survey) but also much less serviceable and legitimate than they once seemed. In noting, therefore, the widespread restlessness with these concepts and calling to mind the many reasons for that dissatisfaction, I shall in effect be developing an argument in favour of changing this particular conceptual scheme. Even the considerable pressures to abandon the present pattern of thought, however, can hardly prove effective until some alternative pattern is available. Accordingly, in our next two chapters I will proffer concepts by which, it is my suggestion, the phenomena of man's religious life across the centuries, across the world, and in man's heart can more adequately be understood.

That is, having surveyed the historical process by which this particular analysis has come into being among a section of mankind, I will now ask how well suited it is to its purposes, especially now that these have expanded in scope; and then in the remainder of the work will inquire whether a different conceptual framework, to be proposed, may not more adequately handle the data by which, in today's new panorama, we are so richly confronted.

ii

We may begin by noting certain factors in favour of the use of our concepts. My historical survey has tended to be in terms of the history of ideas. Yet I trust that I have made clear my recognition that ideas do not have a quite independent history of their own, unrelated to the evolving processes of surrounding reality. Although I will argue later that these concepts are inadequate, nonetheless they are not arbitrary or grotesque. They have arisen in relation to concrete situations, and they represent something real (even though they may not represent it well).

One may take as example the naming in the West of specific religions around the world. We have seen that this has been a recent process; a selective process; and from the point of view of those who know the religious traditions closely, whether as men of faith within them or as careful scholars on the outside, a misleading and inadequate process. Nonetheless we have also seen that it has been a coherent process: that names have not been devised wherever social groups have had religious integrity, and have been in those cases where religious communities have emerged in history distinct from the other social groups to which their members belong. Now this process of differentiation, leading to the rise of what has been called Buddhism, Christianity, Islam, Zoroastrianism, and so on, is unquestionably one of the most profoundly significant and consequential processes in the whole of man's religious development, and indeed in human history generally. That these movements extricated themselves from being tied, as the religious life of man in all previous instances had been, to one particular society and have lived on in some sort of autonomous existence; and have in some cases given rise to, and have even, as Toynbee has recently stressed, survived the fall of, great civilizations; these are matters of monumental importance. That something special was happening with the development of these great movements is undeniable; and to this their distinctive nomenclature bears some sort of testimonial. My contention is not that these emergences may be ignored; but on the contrary, that what was happening in these cases needs to be understood more carefully and more adequately than the single noun formulation makes possible. The interpreting of this major process in man's development is a very elaborate and intricate question.

It has been remarked that a number of great thinkers and prophets arose in scattered parts of the world somewhat simultaneously: Plato, Isaiah, Zarathushtra, Gautama, K'ung[1]. Another way of commenting on the same phenomenon is to remark that during a millennium or so following that period men for the first time organized themselves into large-scale groups cherishing the memory of great leaders. I do not wish to belittle these major figures; human history owes immeasurably to such individual persons. Yet the world historian must take note of the fact that not only did such figures arise; equally striking, there evolved in these centuries the unprecedented sociological phenomenon of a mass response to them.

We have no way of knowing that there may not have been one or more persons in China in the centuries or millennia before K'ung as wise as he. What we do know is that in his case what he had to say was remembered and honoured, and that in Han times the tradition that he championed and came to symbolize was organized on a national scale into some sort of systematic pattern. The fact that K'ung said what he said is no more important for the history of China, and in some ways is less illuminating for the history of man, than that, once he had said it, hundreds of millions of Chinese since have felt that what he said was supremely important and in some sense ultimately true, and have acted to preserve and cherish it.

Similarly with regard to 'Buddhism'. No historian can fail to recognize that something distinctive and major was launched that is designated by this name. Yet no historian, also, can understand the rise of this movement, let alone its subsequent development in India, China, and elsewhere, who does not give at least as much importance to the creative response of the followers as to the activity or ideas of its 'founder'.

What have been called the religions are at least the active and continuing responses of men.

The emergence in human history from some 2,500 to some 1,500 years ago of major instances of such self-organized responses, and, cutting across social, ethnic, and cultural frontiers and continuing across epochal vicissitudes in history, their development into the half-dozen great living religious communities of the present day, sharing among them the allegiance of almost the whole of mankind—these are mighty matters. The concept of 'the religions' recognizes them, and certainly any alternative conceptualization must prove itself by intellectually coping with them more adequately, not less.

Another example of a tie between the process of conceptual reifying and a process of actual crystallizing in human history and society, is that of 'religion' as a generic abstract. The modern West's adoption of this concept, though misleading for an interpretation of the religious life of the Aztecs, the classical Hindus, mediaeval Europe, contemporary Bushmen, and most other peoples, is nonetheless neither fortuitous nor absurd. Its rise in recent centuries in the West has had to do with a great process of differentiation in those recent centuries in that area—a process whose diffusion around the world can be discerned in the present century. This is a process whereby the complexity and proliferating novelty of life have advanced relentlessly and spectacularly. A result has been that religious traditions that were once in practice and are still perhaps in ideal coterminous with human life in all its comprehensiveness, have actually found themselves supplemented more and more by considerations from other or newer sources, so that the religious seems to be one facet of a person's life alongside many others.

The rise of what is called secularism (the term was coined in Europe in 1851[2]) and its spread throughout the world are indeed a symptom of an evolving sociological situation in which an earlier cohesiveness or integrity of man's social and personal life, once religiously expressed and religiously sanctified, has been fragmented. In this situation those who wish to preserve that quality of their existence to which their religious tradition nurtures their sensitivity, are often able to do so only as one item in an otherwise heterogeneous or distracted life. The concept 'religion' as designating, however vaguely, one aspect of life among others bears testimony to this differentiation.

Once again, any new conceptualization must do at least equal justice to the modern situation that has arisen, as well as dealing more adequately with the perceptive religious man's unwillingness—or the careful observer's inability—to segment off one area of his living to which he will confine, in theory or in practice, the relevance of his faith[3].

I do not contend, then, that the old concepts are meaningless; rather that they are imprecise and liable to distort what they are asked to represent.

. . .
iii

Before presenting my own arguments in favour of dropping these concepts, we may note that I am far from being alone in modern times in a dissatisfaction with them. We have already seen, in our historical survey, not only how limited has been their use, but also how hesitant many have become with regard to them. One may now cite several instances of overt protest, from among participants in religious life, both Western and other.

Among Christians, the best known disclaimer is Karl Barth, perhaps the Church's most prophetic contemporary voice. He has devoted in his most substantial work a vigorous section to the topic 'The Abolition of Religion'[4]. 'Religion', he proclaims flatly, 'is unbelief'[5] . . . 'and unbelief . . . is sin'[6].

Similarly, Emil Brunner has written: 'This [Christian] revelation ought not to be called "religion" ' . . . ' "Religion" is the product of man's sinful blindness'[7]. In America, the leading theologian Paul Tillich has apologized in a recent study for his use of the term[8]. In Britain the engaging writer C. S. Lewis remarks in passing: ' "Religion" (how odious a word, by the way, how seldom used in Scripture, how hard to imagine on the lips of Our Lord!) . . .'[9]. Currently growing attention is being paid to the recent German thinker and martyr Dietrich Bonhöffer, who looked forward to a 'religionless Christianity'[10].

Among representatives of other traditions, one may cite the following:

A modern Jewish thinker: 'The attempt to reduce Judaism to a religion is a betrayal of its true nature'[10a].

Jawaharlal Nehru: 'It is hardly possible . . . to say whether [Hinduism] is a religion or not'[11].

A prominent Buddhist religious leader: 'Buddhism is not a religion in the sense in which that word is commonly understood'[12].

A Muslim: 'Islam is not merely a "religion" in the sense in which this term is understood in the West'[13].

The difficulty is not only, however, for those perceptive thinkers who repudiate the concept. More important is the problem with those less alert who succumb to it. It has led them, I would urge, into many serious confusions. For example, the dilemma of the modern Jew is acute who has accepted the belief that there is somewhere something called 'Judaism', though he cannot find it. He may pass his life haunted by the shadow of this entity that, he supposes, somehow confers on him his identity, yet always eludes him. It is impossible to define Judaism, but the conviction that it exists and deserves his ultimate loyalty can become almost the central concern of his therefore unpatterned life.

Similarly many Muslims have come to hold that God has given them something called Islam, and that it is something that can therefore guide and save them, and that conceptualizable parts of it called Islamic law, Islamic economics, Islamic education, and the like are waiting to be discovered and can somehow be applied to their social living in such a way as to solve all problems. Yet, for instance in Pakistan where the opportunity to work this idea out in practice was central, none has been able to say just what this Islam actually is; and those who have seemed to come closest to it, such as Mawdudi, are seen by other Muslims as little helpful in meeting the actual problems and challenges that their country faces. In our previous chapter we have seen that originally 'Islam' named not something that God gave to men, as is now widely imagined, but rather something that God asked them to give to Him—a quite different matter. We have had occasion to suggest elsewhere that the essential tragedy of the modern Islamic world is the degree to which Muslims, instead of giving their allegiance to God, have been giving it to something called Islam[14]. To those embroiled in this misapprehension, God has seemed remote, as well as mundane life seeming intractable. To think of Islam as the name of a religion is proving a spiritual as well as a sociological calamity.

Similar considerations apply in the Christian case. It is as Christians' faith in God has weakened that they have busied themselves with Christianity; and as their personal relation to Christ has virtually lapsed that they have turned to religion for solace[15]. The notion that religion is a nice thing to have, even that it is useful, has arisen, as it could arise only, in a secular and desperate society. Such a notion is a kind of blasphemy, to those whose faith is sensitive. One has even reached a point today where some Christians can speak of believing in Christianity (instead of believing in God and in Christ); of preaching Christianity (instead of preaching good news, salvation, redemption); of practising Christianity (instead of practising love). Some even talk of being saved by Christianity, instead of by the only thing that could possibly save us, the anguish and the love of God.

So much is this so, that a task of the modern religious reformer is to help men not to let their religion stand between them and God. Faith, we shall argue in a later chapter, is deeply personal, dynamic, ultimate, is a direct encounter relating one in anguish or in ecstasy or in intellectual integrity or simply in humdrum household duties to the God of the whole universe, and to one's Samaritan neighbour—that is, to persons as such, oblivious of the fact that he be outside one's organized religious community. If faith is vivid, therefore, one has little concern for abstractions, and at most a secondary interest in institutionalizations.

And if this be true of men, how much more of God Himself. A Christian who takes God seriously must surely recognize that God does not give a fig for Christianity. God is concerned with people, not with things. We read that God so loved the world that He gave His Son. We do not read anywhere that God loved Christianity.

Again, for the devout Jew, revelation proclaims not Judaism but justice; and man's proper response is an ultimate loyalty not to a system but to a community and to the Most High. Similarly, in the Bhagavad Gita, when Krishna the Lord, previously disguised as Arjuna's charioteer, has led Arjuna to a point where he is capable of receiving a divine revelation, he does not reveal 'Hinduism' to him, but reveals Himself, a personal God.

We noted previously[16] the introduction into eighteenth-century Europe of the notion of revealed religion. This has led those who have taken the idea seriously (Muslims as well as Westerners have been involved) into no end of trouble and confusion. God does not reveal religions; He reveals Himself.

At least, this is what genuinely religious people aver[17]. One need not necessarily agree with them. One need not necessarily agree that God exists. Whether or not one is persuaded that there is a God is for the moment immaterial to our argument. One is asked but to concede that those who do believe in God, and genuinely have faith in Him, adopt this attitude. I am not yet saying that the concept of religion is inadequate; rather, so far, that it is inadequate for the man of faith.

The more direct, immediate, and profound his faith, the more he is concerned with something, or Someone, that far transcends anything that can be denominated as religion. This concept is fundamentally a distraction to his religiousness.

This is why, historically, no great religious leader (except Mani?) has 'founded a religion', or preached one. Almost to a man, religious reformers, prophets, eponymous geniuses have severely criticized or attacked the religious environment in which they found themselves, calling men away from a concern with mundane institutions and systems to a transcendent reality, behind and beyond these. A religious reformer does not seek to reform religion, but seeks to reform men's awareness of their total environment, and men's lives; and in the process reified religion has often to be shattered, in order that that awareness and those lives may be restored to wholeness.

This is true not only of Jesus but of Luther and of Wesley; not only of Gautama the Buddha but of Nichiren; not only of Muhammad but of ibn Taymiyah; not only of Amos and Isaiah but of Buber. Throughout human history no man has been religiously great who was not dissatisfied with those aspects of his age that the modern observer would call its religion[18].

A lively faith involves a limpid sincerity of relationship to one's fellow men, and to oneself, and to the Creator or ground or totality of the universe. For these things the formalities of one's religious tradition are at best a channel, and at worst a substitute.

No doubt the leaders of religious movements are preeminently preceptive of the transcendent and immediate qualities of that of which they speak, and more than ordinarily sensitive to the inevitable inadequacies of men's response. Yet even the followers, whose response with all its human frailties constitutes the movements, must have some sense of that transcendence and immediacy, or else they would not follow. God, we have said, does not reveal a religion, He reveals Himself; what the observer calls a religion is man's continuing response. The response is interesting, but to the man of faith at only a subordinate level. The keener his faith, the greater his awareness that it is subordinate, and that it is inadequate[19]. No man has seen the point of his own religious tradition for whom the concept religion is an adequate indication of what it is all about. To be a participant in a religious movement is to recognize that that movement points to something or Someone beyond itself.

The observer sees the movement; the participant sees what it signifies.

iv

Fundamentally it is the outsider who names a religious system. It is the observer who conceptualizes a religion as a denotable existent. To grasp this fact is of the utmost importance; and to grasp its profound and crucial implications.

It is quite impossible to understand man's religious life if one does not understand that that life has necessarily and rightly looked differently when viewed from within and when viewed from without. That this has been so is not an aberration, nor some casual or fortuitous development; it is inherent in the situation in which man in his religious life has been caught up. I shall presently set forth a conceptual framework endeavouring to analyse this and adequately to handle its implications. For the moment I am concerned only to stress that, whatever its implications, the fact has been so[20]. A religious tradition has no meaning unless it enables those within it to see something that those without do not see[21].

Phrased differently, there are some for whom the tradition has a transcendent reference—and for whom this is indeed its point; and these are by that very fact in a different position from those (whom we therefore call 'outsiders') for whom it does not. It therefore follows that the latter's conception of that particular religious complex must be inadequate and unserviceable for the former.

The external observer's awareness is different from that of the *engagé* participant. A relationship of which you stand at one end, with your whole personality and perhaps your eternal destiny at stake, and at the other end stands God, crushingly overwhelming in His majesty and frightening in His imperious demands and yet utterly winsome in His unfrustratable love and concern for you as a person—this is a very different matter from those relationships that you may write down in your notebook as you observe other people's exotic behaviour, or even that you may infer from a careful study of others' symbols which, even if you finally come to understand their meaning, do not reach out and lay hold upon your life. It is this latter complex to which the terms 'a religion', 'the religions', and the names of the various religions, have come to refer. Even if one goes back a couple of centuries and elevates them to a level of designating not mundane historical response but ideal theory, still this level remains inadequate to that in which the man of faith is involved. No matter how idealized, these concepts inevitably retain some measure of the outsiders' interpretation.

Heaven and Hell, to a believer, are stupendous places into one or other of which irretrievably he is about to step. To an observer, they are items in the believer's mind. To the believer, they are parts of the universe; to the observer, they are parts of a religion.

In historical fact, as we have previously seen, except for representing personal piety, the religion concepts arose to serve these outsiders' purposes. Despite some modification (and therefore ambiguity) in being used since also by believers who have uncritically taken them over, one may confidently repeat the assertion that they are inadequate for the man of faith.

v

The participant is concerned with God[22]; the observer has been concerned with 'religion'. I propose now to contend that this latter concept, despite appearances and despite usage, is inadequate also even for the observer. In the first contention, that the concept was inappropriate for the man of faith himself, I have had, despite recent Western custom, the support of sensitive representatives of various communities in their protest against the use of the term for their own faith, and the support of rather massive historical evidence showing that in the Orient men have on the whole not used such a concept for their own faith, and not even in the Christian West until the rise of unbelief. In this second contention, however, that the concept is inadequate also for the outside observer, for the student, I shall appear to be proceeding more alone. It would seem that I am breaking rather new ground. My suggestion that here too the concept should be dropped may seem at first a somewhat bold and radical one.

On more careful deliberation, however, it can be seen that even here there is a fair amount of empirical data to support the contention, in addition to the more speculative and analytic reasons that I shall presently adduce. Before setting forth these more theoretical considerations, therefore, which elucidate the point and seem to justify the move that I propose, we may first note various indications that such a move is in fact not quite so novel as it may sound, and indeed has already covertly begun. I would bring into consciousness factors in an objective situation that point in a direction that, my argument will then advocate, is one of promise.

First of all, we may recall that what appears to many to be natural has proven on inquiry to be characteristic of a limited time and place; and has already shown itself not altogether successful. The custom of interpreting other people's religious life under a series of rubrics of the several religions, some of them named, is Western, is recent, and has already passed its zenith. Although the general public still uses the terms which an earlier generation composed, we have seen that careful scholars have in fact begun to abandon them. One could multiply illustrations of this, beyond the instances previously given. Evidence is particularly abundant, as one might expect, for studies of religious life in the Far East: in recent work on Japan[23] and especially China, where reification is least of all appropriate[24]; but also on India[25] and the early civilizations[26] and modern 'primitives'[27].

One may generalize that the present-day retreat is abandoning reification more or less in the reverse order of its development. This is illustrated in titles, where the individual proper names are the first to be giving way, to less specific denominations such as 'The religion of . . .'[28]; and then this latter is further being replaced either by generic and potentially more personalist and, anyway, still less specific phrases—in English without an article —such as 'religion in' or 'religion among . . .'[29] or by an adjective, as 'the religious life of . . .', or, still less specifically, 'religious life in . . .'[30]—or by simply referring to the people concerned as people, with some indication of a religious orientation[31]; or else each concept is being fragmented by the use of plurals[32] or partial[33] or composite[34] titles.

A generation that imagined that there was a series of things in the world that could be identified as 'Hinduism', 'Christianity', 'the religion of the Sumerians', is being superseded by a generation that is becoming exposed to the idea, and by scholars who unwittingly know very well, that a closer understanding of these matters involves vaguer or different headings. This is so not only for the more amorphous Oriental tradition. That the concept 'Christianity' is inadequate for close knowledge is being implied, however unconsciously, in such new usages as *'das Urchristentum'*[35], 'Protestant Christianity'[36], and *'Les christianismes orientaux'*[37].

Present-day study of what used to be called 'the religions of the world' is reporting what it finds more and more in terms, if not of other concepts, at least of modifications, conscious or unconscious, of the traditional ones. It seems time, therefore, to challenge the whole tradition. So far, each student wrestling with some particular segment of mankind's religious life has tended in effect to say, explicitly or by implication, 'The concept of a specific and namable religion, one among others, does not quite apply in the case that I am studying. It cannot do full justice to this particular situation—though it doubtless is all right for other parts of the world, or other periods'. This last is not, of course, so formulated, but is tacitly assumed or tolerated.

To the point, then, that this concept is demonstrably inadequate for any member of a religious community to portray his own faith, though he may use it to describe that of other communities, we may now add this further point that careful investigators are increasingly finding that it is inadequate for representing the religious situation about which they themselves are well informed, though they feel that it may be used by other observers for other situations.

vi

Let us turn, next, to theoretical analysis. My own reasons to be urged for abandoning the concept altogether, are basically two. There are two considerations in the light of which a notion of the religions can be seen to be inherently and necessarily inadequate for interpreting man's religious life. Aphoristically, these are God, and history.

Not all observers believe in God, and not all the devout are concerned with history; but it is difficult to escape both.

In the European Age of Reason, when these concepts were developed and flourished, men might think to conceptualize their world without much tremulous sense of the numinous or much dissolvent sense of historical flux. Now that the presuppositions of that particular time and place are superseded or outflanked, we may well seek more appropriate terms than theirs in which to depict man's variegated and evolving encounter with transcendence. In our final synthesis we shall argue that the two considerations are two faces of a single issue, with both of which my essentially personalistic interpretation will endeavour simultaneously to cope. In the meantime, we may look at the points one by one.

The first score on which I see the concept of a religion as tending to deceive the observer of a community's religious life is, basically, that the concept is necessarily inadequate for the man who believes and therefore cannot but be misleading for the outsider who does not. There is a serious and tricky problem here. We noted in our introductory chapter the position of those who hold that only a Christian can understand the Christian faith, only a Muslim can understand Islam, and so on. Although I hope to surmount this problem presently, I do not wish to underestimate it. The observer's concept of a religion is beautifully suited to ignore it. The participant can see very clearly that the outsider may know *all about* a religious system, and yet may totally miss the point. The outsider may intellectually command all the details of its external facts, and yet may be—indeed, as an outsider, presumably must be or demonstratively is—untouched by the heart of the matter.

There is a difference between knowing a doctrine of salvation, and being saved. There is a difference between knowing that

134

Islam involves submitting one's will to God's will as revealed in the Qur'an, and actually submitting one's will. There is a difference between having in one's mind an accurate picture of a sacrificial pattern, and actually sacrificing what one values, or being sacrificed. All this is evident enough (though it has sometimes not been stressed). And indeed the student may not merely know the doctrines and patterns, but know also that that difference exists. The relevant point here is that the significance of their involvement for those who are religiously involved lies on the far side of that difference. To know 'a religion' is not yet to know the religious life of him whom one observes.

Christian life is a new life, lived in a supernatural context. To understand Christianity, or to think that one does, is not yet to understand Christians. This latter requires an understanding of that supernatural context, in which what the outsider calls Christianity enables them now to live. The Christian may affirm that no one can understand it who has not known it, and that no one can know it who has not been salvaged out of men's innate limitations by the only procedure in the universe capable of doing that. One may challenge the validity of either of these two propositions; but not their relevance. No amount of attention to the procedure's outward form, which is what concerns the outside student of Christianity, can give, or is even designed to give, an understanding of that transformed life in its spiritual dimensions.

The above argument will in most cases not carry much weight with those who are not believing Christians—a fact that in itself illustrates the very point that I am making. We shall return to this. In the meantime, one may make the further point that the outsider, if he is a skeptic, may reject the statement that the Christian life is lived in a supernatural context on the grounds that no supernatural exists. If so, then for him the Christian is induced by something called Christianity to live in an illusion. Here one must insist that the significant point to understand about this Christian is still not that something called Christianity but what it is like living in an illusion.

The important matter in the life of any religious community is what their religious tradition does to them. This is not easy for an outsider to ascertain. Yet if he is to succeed at all, he will need to conceptualize it in personal, not impersonal, terms.

What is profoundly important in the religious life of any people, and elemental to all our discussions, is that, whatever else it may be, religious life is a kind of *life*. Participants know this, consciously or unconsciously. Observers may have to learn it. In learning it, they find that they must leave behind the distraction of congealed concepts postulating entities different from the living persons before them, or even theoretically independent of them.

Not only do reifying concepts of 'a religion', in terms such as 'Buddhism' and 'Zoroastrianism', misrepresent by freezing the inherently personal, living quality of men's religiousness. Further, they do so by omitting not only the vitality but the most significant of all factors in that vitality, namely its relation with transcendence. The observer's concept of a religion is by definition constituted of what can be observed. Yet the whole pith and substance of religious life lies in its relation to what cannot be observed.

The significant thing about a Christian's life, we have remarked, is that it is lived in a supernatural context. What signifies is not what the Christian does, but that he does it as a child of God; not what he believes, but that God has granted him the gift of believing; not that he is in the Church, but that in the Church he is in living communion with Christ as a personal friend and with fellow members in a fellowship not merely human, not merely social; not that he loves, but that he loves because of Christ; not that he sins, but that he sins to Christ's hurt, and yet forgivably.

The same consideration applies with equal force to other communities. The Muslim theologian al-Ghazzali learned (he phrases it, 'God taught me') something of the shallowness of mere theology from an old peasant woman who, unlike al-Ghazzali with his formidable dialectic by which he controlled a score of proofs for the existence of God, knew no proofs at all and yet lived in God's presence.

It is quite possible and even easy for a modern Western graduate student to know more 'about Islam' than that woman with her simple faith ever knew—or ever wanted to know. The question as to whether he understands *her* is a different sort of question.

Being a Muslim means living in a certain context, sociological, historical, ideological, *and transcendent.* The significance of being a Muslim lies in this fact, not in some prolegomenon to it. The concern of the observer with something that he calls Islam shifts attention from the heart of the matter, namely people's living within this context, to the context itself, which is damaging enough; and disrupts the whole procedure still farther by omitting from his purview the context's transcendence. It does this not perversely but inherently; since the observer by the very fact of being an outsider, a nonacceptor of the context, has ruled out its transcendent quality in theory *a priori.* He has conceptualized what for the man of faith does not exist, namely a context for his life shorn of its most significant dimension. The concept 'Islam' in the mind of a nonbeliever has represented at best an element in the life of such Muslims as have lost their faith.

'Islam' comes alive for the Muslim through faith, which is not an item in a religion but a quality in some men's hearts—a personal quality in several senses, including that of varying from person to person and even from day to day[38]. Once it has come alive, it is *ipso facto* no longer what it appears to be to him for whom it is not alive. The commands of God, for instance, which for an observer appear to control and even to confine a Muslim's behaviour, for the Muslim himself, in accord with the degree of vitality of his faith, rather liberate that behaviour. They free it from the confines of purely human floundering and the ignorance of mundane device; and elevate it to a quite new plane—the in one sense unbounded, certainly eternal plane of cosmic appropriateness and validity. To live a life of which even the apparently petty details now have ultimate significance, of which even the humdrum routine has been raised to cosmic stature and touched with divine splendour; to live in a community of which only the less interesting, mundane side is open to outsiders' observation while one can oneself catch at least a glimpse of its real import, its cosmic role; all this, at least, is part of the meaning of a Muslim's faith. Those of us on the outside who would interpret to ourselves the Muslim must understand not his religion but his religiousness.

So for the Hindu, the Buddhist, the Tierra del Fuegan. If we would comprehend these we must look not at their religion but at the universe, so far as possible through their eyes. It is what the Hindu is able to see, by being a Hindu, that is significant. Until we can see it too, we have not come to grips with the religious quality of his life. And we may be sure that as he looks around him, he does not see 'Hinduism'. Like the rest of us, he sees his wife's death, his child's minor and major aspirations, his moneylender's mercilessness, the calm of a starlit evening, his own mortality. He sees these things through coloured glasses, if one will, of a 'Hindu' brand. He sees also certain gods and institutions that may carry this label, though the deeper and more sophisticated his faith, the more he sees through these. His neighbour, also Hindu, sees the foreground differently; if their vision finally converges, it is because both have been sufficiently penetrating to see through and beyond their foreground to a Reality that, if not yet altogether attributeless, is certainly quite without the attribute of being in any sense *Hindu*.

Of primitive peoples the religious system often seems, to sophisticated outsiders, grotesque. They have not appreciated the religious life of such peoples if they have not grasped the point that it is constituted not only of that system but at least equally of the fact that through it the participants are enabled, one might be tempted to say, to feel at home in the universe (which is anything but grotesque!). Yet one has not truly construed the situation unless one can go beyond this and recognize their life as one in which, by being religious, they not only feel at home in the universe but indeed are at home in it. To omit this fact from one's apprehension is sorely to misconceive.

We return, then, to the Christian's flat assertion: 'The Christian faith is not one of the religions of the world'[39]. Students of comparative religion have been wont to decry such sentiments, even dismissing them as ridiculous. I, in contrast, would argue vigorously that the Christian who says this—for instance, Brunner—is profoundly and critically right. Only, I would go on to assert, with equal vigour: *Neither is the faith of any other people.*

Those who ridicule have failed to understand all faith. Brunner has failed, as has his community generally, only to understand the faith of other men.

We are now in a position to recognize that it was not fortuitous that the religion concepts, having arisen in Western Europe, are inherently depreciative. For the Christian tradition, particularly in its Protestant form, has historically been unusually disparaging of other religious traditions; and the rationalist academic tradition has been skeptical, if not disparaging, of all. The concept 'a religion', and the conceptualizing of named religions, omit, we have argued, the transcendent dimension from what they seek to represent. This has to do with the fact that Christians have regularly failed or refused to recognize that the faith of non-Christians has that transcendence; that God does in fact encounter men in Buddhist, Muslim and Hottentot forms, as he does in the Christian. Secular academics have regularly failed or refused to recognize that there is a transcendent dimension to human life at all. (The very notion of transcendence will, I realize, disquiet them not a little.)

Both these groups, therefore, surveying the religious history of man, could attempt to interpret it, leaving out of account the very quality that gives it significance. They have suspected, or affirmed, that that significance just is not there.

All religions are illusory, they have held; or, all religions other than ours.

Thus also many Muslims. More appreciative or tolerant traditions, on the other hand, such as those of India or farther East, have accordingly not developed this sort of concept not only for interpreting their own faith but also not for interpreting that of their neighbours. (Something similar has been true also of the mystics of all traditions—including Sufis and Christians—who, it is well known, have been the one type in their communities most successful in understanding men of divergent faiths.) Hindus, Buddhists, and their like, whatever their other faults, have usually not failed to recognize those who differed from them in outward pattern and formal grouping as nevertheless engaged on fundamentally the same enterprise, as attuned to the same kind of melody. In the positive hypothesis that I shall proffer in our subsequent chapters, in an attempt to handle religious diversity without distorting it, informed students will perhaps detect elements suggesting the influence on my thinking of certain Indian and Chinese orientations. At the same time I hope that the concepts proposed will also be serviceable within the Western academic tradition, and will be recognized as methodologically continuous with it, and indeed in part derived from it.

Among the Christian writers cited above[40] as protesting sharply against the application of the concept 'religion' to their own faith, none was hesitant to apply it to other people's. These men have not criticized or protested against the concept in itself, but have been content to reject it as applied to themselves, insisting that it does not do justice to that in which their own group is involved. Indeed they reject it in their own case because it compromises, and apply it to others because it compromises. Emil Brunner writes: 'The God of the "other religions" is always an idol'[41]. This judgement can be seen as expressing the arrogance of a narrow-minded Christian. I would suggest that it can also be seen as a perceptive remark, more universal than its author himself intended—but at another level.

The concept 'other religions', religions of other people, inherently turns their gods into idols, into false deities, the product of human phantasy. This applies also to the Christian case. For those for whom Christianity is an *other* religion, for example Muslims, the Christian God is an idol, at least the second person of the Trinity.

Once again the concept serves those who would deny to the religious life of those whom they observe transcendent involvement[42]. Actually, no one in the whole history of man has ever worshipped an idol. Men have worshipped God—or something—in the form of idols. That is what idols are for. Yet that is quite a different thing. 'The heathen in his blindness', sang the nineteenth-century hymn, 'bows down to wood and stone'[43]. Yet it is not the heathen here who is blind, but the observer. Even at his most restricted, the 'idolator' worships not the stone that I see, but the stone that he sees.

Outsiders, then, in their conception of other men's religions, have tended to drain these of any but mundane content. They have done this by throwing a conceptual boundary around their interpretation, thus imposing on other people a limit to which their own mind has given birth. Yet the point of man's religious life lies in man's being introduced in it to that which is without limits. Any attempt to conceptualize a religion is a contradiction in terms.

The student's first responsibility is to recognize that there is always and in principle more in any man's faith than any other man can see.

(Within any community, a sensitive awareness must recognize that there is more in one's own faith than one can oneself see, let alone formulate.)

vii

So much for my first point. My second is at a more mundane level. Those down-to-earth readers who may have been restless at my concern for transcendence will be the first to recognize the cogency of our next, historical consideration. If one rejects the fixity and neatness of formulated patterns because they presuppose some definite upper limit to men's faith, one rejects them also because they presuppose definiteness all round, whereas every historian now knows that in fact there is flux.

Neither the believer nor the observer can hold that there is anything on earth that can legitimately be called 'Christianity' or 'Shintoism' or 'religion' without recognizing that if such a thing existed yesterday, it existed in a somewhat different form the day before. If it exists in one country (or village), it exists in somewhat different form in the next. The concepts were formed before the ruthlessness of historical change was recognized, in all its disintegrating sweep. They have in practice been being abandoned as awareness has since grown. It is time now definitely to reject them theoretically, as inherently inept.

Aristotle, in his *Posterior Analytics,* remarks of a mythical animal that one may give the meaning of the word that names it but it is not possible to give a definition, since there is actually no such animal[44]. A term such as 'unicorn'[45] is used, and its meaning can therefore be stated; but there is no entity in the objective world to which it corresponds, and therefore no statement of what a unicorn is is possible. The implications of this analysis and the outlook that it implies were fundamental for much of Greek thought, and have been influential throughout much of Western civilization since, not least among those not self-consciously philosophizing: the idea that reality is definable. Language, in such a view, consists of words that can be explained; the real world, of things than can be defined.

In the modern age our embarrassment is the other way around. We are learning to reverse Aristotle's assessment; though confusion reigns when we do so unwittingly, or in a fashion that falls short of being explicit or rigorous. For us, words and concepts are to be defined, while things cannot be. We can speak with precision and elegance in our definition of imaginary constructs: an irrational number, or any of the notions in mathematics; model types in sociological theory; concepts in physics; abstractions of all kinds. In the realm of ideals something similar may perhaps obtain. The world of objective reality, on the other hand, is recalcitrant to our schematizations. We may define anything at all, provided only that it does not exist. Once we are talking of empirical objects, our minds move from the neatness of rational intelligibilities to the more humble approximations of an awareness of what always transcends our exact apprehension—and, in any case, is changing even while we try to apprehend it.

The sciences, while developing their own modified or novel meanings of definition, have abandoned the concept of *essence,* its original concomitant. Science is not interested in essences. A modern physicist cannot define matter; but he can handle it, and can do so because his predecessors eventually learned that the essence does not signify. He understands the behaviour of matter not because he knows what matter is—for he does not; but because he has learned how it operates, and how it changes.

The world of the natural sciences, however, is itself considerably less complex, less phased, than that of man and society. Here more than ever we have discovered that on close scrutiny boundaries shift if they do not actually dissolve. We are learning that we do not live in a universe that can be tidily and finally arrayed in a series of packaged items each intellectually dominable, and the whole kept in neat and docile order The philosophic revolt against essentialism has followed the discovery that the objective world itself revolts against its pigeonholing dominance.

The point is valid generally, it would seem; it may be illustrated lavishly in the area of man's religious history. Understanding in this realm was seriously disrupted, we suggest, when last-century thinkers set out in chase of an essence of religion, an essence of Christianity, of Hinduism, and so on. The knowledge that has accrued over the past century or so as the reward of massive work in the academic field called History of Religions, has made those essences not more but less ascertainable. That work and that knowledge have not unearthed what religion, or one of the religions, is; but they have contributed something else, of revolutionary import. The History of Religions has taught man incontrovertibly that 'the religions' have a history. This may sound tautological but actually is crucial. Many religious people have realized it, if at all, only peripherally. Even scholars have not taken it quite seriously.

For essences do not have a history. Essences do not change. Yet it is an observable and important fact that what have been called the religions do, in history, change.

What exists cannot be defined. What obstructs a definition of Hinduism, for instance, is precisely the richness of what exists, in all its extravagant variety from century to century and from village to village. The empirical religious tradition of the Hindus developing historically in the minds and hearts and institutions and literatures and societies of untold millions of actual people is not a form, but a growing congeries of living realities. It is not to be compressed within or eviscerated into or confused with any systematic intellectual pattern.

As an ideal, 'Hinduism' might conceivably be defined (though only by a Hindu) [46], but not as an historical reality. The sheer facts, in all their intractable toughness, stand in the way.

'Hinduism' refers not to an entity; it is a name that the West has given to a prodigiously variegated series of facts. It is a notion in men's minds—and a notion that cannot but be inadequate. To use this term at all is inescapably a gross oversimplification. There is an inherent contradiction between history and this order of idea.

I do not mean merely that to define Hinduism, or Taoism, or Protestantism is difficult. That, everyone knows. My point rather is that it is in principle impossible, and almost perverse. One has radically misunderstood our world if one imagines that things can be defined; and especially living things, and especially human involvements. Not to have recognized that mundane reality—in its complexity, its particularity, and its givenness—outpaces our conceptualizations of it is not yet to have adopted that humility before facts that normatively characterizes modern study.

Obviously, I am not suggesting that what men have called the religions do not exist. The point is rather that, as every historian of them knows almost to his bewilderment, they exist all too copiously. It is the richness, the radical diversity, the unceasing shift and change, the ramification and complex involvement, of the historical phenomena of 'religion' or of any one 'religion' that create the difficulty. What has been called Christianity is, so far as history is concerned, not one thing but millions of things, and hundreds of millions of persons. 'Islam' could perhaps fairly readily be understood if only it had not existed in such abundant actuality, at differing times and in differing areas, in the minds and hearts of differing persons, in the institutions and forms of differing societies, in the evolving of differing stages.

And even if somehow one came to know all that Judaism has been, how is one to make room for what Judaism may yet become?

For there is this further point, of great significance. Not only has the past been various; a future also must somehow be taken into account. And it is inherently unknowable. There is no more befuddling misconception of human history than not to recognize that it is free; if not absolutely, at least free from any limitations that our intellects may attempt to impose upon it. To define is to set limits; but no man can set limits that other men cannot transcend.

To define Hinduism is to deny the Hindu his right to the freedom and integrity of his faith. What he may do tomorrow no man can say today.

It might be felt that, by considering the Hindu case, I have unduly favoured my contention, selecting the admittedly freest, least definable, most amorphous of all the world's 'religions'. Let us look, then, at 'Christianity'. Some might hold that St. Thomas Aquinas, or the framers of the Westminster Confession, or someone, has defined Christianity. I myself would not phrase this so, nor would those named; but we have already treated at sufficient length the question of the inadequacy of these concepts for the man of faith, and I do not wish here to press into service again that side of the argument. For present purposes, let it even be conceded; it would still be an ideal Christianity that was defined, not the empirical Christianity of history, not the actual religious life or the actual institutions of Christians in all their ramifying and diverse objectivity.

This would corroborate my contention that one cannot define what exists. A Christian theologian who attempted to define Christianity would be attempting to define it as it truly is in an idealistic sense, up in the sky; not as it historically has been in concrete actuality. The definable is the pure; and purity is to be found only in theory and in God. Whatever exists mundanely cannot be defined; whatever can be defined does not exist.

Some few have indeed taken refuge in this kind of intellectualist idealism, conceiving a religion unsullied by the world, a transcendent form. To the unserviceability of such a concept for the historian's purpose, on many counts, we shall return. For the moment, we simply note that it evades rather than solves our problem, which would then become that of understanding (and somehow conceptualizing) the ever varying impingement of such a transcendent entity on man, caught in the sublunar flux. In the ambiguity between the ideal and the actual, not only is the manward side of even the most transcendentally conceived 'religion' involved. More heroically, to be involved in it is presumably its very business and significance.

We are in no wise concerned—neither as worshippers nor as observing historians—with an ideal realm of essences unless, and except insofar as, it is somehow, somewhere, involved in the life of man. And this involvement in human history of what some have wished to call the religions decisively compromises the purity of any idea that the human mind might form of them.

The history of the Christian Church, the most orthodox of Christians must assert, is the history of a congregation of sinners. The Buddhist ideal of universal compassion would be evacuated of all relevance if it were not related to men who in their actuality stand sorely in need of compassion. The Hindu equation *atman* is *Brahman* is not an analytic statement tautologically describing the transcendent world, which is unanalysably one, but is a synthetic statement linking to transcendence this world of *maya*, through the soul of man. To say that man's soul is divine derives its truth from the quality of ultimate reality and of man's innermost and abiding nature, but derives its significance from the quality of man's involvement in outer flux. Like that of Jesus, other religious messages too come to call not the righteous but sinners to repentance, not to underwrite the wise but to enlighten the ignorant, to seek and to save those that otherwise would be lost in the confusions of actual living. The religious proclamations of the world have been neither irrelevant nor redundant; not one but is addressed to real men and women, not ideal ones, to actual persons in actual, and differing, situations.

What sort of thing is Buddhism, of which we see one instance or part or manifestation in the life of the emperor Asoka, another in a piece of art of Gandhara, another in the doctrines of Jodo Shin, another in a ceremony in a seventeenth-century Burma village, another in the organization of a nineteenth-century Tibetan monastery, another in the *Weltanschauung* of a twentieth-century Ceylon prime minister or assassin monk, or of a Taiwan organic chemist? Such an enumeration is, of course, absurdly selective. The actual historical evidence as to what Buddhism has at various times and places been seen to be, comprises an immense literature, a vast quantity of works of art, innumerable institutions, and finally the personal lives, devout or almost insouciant, saintly or sinful, great or petty, dramatic or humdrum, of literally thousands of millions of persons, each one different, each one important. In addition to all these unique items, the history of Buddhism comprises also in some sense the social cohesion that has bound the community or parts of it together at various times and places with varying force; and comprises further, in some sense, the process of development that has linked the items historically in some sort of dynamic continuity.

Nor have we yet done. The above is what we see. Not to be ignored, however, is what we do not see: the Buddhist faith in the quiet corner of a man's inner heart; the inspiration in the mind of the artist of which his completed artefact before us is the inadequate expression; the moral ideal in the life of the believer to which his actual behaviour is but a partial and perhaps even sorry approximation.

And beyond these things, which, though they are not observable, yet actually existed in history interior to the lives of those who made it up, what of the transcendent truth of this Buddhism which, the convinced Buddhist could aver, even the most saintly, brilliant exponent of the faith has here on this earth only partly grasped?

In the face of all this, what are we reasonably to mean when we say 'Buddhism'?

viii

Before turning to my own view that we should not say it but learn to say something else, we may consider critically five major types of answer that have been proffered to this sort of question.

One view, perhaps hardly worth serious consideration any more though popular at the turn of the century, is the 'nature and origin'[47] theory, according to which the earliest form of religion or of a particular religion is somehow the true form, with all subsequent development an aberration. Apart from various facts such as that it is and probably always will be impossible to know in any depth or subtlety the earliest, prehistoric forms of man's religious life, and almost impossible to know well the earliest form of several major traditions, such as the Buddhist or Zarathushtrian, there is the evident point that, 'true' or not, subsequent developments are certainly interesting. To equate Buddhism starkly with the Buddha's teachings or the first decades of the Sangha's life is to dismiss with scant justice the rich elaboration of the Mahayana tradition in China and Japan. This is virtually to posit something called a religion and then to assert that it has had no history; to leave unexplained and unnoticed almost the whole religious history of man.

Another device is to propose that we should consider as religion or any one religion what is common to all its instances. This is the traditional Aristotelian notion of the essence of many particulars that belong to a single species, but shorn of Aristotle's subtleties and qualifications[48]. It is rather surprising that this view should still find the support that it does[49], so little tenable does it appear under scrutiny. Indeed, in any realm at all involving historical development, this surely quite breaks down. In the first place, there is no *a priori* reason, and perhaps no historical evidence, for believing that all instances of 'Hinduism', for example, or 'Taoism' or 'Buddhism' must have something in common. It is both logically and historically possible that two quite different things can both be Hindu. Two very different things indeed, or a hundred different things, have all been Buddhist. Secondly, even if there were a least common denominator, it does violence to such religious faith as men have historically had to discount as unessential and irrelevant whatever is particular or special or unique in any case. Are we to regard as insignificant anything in the history of Chinese Buddhism that was not duplicated in Ceylon? Is a student to dismiss as no part of Christianity anything in the Puritan movement that Mexican villagers do not share?—or anything that Aquinas thought, with which the mystic Meister Eckhart and the evangelist Billy Sunday do not both agree? Do an Ash'ari and a Rumi cancel each other out, rather than enriching Islam by their divergent originalities? By this definition, the more elaborate and varied a tradition historically becomes, the thinner becomes the religion of which it is the embodiment. Sufficient external variety could reduce internal meaning to zero.

On a humbler plane, and yet conspicuously in the religious field, surely some people are more religious, are better Buddhists, are more illustratively Christian, than are others. If Buddhism is constituted only by what two Buddhists have in common, then the one who takes his faith more seriously is presumably wasting his time.

The common element theory has just not seriously faced the very problem with which, in a less informed day, it was put forth to deal: the inebriating variety of man's religious life not only in general but within each one of the great traditions.

There are serious difficulties, thirdly, in attempts to intellectualize the phenomena by postulating a transcendent ideal of which the historical actualities are a succession of mundane and therefore imperfect, compromised manifestations. At first blush, this might seem to work reasonably well for those traditions that start, as it were, with a bang, such as the Christian and the Islamic, in which the subsequent history may be interpreted as a series of echoes, more or less faint or distorted, of the great originating note. It is less serviceable, however, in instances where the tradition is rather of the type of a crescendo, such as the Jewish or the Hindu, where in the course of the development additions have been made and even acknowledged.

And in any case, this idealistic interpretation can at best serve only as self-interpretation. This is so for a number of reasons, of which a dominating one is that men cannot go about postulating transcendent realities as a convenience. A Muslim might believe that true Islam is an idea in the mind of God, with earthly Islam an historical series of shadowy reflections. An agnostic or a Jew or a Christian, however, cannot see it so. How are they to interpret the rich development of Islamic religious life? What is a Theravadin to make of Mahayana Buddhism? Or a Parsi of the history of Shinto? A Christian may thus understand his own tradition, but is precluded from understanding anyone else's (which, indeed, is what has too often happened).

This is quite apart from the point, which I have argued vigorously in another connection, that actually such Platonic ideals do not really serve the believer himself. For the perceptive Muslim, the idea in the mind of God is not some transcendent Islam whose unblemished nature becomes corrupted once men lay historical hands on it and bring it down to earth. On the contrary, for him that divine idea is precisely one by which man—the only man there is: actual, imperfect, conditioned, embroiled in the historical—is related within time to eternity. The relationship may be ideal, but one term in it is, even in theory, human. Similarly for the Christian: first, his ideal is not Christianity but Christ; and second, even that Christ is not a purely supernal, transcendent person but one whose nature it was to come into the turmoil of history in the most *engagé* and compromised of fashions, and whose significance now is his presence with the Christian not in heaven but on earth.

If religion or a religion is anything at all, it is not only in fact but in theory something in which actual living, historical persons are involved.

A modification of this idealistic essentialism is for the historian to define Islam as an ideal not in heaven but in the minds of Muslims. 'Islam', then, becomes what Muslims conceive it to be. More accurately, the historian posits an Islam that has been the ideal (the series of ideals) that Muslims have held of Islam. This is somewhat attractive. It is for working purposes a considerable improvement over less personalist essentialisms, chiefly because it induces a careful attention to what has been going on not only overtly but in the Muslims' head and heart. Yet again there are serious difficulties. It omits the imperfections that the believer does not choose to see. The Christian Church in history has often been worse than Christians have recognized; and while believers' ideals are important, and an observer disregards them at his peril and often all too readily, yet so are their failures and self-deceptions, for any adequate understanding of their religious life.

Further, the proposal will not serve the participant. An outsider defining the Muslims' 'religion' thus, though it be the most complimentary definition that an outsider can give, yet must accordingly recognize that he is using the term 'Islam' to refer to something other than what Muslims can understand by it. This is partly so in that for outsiders this 'Islam' is—inescapably—multiform, human, and unstable. Although an ideal, or rather an evolving series of ideals, it is not transcendent but a part of this mundane world. It is a victim of both the flux and the imperfection of history—as for an observer it must be, and as for a Muslim it must not.

Against this type of interpretation is the further fact that Muslims, as in our earlier chapter we discovered, have conceptualized

Islam as a religious system only in part, and on a large scale only in recent centuries and to some degree under the influence of Western thought. The idea largely breaks down, therefore, for the classical centuries of Islamic history. It breaks down for any religious tradition that is not, and for all religious traditions (even the Islamic or Christian) in so far as they are not, conceptualist or intellectualized. In so far as a tradition is other than doctrinal, for example that of the Trobriand Islanders, or that of the Taoists in China, its participants do not form an *idea* of it, and therefore if we are to form an idea of it we cannot rest dependent on their conceptualizations.

To revert to our Buddhist case: we cannot decide to call Buddhism whatever the Buddhists have called that for, as we have seen, they have been innocent of such a concept.

Finally we may mention the theory that would cut the Gordian knot, like the transcendentalists', but choosing the other part, by identifying a religion with its history. The thread running through all the diverse phenomena of any tradition, linking them together, would thus be simply that of continuity, some being related to others only in that they have grown out of them. This does justice to the richness and complexity of the traditions, ever growing, ever changing; to their humanity; and to their openness towards the future. Yet it cannot satisfy a believer; nor, indeed, a student sensitive to the believer's unfulfilled aspiration.

All the things that have happened to, and in, the community since Gautama launched it are relevant to the history of Buddhism; but it is precarious to argue that Buddhism is constituted of all of them without discrimination and without remainder. If some obscure Thai villager commits adultery with his neighbour's wife, that fact is hardly to be reckoned as part of Buddhism. Yet if some obscure Thai villager does *not* commit adultery with his neighbour's wife when tempted to do so, that fact perhaps somehow is. It, like the monument of Borobudur, is one expression of Buddhist faith.

The history of a religion is relevant to an understanding of that religion, surely; at least the scholar must insist upon this.

Buddhism, if one would use the term, is not to be equated with everything that has ever happened n the Buddhist world; yet neither is it to be known apart from what has happened there. Yet one has misunderstood a people if one does not sense that their faith is greater than its history, is above the sins and foibles and distractions of those who profess it. I once heard a Muslim say, 'Anyone who wants to understand Islam must put out of his mind the entire history of the Muslims'; and while one would not agree with him (the remark itself is part of the history of the Muslims), I nonetheless would argue strongly that to understand Muslims, and to understand their religious history, one must recognize what he meant and why. Serious Christians have similarly said, 'Christianity has never been tried'—a remark that I feel cannot stand up to serious analysis, but that nevertheless must be taken as illuminating of something that those Christians legitimately, if confusedly, feel.

What have been called man's religions, then, are as any historian can see involved in history; that is, in change, in imperfection, in the hurly-burly of the mundane. Yet also, as any participant can testify, they involve the transcendent—the abiding, the ideal. How is one to handle this dilemma intellectually?

The problem is the old one of the relation between the many and the one, between time and eternity, existence and essence, process and reality, historical change and abiding truth, the world and God.

Rather than awaiting an agreed answer on these issues, and rather than criticizing further[50] others' attempts to solve these problems, we turn finally to my suggestion that both the worshipper and the student of religious history can do better with an alternative analysis.

The concept of religion and the religions, we conclude, both in practice is being dropped in part and in principle ought to be dropped altogether. The cause of the first and the purpose of the second are a truer understanding of the actual life of men.

For fundamentally one has to do not with religions, but with religious persons.

CHAPTER SIX

The Cumulative
Tradition

THE MAN of religious faith lives in this world. He is subject to its pressures, limited within its imperfections, particularized within one or another of its always varying contexts of time and place, and he is observable. At the same time and because of his faith or through it, he is or claims to be in touch with another world transcending this. The duality of this position some would say is the greatness and some the very meaning of human life; the heart of its distinctive quality, its tragedy and its glory. Others would dismiss the claim as false, though not uninteresting. However that may be, the duality raises problems not only for the man of faith himself, for the formulator of faith whether theologian or artist, and for the philosopher. It raises problems also, we have seen, for the student of religious history. My suggestion is that these latter issues might be treated differently from what has been customary and more effectively, in such a way as to enable the more ultimate questions to be appreciated in truer perspective, and not prejudged.

We speak of the life of religious man seeming to be somehow in two worlds, the mundane realm of limiting and observable and changing actuality and a realm transcending this. What is the nature of that transcendent sphere, and what the nature of its relation to this mundane one, are questions on which, to put it mildly, there is no general agreement. Whether the transcendence is the human imagination at work or the fantasy of subconscious neuroses, or the meaningless patter of language gone awry, or the ideological superstructure of a particular economic situation; or whether it is a real world, or more real than this immediate one, or is this immediate one perceived more truly; and whether, if it is real, it is personal, Jesus-like, rational, formless, moral, punitive, unknowable—all these are questions on which intelligent men have taken varying stands. It would seem evident that if the study of man's religious history is to make progress at all as a cogent scholarly pursuit, it must do so without waiting for, or presupposing, agreement on these matters. In fact the divergence of answers is one part of the very matter that one is trying to understand. Room for this multiplicity must therefore be provided in the conceptual framework with which one approaches the task.

The nature of the mundane world, on the other hand, is becoming increasingly known, in a fashion that admits less and less of divergence. This is true also of the mundane aspect of man's own living. Men may differ as to the content of faith or as to its validity, but there is in principle little room for differing as to its overt manifestations across the centuries in their resplendent or grotesque variety. The unobservable part of man's history, especially his religious history, may and indeed must be acknowledged an open question so far as scholarship is concerned[1]. Meanwhile the observable part, including that of his religious history, is because of that very scholarship accessible to open scrutiny.

From this ambivalent quality of religious life, our difficulty ineluctably stems. What is needed, then, is a device to give the ambivalence full play. Such a device is in fact fairly readily to hand. It may seem disarmingly simple, and at first blush just a trifle evasive, although this in fact is part of its virtue. For as scholars we cannot but also as scholars we need not and must not begin by 'solving' the problem of the relation between transcendence and the world. It is both possible and rewarding to postpone it. Our academic and intellectual skills are not capable of letting us climb over a mountain whose summit is in the skies. While staying on the ground we may, if the road that I discern does not deceive me, quietly outflank it, and so get on with our task.

This is because, whatever the relation between our two realms may be metaphysically or theologically, so far as the historian is concerned the link is quite clear. It is man.

The history of what has been called religion in general and of each religion, is the history of man's participation in an evolving context of observable actualities, and in a something, not directly observable by historical scholarship.

Any historiography, we suggest, distorts what it is reporting if it omits either of these two aspects; and yet is doomed to flounder if it attempts to combine them. My suggestion is the basically rather simple one that we separate them in intellectual analysis, retaining both.

Phrased more historically: the study of man's religious life has in the past been inadequate in so far as its concept of religion has neglected either the mundane or the transcendent element in what it has studied, and has been confused in so far as its concept has attempted to embrace both. I ask whether these studies may not proceed more satisfactorily in future if, putting aside the concept 'religion' or 'the religions' to describe the two, we elect to work rather with two separate concepts.

I propose to call these 'cumulative tradition', on the one hand, and 'faith', on the other. The link between the two is the living person.

By 'faith' I mean personal faith. I shall endeavour to elucidate this in our next chapter. For the moment let it stand for an inner religious experience or involvement of a particular person; the impingement on him of the transcendent, putative or real. By 'cumulative tradition' I mean the entire mass of overt objective data that constitute the historical deposit, as it were, of the past religious life of the community in question: temples, scriptures, theological systems, dance patterns, legal and other social institutions, conventions, moral codes, myths, and so on; anything that can be and is transmitted from one person, one generation, to another, and that an historian can observe.

It is my suggestion that by the use of these two notions it is possible to conceptualize and to describe anything that has ever happened in the religious life of mankind, whether within one's own religious community (which is an important point) or in others' (which is also an important point). Also, so far as I can see, it is possible for these concepts to be used equally by sceptic or believer, by Muslim or Buddhist, Episcopalian or Quaker, Freudian or Marxist or Sufi.

These are rather sweeping claims. They would seem pretentious, did one not remember that I do not pretend to have solved vast problems that have outwitted better men; I am suggesting rather a method that will humbly yet deliberately allow man's long wrestling with those problems to be investigated without prior solution[2].

ii

To illustrate the thesis, let us look at what has been called Hinduism.

Among the Hindus, the cumulative tradition does not begin at any particular time or place. When we first become aware of it, it was already diverse. For illustrative purposes, let us arbitrarily begin by considering the person, whoever he was, who composed what is now the well-known Creation Hymn in Book X of the Ṛg Veda[3]. That one particular person composed it in its present form is not an assumption requisite to my argument: presumably some person did once compose a significant contribution to this poem.

Now that person, about whom we know almost nothing but can conjecture a little, was born into a specific historical context which included the cumulative Hindu religious tradition up to that point, or at least that branch of it that existed within the range of his awareness. The tradition was different for him from what it was further south, and was different also from what it later became. The basic point in this latter difference that I would here stress is that in particular it did not include in his day what it has included since, namely this particular poem. It did include, almost certainly, many of the other hymns now collected into the Ṛg Veda, and this is a fact obviously important for understanding the historico-religious event of his composing the new poem. It would be fascinating to know how much of the indigenous (pre-Aryan) cumulative tradition it included. Did he know any language other than Sanskrit, or ever talk with anyone who did?[4] —and so on; there are many questions.

These questions need not be answered, or answerable; all that I am concerned to show is that he received, external to himself, in the form of rites and practices, norms, ideas, group pressures, family influences, vocabulary, social institutions, and what not, a religious tradition; and that he changed that tradition by adding to it. He added to it something that emerged from the interaction within his personality between that external tradition and some personal quality of his own that we may cheerfully leave undetermined. Orthodox Hindus may believe that he 'heard'; Christians may believe that either the Logos or the devil was at work; literary critics may apply the same explanations that they use for poetic creation wherever they find it. However one may choose to interpret how it took place, the fact is, and on this surely all may agree, that inside that man's person something unobservable happened of which the outward consequence was a new hymn. And this product of his faith was thereupon added to the cumulative tradition, which has therefore never been quite the same since.

That man's faith could not have been what it was had it not been for the particular form of the cumulative tradition to that point. Yet it was not simply the product of that previous tradition; if this poet had perchance died of malaria as a child, probably few would wish to argue that that hymn in just that form would have got written anyway. Therefore the subsequent form of the Hindu cumulative tradition, including this hymn, is not simply the continuation or extrapolation of its earlier history, not including it. Rather, its later history is the prolongation and enrichment of its earlier existence *as modified by* the intervention of the faith and activity of this man.

Multiply this kind of incident a thousand million times, I suggest, and one has the development of the Hindu religious tradition. It is a part of this world; it is the product of human activity; it is diverse, it is fluid, it grows, it changes, it accumulates. It crystallizes in material form the faith of previous generations, and it sets the context for the faith of each new generation as these come along. But it neither includes nor fully determines that later faith. It conditions it, certainly. Yet each man's faith is his own, is partly free, and results from an interaction within the personality between that confronting tradition along with all other mundane circumstances, external and inner, and the transcendent. A man's faith is what his tradition means to him. Yet it is, further, what the universe means to him, in the light of that tradition.

By choosing the author of this hymn, one may perhaps feel that I have invidiously selected genius. Certainly some persons are more important for the cumulative tradition than are others; and it is almost excusable to oversimplify the immense array of Hindu religiousness by thinking of its history in terms simply of those persons and movements that have conspicuously modified and ramified and enriched (or debased?) it in its developing course. Almost, but not quite. The tradition was what it was until it was changed by the creative activity of those who wrote the Upanishads and the Bhagavad Gita, who built the temples and introduced the dances, who formulated the rules and elaborated the practices, who fought it out with the Buddhist sectarians and took up the challenge of Islam, who developed and spread the Bhakti movement, who innovated with the West and against it, who reformed and revitalized and rethought. Almost, but not quite. The great creative leaders have been great and have been creative, and have led. They have led the cumulative tradition to new accumulations; the enormously multi-faceted panorama of Hindu life would not be what it is today without them. Yet the obscure, the average, Hindu is not to be neglected in the story. In the total, his role has been no less crucial. And indeed, finally his role has been in principle no different.

A Sankara or a Ramanuja, on the one hand stimulated and conditioned by an inherited cumulative tradition, and on the other inspired by his own understanding of its meaning and his own vision of a transcendent truth, conceived something new and bequeathed to the subsequent ongoing tradition an objective, public formulation of that private vision. Yet in the same way, though of course on a drastically smaller scale, some remote village mother receives that little segment of the cumulative tradition that obtains just then in her small corner of India, interiorizes it to make what she can or will of its meaning, translating the outer forms into a personal faith, petty or profound; and then in turn she hands it on to her son, modified in an outward sense perhaps only minutely or negligibly, yet personalized. If it meant nothing to her inside, the historian may be sure that the next generation would handle even its externals differently. No less important, in the religious history of man, than the creative faith of innovating leaders is the preservative faith of receptive followers.

It is because the materials of a cumulative tradition serve each generation as the ground of a transcendent faith that they persist. The objective data of a tradition exist in this world and are observable by an historian; but they continue to exist and to be observable because for the men and women who use them they serve as windows through which they see a world beyond.

Anyone familiar with the piety of the common Hindu will appreciate the observation that whatever role exceptional persons may play in setting up particular matters in the tradition, once those matters are launched they are entrusted to the entire community, and their subsequent history is in the hands of the whole.

Furthermore, although changes that are creative advances are perhaps largely the result of the work of outstanding individuals (though even this is disputable[5]), there is another type of change, historically hardly less important, which perhaps more usually is brought about by the action of quite ordinary folk, often acting together in numbers. This is the change of neglect, decline, and retrogression. Elements in a cumulative tradition may be dropped as well as added; customs disappear, observances are not observed, temples fall into ruin. Lofty insights are degraded, warm spontaneities are gradually institutionalized, novelties become traditions. The community not only preserves the insights of its leaders, it can also misinterpret or lose them.

It should be clear that my analysis differs crucially from that of positivists or naturalists or any who would 'reduce' 'religion' to anything less than its devotees see. The cumulative tradition of which we are speaking lies wholly within this mundane world and is fully open to historical observation. Yet this is very different from saying that the whole history and nature of a religion lies within this sphere, so that a religion may be equated with its mundane observable career. From the position here proposed, one may insist that the mundane traditions persist only in so far as they are refreshed, each generation anew, by the faith of each of the participants; and that this faith, being personal, is not confined to what lies within history. The cumulative tradition is wholly historical; but history is not a closed system, since as agent within it stands man, his spirit in some degree open to the transcendent[6].

iii

The significance of all this becomes sharper if we look to the Islamic or the Christian traditions. This analysis may seem apt enough in the rather amorphous Hindu case, and therefore not very novel or revealing; it does not differ radically from the account that Hindus give of their own tradition. Hindus have not used a concept 'Hinduism', and on the whole they are quite happy to acknowledge that their tradition has changed and diversified, and that in form it is a human construct.

In the Islamic case the position is very much trickier. For here, as with Christians, an event in history is part of the content of faith. That is, a man's faith consists, according to his own loyal conviction, not only in an immediate relation with transcendence but also in a conceptualization of the mundane. A Hindu is enabled, he affirms, by the material of his religious heritage, to see beyond this phenomenal world to a unruffled truth beyond; whereas the truth that the Muslim is enabled to see includes something that historians can also see and study, since for him God has acted in history, that is in the realm of contingency and the particular. In the Muslim view, time and eternity come into contact or relation not only in the person of the believer (who is oriented to God in obedience and faith) but also in the pages of the Qur'an, a work that is available also to the outside historian, who has in fact studied it closely. The nonbeliever, indifferent to the Muslim's conviction that this scripture has its source in God, looks for its origin on earth and finds it there, in various strands of the historical background and in the psychology of Muhammad. Similarly the Christian not only knows a transcendent Christ in personal experience, but also sees the historical figure of Jesus on earth as divine, while the mundane historian also can see and study that earthly figure, without perceiving transcending connotations.

This kind of religious situation is indeed tricky. Yet it poses a problem primarily for the Muslim or Christian as believer, a problem of theological acuteness and even of much potential distress[7]. My present analysis in no sense creates the difficulty here. Rather, I would urge, it clarifies it, and perchance offers terms in which it can be more adequately handled, both by men of faith and by non-*engagés* observers; and certainly for a discussion between these. Believers with an historically oriented faith can no longer nowadays solve its inherent dilemma by underestimating the unmitigatedly historical character of its terrestrial aspect. My formulation may make conspicuous and conscious what is otherwise liable to being covert or confused, but it does no more than squarely face and honestly register the facts. It would fail if it did not help the believer to conceptualize that in which he is involved, as well as the observer that with which he is confronted.

The problem for both is real, and serious. For example, for many Muslim believers today, if they think of Islam as a religious system, that Islam is a transcendent truth, stable, free from vicissitudes and contingencies, and it includes a law *(shari'ah)*. Several are discussing whether or how this presumably immutable law is related to conspicuously changing circumstance. This problem is minor compared to the fact that on the basis of modern research historians can today point out a time when 'Islam' did not include this law. By this I mean that the Islamic cumulative tradition as an evolving historical phenomenon can be seen to have developed from a point where it was constituted by several phenomena of which the *shari'ah* as an elaborate legal system was not one, to a later point where that system had been (the historian must assert) constructed by persons whom he can name and whose work he can study. It is a failure of imagination on the part of the student, and a failure of either information or honesty on the part of a believer, not to recognize how different religiously was the situation in which the crucially important legal thinker al-Shafi'i grew up, from what has subsequently come to be known as Islamic. For everyone since that time who has used the term 'Islam' to refer to a religious system has by it inevitably meant an Islam into the stream of whose historical development al-Shafi'i injected the ideas that he crystallized, with the fruitful consequences and reactions and institutional elaborations that emerged, as a result not only of his activities but of those of his contemporaries and successors; and *that* Islam al-Shafi'i himself did not know.

If al-Shafi'i had not lived, or someone whose work would have been curiously like his (or if Ibn Sina's endeavour to construct an Islamic interpretation of life consonant with both the ideas and the principles of the Greek philosophic tradition had not been confuted by al-Ghazzali's brilliant exposition and interpretation of his own rather different faith—or shall we say, confuted by the general trend of events to which al-Ghazzali gave brilliant exposition; or if other things in Islamic history had not developed just as they actually did), then, an historian must assert, the Islamic complex that exists today would have been different from what it is. A Muslim may be quick to retort, out of his faith, that God would not have allowed an al-Shafiⁱ or an al-Ghazzali and all the other establishers of what has come to be the established and recognized form of Islam not to exist; that God has been concerned to see to it that this community's religious interpretations developed correctly[8]. Such a conviction cannot be gainsaid, but it is irrelevant to the argument for the moment (it is a part of men's faith, and therefore comes under our second heading). For whatever reason, it is a fact irrefutable and profoundly significant that the Islamic tradition has *become* (and one can hardly emphasize that word too strongly) what it has observably become; that it has become so by gradual and complex historical processes that can be studied, and through the activity of human beings whose particular and human role in the cumulative process of that becoming can be examined.

The Islamic tradition that modern Muslims inherit, and that observers see, has been the handiwork of Muslims. The process of their constructing it has been mundane. Any divine pattern in it that Muslim faith may discern, God has put in it by working through the intermediacy of persons[9].

iv

The development of a religious tradition, then, is not only within the realm of the contingent. It is also within the realm of change that not merely is possible but is inherent and inevitable. Even after the Islamic legal schools, for instance, came into existence (and one may stress the word 'existence'), there is substantial difference even *religiously* between a law that is known in the fresh and vivid version of its early and fairly simple formulation, and one that sheerly by being used has become over the centuries encrusted with meticulous elaborations and embedded in increasingly nice refinements of supercommentaries. This fact is not evaded by imaging that the later constructs were somehow there all along, just waiting to be worked out. Some choice few of them may have been there metaphysically, though only a Muslim of a certain school can assert this; but they were *not* there historically, and it is the task of the historian to make this graphic.

Accordingly, it is not only the quality of historical existence that is significant, even religiously; but the sheer fact of it. To have existed for a long while is in itself different from not having existed for a long while; also for an institution. To be a member of a new community is seriously different from being a member of one that has fourteen centuries (or twenty centuries) of history behind it. In so far as 'to be a Muslim' means to participate in the mundane existence of the Muslim community and to have available the institutions, the literature and ideas, the interpretations and traditions that that community has produced—and this is certainly part of the meaning of being a Muslim—to that extent 'to be a Muslim' today in the fourteenth Islamic century means something different from being a Muslim in the first or the sixth—quite apart from the differences in the centuries themselves. A corresponding truth applies to the very meaning of 'being a Christian'. Even if life did not change, this would be so[10]. The fact is obvious enough in practice, but room must be made for it also in theory.

Our suggested theory is that al-Shafiꞌi, like the founder of every other major or minor innovation[11] in Islamic history, was a person of a particular time and place, of a particular temperament and personality, who found himself in a milieu including a particular part of the always changing Islamic cumulative tradition; and that the interaction within his spirit of that environment with the transcendent to which that tradition introduced him, enabled him to produce the innovation by which the tradition was thereby modified.

A religious tradition, then, is the historical construct, in continuous and continuing construction, of those who participate in it. These are in interaction, also, and this can be highly significant, with those who do not participate. They are in interaction also, and this too can prove highly relevant, with a total environment that may include earthquakes or modern medicines, moonlit lakes or tyrannous governments.

v

That all this is so is conspicuously true for the outsider looking in. Every informed observer, I believe, will see that some such analysis applies to the development of the Buddhist tradition and the Hindu, the Islamic and the Jewish, the Shinto and the Babylonian; and though we have less information in the case of non-literate ('primitive') communities, presumably something of the sort is true for their history also.

It is equally true, even if somewhat less conspicuous, for the participant. Those of us who are Christians, especially those who have been brought up to think of something that is to be called 'Christianity', are unaccustomed perhaps to thinking of Christian history in these terms, but can hardly gainsay the validity of the observation if pressed, and presumably do not wish to do so, if honest. We are participants in an overt tradition that has become rich and varied, because men at successive stages in its accumulating development have contributed each his share to making it so. Later memory hardly goes back to those times in the community's history before a New Testament had yet been added to the Old to make a Christian Bible, or before the theological debates had hammered out creeds. The mediaeval Church with its structured order, its far-flung network of power and responsibility, its comprehensive vision of an integrated social life, its art and its music, its prestige and majesty, was not the same religious situation for a Christian child to be born into and to grow up within, as had been the precarious Church that gathered an harassed plebeian minority in a corner of some great Roman city centuries before.

Theologically, ecclesiastically, emotionally, morally, the Reformers manifestly modified profoundly the historical complex available as a religious tradition to those generations that came after them; as did also, though on a smaller scale, the Council of

Trent for those who, though they remained within the Roman fold, yet now were members of a sundered Church. The religious ideas and practices, the hymns and the church buildings, the Christian pressures and incitements, surrounding a sophisticated urban Christian in Western Europe at the beginning of the twentieth century after the recent liberals had championed their new cause, were different from those that constituted the religious context of the Russian peasant even in the same decade. It is a failure of imagination not to recognize what profound divergencies differentiate the Christian environment of a Charlemagne from that of a Kagawa, or of the young man named Eutychus who fell asleep under St. Paul's preaching from that of Pascal. To be in the mediaeval times a prelate of the first generation to worship at the new cathedral of Chartres, is not the same thing as to brought up as David Livingstone was, a Puritan among the cotton mills near Glasgow.

Does all this matter? Perhaps the answer is 'yes and no'. Whether it matters cosmically we leave for the moment untackled. That it matters historically is obvious. One cannot understand the religious life of men unless one sees them as men, vividly; living, actual men in real—and differing—situations, participant each one in a religious tradition that in its concrete actuality is particular for him. The Christian Church, whatever it may be ideally, has an earthly history, which we must intellectualize in such a way as to do justice to the diversity of the phenomena and at the same time not to do violence to a conviction of those involved that through it all there is a common element of transcendence. Once one postulates or allows transcendence in each case, as I claim one must, then the outsider need not be concerned with whether it be common or diverse, genuine or fictitious. For him the data are bound together by the genetic bond of continuity, and by the sociological one of cohesion, such as it be (its varying strength can be observed). He can therefore see those data as historically related without necessarily being uniform; for the existential association, no essential identity is required (or denied). The historical reality can thus be seized.

vi

The cumulative tradition, then, of what has been called religion and each particular religion is dynamic, diverse, and observable. It is, I suggest, historically intelligible. It is even objective, in one of the modern senses of that term, in that Marxists, Muslims, and Mennonites should in principle have no difficulty in agreeing on what in fact the Christian cumulative tradition has so far been.

It is not a unit. By the very words 'cumulative' and 'tradition' I have meant to stress that the concept refers in a synthetic shorthand to a growing congeries of items each of which is real in itself but all of which taken together are unified in the conceptualizing mind, by process of intellectual abstraction. Like the total religious tradition of mankind, so each particular tradition has, is composed of, parts, and for many intellectual purposes it is convenient or necessary, and certainly legitimate, to abstract and synthesize at a lower level of generality: the Mahayana Buddhist tradition, the Zen tradition, the Zen tradition in the seventeenth century in a particular island or village; the Presbyterian branch of the Christian tradition in the particular congregation in Toronto in which I grew up; contrariwise, the religious tradition of the globe from the fiftieth to the twentieth millennium B.C. Ultimately again one comes back to literally individual persons. The units of which man's religious history is composed are on the one hand persons, and on the other those segments of the total cumulative tradition available to each of those particular persons. Out of the whole mass of data that we may legitimately call the Buddhist tradition, just that much is relevant to Buddhist X as exists at his time within the range of his conscious or unconscious awareness—a range that depends in part on his own initiative (I can by the expenditure of vigour increase greatly the fraction of the total Christian tradition accessible to me), though it depends chiefly on other, historical factors.

'The cumulative tradition' as a concept, therefore, is not inflexible or final, either in content or in form. It is not given by the world, but is a human construct offered to order what is given. It is a device by which the human mind may rewardingly and without distortion introduce intelligibility into the vast flux of human history or any given part of it. It refers, I contend, to something intelligible, and empirically knowable, though not to an independent entity, intrinsically coherent or self-subsisting. The concept abstracts from out a total dynamic historical complex a part to which there is legitimacy and value in giving intellectual attention[12].

So far as I can see, no one can deny that that to which it refers, both in general and in each particular case, does in fact exist and is important. From the earliest ascertainable times, a cumulative tradition has been an influential factor in the life of every religious man.

What then of faith, the other element in our analysis, and always a further factor in the life of every religious man? In one sense, one might contend that what it is the historian does not need to know. To make sense of human history he needs to know that it has been there. Yet he might not characterize it beyond noting that the term refers to something within the personal lives of men and women, and be content to leave it there. What he can know, and as historian cannot help knowing, are the expressions of faith. These are many, and together constitute the accumulating and varied traditions of which we have been speaking.

Yet not merely can one not adequately understand mankind's active and continuing participation in the various traditions apart from it. More crucially: apart from men's faith, those traditions themselves would not be there.

Besides, some of us are not only historians and observers but participants; and some, would-be participants. Every man is at least potentially himself religious. There is, therefore, not only the delicate and complex question of other men's faith, but also the possible and searching question of one's own.

Let us turn, then, to considering these next.

CHAPTER SEVEN

 Faith

ON THE ONE HAND, great religious minds have regularly affirmed that faith cannot be precisely delineated or verbalized; that
it is something too profound, too personal, and too divine for public exposition. And I myself have been at pains to stress throughout this study that men's faith lies beyond that sector of their
religious life that can be imparted to an outsider for his inspection.

On the other hand, different men, at differing times and places,
adherents of differing traditions, have differed conspicuously in
whatever they have had to say on the subject. Again, our own
study has not failed to emphasize the arresting diversity of mankind's faith.

Is it not then presumptuous, or vain, and perhaps both, for me
to hope to establish anything significant on this matter where
better men have been reticent, or at odds among themselves? I
recognize that it would be neither seemly nor persuasive, and for
our purposes not even helpful, to pronounce on the quality or
the content of the personal faith of many myriads of men. My
concern is rather to devise an analysis explicitly to do justice to
the unfathomability of that personal faith. As with the cumulative traditions, so here our aspiration must be to contrive a method
that will not have prejudged, by the very shape of its concept, the

aspect of man's life that it is proffered to handle. My interpretation will have failed if any man is precluded in its representation from seeing whatever vision it may be to which in fact he may have risen or have fallen. Yet it will also fail if it does not help us to recognize that he has seen it.

A first step, accordingly, may be a flanking one, that of endeavouring to understand not the nature of personal faith, but the role that it has played in the religious history of mankind. In our previous chapter we noted that the observer, and indeed a man's own fellows, do not see a person's faith, but see the expressions of it. These are many; and, as they accumulate in history, they constitute what we have called the various religious traditions. One fact, then, is already clear: that men's faith finds expressions in many forms.

Faith can be expressed—more historically: faith has been expressed, observably—in words, both prose and poetry; in patterns of deeds, both ritual and morality; in art, in institutions, in law, in community, in character; and in still many other ways. Let us look at some of these.

A preliminary insistence must be that when any of these things is an expression of religious faith, then it cannot be fully understood except as an expression of religious faith. This point has been made already in our historical considerations: the traditions cannot be interpreted in human history if the fact of the transcendent element in men's participation in them is denied or neglected. We shall return to the point later also, since it is crucial for any just apprehension of human life. For the moment, my point is that the particular expressions, and types of expression, of which we speak illustrate the elemental verity that men's involvement with them is an involvement through them with something greater than they. Without yet knowing what it is, we may nonetheless affirm with confidence that there is some personal and inner quality in the life of some men, and to it we give the name faith, in relation to which overt observables are for those men religiously significant.

This is not the place to enter on a systematic study of faith's expressions. That would be a captivating task, but large. It would be distracting from our main purpose if we did more than consider a few instances from among the many, as illustrative of some of the general principles involved. The field is so rich, one is embarrassed to know where to start. Instructive, perhaps, will be not to begin with what to many in Western Europe has come to seem the prime area of such expression; namely, ideas—the expression of faith in the form of belief. We shall consider this rather special case later on. It is complicated by the further point that ideas and beliefs are not as such observable (though they are important). They may for convenience be treated under the form through which we chiefly come to know them, their formulation in 'statements of faith'; that is, under the rubric of verbal expressions in prose. I trust, however, that this arrangement will not be taken as corroborating the prevalent, but perhaps misleading, notion that there is a final difference between theology and poetry.

ii

Perhaps the gentlest introduction to our subject may be gained by considering first men's expression of their faith in art. This can be readily illuminating, because on the whole it has been less customary here than in other areas to treat such expressions as something else. In the case of works of religious art, it is relatively clear that they give overt expression to the religious faith of the person who made them, and continue to give expression to that of the persons who continue reverently to cherish them. It is relatively clear also that for the observer who wishes to infer that faith, which he can never see, here is a clue that will serve him if he can bring to it the appropriate qualities of human sensitivity and disciplined imaginative insight and appreciation—along with, of course, all pertinent historical scholarship.

The work of art itself is prey to all the specifications of the ma-

terial out of which it is constructed, is subject to the limitations
of the human agent who conceived it and, once launched, it becomes an item in the play of historical forces. It is always imperfect, and it is always totally mundane. Yet its significance lies in
the fact that it points beyond itself, to the spirit of the man who
framed it and beyond him to the transcendent vision that he saw.
If it is in stone, it is subject to the mundane qualities of that particular stone, including perhaps perishability; if it is a poem, it
is subject to the grammar of the language in which it is composed; if it is music, it is framed within the particular tradition,
with the particular instruments and structural patterns of the
time and place out of which it comes. Yet it is not art if these
concrete particularities do not serve to express something to which
man has access while these particularities in themselves do not.

How important an expression of the faith of Buddhists are the
*mudra*s in statuary; of the faith of Sufis, the poetry of Jalal al-Din
Rumi; of the faith of certain Hindus, the temple architecture of
Ellora or a carving of the dancing Nataranjan; of many Christians, the B Minor Mass.

On a wall of Aya Sofia in Istanbul there stands, recently uncovered, an ancient mosaic depicting the first confrontation of
the courtesan Mary Magdalene and Christ. To portray Christ's
face, the unnamed artist has put together a few bits of coloured
stone in such a fashion as to portray, in a way that was to me more
forceful and more effectively unified than I have met in any theological statement, what in prose I call simultaneous judgment and
forgiveness, the integration of rebuke and love. I recognize that
others may not see it so, and this is an important theoretical point.
It is germane to our whole presentation to note that I brought to
the mosaic my faith previously fed from other sources, and this is
not irrelevant to the fact that this work of art could thereupon
become for me a new expression of that faith. Yet, I having seen
it so, no one can now persuade me that the artist did not see it
so also; this manipulation of pebbles was an expression of his
faith. Had he not been a consummate artist, he could not have

done this; but neither could he have done it, had he not been personally Christian.

The stones themselves do not synthesize condemnation and mercy. This is done in the heart of the artist, as it can be done again in the heart of the observer.

Similar considerations apply, of course, to, for instance, those superb statues of the Buddha that, again to belittle them by prose, present a figure where a total joy and peace have been attained, not by abstracting oneself from this world but by living through it in compassion and righteousness until, as it were, one has come out on the other side in the most utter serenity. The hint of a smile almost playing on the lips of the Buddha and the eyes that almost seem closed in not a faraway look but a look that sees far through the world of tumult to quiet (in what seems at first a startling contrast to a Christian crucifix, where the ultimate truth of the universe is imaged as in agony within the tumult) —this tranquil truth, this incarnate TRUTH, this ultimate serene: this is the work of a man of a faith powerful and personal.

The statue is of stone, and cannot see. But its contriver saw something, very clearly; something beyond this world. And we, in looking at it, are surely obtuse if we see nothing more than the statue.

• • •
iii

Secondly, let us look for a moment at faith's expression in community.

We have throughout stressed, and will yet reiterate, that religious faith is personal. In this we run the risk perhaps of seeming to make out that it is individualist, which is certainly not the same thing. One knows God in so far as one loves one's neighbour, sees the Christian; and the tribalist may derive what personal ecstasy he knows from his participation in a group dance. Even so primarily religious a community as the Jewish has, no doubt, certain economic and other sociological and mundane aspects; yet these are not sufficient to sustain it. The historian recognizes that this community would have ceased long ago had its existence not expressed and embodied the personal religious faith of Jews.

The Christian Church, the Muslim *ummah*, the Hindu caste, the Buddhist Sangha and much more are in primary part the expression of the personal faith of the men and women who constitute and have constituted these groupings. Once in existence such communities develop, no doubt, a certain social momentum of a mundane sort; particularly so highly organized a structure as the Christian Church in some of its parts, or so highly functional a one as a Hindu caste. This momentum can be massive, and would be presumably adequate to keep each community in being for a certain time on its own in only gradually disintegrating force even if its members' attitude to it as a necessary and basic expression of their personal faith should lapse. Nonetheless one may be sure, as with the Jews, that this would be but temporary. Neither the original existence nor the continued history of religious communities can be understood apart from the personal faith of their members. In highly articulate and intellectualist instances this corporate quality is theoretically formulated, into, for instance, a doctrine of the Church; in the case of a Polynesian or African tribe this may be virtually absent, while the social cohesion and felt loyalty are certainly no less.

The matter is in some ways clearer, and in some more complicated, where the religious community has developed divergently from other social groupings, as with the Christian Church penetrating the Roman Empire, the Islamic *ummah* invading India, the Buddhist community expanding into Southeast Asia, the Jewish community existing within Western society. Yet it is relevant also to simpler societies where religious loyalties and other social loyalties and contacts are coterminous; where the religious grouping is the only grouping there is or, put another way, where the only social grouping that men know they know religiously, and constitute religiously. Here it is their faith that constitutes their society as a community[1].

We need not labour the point; so basic is the tie between personal faith and community, that some moderns would follow Durkheim[2] in identifying the two, or in deriving 'religion' from society. This is suggestive, but not adequate. When I asserted earlier that fundamentally in humanity's religious history one has to do not with religions but with religious persons[3], some would incline rather to say 'but with religious communities'. Religious communities are extremely important, as every man of faith knows and as every historian knows. It is almost impossible to exaggerate their significance—almost, but not quite. For it is an exaggeration to see them as ultimate or elemental. If one takes the community as a prime concept in one's attempt to understand man's story, one cannot reckon with a social rebel in the name of the Lord like Amos, or with a hermit or forest dweller, or with an innovator like Jesus or Muhammad from whom communities arise. Nor, for that matter, can one reckon with the modern man who feels his way towards a faith but adheres to no community, or who belongs to one community but finds his faith not confined within it: the Presbyterian who reads Methodist books, the Methodist who reads Buber or the Bhagavad Gita, the Muslim who is a sincere Indian nationalist, and, indeed, any religious man who sees the value of human brotherhood. Further, one cannot understand the situation in China, where, as we have seen, the compartmentalization of men into boundaried religious communities each around one religious tradition, on the Western pattern, hardly obtains.

Moreover, historically we have seen a situation in the eastern Mediterranean world and western Asia, something less than two thousand years ago, when religious communities, as with a Kartir or the later Mandaeans, were gradually coalescing into organized actuality, or with the evolution of a Church were superseding previous socializations, or with a Mani or Muhammad were being deliberately launched. What has become for many—though not for all—the standard pattern of religious community has *become* so, gradually, through an historical process that can be observed and has to be understood.

Such situations as the Chinese are relevant, as are these theoretical considerations, to the contemporary scene. For as suggested in our opening chapter, one of our modern problems is to construct a world-wide community even though it be composed of a diversity of religious traditions. For some of us insist that our faith impels us towards a fellowship larger than that of the denominated group of which we are members. The community expression of the faith of a Chinese has not on the whole been of that kind that Europe has manifested in the Thirty Years' War, and Christendom in anti-Semitism and *Apartheid,* and India in Hindu-Muslim riots. And it is only as persons that we human beings can learn what most of us have to learn, how to keep our faith but extend our loyalty, how to express our faith in a community that is not closed.

Religious communities have been extremely important; but they are not final, either historically or conceptually[4]. To be religious is an ultimately personal act. It is, to an important degree, an act that one makes in community; but is not one that any community can make for one.

Faith finds expression not only in community as such, but in a number of social institutions, from monogamous marriage to temple prostitution, from Sunday schools to the Caliphate. Such matters have come into historical existence and have remained there modified or developed, for a number of historical reasons, of which a quite fundamental one is that the particular religious faith of particular persons has found expression in them. These like other religious actualities have unquestionably existed not only in this world but of this world, within its imperfections and corruptions and ambiguities and drift. This fact is not precluded by, nor does it preclude, the other fact that they have expressed a partly unworldly faith within men's hearts.

iv

Of expressions of faith, one of the most immediate but exacting, one of the most obvious but rarest, is in what we may perhaps imprecisely call 'character'.

From time to time one meets a person the winning quality of whose living is an immediate embodiment of his faith in so spontaneous yet compelling a way that one at once recognizes the incomparability and finality of human character. When we do meet such a person, we realize how secondary, if not actually irrelevant, are other religious expressions. It matters little if that person's faith may be related perhaps to a systematic verbal statement that to us is curious or alien, to a form of worship that to us is remote, and so on. Or within one's own tradition one may know two persons who express faith identically in formal statements of belief, in formal patterns of ritual, in formal community membership and what not, yet in the case of one of them that faith finds embodiment in his character, while hardly in the other. One then understands how it is that some have been prompted to hold that nothing ultimately matters to God or to man but character.

Certainly to assess a religious tradition by the kind of character that its faith produces would seem more legitimate than to do so on grounds of reason, or revelation, or any impersonal standard, were it not that none of us is in a position to judge.

v

Turning to expressions of faith in less personal, more abstractly considered modes of behaviour, particularly as patterns to which behaviour ought to conform, we may note these, as already suggested, as falling under two chief headings, ritual and morality. In some instances these may overlap, especially when ethical imperatives are systematically arranged into a formal pattern, as in the Jewish *Torah* and the Islamic *shariʿah,* where morality is ritualized. In other cases, such as the Puritan or Roman Catholic or Confucian or Theravadin, rites and precepts tend to be more discriminated, at times rather sharply so. In any case, much religious faith has sought and found for itself an expression in ritual practice, and much in a moral code or in moral striving. So much is this so, that some students would assert that one or both of ritual and morality is a universal or generic characteristic (a point on which we need not have an opinion[5]) ; and some theologians, that 'faith without works is dead'[6].

Christians have not been behind others in holding that religious faith must eventuate in faith-inspired practice. They have, however, often failed to recognize the more immediate modes in which other traditions have formulated the relationship. Since the Christian tradition historically arose with an explicit repudiation of law-centeredness in the Jewish one, and since its interpretation of ethics has almost always formulated it as at least logically subordinate to something else, Christians have seldom appreciated the significance of a tradition such as the Jewish or Islamic where law has been faith's primary and controlling expression, both for the person and for society—where the Christian's 'orthodox' and 'heterodox' have as counterpart 'orthopraxy' and deviation, where the mediator between man and God is righteousness, and where the final requirement of man is a recognition of God and of the rightness of right actions[7].

Despite the disparity here between Christian and Judaeo-Islamic understanding, all three of these traditions have seen right action as the will of a personal God, and all have found great difficulty in appreciating the still more immediate formulation of, for instance, the Theravadin Buddhist tradition, where ultimate reality as *dharma* is itself a transcendent pattern of right conduct, so that even the intellectual expression of faith, let alone the practical, is in ethical terms. This has at times left the Westerner uncertain as to how a faith of which this is the expression is to be classed as a religious faith at all. In our analysis the question of religious faith is a question concerning a living quality of the particular persons who may hold it, rather than of any traditional form of its expression; and that this should be primarily moralistic is not in itself an argument against it.

vi

We will leave aside consideration of many other ways in which faith has been, or in which men have thought that it ought to be, set forth; and turn our attention finally, in necessarily a brief conspectus, to the elaborate and thorny question of faith's expression in ideas and words. As previously indicated, we may for convenience restrict ourselves to prose, poetic expression being adequately treated as art, already touched on.

There are at least two complications to our dealing with faith as intellectually formulated, two reasons why the issue must be exceedingly delicate. One is the evident point that this book is in itself something being written in prose. Nor is this an accident: my own approach is incorrigibly that of the intellectual, both in outward expression—the book form—and in motivating spirit. And this approach the reader has at least for the moment made himself willing to share.

Secondly, in the Christian tradition, radically more so than is true of most others, there has been a sustained and central emphasis on formulating the faith in prose, from the Apostles' Creed to the most recent volume of Tillich's systematic theology[8]. Much more attention in the Western world has been paid to the evolving content of this particular form of expression, than to the fact of it, which has tended to be taken rather uncritically and unselfconsciously for granted. The peculiarity of the place given to belief in Christian history is a monumental matter, whose importance and whose relative uniqueness must be appreciated. So characteristic has it been that unsuspecting Westerners have, as we have seen, been liable to ask about a religious group other than their own as well, 'What do they believe?' as though this were the primary question, and certainly were a legitimate one.

One factor contributing to this peculiarity, there would seem no question, has been the circumstance of Greek thought as a massive influence in Christian history. Greek thought is intellectualist *par excellence*. The tradition that over the centuries has stemmed from Greek philosophy has nourished and has been sustained by a faith in reason among those persons by whom it has been carried[9]. The value of this in the stream of Western life in general has been incalculable; but so also has been the degree to which it has coloured other elements in Western society.

It is not the intention here to consider the role of reason in human life generally, even though this problem is recognizably in some ways involved in our concern, and even though there is an historical as well as theoretical plane on which that problem can profitably be viewed[10]. Rather we confine ourselves to the separate or sectional issue of the intellect's giving formulated expression to religious faith, in creeds and doctrine.

Western man has viewed his own quite special situation here usually without the help of seeing it in the wider context of men's experience in other civilizations as well. He has hence tended to absolutize certain problems that are more manageably solved when seen in perspective.

Another factor in the later Western situation, or symptom of it, has been the fact that neither Latin nor modern Western languages have a verb to go along with the technical term 'faith' (*fides, foi*, etc.), and have made do with words for 'believe' (*credo, croire*, etc.)[11]. Recently strenuous efforts have been made to discriminate between 'believing in' and 'believing that'. And in other ways Christians endeavour to take note of, or to make allowance for, a divergence between that about which religious people are talking and the ways in which, following tradition, they talk about it. Nevertheless monstrous confusion, I would suggest, has arisen from this ambiguity, and its implication that belief is identical with faith, rather than an expression of it. In modern times in its traditional forms it has become, even, a perhaps increasingly inadequate expression.

In calmer days, when Europe's faith in reason was less troubled and its knowledge less wide, and less scientifically and securely based, the concentration on this one particular expression of religious faith and even the confounding of faith with belief worked perhaps tolerably well, or anyway wrought less mischief. Today, however, it has run its course.

For intellectuals, if not for all men, a conceptual explication of faith is no doubt requisite and certainly salutary. Yet it can be serviceable only if it is utterly honest, and it must be recognized for what it is, both in one's own case and in that of others. In fact a certain school of modern philosophers have come from their studious examination of language to deny that prose is inherently a possible instrument for reporting transcendence. Since they have mostly failed themselves to see that the transcendence is nonetheless there, perhaps their opinion is none too weighty. Yet their analysis has shown up a perhaps significant difficulty.

Yet they have erred, we feel, in working on a foundation principle that words and sentences mean something. In fact, it is only persons who mean something; language is their instrument. Though convenient enough for certain everyday purposes, it is ultimately wrong to suppose that a statement can in itself be true or false. It is what the statement means that is true or false. This apparently innocent point becomes enormously important when the same statement means different things to different persons. Linguistic philosophic schools have arisen at a time when the world of natural science has in fact to a large extent arrived at a use of language that is impersonal. It is the ideal of a natural scientist to construct statements whose meaning and whose truth will both be independent of the person who makes them. This is admirable in discourse about what is impersonal; but one commits a massive blunder, radically failing to recognize what it is with which one is confronted, if one would apply so inappropriate an ideal to the realm of human affairs.

It is a misguided enthusiast who, bedazzled by the success of the natural scientist in dealing with his material, hastily would imitate his formalities, rather than emulating the spirit of the scientist's humility before that which he studies, and the scientist's constant readiness to modify his assumptions and his method in the light of the material and the problem to hand. One betrays the spirit of science and succumbs to an authoritarian secondhand scholasticism, if one undertakes the study of human life and human history with dogmatic presuppositions (such as that human beings behave essentially like molecules or guinea pigs) rather than being ready to adapt such hypotheses and interpretations as the evidence induces.

My particular hypothesis here is that religious statements express the faith of persons, who as persons are involved in transcendence. Certainly it can be shown historically that such statements have meant different things to different men. This is appropriate if they express the personal encounter of each—in his finitude and particularity—with infinity, or at least with what is greater than the objectively mundane. (In this at least there is a resemblance between creed and poetry.) The proper way to understand a religious statement is to endeavour not to see what its words and clauses mean (which may too easily become, what they mean to me), but to see what they meant to the man who first uttered them, and what they have meant to those since for whom they have served as expressions of their faith.

As with all other elements of a religious tradition, theological propositions are to be understood in relation to the personal life, a life of personal faith, of the men and women who use them. As we have seen also with all those other elements, these expressions have a form that is mundane, and that is historically related to the particularities of the time and place where they are fashioned —as it is the business of the observing historian to descry—and once launched they develop a certain momentum and independence of their own, and play their role in the historical vicissitudes of specific situations. Yet religiously they, like the others, I would contend, can be understood only as they serve each generation anew, and concretely in each town, each hamlet, ultimately in each human heart, as an expression of a faith by which those particular persons are oriented, within their mundane situations, to transcendence.

I submit also that there is no final difference in principle between the doctrinal and the artistic, moral, communal, and other sorts of expression. By this I certainly do not mean that all religious doctrines are equally true, just as one would hardly hold that all works of art are equally beautiful or all ethical systems equally good. The purpose of constructing the proffered analysis for these expressions, however, was not yet to assess their validity nor that of the faith that they expressed, but rather to enable us to conceptualize without undue distortion and without prior assessment what it is with which one has here to do. Until this is done, questions of truth and goodness are not even adequately posed. (To such questions we shall return.)

The suggestion that intellectual formulations in the religious realm refer not directly to a transcendent reality but only indirectly, through the inner life of persons, is not so radical as may at first blush appear. Particularly since the Enlightenment with its highly rationalistic views, many in Europe have tended to treat intellectual statements of religious faith, whether other people's or their own, as though they were straightforward, immediate, and independent descriptions of a metaphysical realm. Not only in other parts of the world, however, but also in other major strands of the Christian tradition itself, a less intellectualist interpretation has obtained of the transcendence in which the man of faith is involved. Several theologians have been at pains to emphasize that the Christian revelation is not a revelation of propositional truths[12].

Indeed among all traditions the Christian has had perhaps more reason than most to insist that the ultimate reality with which man is concerned is personal. Christians have certainly claimed that they (as persons) are (through faith) in touch with Truth, absolute and final. Yet this truth for them is not a theological system, but is itself a Person. Many Christians have traditionally been unwilling, perhaps, to go as far as I am ready to do in seeing the implications of the fact that their doctrinal systems and creeds, then, are both in practice and in principle derived; that is, are historical human constructs. Yet it hardly does violence to the spirit of the tradition to say, in the words of a respected and in some senses orthodox contemporary theologian, 'The function of systematic theology is to make clear the meaning and significance of Christian faith' . . . 'Theology . . . does not determine faith, but analyses Christian faith as it actually exists'[13].

In my submission it liberates and deepens rather than undermines one's own faith to see past intellectual statements of one's tradition in this light. There can be little question but that it illuminates to see those of other traditions so. Doctrinal formulations, theological systems, creeds, and the like, in their historical profusion, variety, consequence, and seriousness, can be understood, and I would feel can be understood only, as statements by and for persons—and also, in a primary and immediate sense, about persons. Ultimately and indirectly they are statements about transcendence. Primarily and immediately they are about persons, whose faith means that they are involved in such a transcendence. The transcendence, and even the involvement, are something to which their statements may be an attempt to give intellectual expression, but which those statements cannot capture but can only indicate.

Theology is part of the traditions, is part of this world. Faith lies beyond theology, in the hearts of men[14]. Truth lies beyond faith, in the heart of God.

vii

Faith, then, is a personal quality of which we see many sorts of expression. It will be perhaps not distracting to draw an admittedly inadequate analogy between faith and another human involvement—one that, though of a different sort, yet also receives many expressions; namely, love. By love one means not merely an emotion, which by itself is a sentimental substitute; though true love—the adjective is revealing—has deep emotional implications. It too can be expressed in words—'I love you'[15]—though the potential ambiguity of that expression is evident[16]. It can be expressed also in a wide range of behaviour, from holding hands to composing a symphony; certainly in moral obligation, that may exact one's life. Yet love itself, behind its expressions, is closer to the involvement itself, of person with person; and its full meaning is not less than a life lived out in terms of that relationship, personal and total. The analogy with faith is inadequate but not absurd, not even remote.

I have spoken of expressions of faith, in order to elucidate the interpretation, but one final and quite basic point needs yet to be made in order that the analysis may be proffered as an integrated hypothesis. The point was illustrated in our initial observation of the accumulating Hindu tradition. It is this: that if all the matters that we have suggested, theologies, rites, music, dances, congregations, moralities, and much more, the materials of religious history, are in significant part the expression of the faith of the persons who have produced or maintained them, so also are they, do they become, the ground of the faith for those persons who come after. Handel was able to write "The Messiah" in part because he had the faith that he had. I have the faith that I have, in part because Handel wrote "The Messiah". Aquinas's personal faith is to be understood in part because the Christian cumulative tradition had been what in fact it was up to that point; his theology was the expression of his personal faith, and it has become the 'impression', as it were, of that of later Thomists. The cumulative tradition is the mundane result of the faith of men in the past and is the mundane cause of the faith of men in the present. Therefore it is ever changing, ever accumulating, ever fresh. Every religious person is the locus of an interaction between the transcendent, which is presumably the same for every man (though this is not integral to our analysis), and the cumulative tradition, which is different for every man (and this is integral). And every religious person is the active participant, whether little or big, in the dynamics of the tradition's development.

This, then, I make bold to suggest, is how what used to be called a religion actually works in human history. It is a dialectical process between the mundane and the transcendent, a process whose locus is the personal faith and the lives of men and women, not altogether observable and not to be confined within any intelligible limits. It is a process of which the mundane, overt results are available for scrutiny by the historian, in the ever expanding deposit of what I have called an accumulating tradition. What the non-overt and perhaps even non-mundane results of this process are to be in the faith of those persons who subsequently confront or participate in the tradition, is up to them to say. Or it is for the later historians to infer from the new contribution that, out of that faith, they then may make to the ongoing development.

Each person is presented with a cumulative tradition, and grows up among other persons to whom that tradition is meaningful. From it and them, and out of the capacities of his own inner life and the circumstances of his outer life, he comes to a faith of his own. The tradition, in its tangible actualities, and his fellows, in their comparable participation, nourish his faith and give it shape. His faith, in turn, endows the concrete tradition with more than intrinsic significance, and encourages his fellows to persist in their similar involvement. His faith is new every morning. It is personal; it is no more and no less independent of his mundane environment (including the religious tradition) than is his personal life at large.

If we have observed, then, something of how faith operates in human history, are we in a position to say something further about it? Or if faith comprises a transcendent factor, does this mean that it is and must remain itself quite unknowable? I have insisted that it cannot be observed. Yet this is true of virtually everything really important in human life. All serious study of man as personal is a study of matters not directly observable. Ideas, ideals, loyalties, passions, aspirations, love, faith, despair, cannot be directly observed, but their role in human history is none the less consequential for that, nor the study of them the less legitimate. 'The proper study of mankind is by inference'[17].

Procedures here are more delicate, than in an epistemology by experimental observation; but some of us, undaunted, are happy and bold to affirm that man must study man in his full humanity, and not try to circumvent this by wishing that human life were less than human. By the exercise of imaginative sympathy, disciplined by intellectual rigour and checked by elaborate procedures, cross-checked by vigorous criticism, it is not impossible to infer what goes on in another's mind and heart. Those distrustful of the humanities disciplines may carry their distrust beyond tentativeness to outright dismissal. For them the faith of mankind, one element in our twofold analysis, though it cannot be exorcised, must remain foreven an unknown—conspicuously operative throughout history yet intrinsically elusive. Others may be willing to join in believing that careful study may succeed in attaining some appreciation, at least, though no final grasp, of the personal life of one's friends[18]. I have argued throughout that men's faith is their own, and is in principle beyond external domination. Yet, like other of man's personal involvements, in art, love, ambition, joy and sorrow, though it cannot be comprehended, it can be apprehended. Though as a privilege and never as a right, man can know in part what other men know at heart.

In my submission, then, it is in principle possible for men to become significantly aware of each other's faith. We should be able to arrive at a point where we can understand, not with complete assurance but with reasonable confidence, and not fully but in significant part, what the faith of other persons, other groups, even other ages, is and has been. This becomes the new and challenging business of 'Comparative Religion' studies—a task that is just beginning at this level, and is assuredly difficult but assuredly rewarding. For a century now serious historical studies have made major advances in uncovering and making known what I am calling the cumulative traditions of mankind's religious life. The next step is to discover and make known the personal faith of men that those traditions have served. This can be done, I affirm, by treating the observable items of the traditions as clues to the understanding of a personal and living quality of the men whose faith they have expressed.

A century from now, one may venture to predict, much will have been accomplished in this matter if an effort of this kind is, as we hope, made on a scale and with a seriousness comparable to those devoted to the observable side of religious life, and commensurate with the need of modern man for understanding in this realm.

We have not answered, then, the query 'What is faith?' beyond asserting that the term refers to a personal quality of human life and history, and indicating an empirical procedure by which, through disciplined investigation, it should be possible over the years to give a progressively more adequate and accurate answer as to what is, what has been, the particular faith of particular persons.

Once again, the analysis that we have been at pains to proffer does not answer a philosophic question so much as provide a method by which men may proceed to answer an historical one—gradually and partially—and yet to answer it in its variety and actuality. Not what faith is, perhaps; but what faith has been.

Yet this is not evasive, nor in the end is it even unphilosophical. For if faith is personal, then even in principle it is not a generic entity, but a living quality. It is not a fixed something, but the throbbing actuality of a myriad of someones. There is no such thing, I have argued, as religion or a religion; and when one divides what has been called that into two parts, an overt tangible tradition on the one hand and a vital personal faith on the other, neither of the resultant parts is a thing either, definite, stable, static, complete, definable, metaphysically given. To see faith truly is to see it actually, not ideally.

This means historically; with continuity but not identity.

No man has had faith who has not been in part educated to it by the legacy of others. Yet the religious history of mankind is ununderstandable if one does not allow that the faith of many men has fallen short of, diverged from, or transcended that expressed in the tradition available to them[19]. Far from accepting, then, any suggestion that the faith of men in all communities is really the same, I would stress rather that the faith of men even within one community has not been the same. In the traditions the historian sees variety; in faith, the appreciative senses a similar variety.

Indeed, with the personalist emphasis I would urge not only that the faith of men is the actual faith of actual men, and hence no two are the same. Only in abstraction can one arrive at identities. Going further, I would recognize that any one man's faith is different any given morning from what it was the preceding afternoon. Faith is personal, and one must take this seriously.

My faith is different from my brother's. This is a fact. The faith of one of my neighbours (or readers) is different from that of another. This is an inference, but can hardly be gainsaid by anyone who takes evidence seriously. From data such as these the historian must start. Looking further afield and more widely in time, if one may infer anything at all in these matters one can hardly but recognize (and the more sensitive one is, the more surely one recognizes) that Tertullian's faith was different from Abelard's, Constantine's different from Zwingli's, St. Teresa's different from John Knox's, Harnack's different from William Jennings Bryan's. At a less élite level, the faith of a Roman proletarian catacombist or martyr was different from that of a hanger-on of the Crusades, and both these from the faith of a modern Bible-belt farmer.

The cumulative tradition for me and for my brother is relatively similar, since we were brought up with the same rites and hearing the same sermons, and we have the same number of centuries of Christian history to look back upon; though it has diverged somewhat as we have grown older, as we have read different books and paused before different paintings. These minor divergencies dwindle, however, beside those that differentiate the religious environment, and so far as one can sense, also the faith of a Bede from a Berdyaev.

Yet I have insisted that an analysis is lopsided and faulty if it serves only the observer, not the participant. Is the worshipper also to be content with no ideal of faith? The historian and even the philosopher may accept faith for what it has been, and look no further for some final essence. But can it be reckoned an ultimately personal matter not only for others but also for oneself? I believe that it can, and must. I see this interpretation of the issues as not only required by the evidence for an observer's understanding of mankind's religious history, but required also by his own involvement for a participant's understanding of the universe and of his place in it. One's own faith cannot be lively and deep and true until it too is personal. It is not self-conscious until one has recognized this.

My faith is an act that *I* make, myself, naked before God. Just as there is no such thing as Christianity (or Islam or Buddhism), I have urged, behind which the Christian (the Muslim, the Buddhist) may shelter, which he may set between himself and the terror and spendour and living concern of God, so there is no generic Christian faith; no 'Buddhist faith', no 'Hindu faith', no 'Jewish faith'. There is only my faith, and yours, and that of my Shinto friend, of my particular Jewish neighbour. We are all persons, clustered in mundane communities, no doubt, and labeled with mundane labels but, so far as transcendence is concerned, encountering it each directly, personally, if at all. In the eyes of God each of us is a person, not a type.

There is nothing in heaven or on earth that can legitimately be called *the* Christian faith. There have been and are the faiths of individual Christians, each personal, each specific, each immediate. Besides, there have been now and then some generalized statements by theologians, intellectual systematizations of what they as persons conceived that that faith ought to be, though these generalized statements have differed among themselves and no one of them has been or could be free of the humanity (particularity, fallibility, historicity) of the man or men who composed it[20]. All these have existed on earth. In heaven there is God, seen by Chris-

too individualistic — what about community? [handwritten margin note]

tians as triune and active, known by them as loving. Neither for the outside observer nor for the believer is there in heaven a generalized prototype of Christians' faith. Faith not only is but ought to be mundane, man's response.

Xian [handwritten margin note]

There is no ideal faith that I ought to have. There is God whom I ought to see, and a neighbour whom I ought to love. These must suffice me; and my faith is my ability to see that they abundantly more than suffice.

The ideal towards which I move is not an ideal of my own faith but is God Himself, and my neighbour himself. Faith is not part of eternity; it is my present awareness of eternity.

Similarly the Muslim's faith is his personal awareness, which takes place on earth, in history, that outside of history there is only God, and that inside of history on earth his duty is to obey only God. This faith has varied across the centuries, and continues to vary, which is another way of saying that it is real.

I certainly do not deny, then, that Christians in their religious life have something in common—or Muslims, or any group, or indeed all men together. What rather I am asserting (conformably both to the historian, who cannot see that common element, and to the man of faith, who therein can) is that what they have in common lies not in the tradition that introduces them to transcendence, not in their faith by which they personally respond, but in that to which they respond, the transcendent itself[21].

The traditions evolve. Men's faith varies. God endures.

The same God for all?
mono?
pan?
God = transcendent?
God as outside the world system?
as inside?
As an ideal? A reality? [handwritten notes]

CHAPTER EIGHT

Conclusion

USUALLY WE SEE the world through a pattern of concepts that we have inherited. Sometimes these windows need cleaning: so much so that almost we may be seeing the windows that we have constructed rather than the world outside. Sometimes too on thoughtful examination we may come to recognize that by re-arranging the windows as well as by cleaning them we could get a better view of the real world beyond. Certainly we may be grateful to our ancestors who have built these windows through which we see. Without them we should still be walled up within the confines of our immediate experience or that of our small circle— as their ancestors before them had been. Yet it is not impious of us to ask occasionally whether we might not see better by enlarging a window here or there, or even by replacing it with new ones of a different shape.

For conceptualization is a human activity. The process of its development can be observed. Thereupon it can also be consciously amended. For the process has thus become one whose further development is self-conscious, deliberate. This is so even in the religious realm, unaccustomed though we are to self-awareness of movement there.

This much at least is clear: that the amalgam of inner piety and

outer institution that at a certain stage in their dynamic development was intellectually reified under the term 'religion' and 'religions' was conceived thus because some people (rather inadvertently) fell into the habit of doing so. And the 'religions' have
names because we have given them names. Once he has become
aware of what has happened, man cannot escape choosing between
whether or not he will continue to use these particular concepts.
To me, for reasons that I have set forth, they seem now clearly
inadequate.

Accordingly, my endeavour has been to devise and propound
a new conceptual apparatus or theoretical framework, more profitable than those traditionally or currently available; one by means
of which the human mind may be able to comprehend more justly
the immensely diverse, fluid, and subtle data of the religious life
of man in history thus far, and to participate in that life from
now on more intelligently.

The proposal that I am putting forward can, at one level, be
formulated quite simply. It is that what men have tended to conceive as religion and especially as a religion, can more rewardingly, more truly, be conceived in terms of two factors, different
in kind, both dynamic: an historical 'cumulative tradition', and
the personal faith of men and women.

On the verbal plane, I seriously suggest that terms such as
Christianity, Buddhism, and the like must be dropped, as clearly
untenable once challenged. The word 'religion' has had many
meanings; it too would be better dropped. This is partly because
of its distracting ambiguity, partly because most of its traditional
meanings are, on scrutiny, illegitimate. The only effective significance that can reasonably be attributed to the term is that of
'religiousness'[1], but for this generic abstraction other words are
available—we could rehabilitate perhaps the venerable term
'piety'. In any case, the use of a plural, or with an article, is false[2].
Certainly much would be gained if everyone who were tempted,
from habit, to use the word 'religion' would stop to clarify to himself just what it was to which he wished to refer. Once he had

done this, it is doubtful that he would then go on to use it anyway; especially if he hoped to clarify it also to his hearer or reader.

I am bold enough to speculate whether these terms will not in
fact have disappeared from serious writing and careful speech
within twenty-five years.

Such a disappearance could mean for the devout a truer faith
in God and a truer love of their neighbour; and for scholars, a
clearer understanding of the religious phenomena that they are
studying.

Perceptive readers will have noticed that in the course of this
present inquiry the adjective 'religious' has been retained in use
even while the noun is rejected. This has to do with a contention
that living religiously is an attribute of persons. The attribute
arises not because those persons participate in some entity called
religion, but because they participate in what I have called transcendence. That adjectives may come closer to describing reality
than do nouns, especially in the personal realm, is perhaps an important philosophic orientation[3].

I have proposed my pair of concepts, tradition and faith, to replace the currently established single one, without inquiring at
length into the nature of the two. This is partly in line with my
concomitant thesis that the 'nature' either of religious traditions
or of faith is not an intellectual desideratum nor a metaphysical
reality; we are dealing here rather with historical actualities,
which must be explored as such. This point, however, though important, will admittedly not in itself satisfy. The matter of
cumulative traditions will involve less difficulty, doubtless; but
'faith' in my argument, as otherwise, is open to much further exploration.

This, however, would require another book, someday perhaps
to be written. A little below, the point will be touched on once
again, in a consideration of the proffered analysis from the viewpoint of a man's own potential faith, in relation to authority. Yet
a full treatment of the question is, I suggest, a corollary rather
than an antecedent to our hypothesis.

Rather than arguing further the position put forward, we may consider how it may be tested. The thesis has been inductively evidenced, and theoretically analysed. To me, it seems that the evidence of our modern knowledge impels the new position, and that the logic of reflection corroborates it. There remains one important check: to test it in practice. Three areas here may be noted.

The first is that of the study of other men's religious life. Here I have few qualms. Recent studies in the 'History of Religions', as we have previously noted, would seem to indicate that an unwitting movement in this direction has in fact already begun[4]. There would seem small doubt but that the conscious application of a tradition-faith analysis to an understanding of outside cultures would prove quickly and richly effective. My suggestion will have to be withdrawn or modified if scholars willing to try it out in the case of their particular province of study do not find it apt and helpful. To me it seems clear that in this area the theory fits; but by all means let it be tried by other observers.

Particularly interesting will be the special case where outsiders may approach Christian study[5]. I should guess that rather than attempting to answer the question 'What is Christianity?' they would find it rewarding to set as their goal the ascertaining of what has been historically the Christian tradition, and what has been the personal faith of Christians. If my theory is valid, they should find this both more manageable and more revealing[6].

Secondly, there is the developing area of intercommunication among religious communities. 'Dialogue' between members of differing traditions is nowadays replacing polemics, debate, and monologue preaching of traditional missionary policy. Terms in which it can be conducted have not yet, however, been widely found[7]. It will be illuminating to discover whether among diverse groups conversation in the terms propounded here could prove fruitful, or at least mutually intelligible. This will be a highly significant test of the theory, especially in view of the possible importance of this activity for the world's future religious development[8].

Thirdly, there is the position of the believer. This unquestionably is the most delicate and difficult area. It is here that problems will most searchingly arise, and that vindication if it comes at all will come most dearly.

At least, this will be so for Christians and Muslims. For the other half of the world's religious population I anticipate no major disquiet. Hindus and Chinese especially will, if I mistake not, find the proffered analysis acceptable enough, apparently almost straightforward. Some pious Jews perhaps will, and others perhaps will not, find difficulty in applying the thesis to their own position, however appropriate it may seem to them for representing the situation of those whose form of faith they do not share. It is Christians and Muslims, however, who will provide the crucial test[9]. If it proves ultimately possible to express within the terms of the intellectual framework that has been here propounded whatever a Christian or a Muslim wishes to say about his own faith, his own religious position, his own tradition, then certainly the theory will have demonstrated a rather considerable vitality.

More important, however, than the significance of this for the theoretical orientation will be the significance for the traditions themselves. For while the question of the serviceability of the suggested theory for the participant involves the most delicate and difficult area of its validity, it is at the same time by far the most important, and potentially the most valuable. If Christian theology can be adequately expressed in these terms, then the gains for Christians themselves could be striking. If the Islamic community can reformulate its position in the modern world in a way that thus takes fully seriously not only the faith of other men but also the historicity and dynamic of its own tradition past and present, the profoundly personal quality of faith and the profoundly transcendent quality of its immediate reference, then it would seem if the opinion of an outsider may be tolerated that its contemporary religious crisis will be solved[10].

In the Christian case, where I have more right to speak, the first point to be remembered is that present Christian theology is inadequate. No doubt theology is always inadequate to faith[11], but the contemporary crisis is unusually grave. We return at this point to the problems noted in our Introduction above. The Christian Church is seriously and rightly striving for a new intellectual-verbal expression of faith that will be more intelligible to others than is any currently available, and more satisfying to its own members and especially to its own theologians. Such an expression must function in a world increasingly characterized by science in all its ramifications, by conspicuous and rich religious diversity across the world and also within the Church, by rapid and self-conscious change, and all the rest; but also in our world where, not least because of this newness, faith itself continues to be precious and of transcending significance. It is no secret that the Church is consciously in need of a new theology that will empower Christians to be at once more modern and more devout, that will nourish a faith more closely attuned both to contemporary history and to the fullness and majesty of God. The two important movements of Christian thought in the twentieth century so far, liberalism and neo-orthodoxy, have been oriented to one or other of these, not to both.

To such a Church the present analysis is offered, in the bold hope that conceivably it might be able not to answer the questions that press hard but to provide prolegomena of thought within which those questions could be tentatively answered by men of sufficient faith and intelligence.

In the process of answering them, of reformulating a theology, if it were to be along such lines as these, many problems would obtrude. I do not wish to suggest otherwise. Salient among them would doubtless be, for instance, the question of authority[12], a doctrine of the Church[13], and others. The present analysis, however, perhaps does not itself generate such problems, but rather only brings them into the open. Conceivably it might even provide the terms in which a solution for them must be found, if it is to be one consonant with modern knowledge of science, of one's own history, and of other men's faith.

Somewhat comparable considerations apply also in the Islamic case[14]; although of course differences remain significant.

In neither case, however, is it simply a question of whether traditional theology can be re-expressed in new terms. This would contradict the analysis itself, which has been elaborated in order to deal with the fact that the modern situation of mankind, including that for religious communities, is recognizedly new. Those whose faith theology formulates and those to whom it is addressed are men of new knowledge, new opportunities, new responsibilities; and they know it. To express either Christian or Islamic theology in terms dynamic enough to be appropriate for today, inescapably involves real novelty. Presumably, whatever the theory, it must recognize the demonstrable fact of novelty in the past, and innovate by inherently providing for its becoming self-conscious but disciplined in the present.

The advent of self-consciousness in human religious history is a drastic emergence. Its consequences no one can conceivably foresee.

This closing section of our study I have ventured to entitle 'conclusion'. Yet I trust that no one will take this too seriously. In intellectual formulation in these matters not only can there not be, but emphatically there must not be, any final conclusion. For the religious history of mankind is not yet over.

It would be foolish to predict the future. Yet not least foolish are those who tacitly prophesy, or whose attitudes imply, that the present state of affairs will continue. Other men's cumulative traditions are manifestly in continuing development. So is one's own. Not least significant for our purposes, the relations among the various communities are becoming changed. The total religious history of mankind is entering a new phase—as every day it has always entered one, though now more rapidly and conspicuously and more corporately.

The Christian tradition is still in process. The Islamic has not ceased to evolve. Nor the Jewish, nor the Buddhist. The Hindu's is always in transition. The only traditions that are not changing before our eyes are those that have ceased to exist—as those of the ancient world, though even these persist more actively than is usually recognized[15]. The position of almost every religious person on earth today, and surely tomorrow, is manifestly novel both in terms of his own tradition and also in the relation to him of other men's.

Until now, we have been concerned chiefly with two types of person whose business it has been intellectually to understand religious matters: the outside observer, endeavouring to interpret what he sees, and the participant in a tradition endeavouring to interpret what he knows or feels (or endeavouring to know and feel what he has inherited). We may now add a third type: coming generations, whose business it will be to some degree to decide, to choose, to explore, to innovate. One reason why it has been necessary, and indeed one reason why it has been possible, to construct a single theory adequate to serve simultaneously both observer and participant, is that in our day these two roles are beginning to coalesce, as men of faith become aware of themselves as incipiently or potentially members of the total corporate religious complex of mankind, composed of different but no longer separated communities.

The need for new conceptual patterns has become evident not only on the one hand because of new and wide-ranging knowledge that has become available about other traditions, and on the other hand because of the crisis of knowledge regarding one's own. Beyond both of these, the contemporary interpenetration of men's traditions, on the religious as on other planes, may be inaugurating a radically new age. Still further novel, man's new awareness of all this and of his own involvement in it, as a process in which he is a conscious and responsible participant, is radical.

All man's history is becoming self-conscious; including his religious history. It is also becoming more unified, for good or ill. How man will work out the unification on the religious plane is as yet far from clear. What is clear already is that the responsibility for this too is becoming his. Men of different religious communities are going to have to collaborate to construct jointly and deliberately the kind of world of which men of different religious communities can jointly approve, as well as one in which they can jointly participate[16].

This is an immense task, and a new one. To undertake it many things will be needed, including new ideas. In addition to the tests that have already been mentioned, the requirements of such a movement are the new and challenging test for any new religious theory (or theology) today. This test will be applied (or rather, in the hands of exploratory participants, will be enacted) by those coming generations whose function, consciously or otherwise, it will be to construct the next phase of the world's religious history.

They will play their role more intelligently, and the scholars among them will observe and interpret it more truly, if they can bring to their task an apprehension of the processes that are involved, more flexible and more embracing, more penetrating and truer, than in the past has been either available or necessary.

On the threshold of that new age, I close.

May we perhaps, then, summarize our argument?

The meaning of 'religion', as a term, elucidated under our historical and theoretical inquiry, may I hope have let us see a little more truly the meaning also of man's religious life itself.

The end of religion, in the classical sense of its purpose and goal, that to which it points and may lead, is God. Contrariwise, God is the end of religion also in the sense that once He appears vividly before us, in His depth and love and unrelenting truth all else dissolves; or at the least religious paraphernalia drop back into their due and mundane place, and the concept 'religion' is brought to an end. This occurs also even when the unrelenting truth is only that of scholarly inquiry.

Written from within the Christian Church, this present study is offered to fellow Christians in the hopes that it might contribute to our doing justice intellectually both to what we now know of the world in which we live and to what we know of God as Christ has revealed Him to us. Written from within the universities, it is offered to fellow scholars in the hopes that it might contribute to our ability to understand and to interpret to the world the long and rich religious history of man. Written from within mankind[17], it is offered to fellow human beings throughout the world, including those whose religious faith is derived from other traditions and also those whose faith is not religious, in the hopes that it might contribute to the intellectual aspect of our new task of together constructing a brotherhood on earth deserving the loyalty of all our groups.

Such aspirations would seem fantastical and pretentious, were it not that today surely no man's faith is finally legitimate unless it can so aspire.

Notes for Chapter Two: 'Religion' in the West

1   Some of my readers, abreast of recent trends in analytical philosophy (especially British) and in linguistics (especially American), may be disquieted at my conserving such classical notions as 'mind' and 'concept'. My not adopting some of the newer fashions, however, is not entirely due to a backward-looking orientation. It is related also to my belief—perhaps, of course, erroneous—that a recognition greater than current terminology concedes of the specifically personalist quality of human behaviour, will presently prevail. In any case, whether this prevail or not, my own conviction is that language and other human affairs, including religious, can best be understood in terms that combine with scientific rigour a specific humanistic appropriateness, without sacrificing either. At all events, I hope that as we proceed my meaning may be clear, and that readers will be patient enough and gracious enough to assess the validity of the argument in its own terms as it develops.

2   'Religion is universal in human societies. This is an empirical generalization, an aggregate of a multitude of specific observations'—Raymond Firth, *Elements of Social Organization*, London and New York, 1951, p. 216. The 'specific observations' here are those of anthropologists. Another anthropological writer states, 'Primitive societies without religion have never been found'—William Howells, *The Heathens: primitive man and his religions*, New York, 1948, p. 11.

3   The skeleton designated *Palaeoanthropus palestiniensis*, now in the Rockefeller Museum, Jerusalem, Jordan, was found carefully buried. It is dated conservatively at 100,000 B.C. As the religious traditions of man extant today are traced backwards in time through recorded history and into the neolithic and eventually the palaeolithic period, the observable data serving as evidence for them became, of course, progressively more tenuous; gradually materials fall away, until eventually one is left with only burial. This, however, persists very far back indeed. Interpretations of the data naturally vary. Yet there would seem no question but that early burial of the dead, whatever it may have meant to those who practised it (which we shall never know), was careful and deliberate and is historically related to customs in more recent and more manageably knowable times that are everywhere religious. (Some scholars discern death rituals even earlier, from the remains of Pekin man found at the Choukoutien caves, going back perhaps half a million years, but I find their arguments speculative and precarious.)

4   On these discussions, see the following:
W. Warde Fowler, 'The Latin History of the word "Religio" ', in *Trans-*

NOTES FOR CHAPTER TWO

actions of the Third International Congress for the History of Religions, 2 voll., Oxford, 1908; II, 169–175; and *Social Life at Rome in the Age of Cicero,* London, 1929, chap. XI (pp. 319–352) , 'Religion'.

M. Kobbert, *De verborum* religio *atque* religiosus *usu apud Romanos quaestiones selectae,* Königsberg, 1910, and his articles RELIGIO, RELIGIOSI DIES, RELIGIOSA LOCA, in *Paulys Real-Encyclopädie der classischen Altertumswissenschaft, Neue Bearbeitung begonnen von Georg Wissowa,* . . . *Zweite Reihe,* Stuttgart, 1914.

Walter F. Otto, 'Religio und Superstitio' in *Archiv für Religionswissenschaft,* 12: 533–554 (1909) and 14: 406–422 (1911) .

J. B. Kätzler, 'Religio. Versuch einer Worterklärung', in *20. Jahresbericht des Bischöflichen Gymnasiums Paulinum in Schwaz* (for 1952–53) , pp. 2–18.

Henry Toomey Wilt, 'Religio: A semantic study of the pre-Christian use of the terms religio and religiosus', unpublished doctoral dissertation submitted to Columbia University, New York, 1954 (consulted in microfilm) .

Of these studies, the German are the most cogent.

5 The two points of view on the original meaning of the word are reflected already in the discussions among later Latins themselves as to its etymology. Cicero (in a passage given below, note 18) has Balbus the Stoic propound a derivation of the adjective from *relegere,* with the implication that a 'religious' person is one who is careful in his worship and is, as it were, the opposite of a 'neglectful' one. The Christian writer Lactantius, in his *Divinae Institutiones,* IV, 28, rejects this on the grounds that piety turns not on the subjective question of how men worship, but rather on the objective one of whom; that there are real obligations to be fulfilled, and this is the root of the matter. He accordingly derives it from *religare* 'to bind':

Hoc uinculo pietatis obstricti deo et religati sumus: unde ipsa religio nomen accepit, non ut Cicero interpretatus est a relegendo . . . nam si in isdem diis colendis et superstitio et religio uersatur, exigua uel potius nulla distantia est. . . . nimirum religio ueri cultus est, superstitio falsi. et omnino quid colas interest, non quemadmodum colas . . . . diximus nomen religionis a uinculo pietatis esse deductum, quod hominem sibi deus religauerit et pietate constrinxerit, quia seruire nos ei ut domino et obsequi ut patri necesse est (text used: Samuel Brandt & Georgius Laubmann, edd., *L. Caeli Firmiani Lactanti Opera Omnia . . . pars I* [*Corpus Scriptorum Ecclesiasticorum Latinorum,* vol. 19], Venice, 1890, pp. 389–391). ('By this fetter of piety we are bound and tied to God; which is where religion itself took its name, not, as Cicero explained it, from "carefully gathering" . . . . For if both religion and superstition are involved in worshipping the same gods, then the distinction between the two becomes thin or, rather, disappears . . . . Surely religion is the worship of the true, superstition of the false [or, religion is the worship of Him who is true, superstition of that which is false]. And what makes all the difference is what you worship, not how you worship. . . . The name of religion, we have said, is derived from the bond of piety, because God has tied man to Himself, and bound him by piety; for we must serve Him as a master and be obedient to Him as a father') .

(Cf. also *hominem deo pietatis uinculis esse religatum, unde ipsa religio nominatur,* ibid., IV, 64 [69], ibid., p. 753) .

A great deal of all studies of religion since, including the most modern, can

204

be arranged in effect on one side or the other of this dichotomy. There are those on the one hand primarily concerned with objective realities, with that outside man to which he is related in religion; and those on the other hand primarily concerned with subjective attitudes, with the involvement by which he is related. On the etymological question, earlier pronouncements were made with no basis for any learned decision: the ideas put forward by any writer reflect his own position on the significance of religion in human life, rather than any philological wisdom about its name. These writers' expositions are valuable to the modern student as indicating authoritatively, and often quite forcefully, what *religio* (more recently, 'religion') meant to them.

I would like to suggest that consideration be given to the possibility that two roots (or even two original words?) may have coalesced in Latin *religio*. (It is evident, at least, that the meanings of two roots coalesced in the minds of those who used the word. It is not unknown for a word's meaning to be influenced by a 'false' etymology, which is another way of saying that two streams of meaning converge. An example is the word 'sect' in English.) This would happily explain the divergent interpretations later given, and the fact that many writers actually use the word now in a subjectivist, now in an objectivist, sense. Certainly from the earliest records that we have, the word has meant different things to different people, many of whom have felt very strongly that the word *really* means this or that. For those who tend to equate their interpretation of that which they call religion with the 'real' meaning of the word, and further to equate the 'real' meaning of the word with its original meaning, it is important to point out that at the time of the earliest extant records of the Latin language, *religio* as a word and also the quite different matter of what we today call the religion of the Latin people, both had already many centuries of development and perhaps decline behind them.

6 Recent studies (see esp. Kätzler, note 4 above) have assembled reasons for believing that the root is neither that of *ligāre* 'to bind' nor *legere* 'to gather, to study, to read' but a third root *lig-*, cognate with Greek ἀλέγω and Albanian *•log-*, meaning 'to pay attention, to give care', and appearing also in the Latin correlative negative (*nec-legere*) *neglegere*, 'to neglect'. This is etymologically attractive; so far as interpretation goes, it amounts to a more plausible statement of the case in favour of the subjectivist side, in the Cicero tradition. Those aligning themselves on that side of the argument have in fact assumed a meaning implying 'pay heed, etc.', but have had to assign this to the root *leg-*; the contrast with *negligence* has been tacit or noted. Wilt argues that the earliest meanings of the ancient verb *relig-* (traces of which survive in the ἀπαξ *religentem*, preserved from an ancient song) and the noun *religio*, were secular, implying a redirecting of effective attention. His arguments are not very persuasive, and at best could be taken as supplementing, but not answering, Kobbert.

7 Remarking that Greek mythology is much richer than Roman in its presentation of the gods as figures, a major scholar writes 'The *numen* for the Roman is expressed not in the figure, but in a succession of acts, in which it encounters man'—Franz Altheim, *A History of Roman Religion*, translated by Harold Mattingly, London, 1938, p. 181.

8 Or four, if one counts only once the two repetitions: I. 931–932 =
IV. 6–7; V. 86 = VI. 62. I have used the excellent edition *T. Lvcreti Cari De
Rervm Natvra libri sex. Edited with introduction and commentary by William
Ellery Leonard [&] Stanley Barney Smith*, Madison, 1942. I have consulted also
the commentary in *Titi Lvcreti Cari De Rervm Natvra libri sex. Edited with
prolegomena, critical apparatus, translation and commentary by Cyril Bailey*,
3 voll., Oxford, 1947. Lucretius's dates are approximately 99–55 B.C.

9   *humana ante oculos foede cum uita iaceret
in terris oppressa graui sub Religioni,
quae caput a caeli regionibus ostendebat,
horribili super aspectu mortalibus instans—I.* 62–65

10 Especially the reverberating I. 101:
        tantum Religio potuit suadere malorum!

11 1. 83; cf. Leonard's introduction, op. cit., especially p. 77.

12 V. 1194–1203. His word is *pietas*.

13 An example is I.61 (Cotta is speaking) : *caerimonias religionesque
publicas sanctissime tuendas arbitror.* I have used as text *M. Tulli Ciceronis,
De Natura Deorum, Edited by Arthur Stanley Pease, Bimillennial edition*, 2
voll., Cambridge, Mass., 1955–1958. Cicero lived from 106 to 43 B.C.; this particular work appeared in 45 B.C.

14 E.g., in the opening sentence (Cicero himself) : *quaestio est de
natura deorum, quae et ad cognitionem animi pulcherrima est et ad moderan-
dum religionem necessaria.* Pease's comment is: '*Religio* seems here used in
the meaning of "attention to religious observances" '—op. cit., ad loc.

15 If there is validity in Wilt's thesis that *religio* was originally secular, or even in my subsumption of his derivation under a possibility that there
had been a subjective, human notion of *religio* (or a comparable verb or adjective) signifying 'paying attention' (to the ritual) in addition to a transcendent notion of an external obligation or tabu, then Cicero's version of
religio is not a 'softening' of the archaic meaning but a presentation of one of
the archaic meanings.

16 By Cotta, who of the three speakers presumably most nearly voices
Cicero's own views, in I. 121—'Epicurus . . . in abolishing divine beneficence
and divine benevolence, uprooted and exterminated all religion from the
human heart' (*ex animis hominum extraxit*) (*Cicero. De Natura Deorum.
Academica. With an English translation by H. Rackham*, London & New York
[Loeb Classical Library], 1933, p. 117).

17 'The word *superstitio* does not occur in Latin before Cicero'—
Bailey, op. cit., p. 609 (vol. 3) , commentary ad 1.63. From his time on, however, it became standard to range atheism, *religio*, and *superstitio* in a series
of which the mean is good and the extremes are aberrations. Cicero presents
the Academy representative Cotta as referring to *non modo superstitionem*

... *in qua inest timor inanis deorum, sed etiam religionem, quae deorum cultu pio continetur* ('not only superstition, which involves a fatuous fear of the gods, but also *religio*, which consists in duly worshipping them') —I. 117.

18 In the oft-cited etymological derivation of the term, II. 72 (Balbo the Stoic is speaking): *qui autem omnia quae ad cultum deorum pertinerent diligenter retractarent et tamquam relegerent sunt dicti religiosi ex relegendo, ut elegantes ex eligendo, ex diligendo diligentes, ex intellegendo intellegentes; his enim in verbis omnibus inest vis legendi eadem quae in religioso.* (Pease, op. cit., vol. 2, p. 739.) The discussion here is of adjectives; elsewhere it is the noun that is more often used, but still referring, it seems to me, in virtually every case to a quality rather than a substance, to a subjective attitude of the person concerned rather than to an objective act or entity. A discrimination between *religio* (or its correlative *pietas*) and *superstitio*, the former a laudatory and the latter a pejorative term, is made not only by Balbo but also by each of the other participants in the discussion: Velleius, expounding the Epicurean position, I. 45 (*ut deos pie coleremus et ut superstitione liberaremur*), and Cotta, the representative of the Academy, I. 117 (cf. our previous note); in each case it is the *manner* of worshipping on which the distinction turns.

19 Greek πιστις, Latin *fides*. The Christians did not coin these words, but it was they who gave them a new religious connotation, having taken them from the secular vocabulary. There the basic notion had been 'trust'. In Greek they used a corresponding verb, but not in Latin; in the latter, for the idea of 'having faith' or 'practising faith' the Church took over *credere*. This was perhaps unfortunate, since the misleading and even disastrous confusion between faith and belief has been promoted by this. On this point see further below, chap. 7; on πιστις as a term see below, chap. 3, notes 26, 27.

20 Apart from Lactantius and Augustine, who are discussed below, and Jerome's Bible, I have observed usage in Tertullian, Minucius Felix, Arnobius, and Firmicus, and isolated passages elsewhere. My study, however, has been preliminary only; and I know of no complete investigation. The studies of Latin usage generally (such as those in note 4 above; except Fowler briefly, and I find rather inadequately) stop short of the Christian period. A systematic examination would be most helpful.

21 Constantly, for the cults of the pagans. As illustrations of this use also for their own Christian practices: from Tertullian, in the singular, *religio orationis*, the form of the prayer, which God has taught us (*deus solus docere potuit, quomodo se uellet orari, ab ipso igitur ordinata religio orationis* . . . —'God alone could teach man how He wished to be prayed to. Therefore the pattern of prayer [was] ordained by Him Himself . . .'—*De Oratione*, 9.8) (see *Quinti Septimi Florentis Tertulliani Opera*, Augustus Reifferscheid & Georgius Wissowa, edd. [*Corpus Scriptorum Ecclesiasticorum Latinorum*, vol. 20, part 1], Vindobonae &c, 1890, p. 187); from Arnobius, in the plural, Christians are being said *inauditas incognitas repentinas agitare atque inducere religiones*—'to be practising and carrying on unheard of and unknown and novel *religiones*'—*Adversus Nationes*, II, 72 (Augustus Reifferscheid, ed. [*Corpus Scriptorum Ecclesiasticorum Lat.*, vol. 4], Vindobonae, 1875. p. 107).

NOTES FOR CHAPTER TWO

22 *Et promouebitur quidem, cum Deus permiserit, ad ampliorem locum religionis suae*—Cyprian, letter 40: in the Bayard edition, Paris, 1925 (*Corpus Scriptorum Ecclesiasticorum Latinorum*, vol. 3), p. 586.9-10; and again, *Cunctis religionis gradibus ascendit*, letter 55 (ibid., p. 629.11). I owe the reference to these to Alexander Souter, comp., *A Glossary of Later Latin to 600 A.D.*, Oxford, 1949, s.v. Cyprian is the first half of the third century.

23 I have not actually seen this particular usage myself. The quotation is from Souter, op. cit., s.v.

24 This is the basic meaning of the title of Firmicus's work, *De Errore Profanarum Religionum* (ca. 346 A.D.). I sense an appreciable difference between the concepts *falsa(e) religio(nes)*, as found in Lactantius (below, note 30) and *error religionum*. The word 'profane' here, a traditional pagan term, is also highly interesting.

25 If this is indeed the sense of the passage from the *Epitome* of Lactantius, chap. 37: *Nam et Deus . . . quaerendus est, et religio suscipienda, quae sola nos discernit a belluis* ('For God ought to be sought after; and also *religio*—which alone distinguishes us from animals—ought to be observed'. Is *religio* here perhaps 'worshipping'? How is one to know whether the writer had in mind here, for *religio*, an inner disposition or the performance of outward acts?) Text used: *Firmiani Lactantii Epitome Institutionum Divinarum: Lactantius' Epitome of the Divine Institutes; Edited and translated with a commentary* by E. H. Blakeney, London, 1950; Latin, p. 25. His English version is p. 86: 'religion should be acknowledged, which alone severs us from the brutes'. (In the alternative system of chapter numbering, this is chap. 32; e.g., in Samuel Brandt *et* Georgius Laubmann, edd., *L. Caeli Firmiani Lactanti Opera Omnia . . .* [*Corpus Scriptorum Ecclesiasticorum Latinorum*, vol. 19], p. 708, reading *deus* and *beluis*.)

26 Examples: Arnobius, *Adversus Nationes*, II. 72: *religiones vestrae multis annis praecedunt nostram.* II. 73: *religio nostra.* (Cf. II. 71: *religio . . . quam obitis*). Lactantius, *Divinae Institutiones*, V. 19: *nostra . . . religio.* In the editions cited, the references are as follows: for the former (Reifferscheid), pp. 106, 108, 106, respectively; for the latter (Brandt, vol. 19), p. 467.

27 Examples: Lactantius, *Epitome*, 29: *religio summi Dei . . . religio Dei.* Cf. also *Divinae Institutiones*, I. 1: *cuius religionem cultumque diuinum.* II.1,1: *religiones deorum.* (In the editions cited, p. 29, p. 4 fn., p. 95 respectively.)

28 The passage in which I have found *nostra religio* used in its most comprehensive sense (although as something within the worshipper's mind, not an institutional system) is one where it is contrasted not directly with the pagans' *religio* but with 'what they offer to their gods', which he says lacks personal involvement and personal feelings, and with their behaviour at the temple, where alone their *religio* is found, the rest of their life untouched by it. Lactantius, *Divinae Institutiones*, 5.19: *Nihil intimum, nihil proprium diis*

208

suis offerunt, non integritatem mentis, non reuerentiam, non timorem. perac-
tis itaque sacrificiis inanibus omnem religionem in templo et cum templo
sicut inuenerant relincunt nihilque secum ex ea neque adferunt neque refer-
unt. . . . nostra uero religio eo firma est et solida et inmutabilis, quia iustitiam
docet, quia nobiscum semper est, quia tota in animo colentis est, quia mentem
ipsam pro sacrificio habet (ed. cit., pp. 466–467) —'They offer to their gods
nothing personal, nothing their very own; no integrity of mind, nor reverence,
nor awe. Accordingly once their vacuous sacrifices have been gone through,
they leave all *religio* at the temple and with the temple just as they found it.
They bring nothing of it with them, and take nothing back. . . . But our
religio is strong and solid and immutable just because it teaches justice, just
because it is constantly with us, just because it is altogether within the heart
of the worshipper, just because it has for its offering the mind itself'.

29 It is a matter of considerable delicacy and subtlety to sense aright
the meaning of such words, and one can perhaps never be sure that one has
truly grasped what was in the mind either of an author or (what may be different) of his early readers. At least we should be careful to give less weight
to our twentieth-century concepts and more to those that were prevalent in
times just preceding the usage in question. One may also legitimately bear in
mind the point that there is no reason for supposing that these authors necessarily had a clear and sharp concept in their minds to which the word *religio*
gave expression; that this was far from being the case is suggested by the similar situation in modern usage, observable among even careful thinkers, and
is proved by the clearly divergent uses of the word in the same writer at different passages.

30 Among contextual patterns that suggest a still close relation of the
term *religio* to cultic practice, are the following: *Nunc, quoniam falsam re-*
ligionem, quae est in deorum cultibus—Epitome, 36 [41] (Brandt & Laubmann,
ed. cit., p. 711); *cultus deorum . . . ; . . . de falsa religione diximus*—ibid., 25
[30], (p. 699) ; etc. Further, although some passages from these writers can in
themselves be taken in various ways, more instructive and probably more
proper is to read the writers with the earlier and less generic meanings in
mind, and thereby to see where evident innovations come. Some other passages
where he uses *falsa religio*: *Divinae Institutiones, II.1,1 (religiones deorum*
falsas esse) ; II.3,12 *(falsae religiones)* —ed. cit., pp. 95, 105. Most significantly,
the title of Book I of the *Divinae Institutiones* is *De Falsa Religione*. Is this
the first time in human history that such a concept is formulated? (Cf. below,
p. 30 at note 48.)

31 For example, in the *Epitome*, Cicero's *De Natura Deorum* is mentioned in ch. 17 (22) (Blakeney, p. 12; Brandt & Laubmann, p. 688) and is
quoted elsewhere; Lucretius is mentioned and quoted in ch. 20 (25) (p.14; 691)
(Divinae Institutiones, II, 3, 10 [p. 105]).

32 The opening passage of the *Divinae Instituiiones* might seem to
be accepting an interesting divergence between these two, since he speaks of
the learned being led to true philosophy, the unlearned to true *religio* (*ut et*
docti ad ueram sapientiam dirigantur et indocti ad ueram religionem—I. 1, ed.

cit., pp. 2–3; cf. *Epitome*, proem, Blakeney ed., p. 3) . This refers, however, to a possible distinction in the mind of the two groups concerned, a distinction that is resolved in his own mind, and will be in his book. Later he explicitly conjoins them: *Nunc quoniam falsam religionem, quae est in deorum cultibus, et falsam sapientiam, quae est in philosophis, refutavimus, ad veram religionem sapientiamque veniamus. Et quidem conjuncte, quia cohaerent, de utraque dicendum est. Nam Deum verum colere, id est nec aliud quidquam, quam sapientia* ('Since we have, then, refuted false *religio*, which lies in the cults of the gods, and false *sapientia*, which the "philosophers" have, let us now come to true *religio* and *sapientia*. And indeed one must speak of the two together, since they are of a piece. For to worship the true God, is nothing other than *sapientia*'—*Epitome*, chap. 36 [41], Blakeney, p. 27; Brandt & Laubmann, pp. 711–712.) He also coins the important phrase and concept, *vel sapiens religio vel sapientia religiosa* (ibid., chap. 37 [42], p. 28; 712) : 'philosophic *religio*; or alternatively, religious philosophy'. This follows the interesting aphorism *et ideo falsa religio est, quia non habet sapientiam, ideo falsa sapientia, quia non habet religionem* (ibid., chap. 36 [41], p. 28; 712) : '*Religio* is false without philosophy, in just the same way as philosophy is false, without *religio*'.

33   The term thrēskeia occurs four times in the New Testament: Acts 26.5, Colossians 2.18, James 1.26,27. These passages are considered for their original meaning below, chap. 3 at notes 29,30. In all cases the Vulgate renders it by *religio*, and only here is this word employed. In the James passage the corresponding adjective *thrēskos* is also found, which comes out inescapably therefore as *religiosus*. This latter term is found four further times in all in the Vulgate: once in the Old Testament (see our next note) , and three in the New: Acts 2.5; 10.2; and 13.50. Here it renders *eulabeis, eusebēs*, and *sebomenos* respectively ('devout, god-fearing')—terms that occur richly in the New Testament (see below, chap. 3 at note 28) but are normally translated by Jerome in other ways. For the passages with the noun, the Latin is as follows: *secundum certissimam sectam nostrae religionis vixi Pharisaeus;* . . . *religione angelorum. . . ;* and *Si quis autem putat se religiosum esse . . . huius vana est religio. Religio munda, et immaculata apud Deum et Patrem, haec est. . . .*

34   The term *religio* occurs 9 times in the Vulgate Old Testament. Quite typical is the following passage, Exodus 12.43 (in English, the Authorized Version of 1611: 'And the Lord said . . . , This is the ordinance of the passover): Hebrew, חקת הפסח; Septuagint Greek, ὁ νομος του πασχα; Latin, *Haec est religio Phase*. Illustrative also is Exodus 12.26 ('Your children shall say . . . , What mean ye by this service?'): Hebrew, העבודה הזאת; Greek, ἡ λατρεια αὐτη; Latin, *Quae est ista religio?*. The other seven passages are: Exodus 29.9; Lev. 7.36 and 16.31; Num. 19.2; Esther 8.17 and 9.27; 2 Mac. 6.11. Further, *religiositas* occurs three times (all in Ecclesiasticus: 1. 17, 18, 26), translated (AV) 'religiousness' and 'godliness'. *Religiose* is found once: *bene et religiose* (no Hebrew; Greek original, καλως και ἀστειως (2 Mac. 12.43) . The adjective *religiosus* occurs once (for its four further occurrences in the New Testament, cf. preceding note): *Benedicte omnes religiosi Domini* (not in Hebrew; Greek original, . . . παντες οι σεβομενοι τον κυριον . . . 'All ye that worship the Lord'—the Song of the 3 Holy Children, added in the Apocrypha after Daniel 3.23; verse 67,—Daniel 3:90).

35　With *religio* Augustine throughout uses *cultus,* and the verb *colere,* as virtually interchangeable. In an early passage, for instance, he writes of converting men from superstition directed to idols and from worldly vanity *ad verum cultum veri Dei* (*De Vera Religione,* 11.2—text used: J.-P. Migne, ed., *Patrologiae Cursus Completus . . . series latina . . . ,* vol. 34, Paris, 1861, col. 123). This last I would translate 'to true (or, genuine) worship of Him who is truly God'. My use of the word 'genuine' here and as a suggestion for the title of the work, is because Platonic thinking is nowadays rather rare, and yet one misunderstands the term 'true' here if one thinks of it in any but a Platonic sense—that is, that true *x* is an ideal to which actual *x*'s approximate more or less closely. (We preserve this usage in a phrase like 'true courage'.) 'True' in the today more prevalent logical sense, applying to propositions rather than to substances, is misleading if applied to Augustine's (and I shall later argue, to anybody's) conception of religion. We shall return to this consideration.

35a　'I wrote a book *Concerning True Religion* in which I argued at great length and in many ways that true religion means the worship of the one true God, that is, the Trinity, Father, Son and Holy Spirit.' These are Augustine's own words, as translated in *Augustine: Earlier Writings, selected and translated with introductions by John H. S. Burleigh,* London, 1953, being vol. VI of John Baillie, John T. McNeill, Henry P. van Dusen, edd., *The Library of Christian Classics;* p. 218. I write 'comes close to saying' because the Latin original does not bear this interpretation quite literally: . . . *multipliciter et copiosissime disputatur unum uerum deum, id est trinitatem, patrem et filium et spiritum sanctum, religione uera colendum . . .* (*Retractationes,* book I, chap. 12 [or, according to an alternative system of numbering, 13] section 1. Edition used: *Corpus Scriptorum Ecclesiasticorum Latinorum,* vol. 36: *Sancti Aureli Augustini Retractationum libri duo,* ed. Pius Knöll, Vindobonae & Lipsiae, 1902, p. 57).

36　The term occurs once in this book, referring perhaps to the established Church, in the phrase *haereses a regula Christianitatis aversae.* The full passage reads: *Haereses namque tam innumerabiles a regula Christianitatis aversae, testes sunt non admitti ad communicanda Sacramenta eos qui de Patre Deo, et Sapientia ejus, et Munere divino aliter sentiunt et hominibus persuadere conantur, quam veritas postulat*—chap. v, 8 ('Innumerable heresies that have been turned aside from the rule of *Christianitas* are witness to the fact that persons are not admitted to sacramental communion who think, and try to persuade men to think, differently about God the Father, and His Wisdom and the divine Gift, from what truth lays down'. Migne ed., col. 126).

I have not searched Augustine systematically in his other writings for further uses of this term, but have found that it does occur in his treatise on the Sermon on the Mount, book 2, chap. 12, section 41, Migne ed., vol. 34, col. 1287: *qui autem in professione Christianitatis inusitato squalore ac sordibus intentos in se oculos hominum facit*—where I would take it as probably a verbal noun, 'in professing to be Christian'.

In *De Vera Religione* he uses (coins?) the phrase *Christiana religio* as something that we should hold and follow (*tenenda est nobis Christiana religio. . . . Hujus religionis sectandae caput est . . .* —vii. 12, 13; Migne ed., col. 128), should know and follow (*ea est nostris temporibus Christiana religio, quam cognoscere ac sequi, securissima ac certissima salus est*—x, 19; Migne ed., col. 131). He has later on, however, to explain this usage, and almost to apologize for it, assuring his readers that by calling this *religio* 'Christian' he did not mean that it was something new (with Christ), but that it had acquired this new name (*non quia prioribus temporibus non fuit, sed quia posterioribus hoc nomen accepit*—Retractationes, I.12 [13], 3; Knöll ed., p. 59—see further below, at note 46, and all his discussion in this paragraph [Knöll ed., pp. 58–59]). However, in this later work he reiterates the usage (*Christiana religio, quae uera religio est*—ibid., I.12 [13], 1, Knöll ed., p. 57). When he says that Christian worship is true worship, and then considers in what sense the adjective *Christiana* is justified, should his phrase be understood perhaps as 'worship through (*or*, in?) Christ'? Or the usage is formally parallel to what we would mean in saying 'Christian courage is true courage'.

37 The concluding sentences of the work. Burleigh trans., p. 283. Latin text, in the Migne edition cited, col. 172.

38 Cf. chap. vi, section 10 (Migne ed., col. 127), speaking of 'this Catholic Church': *omnibus tamen gratiae Dei participandae dat potestatem*, 'to all it gives the possibility of participating in the grace of God', though not all take advantage of this *potestas*, for- he goes on to say that some of its members are chaff, and also (section 11) there are true Christians (or, men truly Christian?—the actual term is not in the Latin) outside of it. (Burleigh, op. cit., p. 231, translates *potestas* as 'power'.)

39 Especially in chapters iii, iv. Also he elsewhere affirms *non aliam esse philosophiam, id est sapientiae studium, et aliam religionem*: 'philosophy, that is, an assiduity for wisdom, is not something different from *religio* [the worship of God]' (v, 8; Migne ed., col. 126).

40 *Nulla substantia malum est*—in the passage cited below, note 42.

41 xxxviii, 69; the Burleigh trans. (above, note 35a), p. 260. The original reads: *Nego esse quemquam istorum qui nihil colendum existimant* (Migne ed., col. 153). Throughout this discussion (chapters xxxvii, xxxviii; section 68ff., Migne ed., coll. 152ff.) he does not use the noun *religio* much but the (correlative?) verb *colere*.

42 I have reversed here the passage in which Augustine speaks of the descent of man from heaven to earth; man's problem, of course, is to return (and God in His mercy has provided a path to enable him to do this): *Ita homo de paradiso in hoc saeculum expulsus est, id est ab aeternis ad temporalia, a copiosis ad egena, a firmitate ad infirma: non ergo a bono substantiali ad malum substantiale, quia nulla substantia malum est; sed a bono aeterno ad bonum temporale, a bono spirituali ad bonum carnale, a bono intelligibili ad bonum sensibile, a bono summo ad bonum infimum* (chap. xx, section 38, Migne ed., col. 138).

43 This meaning of the term is by implication: the final paragraph of the work opens *Religet ergo nos religio* ('Let therefore *religio* bind us . . .') (lv, 113, Migne ed., col. 172), which implies that at this point at least he is

accepting the derivation of *religio* from *religare* 'to bind'. It is to be noted, however, that twenty-five years later (by which time he had outgrown any feeling that this term could adequately serve to express a Christian's faith: cf. below, note 49) in his *De Civitate Dei* (book x, chap. 3—in the Emanuel Hoffmann edition, *Corpus Scriptorum Ecclesiasticorum Latinorum*, vol. 40, parts 1, 2, Vindobonae &c, 1899–1900, part 1, p. 450) he makes a kind of pun with *eligentes . . . religentes . . . neglegentes*, which favours the etymology from *leg-* 'to collect' or *lig-* (cf. above, notes 5, 6). On this point see also his etymology *ei* (sc. *Deo*) *uni religantes animas nostras, unde religio dicta creditur* (*De Vera Religione*, lv, 111, Migne ed., col. 171) and his later comment thereon, *Retractationes* I. 12 (13). 13 (Knöll ed., pp. 64–65).

44 This translates the opening of the final paragraph (lv, 113; Migne ed., col. 172). The work has built up towards the end in a crescendo of ever more lofty *religio*: a series of sentences and paragraphs each beginning with *non sit nobis religio . . .* ('Let not ours be a worship' of various lesser matters). This series is designed to wean the mind away, in Platonic fashion, from all earthly and visible things to the one pure true God. (Were he writing in the twentieth century, we may imagine that he would add a paragraph *non sit nobis religio religionis . . .* , 'let not our worship be of religion', 'let us not be tied to religion'.) Then the final paragraph opens: *Religet ergo nos religio uni omnipotenti Deo; quia inter mentem nostram qua illum intelligimus Patrem, et veritatem, id est lucem interiorem per quam illum intelligimus, nulla interposita creatura est.*

45 The phrase *vera religio* had occurred earlier in Christian writing, but without explication; and it is sometimes difficult or impossible to be sure just what was meant. I have not found it in Tertullian, but the early third-century writer Minucius Felix uses it once, Arnobius (c. 300 A.D.) twice, and Lactantius (ca. 250–ca. 325 A.D.) often. For Lactantius it is clearly a personal ideal, 'true religion' and not 'the true religion': he equates it with piety ([*uera*] *religio id est summa pietas*) and justice (*religio quae eadem iustitia est*) and correlates it with philosophy or wisdom (*uera religio ueraque sapientia*). Similarly Arnobius writes that the one who, having ousted the old *religiones* from the earth (correlative with *deorum cultum*), is accused of being *religionis extinctor*, 'a destroyer of religion' (correlative with *impietatis auctor*), is rather he who *ueram in orbe religionem induxit* (correlative with *pietatis aperuit ianuas*). I would translate this as 'brought true religion (worship, piety) into the world', rather than 'the true religion', supporting this rendering by the terms to which it is parallel and those with which it is contrasted. Indeed this author proceeds to specify this *religio* as a knowledge (*sic*) of God and of prayer to Him (*an ulla est religio uerior officiosior potentior iustior, quam deum principem nosse, scire deo principi supplicare, qui bonorum omnium solus caput et fons est perpetuus . . . ?*). 'True' here equals 'genuine'.

When Minucius Felix, on the other hand, writes *ad ueram religionem reformauit*, it is difficult to say on the basis of the immediate context alone whether this should be translated 'he converted [him] to true religion' or '. . . to the true religion' (or, to proper worship).

The references for this note are: Minucius Felix, *Octavius*, 1.5; Arnobius, *Adversus Nationes*, II.2; Lactantius, *Divinae Institutiones*, IV. 3, *Epitome*, chap. 64 [69], chap. 44 [49]. The texts are found in the series *Corpus Scriptorum*

Ecclesiasticorum Latinorum as follows: vol. 2, ed. Halm, p. 4; vol. 4, ed. Reifferscheid, pp. 48–49; vol. 19, edd. Brandt & Laubmann, pp. 278 (line 12. For *uera*, see the critical apparatus; also the context, especially the preceding sentence; and see also other edd.), 754, 722. For the last two, in the Blakeney ed. cit., pp. 53,34.

46 *Retractationes*, I. 12 (13) .3. *Nam res ipsa, quae nunc Christiana religio nuncupatur, erat et apud antiquos nec defuit ab initio generis humani, quousque Christus ueniret in carne, unde uera religio, quae iam erat, coepit appellari Christiana* (Knöll ed., p. 58). The translation that I have given is taken from the Burleigh version cited above (note 35a).

47 St. Augustine is too devout a man to use, for what he has in mind, the humanist phrase 'my religion'. Tertullian and Arnobius had earlier used *nostra religio, vestrae religiones, vestra religio*; this indicates, of course, when one reflects on it, that the word *religio* had a different meaning for them. This is made clear, for instance, in that Arnobius can write *religio nostra nunc nata est* ('our *religio* has just now been born') (*Adversus Nationes* ii, 73), which shows that he is thinking of something that has come to exist observably in time, a phenomenon of this world, over against Augustine's *religio* by which he refers to the pre-existent and transcendent ideal that the Church (newly born) makes available. Arnobius is conscious enough of the same point as Augustine; but he is using different terms to designate the eternal and the temporal aspects respectively of that in which he is involved. For he explicitly states, *non ergo quod sequimur nouum est, sed nos sero addidicimus quidnam sequi oporteret ac colere. . . . religio nostra nunc nata est* ('Therefore what we follow is not new, but it is we who only recently have learned what it is that one ought to follow and worship. . . . Our *religio* has just now been born'—II. 72, 73; Reifferscheid ed., pp. 107, 108).

Note, also, Arnobius's correlation between *religiones vestrae* and *nostram* (II. 72; p. 106)—where the former cannot signify an ideal since Arnobius does not believe in it, that is, does not believe it to be ideal. This shows that he is using the word *religio* to represent the outward facts of religious life for both the pagans and for his own group. Arnobius, also, uses the plural for Christian *religiones* (II. 72; p. 107; cf. note 21 above)—which indicates forcefully enough that he has in mind something quite different from modern usage for this word, while 'Christian rites' is normal enough also today.

48 Sir Sarvepalli Radhakrishnan, *The World's Unborn Soul: an inaugural lecture delivered before the University of Oxford*, Oxford, 1936, p. 10.

49 It seems perhaps a little harsh to write this sentence after the exhilarating work of St. Augustine under the heading *religio*. It is prompted, however, by what the 'idea of religion' had become, and has become since, despite his essay. Moreover, it is curious to note (cf. above, note 43) that twenty-five years later when writing his greatest work, *The City of God*, Augustine himself had become disenchanted with the term. At one place in that book he is casting about for a word to express the worship due to the Deity (*deitati debitus cultus*) and settles on a Greek one, λατρεια, stating dissatisfaction with various Latin terms (including *cultus*) and remarking that even

religio (*ipsa religio*: the *ipsa* is interesting), though it seems to signify this, and is used for θρησκεια, is yet not quite right because in Latin usage, among not only the uneducated but also the most learned, it refers to human ties as well as to those to God. (This might perhaps support slightly Wilt's thesis of a secularist element in the verbal tradition: cf. note 6 above.) He goes on in similar vein for *pietas* and its Greek equivalent. Evidently he is searching for words that will express something for Christians that the vocabulary of earlier Roman faith did not have. And he has come to the conclusion that *religio* will not quite serve. (*De Civitate Dei*, chap. X, section 1). A little later on (section 3) he sums up in the words, *Hic est Dei cultus, haec uera religio, haec recta pietas, haec tantum Deo debita seruitus.* (Hoffmann, ed. cit., part 1, pp. 445–447, 451.)

50 Salvianus (*fl.* 440 A.D.) is the earliest entry for the subsequently standard use of *religio* as meaning 'vita monastica' in Du Cange, *Glossarium mediae et infimae Latinitatis*, 8 voll., Paris, 1840–1857; s.v. *religio* (vol. 5, 1845).

51 James A. H. Murray *et al.*, edd.: *A New English Dictionary on historical principles*, reissued with supplement, 12 voll. and several parts, Oxford, 1933; s.v. 'religion'. Hereafter this work is cited as *Oxford English Dictionary*.

52 *Ibid.*, for the English; for Latin, this is first attested in Du Cange, op. cit., for 1143 A.D. (*religiosus ordo, monastericum*). Cf. *religio nova* for the Cistercian order, 1201, ibid., s.v.

53 Of Aquinas's numerous writings, the word *religio* appears in the title of two, both minor ones (*opuscula*); and in both cases the significance is the monastic life. *Contra impugnantes Dei cultum et religionem* (an address delivered 1257 and published 1266, in answer to an attack on the religious orders by one William of the French village St. Amour), and *Contra retrahentes a religionis ingressu* (1270). These are available in English as follows: *An Apology for the religious orders, by Saint Thomas Aquinas, being a translation of two of the minor works of the Saint. Edited, with introduction, by the Very Rev. Father John Procter . . .* , London, 1902.

54 Devoted to this matter is Question 81 (*De Religione*) of the Second Part of the Second Part. This question is discussed for eight articles. For the Latin text, I have used the Ottawa edition, *S. Thomae de Aquino ordinis praedicatorum Summa Theologiae, cura et studio Instituti Studiorum Medievalium Ottaviensis*, Ottawa, 5 vols., 1941–1945. I have consulted also the indices reprinted as vol. 4 (n.d.) in the Marietti [reprint] edition, 3 vols., Taurini/Roma, 1948–1950. The English translation: *The 'Summa Theologica' of St. Thomas Aquinas. Literally translated by Fathers of the English Dominican province*, London, New York, &c, 21 vols., 1911–1922 and index, 1925. II.2.81 appears in these editions as follows: Latin, vol. 3, pp. 1829–1836; Eng. trans., vol. 11, pp. 7–22.

55 The phrasing here is my own, not Aquinas's; I believe it is a fair statement in modern terms of his position in, for instance, *Summa Theologica*, II.2.81, article 1 and II.2.82, article 2. (Ottawa ed. cit., vol. 3, pp. 1829–1831, 1837–1838.) (See also note 57, just below, the *Summa* references.)

56 '*Religio* is not faith, but a witnessing to faith through outward signs' (*religio non est fides, sed fidei protestatio per aliqua exteriora signa*) —ibid., II.2.94, article 1, *ad* question 1. (Ottawa ed. cit., vol. 3, p. 1911a; English trans., vol. 11, p. 182, reading, '. . . a confession of faith by outward signs'.)

57 Cf. above, note 55. Also, '*Eusebeia* [the Greek term, designating an attitude towards holiness] is the same thing as *religio*' (*eusebeia . . . est idem quod religio*), ibid., II. 2.80, art. un. ad 4 (Ottawa ed. cit., vol. 3, p. 1829a); again, '*religio* primarily and chiefly signifies *latria*, which renders worship to God by the expression of true faith' (see next note). In the *Summa*, he affirms that *religio* has both internal and external acts, the latter being 'secondary and subordinate' to the former (II.2.81, art. 7; this point is reasserted in the next Question, 'Of Devotion'—II.2.82. Latin text, ed. cit., vol. 3, pp. 1835, 1836– 1840; English trans., ed. cit., vol. 11, pp. 19, 23).

58 In the *Summa Theologica* he is etymologically undecided (II.2.81, art. 1; ed. cit., vol. 3, p. 1830), but in *Contra impugnantes* he explicitly follows St. Augustine in accepting the etymological derivation from *ligare* 'to bind', and speaks of the creature having become—by creation—in a sense separated from his original existence in God. 'Hence, every rational creature ought to be reunited to God. . . . Therefore, St. Augustine says [*De Vera Religione*], "*Religio* reunites us to the one Almighty God." . . . *Latria*, which is the worship of God as the Beginning of all things, is the duty of man in this life. Hence, *religio*, primarily and chiefly, signifies *latria*, which renders worship to God by the expression of [true faith]. Hence, all that belongs to [true faith], and the homage of *latria* which we owe to God, are the primary and chief elements of *religio*. But, *religio* is affected, in a secondary manner, by everything by which we manifest our service to God. . . . *Religio*, then, bears a two-fold meaning. Its first signification is *that* re-binding, which the word implies, whereby a man unites himself to God, by faith and fitting worship. Every Christian, at his Baptism, when he renounces Satan and all his pomps, is made partaker of [true *religio*]. The second meaning of *religio* is, the obligation whereby a man binds himself to serve God in a particular manner, by specified works of charity, and by renunciation of the world. It is in this sense that we intend to use the word *religio* at present' (Procter, *op. cit.*, pp. 50–51, except that I have substituted *religio* here for Procter's translation 'religion', and further have taken the liberty of rendering *vera fides* and *vera religio* according to my own interpretation of Aquinas's meaning for these phrases, as [true faith] and [true *religio*], rather than Procter's 'the true faith', 'the true religion').

One gets perhaps from this passage a sense that *religio* is taken (unlike St. Augustine's more Platonic view) more as a binding than as a bond, and therefore, as in our preceding note, as something that man does, worship, rather than something that touches him. Yet the final sentence of the non-monastic part, in which man participates in a true something, restores the Augustinianism.

59 At another place he speaks of *religio Christi: Contra retrahentes* . . . , opening sentence. To relate this to any of the things that the author says elsewhere about the word, such as those that we have cited, I find that I must take this as an objective genitive: 'the worship of Christ' (or, the bond uniting us with Christ). Procter, op. cit., translates it as 'the religion of Christ':

'The religion of Christ appears to aim chiefly at diverting the attention of mankind from material things, in order to concentrate their thoughts on such as are spiritual' (p. 377). This may not preclude an objective genitive, though it is hardly usual in current English; taken in any other signification (the religion that Christ instituted? or in a much later, systematic sense as 'the Christian religion') this would make a fourth and very novel Thomist usage. At least, as something that seemingly acts, impinging upon man from the outside, I personally cannot quite fit it under any of the other three.

60 For example, the very considerable work of a recent scholar illustrates and clinches this in its title as a study of the Middle Ages: G. G. Coulton, *Five Centuries of Religion*, 4 vols., Cambridge, 1923–50. Yet as the author himself remarks, the first volume 'deals mainly with Religion in the medieval sense, in which the Religious was the cloistered soul' (vol. I, p. xxxiii). He justifies this by remarking that 'cloistered religion . . . is one of the most striking examples, in all world-history, of institutional religion on a great scale' and that 'no modern study of medieval piety [*sic*] could avoid putting it in the foreground' (*loc. cit.*). He says 'having dealt in these volumes . . . with the cloistered religion of the later Middle Ages, I hope to pass on later to a study of other religious currents during these five centuries' (*ibid.*).

61 It is always impossible to be sure, and difficult even to be quite sanguine, that something is not to be found. All that one can report is that one has not found it. Excluding the two works of Aquinas previously mentioned (above, note 53) and one other work in which *religio* means the religious orders (Stephanus of Bohemia: *Apologia pro sacris religionibus monasticis, ca.* 1400—reference in the Hurter work about to be described, II, col. 1388), I have objective reasons for doubting that works are known from this period in whose title the word *religio* occurs. These reasons are chiefly that, apart from other general inquiry, I have systematically searched the indexes of Hurter and of Migne. These are as follows:

H. Hurter, *Nomenclator literarius theologiae catholicae.* Tomus I, . . . *Aetas prima: ab . . . initiis ad . . . (1109)*, 3rd ed., Oeniponte, 1903; Tomus II, . . . *Aetas media . . . ab anno 1109-1563*, 2nd ed., Oeniponte, 1906. (The third volume, covering the period 1564-1663, was not considered relevant for this segment of our work.) J.-P. Migne, ed., *Patrologiae Cursus completus . . . ab aevo apostolico ad tempora Innocentium III* (anno 1216) . . . *series latina*, Paris, 221 volumes, 1844-64 (reissued, 1866-1890): . . . vol. 218, *Indices*: xiv, *Index alphabeticus omnium patrologiae latinae operum, juxta eorum titulum digestus* (columns 659-798).

This last enters 8,000-some titles not merely of works but of sections (*libri,* chapters) and even of topics treated. (See also the indexes remarked below in the next note.) Of this considerable number only three (unless my hurrying eye has failed me) include the adjective *religiosus*, each time in the plural and in the sense of members of monastic orders (a passage from St. Yves's *Decreta*, Migne, vol. 161, coll. 1171-1176; an opuscule of St. Peter Damian, vol. 145; an anonymous opuscule *Liber de religiosorum poenitentia et tentationibus*, vol. 213). The noun *religio* occurs in eight entries. Five of these pertain to the early (pre-medieval) writers that we have discussed for the Roman Empire period: Firmicus (see above, note 24) (wrongly attributed in the Migne index to St. Eusebius, the immediately preceding author in the volume cited; the column number, however, is correct for Firmicus) ; the first chapter (*liber*) of Lactantius's *Divinae Institutiones* (above, note 30); Augustine's *De Vera Religione* (above, at notes 35–44); and modern commentaries on these. Another is a passage (a few sentences) in St. Isidore's *Etymological Dictionary* (Book VIII, chap. 2; Migne, vol. 82, col. 295) in which the word *religio* is entered and briefly considered; and another a passage (vol. 161 '1267', lege 1265–1272) from the *Panoramia* of St. Yves (Ivo) of Chartres, where the question of Christians' marrying Jews is considered, along with the question of marriage between pagans of whom one subsequently is baptized (*Sancti Ivonis Carnotensis episcopi . . . Panoramia seu Decretum*).

In this last case, it is interesting and perhaps significant to note, St. Yves himself does not use the term *religio*. It is apparently his nineteenth-century editors that have added to his text a heading *Conjugum debet esse inter homines ejusdem religionis* ('Marriage must be between persons of the same religion') , and the nineteenth-century indexers that have in the index entered this passage under the title *Religionis diversitate in matrimonio (decreta de)* ('Prescription concerning difference of religious affiliation in marriage') .

There remains, then, one work. About it I am far from clear, but one must record that it may be one exception to my generalization about the appearance of the word *religio* in mediaeval book-titles. Migne (vol. 184, coll. 771-792) publishes *S. Bernardi Clarae-vallensis . . . Instructio sacerdotis seu Tractatus de praecipuis mysteriis nostrae religionis* ('St. Bernard of Clairvaux: Priest's Instruction, or, Treatise on the outstanding mysteries of [our religion? or, our order?]') . The attribution of the work to St. Bernard is to-day generally questioned (see Leopoldus Janauschek, *Bibliographia Bernardina*, Vindobonae, 1891, p. vii) ,and there is some uncertainty about the title (it is also known as *Gemina Crucifixi;* Janauschek enters it as *Instructio Sacerdotis, seu: Tractatus de praecipuis mysteriis* nostrae religionis, al. *Gemina Crucifixi;* why the last two words of the second possibility are not in italics here I have not been able to clarify) . The Cistercian order has currently under weigh a considerable enterprise of studying and publishing the works of St. Bernard (see Jean Leclerq: *Etudes sur Saint Bernard et le texte de ses écrits,* Analecta Sacri Ordinis Cisterciensis, *annus* ix, fasc. 1-2, Romae, 1953) . Whether this work will be examined is not clear (see Leclerq, op. cit., p. 39, para. 2) . Although it may turn out that, whoever the author, the word *religio* in this title is genuinely mediaeval, nonetheless I think that the statement in my text about books 'written specifically on "religion" ' may not need to be modified. One may note that, whatever the title, the noun *religio* does not occur in the text of this treatise.

More problematic is the situation in the later midde ages, since Migne covers the period only until 1216. We have already dealt with Aquinas; and Pietro de Monte (*ca.* 1440) is considered below (note 64) . Hurter, op. cit., is perhaps not so careful as one might wish, but in any case his fairly substantial material has been used to induce my generalization; and it seems perhaps not unreasonable to suppose that if he (and at a much reduced level of probability, I, working also from other less systematic sources) has missed a book on *religio* then perhaps it was a relatively minor one. I may add, however, that of course I should be more than grateful to have my attention drawn to any items that I have missed.

62 Apart from the question of book-titles, which I have tackled in a somewhat systematic way, the larger issue of the use of the word generally in

the mediaeval period is one on which, not being in any sense a scholar in this field, I am unable to give any but superficial impressions. These, however, are that the term (except in the sense of monasticism) was little prevalent. Some objective support to this view is given by the facts that emerge from a study of the other indexes of Migne. In vol. 219 he has (index 53, coll. 317–320) an index of 'religion' very much 'in general' (*Index de religione generatim spectata*; it is also truly remarked *Agimus de Religione sensu generaliori sumpta* —coll. 317–318); and in vol. 220, his index 155, *Index de Virtutibus*, has a heading 'On faith, as worked out in practice through the virtues of *religio* and piety' (coll. 610–612, of which *de religione* is coll. 610–611), which contains 141 references. I have examined only a few of these at random; to study them all might prove rewarding, though one must constantly bear in mind that the nineteenth-century editors' minds are at work here as well as the mediaevals'. This is true of all indexing of ideas or things rather than of words.

A more complete study would seek the help of the eight entries s.v. *Religio* in the index to Migne's indexes: *Elucidatio in 235 tabulas Patrologiae Latinae, auctore Cartusiensi*, Rotterdam, 1952, Pars Prima, p. 71. Again, however, not all of these entries are references to the word; for example, the *Elucidatio* entry *religio Judaica* refers to A 1205, i.e. Migne, vol. 218, col. 1205, where an entry is *De religione Judaica*, which in turn refers to II. 595 and II. 355. Of these the former is *Tertulliani Liber Adversus Judaeos* and in the latter case Tertullian uses the phrase *vero Judaeo* and speaks of the true Jerusalem. In other words, the term *religio* itself is not found in the original texts.

The dictionaries, of course, are also helpful though they indicate the meanings in which the word was used rather than the frequency of usage, and most dictionaries of mediaeval Latin give only those mediaeval usages that are not also classical.

The matter might be summed up negatively: that I have not found much evidence to suggest that the term or concept *religio* was frequently used in the European Middle Ages.

63   One method of my investigation here has been through book-titles. Of those in which the term 'religion' or its cognates occurs (also, rarely, *Godsdienst*) I have been able to find in all, fifty-nine for Western Europe in the sixteenth century, 103 for the seventeenth (including translations where relevant, but not counting re-editions unless the title changed). After 1700 I have collected not all such titles that I could find, but such as seemed to me significant. I have noted also every instance that I could find, up to about 1850, of the name of 'a religion' ('Christianity', 'Judaism', 'Mahometanism', etc., and their counterparts in other languages) in titles. After that date, I have studied such as seemed significant. More thorough and systematic search would undoubtedly uncover more examples, particularly of pamphlets, but I have reason to believe that the material on which my study is based is reasonably representative, at least of influential works. I realize, however, that there is no way of being sure that what seems the first instance of a particular usage may not have had precedents beyond my ken. It would seem, however, that general tendencies must be adequately reflected in the material here surveyed.

In defense of the use of titles as a potentially fruitful method for the study of the history of ideas, three considerations may be brought forward. First, on the practical level, it can be reasonably manageable as an objective and controllable index of terms, frequencies, and the like. Secondly, it seems to

me both that an idea if it is really important to a literate society will probably
be reflected in the titles of books, and contrariwise that the occurrence of
an idea in a book-title is a fairly significant factor in fixing that concept in the
thinking of the society in question. Third, if a man writes a book on a designated notion, one may be reasonably sure of being able to know what he
means by it, which is not always the case if he uses the term only incidentally
in the course of his writing.

I certainly do not put forth the method as foolproof, but simply as one
handy and perhaps useful way of dealing with otherwise bewilderingly vast
material.

64 In 1524 in Rome the following was published: *Miraculum Eu-
charistiae per Epiphanium a Petro de Monte Episcopo Brixien. Latinis lit-
teris traditum & e Bibliotheca palatina in lucem editum.* The first page
begins with the heading *Opusculi de sacramēto Eucharistie ex Epiphanio in
latinū a Petro de Monte traducti, ad . . . Nicolaum . . . cardinalem Phrohę-
mium;* signature B reads *Explicit prohęmium, incipit Epyphanius.   Christianae Religionis . . . .* The text from this point on is the same as that
presented in J.-P. Migne, *Patriologiae Cursus Completus . . . series graeca*,
Paris, vol. 120, coll. 273–286 under the following heading: *De religione christiana libellus. Ex Epiphanio in Latinum a Petro de Monte traductus.* If the
latter title is original, it is the earliest occurrence of a book bearing the
phrase *religio Christiana* as its title that I have found. This would seem to
me then a matter of prime importance. Who wrote the original Greek seems
uncertain, and what its Greek title may have been is unknown (the Greek
text seems to be lost). Migne (loc. cit.) assigns the original to Epiphanius
Monachus, A.D. 1110. Hurter, op. cit., vol. I, col. 769, states that it may perhaps have been originally by Christophorus, patriarch of Alexandria, who
died in A.D. 836. The British Museum general catalogue enters the 1524 edition under St. Epiphanius, Bishop of Constantia in Cyprus (A.D. 315?–403);
but enters the Migne edition under Epiphanius Hagiopolita.

The Latin translation was made apparently about 1440; in any case before
1443, when the cardinal to whom it is dedicated died (Johannes Haller, ed.,
*Piero da Monte: ein gelehrter und päpstlicher Beamter des 15. Jahrhunderts
—seine Briefsammlung*, Rome, 1941 [*Bibliothek des deutschen historischen
Instituts in Rom, Band XIX*], introduction, p. 87). Haller has seen in the
Vatican library the manuscript containing this work, which he reports as an
autograph (*op. cit.*, introd., p. 109) (he seems perhaps unaware that it has
been published); and gives its title as *Libellus de religione christiana ex
Epiphanio in latinum a me Petro de Monte traductus . . .* (*op. cit.*, p. 87, fn.
219). The *a me* would seem to confirm that this wording is the translator's
own.

On Monte (Petrus/Piero/Pietro de/da/del) see Agostini Zanelli, 'Pietro del
Monte' in *Archivio storico lombardo. Giornale della Società storica lombarda*,
Serie quarta, vol. vii (*anno xxxiv*), pp. 317–378 (1907); vol. viii (*anno eod.*),
pp. 46–115 (1908), though this seems to have no material on this particular
translation. The justification for including him here as Renascence rather
than under the Middle Ages (above, note 61), apart from the date (and he
was Italian, from Venice), is that, as this translation itself suggests, he was in
those circles involved in the revival of Greek learning in Italy. Haller, *op. cit.*,

pp. 79–83, has published letters of his written from England in which he complains sadly of being away from the Greek writings that he much loved.

If this were the first book ever written on '[the?] Christian religion', this would seem interesting. One's excitement is somewhat diverted, however, on realizing that *religio* here refers in a then traditional fashion to ritual practice, and *Christiana religio* is the Christian sacrament, the eucharist.

65 The work was published both in Italian and in Latin: *Libro di Marsilio Ficino Fiorentino della Cristiana religione*, and *Marsilii Ficini Florentini de Christiana religione liber*, both without date. Kristeller (*Supplementum Ficinianum: Marsilii Ficini Florentini . . . opuscula inedita et dispersa . . . ed. Paulus Oscarius Kristeller*, 2 vols., Florentiae, 1937) gives arguments (pp. lxxvii–viii) to show that it was written in Latin in 1474, translated and published in Italian in 1474 (i.e., in the year ending March 1475), and then first published in its original Latin only subsequently, in 1476. It was soon fairly frequently republished, in various parts of Renascence Europe. I have used the Latin version in a 1576 Basel edition of his works: *Marsilii Ficini Florentini, insignis Philosophi Platonici, Medici, atque Theologi clarissimi, Opera*, 2 voll., in which it is the first item, I. 2ff.

66 See note 64 just above. Augustine had used this juxtaposition of words (above, note 36). My feeling that it had not been much used for the intervening thousand years, though impressionistic, has as one basis the fact that the term *religio* itself was, we have seen, not very current. And when used, it was chiefly in senses to which the adjective *Christiana* would hardly apply. Cf. also below, chap. 3, where the practice of naming particular 'religions', including the Christian, is considered historically.

67 I have found fifty-nine instances of book-titles with it to the end of the seventeenth century, and this accounts for one-third of all my titles for that period that include 'religion' at all. I have some evidence that the greatest frequency by far is in the first half of the eighteenth century, though by that time it was giving way to 'Christianity' as a term. See chap. 3, pp. 76, 77.

68 *Diuina prouidentia . . . quamuis permittat uarijs locis atque temporibus, ritus adorationis uarios obseruari. Forsitan uerò uarietas huiusmodi, ordinante Deo, decorem quendam parit in uniuerso mirabilem*—op. cit., I. 4.

69 See *De Christiana Religione*, especially chap. 1 ff. (*Opera*, vol. I, pp. 2 ff.); and also his *Theologica Platonica*, especially Book 14, chap. 9 (ibid., I. 319–321), of which the title is *Religionem esse humano generi maximè omnium propriàm & veridiam*. Note the often quoted *Cultusque diuinus ita fermè hominibus est naturalis, sicut equis hinnitus, canibusúe latratus* ('The worship of God is as natural to men, as is neighing to horses or barking to dogs') (I. 319–320). Skills and speech, even reason, he says, the beasts share with us, in a rudimentary form. *Quid ergo reliquū est, quod omnino solius sit hominis? Contemplatio diuinorum* ('What then is left, that is altogether uniquely human? The contemplation of what is divine') (I, 319).

NOTES FOR CHAPTER TWO

70 *Cum religionem dico, instinctum ipsum omnibus Gentibus communem naturalemque intelligo, quo ubique & semper prouidentia quaedam regina mundi cogitatur & colitur—Theol. Plat.* (Opera, I. 320).

71 *Omnes hominum opiniones, affectus, mores, excepta religione, mutantur*—loc. cit.

72 Ficino, however, did introduce a new idea of his own at this point, in the general theory of idealism: that of the *primum in aliquo genere*, according to which one member of a genus may be the full representative of the essence of that genus, only the other members of the series falling short. See, for instance, Paul Oskar Kristeller, *The Philosophy of Marsilio Ficino*, trans. Virginia Conant, New York, 1943.

73 *Omnis religio boni habet nonnihil* . . . *—De Christiana Religione*, heading of cap. iv (*Opera*, I, 4). Ivan Pusino, in an otherwise valuable study ('Ficinos und Picos religiös-philosophische Anschauungen', *Zeitschrift für Kirchengeschichte*, Gotha, 44: 524 [1925]), takes *omnis religio* as 'every religion', which seems to me seriously to misunderstand what Ficino is saying.

74 *Deus in se ipso summum est bonum, ueritas rerum, lumen fauorque mentium. Illi igitur Deum prae caeteris, imò soli syncerè colunt, qui eum actione, bonitate, ueritate linguae, mentis claritate, qua possunt, & charitate qua debent, sedulò uenerantur. Tales uerò sunt, ut ostendemus, quicunque ita Deum adorant, quem admodum Christus uitae magister, euisque discipuli praeceperunt* (De Christiana Religione, cap. iv; Opera, I, 4). *Christus est idea, & exemplar uirtutum* ('Christ is the type and pattern of the virtues'—ibid., chapter heading of cap. xxiii; I, 25. See also all this chapter; pp. 25-26). The third sentence here cited is more literally, 'Such in truth are those, as we will show, whoever worship God in the way that Christ, life's teacher, and his disciples, set forth'; but I believe that the paraphrase in my text does not distort Ficino's general thesis.

75 *Si philosophia ueritatis sapientiaeque amor ac studium ab omnib. definitur. Veritas autem & sapientia ipsa solus est Deus, sequitur ut necque legitima philosophia quisque aliud, quam uera religio, necque aliud legitima religio, quam uera Philosophia* (from the section entitled *Laus Philosophiae moralis; Opera*, I, 668).

76 One must perhaps stress the 'rather' here: Ficino was not a totally original thinker, of course. The continuity of his thought with scholasticism is discernible, and he is clearly reviving Augustine, nor had the Platonic tradition ever entirely lapsed in the Catholic Middle Ages. Nonetheless it is generally recognized that he was historically significant, and his ideas represent a shift in the general trend of religious thinking.

77 Latin *fides*, German *Glaube*.

78 His works have, since 1883, been in process of publication in a great Weimar edition (*D. Martin Luthers Werke: kritische Gesamtausgabe*,

222

edd. J. C. F. Knaake *et al.*), of which some eighty volumes have so far appeared. I have not, I confess, gone through them to see whether he uses the Latin term *religio* or the German derivative *die Religion*. I have, however, gone through the analytical index in the catalogue of Dr. Williams's Library, London, which enumerates the contents (*Inhalt*) giving 542 headings (titles of individual works and entries). About a quarter or less are in Latin, the rest in German. In these the two terms do not appear; Luther joins the ranks of those who never wrote a book or tract on religion. [I have since come across two instances of Luther's using the word, one in Latin and one in German. The former is in his commentary (Wittenberg, 1532, 1534) on Isaiah 44: 18, where he affirms . . . *Huic de faventi gratis et bene facienti sic credere est vera religio et iustitia vera* (op. cit., vol. 25, p. 287), where the parallel with 'true (sc. genuine) justice' makes evident a meaning in the order of true (genuine) piety (in both these the English definite article would be out of place), and the predicating construction with *credere* suggests that this is in effect a verbal noun, something that a person does. (A century later Europe began to designate by 'religion' what it is that men believe, not the fact of their believing it, their holding it in faith—see below.) The German instance is that in his translation of the Bible he rendered by it the εὐσέβεια of III Macc. 2: 32: *sie verliessen ihre hergebrachte Religion nicht*. The Zurich Bible here uses *Frommigkeit* (piety). *Religion* occurs nowhere in the latter Bible, nowhere else in Luther's.]

79   This point is somewhat developed below, chap. 5; see especially note 9, and notes 4-10.

80   In Luther's titles (above, note 78), the term *Gottesdienst* occurs twice, both times in its literal (and modern) sense of the service (worship service) of God: *Von Ordnung Gottesdiensts in der Gemeine*, 1523, (*Gesamtausgabe*, vol. 12, 1891, second entry), and *Deutsche Messe und Ordnung Gottesdiensts*, 1526 (ibid., vol. 19, second entry). That he had in mind, in writing this compound, its literal significance rather than a later composite entity-idea, is illustrated in that the subtitle to the latter reads *Unterrichtung wie man die Kinder möge führen zu Gottes Wort und Dienst*. One can also observe the process of the forming of the compound in his translation of the Bible: in his 1522 translation he renders James I, 27 as *Eyn reyner und unbefleckter Gottis dienst* . . . , whereas in 1546 he writes *Ein reiner und unbefleckter Gottesdienst*. . . . In both cases, be it noted, he translates in the preceding verse Θρῆσκος, which in English, AV, becomes 'he is religious', and on which the point of verse 27 depends, by *er diene Gott* (*Gesamtausgabe: Die deutsche Bibel*, 7.Band, Weimar, 1931, pp. 390, 391). Similarly, in 1522 he renders Θρησκεια in Acts 26, 5 as *nach der aller strengisten secten unsers Judentums*, but in 1546 as *die strengste Secten unsers Gottesdiensts* (ibid., pp. 520, 521).

Although I have not made a systematic study of the history of the terms in German and Dutch, it would seem that *Godsdienst* has become in the latter language a standard counterpart of 'religion' of the Romance languages and English, in all its senses (although *religie* occurs also early), while in German this latter concept, slow in its acceptance, was rendered by *Gottesdienst* and *Religion* for a couple of centuries after the Reformation, more recently the latter prevailing alone, the former reverting to its use for worship service. The vigorous activity in German university circles in the nineteenth century in the study of *die Religion* as an academic concept, and in the use of this term for it, probably contributed both to the prevalence of the term then in the language, and to the protests against it in our century (see preceding note). The fact that the word *Religion* is virtually not found in the German standard Bible doubtless contributed to the particular development.

81 *De Vera et Falsa Religione, Huldrychi Zuinglij Commentarius* . . . Tiguri, 1525. I have used the edition in the *Corpus Reformatorum,* voll. 88–100: Emil Egli & Georg Finsler (later also Walther Köhler *et al.*), edd., *Huldreich Zwinglis sämtliche Werke,* Band I, Berlin, 1905, Bde. II–XIII, Leipzig, 1908–1944, where the *Commentarius* is vol. 3, pp. 622–912.

82 *De vera falsaque religione Christianorum*—*loc. cit.,* p. 638. It is the opening sentence after the dedication (to the King of France) and the brief *Ad lectorem.*

83 For instance, *additione 'veri' et 'falsi' religionem a superstitione distinguimus* (ibid., p. 639), and elsewhere; as in the next note.

84 *Falsa religio sive pietas est, ubi alio fiditur quam deo* (ibid., p. 674).

85 The remainder of the paragraph explicating the quotation given in our preceding note; and see his later section *De Ecclesia* (ibid., pp. 741 ff.).

86 The phrase *falsa religio* appears here for the first time in a book-title. Moreover, so far as I have ascertained it had not been used at all for a thousand years. Somewhat over a millennium earlier it had served as a chapter-title for Lactantius (above, note 30), and had been a fairly common concept in that century. In the meantime, however, it had lapsed. Indeed it was not a phrase that could serve the Middle Ages; so far as my discernment goes the term *religio* with the adjective *falsa* during all those centuries would have constituted a rather meaningless combination.

The earlier meaning, moreover, in Lactantius's day, was somewhat different from Zwingli's also. The *religio* that the Fathers were denouncing as false was not the *pietas* of the Romans, their inward attitudes, but rather their practices and rituals, and the gods in whose name they worshipped. Those whom Zwingli was accusing of being falsely religious in his day were believers in the same God, 'members of the same religion' to use our modern terminology, as was he. Against Cicero, on whose side Zwingli (below, our next note) aligns himself, Lactantius (above, note 5) had pressed his asseveration that what matters is Whom one worships, not how. Catholics and Protestants both worshipped the same 'whom'; it was by meaning by *religio* something inward that Zwingli was able to apply the terms 'true' and 'false' to it. Moreover, Zwingli looked forward to meeting in heaven 'all the saints and sages and believers and the steadfast and the brave and the good who have ever lived since the world began', a fellowship among whom he names Socrates and several others not members of his Church—for which Luther apparently took him sharply to task (*The Library of Christian Classics*, vol. 24: *Zwingli and Bullinger. Selected Translations with introductions and notes by . . . G. W. Bromiley*, London, 1953, pp. 275, 349 ref. 64).

87 True *religio* for him, however, is not a purely Platonic ideal. The fact that he uses also '*falsa*' suggests already the difference in vision between him and St. Augustine, his one quasi-predecessor whom to some degree he was consciously rehabilitating. Like Ficino, Zwingli sees man's tending towards God (*a*: see references below), which he names *religio*, as God-given (*b*); unlike Ficino, he sees it as effectively given not in creation, so that it is natural, stable, and universal, but in Christ. (For Zwingli, man is created in God's likeness, but sin has intervened) (*c*). Thus he follows his section *De religione* (ibid., pp. 665–674) with a section *De religione Christiana* (pp. 674–91); which phrase his modern German editor translates as *die Christus-Religion* (*d*), and which we might render, 'the piety that Christ has made available' (Zwingli elsewhere uses the phrase *pietas Christiana*). This is certainly not yet 'the Christian religion', but it was doubtless a step in that direction, particularly for those whose perception was less vivid and whose faith less intense.

Further, in accepting etymologically Cicero's notion of *religio* as signifying being solicitous in attending to those things that pertain to the worship of the gods, Zwingli specifies *pietatem totam Christianorum* as embracing all aspects —faith, life, laws, rites, sacraments; and would designate them all in his term *religio* (*e*). There is a difficulty here in that the five things named are not coordinate, the last three existing outside men. The use of *pietas* in this connection is revealing, but I am uncertain whether he means to identify *religio* with these things (which would not cohere either with his usage elsewhere in the treatise, or with the Cicero that he has just quoted) or, more logically, to include them in the sweep of those things to which *religio* in men's hearts is directed. (The last three items listed might perhaps be taken as meaning the performance of these things?)

The references for this note are as follows, all from *Werke*, vol. III: (*a*) *In* [*deum*] *tendit religio, homo . . . religione tendit in eum* (p. 640); (*b*) *Solius ergo dei est et ut credas deum esse, et eo fidas* (p. 642); (*c*) pp. 665ff.; (*d*) W. K. (= Walther Köhler), in his introduction to the *Commentarius*, p. 597: '*Die Christus-Religion (das ist religio Christiana)*'; (*e*) *Nos enim 'religionem' hic accipimus pro ea ratione, quae pietatem totam Christianorum, puta: fidem, vitam, leges, ritus, sacramenta, complectitur* (p. 639).

88 *Christianae religionis institutio, totam ferè pietatis summam, & quicquid est in doctrina salutis cognitu necessarium, complectens: omnibus pietatis studiosis lectu dignissimum opus, ac recens editum. Ioanne Calvino . . . auctore*, Basileae, MDXXXVI.

89 Between Ficino and Calvin probably it was more common but I have found *religio* as a title twice in Catholic works with the adjective *monastica* (Jodocus Clichtoveus, *De laude monasticae religionis opusculum*, Parisijs, 1513; and Johannes Doc [Docus], edidit, *Apologiam monasticae religionis*, Salamanticae, 1528, Antverpiae, 1529, etc. [the second of these I have not myself seen; the ref. is from Hurter, op. cit., II, col. 1388]); once (Catholic) in the plural (see below, note 132), once in the Zwingli work that we have consid-

ered (above, note 81), and otherwise three times with the adjective *Christiana*, forerunner of Calvin's catechisms. These last are not really books but little manuals. The first, n.p., n.d., but presumably Augsburg, 1510, uses *religio* in two senses, first on the title-page, *Tabula Christiane religionis utilissima*, and secondly in a list of the nine kinds of 'benignity', which are *religio*, *pietas, innocentia, humanitas*, etc., of each of which a formal 'definition' is then given; the first is *Religio. Est virtus divinitatis curam gerens cerimoniamque offerens*. The booklet is constituted of mnemonic elements for the Christian: it gives the Apostles' Creed, the Lord's Prayer, the golden rule, the Ten Commandments, the two commandments of grace, ten canonical precepts, a list of feast days, etc. There are thirty-two pages in all; no 'editorial comment'. The word *religio* in the title, then, signifies something of the order of Christian prescriptions or norms?—something that can be arranged in tabular form, anyway, and is closer to the traditional sense of ritual observance or pattern than to the 'virtue' defined later in the booklet. A similar work, *Tabula Christianae religionis*, appeared in three editions, the last dated 1520, the others undated but probably 1515, 1520, probably Rome. The first 'catechism' was on a similar pattern, except that the Ten Commandments, the Apostles' Creed, the Lord's Prayer, etc., are in this case each followed by an expository commentary: *Catechismus: das ist ain anfengklicher Bericht der Christlichen Religion von den Dienern des Evangelions zu Augsburg für die Jugent aufs kürtzest verfasset und beschriben* (n.p., n.d.; sc. Augsburg, 1532–1533). These not only supplied the form of which Calvin's work is a subseqûent flowering, but also apparently popularized among the laity as well as contributing directly to Calvin the subsequently extremely important concept and phrase *Christiana religio*.

90 *Institutes of the Christian Religion . . . translated from the original Latin, and collated with the author's last edition in French, by John Allen*, 3 vols., London, 1813. This translation was soon republished in the United States, and has gone through many editions on both sides of the Atlantic, and is still being reprinted. Presently another translation, also popular, appeared, reiterating this unfortunate wording: *Institutes of the Christian Religion*, trans. Henry Beveridge, 3 voll., Edinburgh, 1845–1846 (another ed., 2 voll., Edinburgh, 1863). The most recent translation also, although apparently carefully and conscientiously done, perpetuates the nineteenth-century misrendering of the title, seemingly on no better grounds than that it has dominated English-speaking usage lately—though there is an awareness by the translators that the first part, at least, of the established phrasing is not truly represented in 'this form [that] has since prevailed' (see fn. 3, p. xxxi; but see also the to me disappointing and unconvincing translation of the full title on p. xxxiii); *Calvin: Institutes of the Christian Religion*, ed. John T. McNeill, trans. Ford Lewis Battles *et al.*, *The Library of Christian Classics* (John Baillie *et al.*, edd.), vol. XX, London & Philadelphia, 1961.

91 That this is at least in part what Calvin himself had in mind for this word is suggested by his own use of the term 'Instruction' in his 1537 French version (see below, note 95) of what he entitled the following year in Latin *Catechismus sive Christianae religionis Institutio . . .* , Basileae, 1538, and later *Catechismus . . . hoc est formula erudiendi pueros in doctrina*

Christi (p. 679 of the Geneva, 1550, edition of the larger *Institutio* and the catechism together). This point is recognized in a modern English version: *Instruction in Christianity by John Calvin—an abbreviated edition of 'The Institutes of the Christian Religion'—newly translated from the Latin into simple modern English by Joseph Pitts Wiles*, Stamford [1920] 1921 (in 'The Translator to the Reader', pp. 6–7, Wiles demurs to the translation 'The Institutes': '. . . But *Institutio* means "Instruction" '—p. 7; I demur to his translation 'Christianity'; on this see below, chapp. 3, 5). I have found a seventeenth-century version, no doubt modelled on this, of 'Institution' in English as a verbal noun in Calvin's sense: *A Short Catechism for the Institution of Young Persons in the Christian Religion. . . . Composed for the use of the schools in South-Wales*, London, 1652 (published anonymously; actually by Jeremy Taylor).

Nonetheless, I somewhat incline to the view that 'instruction' in modern English does not exhaust the reference of *institutio* in the mind of Calvin or of his first readers; that the term carried some sense of 'establishing', 'setting up', 'laying the foundations of'. This feeling is rendered by Scottish translations the following century: *Iohn Calvines Catechisme, contayning at large the whole grounds of Christian Religion*, Aberdeen, 1628: *The Catechisme, containing at large the grounds of Christian Religion . . .* , Edinburgh, 1645. (Note the word 'grounds'.)

92 Calvin thinks of religion *extra Christum* and *sine Christo*, but in the singular; in the 57 volumes of Calvin's works in the *Corpus Reformatorum*, according to the index in vol. 58 [-59], the plural occurs only once, outside 'religions' being mentioned in that the study of them is damned *(religionum exterarum* [lege *externarum?*] *studium damnatur* [with ref. to vol. 27, 217; though on checking this seems inaccurate]. For all these reff., see *Ioannis Calvini Opera quae supersunt omnia . . . edd. Guilielmus Baum, Eduardus Cunitz, Eduardus Reuss,* [=*Corpus Reformatorum,* voll. 29–87], vol. 58 [-59], *Index Nominum et Rerum*, s.v. *religio,* coll. 185–186).

93 § 1. *Omnes homines ad religionem esse natos. Quum nemo hominum reperiatur, quamlibet barbarus sit, ac toto pectore efferatus, qui non aliquo afficiatur religionis sensu. . . . § 2. Quid inter falsam ac veram religionem intersit. Quoniam hoc communi sensu receptum est, si a vita nostra absit religio, miserrime nos vivere, adeoque brutis pecudibus nihilo excellere, nullus est qui a pietate cultuque Dei prorsus alienus videri velit . . .*—the opening passages of *Catechismus sive Christianae religionis Institutio . . .* , Basileae, 1538; in Calvin, *Opera*, vol. 5, col. 323.

94 Under the impact of naturalistic presuppositions, however, this term also has perhaps lost its transcendent reference, suggesting to many a certain attitude on the part of persons without consideration of what it is an attitude towards.

95 An example of Ficino using *pietas* interchangeably for *religio*: the next sentence after his defining his term *religio* as quoted above, note 70, is, *Ad quam certe pietatem causis praecipuè tribus inducimur* (loc. cot.). Zwingli, *passim*: for instance, *religio vel potius pietas . . . ; pietas ergo, sive religio*

NOTES FOR CHAPTER TWO

haec est . . . ; *pietas est, religio est* (all these, op. cit., p. 668) ; *vera religio, vel pietas, haec est* (p. 669) ; *falsa religio sive pietas* (p. 674) . Calvin: see the last few words of note 93 just above; and in his first catechism, which is in French (*Instruction & Confession de Foy dont on use en l'Eglise de Genève,* n.p., n.d. [sc. 1537]) , he couples *religion* with *piété et recognoissance de Dieu* (Albert Rilliet & Théophile Dufour, edd., *Le Catéchisme français de Calvin publié en 1537: réimprimé pour la premiére fois d'après un exemplaire nouvellement retrouvé,* Genève, 1878, p. 4. (In the Latin version of the following year: *falsam ac veram religionem. . . . vera autem pietas. . . . veri Dei cognitionem . . .—Opera,* vol. 5, coll. 323–324.)

96   For Zwingli's own remarks on how he understood *Commentarius,* see his preface *Ad lectorem: Werke,* vol. III, p. 637.

97   *The Institution of Christian Religion, wrytten in Latine by maister Ihon Caluin, and translated into Englysh according to the authors last edition* [by T. N., viz., Thomas Norton], 3 pts., London, 1561.

98   *Catechismus, sive prima Institutio, Disciplinaque Pietatis Christianae, Latine explicata,* Londini, 1570. The author was 'A.N.', viz, Alexander Nowell. The phrasing of this title is significant; cf. also its translation in the next note.

99   *A Catechisme, or first Instruction and Learning of Christian Religion; Translated out of Latine into Englishe,* London, 1570. Note 'instruction' for *institutio,* 'religion' for *pietas.* The translator is again T. Norton.

100   These are taken respectively from: the title; the preface (unpaginated) ; id.; folio 1a, 1b, 2a, 5a.

101   Although these and other instances are, to my mind, quite clear, there are one or two passages that involve perhaps some ambiguity. Norton in his preface uses 'religion', five times without the article (in each of these cases 'piety' or 'religiousness' could reasonably be substituted) , and once with 'his' (=God's) : 'avauncing his religion and glory'. In the translation he uses the word thirteen times, again in twelve of these without the article except where the grammatical construction requires it, in the qualified clauses: 'the religion that . . .'. This last is correlated with the one exception: 'The Religion that I professe . . . is the same whereof the Lord Christ is the author and teacher, and which is therfor properly and truly called the Christian Religion . . .' (folio 1 a/b) , which sounds perhaps objectified. Later on on the same page, however, this is defined, in response to a question: 'Christian Religion is the true and godly worshipping of God, and kepying of hys commandments'. Also, in the previous case it would be not impossible to translate the same Latin as, 'The piety that I profess is the same whereof the Lord Christ is the author and teacher, and which is therefore properly called Christian piety'—which gives a different meaning in modern English, but whether it would have to Mr. Norton I do not know.

In the following passage a plural occurs twice, though strictly a plural of 'worshipping' would be equally possible: 'As there is onely one true God, so

228

there be but one godly worshyppyng and pure Religion of one onely God. Otherwise we should daily forge ourselves new Fayned Religions, and every nation, every citie, and every man, would have his owne severall Religion, yea we should in our doings follow for our guide, not Religion and true godlynesse the begynnyng and foundation of vertues, but superstition and deceitful shadow of godlinesse. Which is most plaine to see, by the sundry and innumerable not religions but worse than dotying superstitions of the old Gentile nations, who otherwise in worldly matters were very wise men.' —folio 2 a/b.

One has a glimpse here of the early stages of that transition that we study next.

102 This particular matter does not operate either in languages such as Latin where there is no article, nor normally in those such as French, Spanish, Italian, and German where the article is usually constant. Calvin's *Institution de la religion chrestienne*, 1541, introduced the phrase into French in a form in which it has remained unchanged until today (except for the spelling *chrétienne*), despite the change in meaning. Curiously, however, in his earliest use of *religion* in French, where he links it with *piété et recognoissance de Dieu* (above, note 95) he does write it without the article in a heading in his introduction to the French Catechism: *Quelle différence il y a entre vraye & faulse religion* (Rilliet et Dufour, op. cit., p. 4). Though many of them do not reproduce the English discrimination between an abstract or generic noun without article and a concrete noun with one, all the languages of Europe do register a change of form between the singular and the plural, which last testifies a major innovation in thought, as we shall see. In the case of French, also, it might be argued that Calvin's first vernacular equivalent for *religio* was not 'religion' but 'foi', in that his 1538 *Catechismus sive Institutio Christianae religionis* of which the 1541 version was that given above, had behind it originally not that but the now recently discovered *Instruction & Confession de Foy* of 1537.

103 *Semper et ubique* is a favourite phrase of Ficino's, in his insistence on the universality and stability of the religious sense.

104 *Deinde quia Deum non infinita ipsius maiestate, sed fatua stupidaque ingenii sui vanitate metiuntur, a vero Deo ita desciscunt. Proinde quantalibet colendi Dei cura sese postea fatigent, nihil efficiunt: quoniam non Deum aeternum, sed cordis sui somnia et deliria pro Deo adorant. . . . Sed veri Dei cognitionem ab ipso petunt, non alium concipientes, quam qualem se ipse exhibet ac declarat*—Introduction to the 1538 Latin catechism (*Opera*, vol. 5, col. 324). In the 1537 *Instruction . . .* : men hold God *en quelque vénération* but conceive Him not according to His own nature but *par la folle & Estourdie vanité de leur esperit . . . ilz adorent, non pas le Dieu éternel, mais les songes & resveries de leur cueur au lieu de Dieu* (Rilliet & Dufour, op. cit., p. 5). (To anticipate considerations of chap. 5 below, it is interesting to note that Calvin could write this way concerning the religious life of other people when in fact he knew virtually nothing about it.)

105 'recognoissance de Dieu'—*Instruction . . .*, Rilliet & Dufour, op. cit., p. 4; *veri Dei cognitio*, Catechismus, 1538, *Opera*, vol. 5, col. 324.

107   The first version of this was a poem in Dutch: *Bewys van den Waren Godsdienst in ses Boecken gestelt, By Hvgo de Groot*, n.p., 1622; there were three editions the same year. The larger and better known prose revision was *De Veritate Religionis Christianae*, Paris, 1627. There were numerous later editions; the Latin text was widely read for at least a century, and was commonly used as a school textbook in, for instance, England into the nineteenth century. Of translations in whole or in part there were scores altogether, in German, French, English, Dutch, the Scandinavian languages, and even Welsh and Hungarian.

108   He speaks of other religions not as false, but as having, in addition to what they have in common with each other (and with the Christian), certain special errors (*cum singula religionum genera quae se Christianis oppunent, . . . praeter id quod inter se habent commune, proprios quosdam errores habeant*, pp. 195–196). He speaks of the Christian as 'surpassing' rather than as contradicting the others (*Christianam religionem praestrare aliis omnibus*; elsewhere, *omnes alias . . . exuperat*, p. 119). He speaks of men participating (*sic*) in so great a good (*sic*) as the truth that the Christian finds (*ut non modo de reperta veritate sibi gratuletur, sed et aliis . . . opem ferat, et eos tanti boni participes faciat*, p. 195). And he is concerned with a pious trustfulness by which man is disposed to faithful obedience to God, with the hope and true love of God and of one's neighbour, to the end of having God because of His own goodness (*. . . pia fiducia; qua compositi ad fidele obsequium in Deum toti recumbimus, . . . unde et spes exurgit, et verus amor tum Dei tum proximi . . . ut . . . ipsum . . . habeamus pro sua bonitate*—p. 122).
However, this orientation is quite overborne by the presentation of *religio* as a system of precepts. This is illustrated all too forcefully in the table of contents, for instance, which comprises chiefly a series of propositions to be proved. And he explicitly speaks of the precepts as the main points on which he commends the Christian religion, and by which it excels all others (*de praecipuis, id est, de praeceptis illis ex quibus Christianam religionem maxime commendavimus*, pp. 135–36; *Quo Christiana religio omnes alias . . . exuperat, est summa sanctitas praeceptorum*, p. 119). Further, even in the passage to which we have just referred as illustrating his concern with what is in man's heart in its direct relation to God and its love of neighbour, he uses the term *religio* not for that inner quality but for a something that rests on that.
Page references are to the Oxford, 1820 edition: Hugo Grotius, *De veritate religionis christianae*.
The work is basically one of apologetics; cf. below, note 115.

109   *Christiana religio Deum, ut mentem purissimam, pura mente colendum docet, et iis operibus, quae suapte natura etiam citra praeceptum honestissima sunt. Sic non carnem vult circumcidi, sed cupiditates; non ab omni opere, sed ab illicito nos feriari; non pecudum sanguinem aut adipem Deo sacrare, sed, si opus sit, pro veritate ipsius testanda nostrum offerre sanguinem; et, quae de bonis nostris egentibus damus, Deo data credere . . .* (p. 121). It is rewarding to reflect carefully on the fact that the subject of the verb *vult* in this last sentence is not God, as an earlier age would have held and as I hope that we may learn to say again, but *Christiana religio* ('The

Christian Religion [or, Christian religiousness, Christian piety?] wishes us to circumcise not our flesh but our desires . . .') .

110 *De Veritate prout distinguitur a Reuelatione, a verisimili, a possibili, et a falso,* Paris, 1624. London editions in Latin appeared in 1633, 1645, 1656, etc. I have seen also the third of a series of editions in French, [London?] 1639.

111 *Christoph Frankens Diss. de religione naturali contra naturalistas et remonstrantes, maxime Eduard Herbertum et Curvellaeum, Kilon, 1666,* and *Georg Titii Diss. de insufficientia religionis mere naturalis ad consequendam vitam aeternam, Helmstad., 1667,* seem to be the first two uses of the phrase. Unfortunately I have not been able to see copies of either of these works. The reference for the first is from Johann Anton Trinius, *Freydenker-Lexicon, oder Einleitung in die Geschichte der neuern Freygeister ihrer Schriften, und deren Widerlegungen . . . ,* Leipzig und Bernburg, 1759, p. 586; that to the second, ibid., p. 303 and also [J. G. Walch] *Io. Georgii Walchii Bibliotheca Theologica Selecta, litterariis adnotationibus instructa,* 4 voll., Ienae, 1757–1765, I. 783 (which gives Ger. rather than Georg in the name of the second author) .

112 The two writers in the previous reference were attacking the notion that they posited, as the titles show; but the term was taken over by men who welcomed it. It is first used in an English title by a Christian bishop in 1675 (*Of the Principles and Duties of Natural Religion; to which is added, a sermon preached at his funerals, by W. Lloyd,* 2 parts, London, 1675 [by John Wilkins]) . Actually this work is, as is indicated, posthumous, the author having died in 1672, but the wording of the title occurs also in the opening sentence, and is therefore presumably Wilkins's own. The circumstances indicate that as well it had the approbation of the introducing editor, J. Tillotson, Dean (and afterwards Archbishop) of Canterbury.

I have found the phrase also in a Frenchman's work towards the end of the century (*De Naturali religione liber . . . auctore Petro Chauvin,* Roterdami, 1693) . It occurs in the highly influential work of another English clergyman, Samuel Clarke, *A Discourse concerning the Unchangeable Obligations of Natural Religion, and the Truth and Certainty of the Christian Revelation; being eight sermons preach'd . . . in the year 1705,* London, 1706 (which was repeatedly reissued and discussed) . And in 1714 it is used (again posthumously) by a Christian writing against it (see next note).

'The religion of nature' occurs from 1725 (William Wollaston, *The religion of nature delineated,* London, 1725—there was a fifth edition already by 1731) . Both phrases have a lively history in the fifty years following the 1730 publication of the highly provocative *Christianity as old as the creation; or the Gospel, a republication of the religion of nature,* London, anonymous (actually by Matthew Tindal). Perhaps the last really major use of the phrase is in David Hume's also posthumous work, *Dialogues Concerning Natural Religion,* London, 1779, though the concept became enshrined also in the Gifford Lectures.

113 The first book in which I have found this dichotomy is Thomas Halyburton, *Natural religion insufficient; and revealed necessary to man's*

happiness in his present state; or, a rational enquiry into the principles of the modern deists: wherein is largely discovered their utter insufficiency to answer the great ends of religion . . . ; and particularly the writings of the learn'd Lord Herbert. . . . , Edinburgh, 1714. It was given wide currency in Joseph Butler, *The Analogy of religion, natural and revealed, to the constitution and course of nature* . . . , London, of which there were three editions in 1736 and a steady stream throughout the eighteenth and into the nineteenth centuries. I have not been able to see a copy of *De Praestantia religionis revelatae prae naturali,* whose title, with the author as 'C. J. Sucro' and the publication as 'Hal. 1741' are recorded in Trinius, op. cit., p. 304. It would be significant to know whether this was by a Roman Catholic.

114 'Christianity is a scheme quite beyond our comprehension'; p. 146 of the Edinburgh, 1824, edition. The qualification modifies the predicate somewhat, but the general presuppositions are evident as to the concept of what religion is. For the use of the term 'Christianity', see below, chap. 3.

115 I have rather come to feel that there is something inherently irreligious in apologetics, wherever it may be found. For an exploration of a modern Islamic instance, see my *Islam in Modern History,* Princeton 1957, London 1958, pp. 85–89, 115–156; New York 1959, pp. 91–94, 119–161.

116 This 'virtually ultimate' practice has recently begun to give way in the United States (on a considerable scale only since the Second World War) to one of categorizing Protestants', Catholics', and Jews' as 'Three Religions'.

117 For example, Iohn Brereley [pseudonym; sc. Lawrence Anderton], *Sainct Austines religion; collected from his owne writinges, and from the confessions of the learned Protestants,* London, 1620.

118 For example: Richard Baxter, *The Grotian Religion discovered, at the invitation of Mr. Thomas Pierce, in his Vindication; with a preface, vindicating the Synod of Dort from the calumnies of the new Tilenus . . . ,* London, 1658.

119 Some examples, which followed on the highly successful work of our next note: George Mackenzie, *Religio Stoici: with a friendly addresse to the phanaticks of all sects and sorts,* Edinburgh, 1663; [anon.] *Religio Clerici,* London, 1681; [C. B., viz. Charles Blount], *Religio Laici: written in a letter to John Dryden, Esq.,* London, 1683; [anon.] *Religio Laici; or, a layman's faith, touching the supream Head . . . of the Church,* London, 1688.

120 *Religio Medici*—the first two editions, anonymous, appeared in London, 1642; the first authorized ed., London, 1643; the author was Sir Thomas Browne. The work was very influential, and was repeatedly reissued. Browne's use of *religio* here comes close to the general practice of his time in designating not, in the sixteenth-century way, his sense of the holy but in the seventeenth-century one, what he believed. Yet whereas in the case of 'the religion of' a large group this age, almost as in a modern anthropologist's description, abstracted the belief system from the lives of the people who lived it, in this case the abstraction is minimal, and the essay is deeply

personal and alive. Illuminating of this and of his sincerity is his reference to his belief, propositionally, 'that there is such a City as Constantinople, yet for me to take my oath thereon, were a kinde of perjury, because I hold no infallible warrant from my owne sense to confirme me in the certainty thereof' (pp. 129–130). The charm and significance of his work surely lie precisely in the fact that the religion that he expresses, though theoretical, is his own; genuine, sincere, and real.

It is interesting to compare what the word 'religion' means in the title of his book with what it means in the phrase 'the Christian religion'. A tendency has developed to feel today that his use of the word is rather special and in some sense secondary, whereas the meaning in the phrase 'the Christian religion' (or 'the Buddhist religion' or whatever) is the primary meaning— which is perhaps the measure of our disintegration. The notion that there is something real that the phrase 'the Christian religion' names, while 'Browne's religion' is only metaphorical or secondary, has surely to be challenged. I shall argue later that the term 'religion' should be dropped; but if there is anything in the world to which it can legitimately be applied, surely it is in the sense that there are as many religions in the world as there are people. It is legitimate, of course, to operate at any level of abstraction or generalization that one pleases, so long as one recognizes that at any level other than that of discussing Browne one has left what is real, and that one *is* abstracting, generalizing.

Readers may have noticed that the Latin *religio* is (by its author) rendered into English by the personalizing term 'faith' in the 1688 work of this class listed at the end of our preceding note.

121 *La religion des Hollandois representée en plusieurs lettres écrites par un officier de l'armée du roy à un pasteur et professeur en théologie de Berne,* Paris, 1673 (anonymous; actually by Giovanni Battista Stoppa— *Catalogue général des livres imprimés de la Bibliothèque Nationale,* Paris, s.v.); *The Religion of the Dutch, represented in several letters from a Protestant officer in the French army* . . . , London, 1680.

122 *The Religion of the Church of England the surest establishment,* anon., London, 1673; 2nd ed., 1678.

123 Some examples: [Richard Baxter], *The Safe Religion; or, three disputations* . . . , London, 1657: (cf. below, next note); Richard Baxter, *The Vain Religion of the formal hypocrite* . . . , London, 1660: [John Goodman], *The Old religion demonstrated in its principles* . . . , London, 1684; [Edward Ward], *Modern religion and ancient loyalty: a dialogue,* London, 1699.

124 These are from the preceding century: Matthias von Zittart ('Matthias Aquensis'), *Catholicae ac orthodoxae religionis adversus lutheranam haeresim Matthiae Aquensis miscellanea assertio,* Coloniae, 1542; *Ruewardi Tapperi* . . . *orationes theologicae, potissimas religionis catholicae controversias, et verum Germaniae pacandae rationem explicantes* . . . [Cologne], 1577 (the title here is apparently by the editor, Tapper's pupil Bishop Lindau, the author having died eighteen years previously). One may compare Faustus Nairomus, *Dissertatio de origine, nomine, ac religione Maronitarum,* Rome, 1679, though this I would translate as 'rite'. On Roman Catholic usage in general, see the next paragraph of our text. 'Reformed Catholike religion' is used

to designate a Puritan Anglican position in the subtitle of the 1657 Baxter work just cited (note 123) : *The Safe Religion; or, three disputations for the reformed Catholike religion, against Popery.*

125   Francis Cheynell, *The Rise, growth, and danger of Socinianisme; together with a plaine discovery of a desperate designe of corrupting the Protestant religion, whereby it appeares that the religion which hath been so violently contended for—by the archbishop of Canterbury and his adherents— is not the true pure Protestant religion, but an hotchpotch . . .* , London, 1643. Richard Baxter, *The Protestant religion truely stated and justified . . .* , London, 1692, is posthumous; I do not know whether the wording is this author's own, who, before he had been excluded from the Church of England by the Act of Uniformity, 1662, had used rather 'reformed Catholike' (above, preceding note) .

126   I say 'apparently', since my evidence for this judgment is certainly short of conclusive, and indeed my investigations on this particular have not been carefully systematic or even deliberate; the somewhat impressionistic generalization has arisen from material unearthed in the course of inquiry into another issue, our main concern. Certainly for the late sixteenth and for the seventeenth centuries many fewer of the uses that I have uncovered are by Roman Catholics; but this could conceivably reflect not much more than the fact that the investigations were carried out chiefly in London libraries. And in any case one could not simply compare the number of Protestant with the number of Catholic uses; the issue is rather the relative frequency of this term in comparison with other terms (faith, rite, etc.) within each group, and the sense (and the weight) given to it. One objective point is that reported in our next note, that the term, where I have found it used in Catholic writing, is primarily in apologetics. The Catholics did not share, so far as I can see, in the Protestants' sixteenth-century use of this word (esp. through Calvin) for piety, almost faith. And in the seventeenth century, for the Catholics it seems to have remained the designation of one element in their complex, not to have named the complex itself, as became the case for Protestant Europe.

To check these impressions in a preliminary and tentative way, I have found that writers picked more or less at random do not seem to use it. To give one example among many, the prolific Cardinal Bellarmino has (in the *Catalogue général des livres imprimés de la Bibliothèque Nationale*, Paris, s.v.) books chiefly on 'Christian doctrine' and (somewhat less) 'Christian faith' (which otherwise continued and has continued a favourite Catholic term) but none including the word 'religion'. One exception to all this is Pascal; see below, note 129. For further discussion of Catholic/Protestant divergence see also below, and esp. note 135.

It should be remarked that doubtless the famous sentence that formulated the settlement of the Peace of Augsburg, 1555, *cujus regio ejus religio*, meant different things to different people; and further that probably those to whom it conveyed an idea that the ruler should set the pattern of institutional procedures, of formal observances, found it more intelligible than those who took *religio* as naming a more personal, subjective involvement.

127   In the century or so following Luther, more than three-quarters of the rather limited number of book-titles by Catholics that I have been able

to find bearing the word *religio* are anti-Protestant; in the latter seventeenth and eighteenth centuries they are anti-deist and anti-'irreligion' as well, or more so. To designate that for which they argue, they use (apart from *fides* and the like) *vera religio, catholica religio, religio Christi* and *christiana religio*. The direct influence of Calvin's writing is presumably to be seen in the titles *Institutio christianae religionis, authore Luca Osiandro*..., Tubingae, 1582, and *Institutionum religionis christianae libri IV ... auctore Jacobo Bayo* ..., Coloniae Agrippinae, 1620 (reprinted Antwerp 1624), though I have not been able to see these books (titles from the B.N. *Catalogue général,* s.vv. Osiander, Lucas, senior, and Bay, Jacques de, respectively).

128 *Hieronymi Plati ... de bono status religiosi libri III*, Augustae Trevirorum, 1601, reprinted Antverpiae 1604, Lugduni 1606, Augustae Trevirorum 1612, and French trans. Lyon 1620, Rouen 1621, Paris 1644 (*Traité du bonheur de la vie religieuse*) (*Catalogue ... de la Bibliothèque Nationale,* s.v. Piatti, Girolamo). Francisco Suarez, *Opus de virtute et statu religionis*..., Lugduni, 1609-10, reprinted ibid., 1625 with the subtitle ...*De varietate religionum tam in genere quam in speciali; de religione Societatis Jesu in particulari....* A compendium of this by Vincenzo Tancredi, *De virtute religionis,* Monte-Regali, is found as late as 1651.

129 Except perhaps since the late-nineteenth-century synthesis, to which we shall presently come—and for the plural, to be considered next: 'the religions' of the rest of the world.
One earlier exception is the perhaps most Calvinistic of all Catholics, Blaise Pascal. In his posthumously published *Pensées de M. Pascal sur la religion, et sur quelques autres sujets, qui one esté trouvées après sa mort parmy ses papiers,* Paris, 1669, he speaks of *la vraye religion,* or more revealingly *la veritable Religion,* which is *la Chrétienne* (also, *la nôtre,* and sometimes *le Christianisme*), over against *plusieurs Religions contraires, . . . toutes fausses* (or, *les autres Religions*). See especially his second chapter. In the Amsterdam, 1712, edition, the reference for that chapter is pp. 12–23; the other phrases that I have cited are common, an illustrative reference for each being, respectively, as follows: pp. 12, 23, 13, 14, 31, 17, 13.

130 An example, which though from late in the period seems illuminating: [Friedrich Spanheim], *Christianae religionis restitutae apud Geneuenses historia, quam ... complexus est F. Spanhemius ... Cum iconibus virorum illustrium quorum opera praecipue Deus collapsam religionem restituit,* Genevae, 1672. In Protestant usage, the phrase 'Christian religion' refers to too ideal a thing for one to speak of its having collapsed. The Catholic, since it designated rather the observances, could use such a phrase in this historical context.

131 Even with the adjective 'Christian', which would make a Protestant almost shudder: *Valent. Alberti: interesse praecipuarum religionum christianarum, in omnibus articulis deductum.* Lipsiae, 1681—ref. from Walch, op. cit., vol. I, p. 656. *Catalogue générale de la B.N.* has the same entry, s.v. Alberti, Valentin, for a fifth edition 1707, and again 1729; German translations are noted in Walch, loc. cit., for 1686, 1708. For the use of the plural among the Church Fathers for Christian practices, see above, note 21.

132 *Dyalogus Johannis Stamler Augustñ. de diversarum gencium sectis et mundi religionibus*, Augustae Vindelicorum, 1508—which is perhaps the first occurrence anywhere of the phrase 'the religions of the world'? An Italian translation, undated, but entered in the British Museum general catalogue as '[1540?]' is: *Dialogo di Giovanni Stamlerno Augustense de le sette de diverse Genti, e de le religioni del mondo*, Vinegia. This is perhaps the first occurrence of a plural for 'religions' in Italian or any modern European language? I have found no further books on 'the religions' until more than a century later—see next note. The 1508 date means that the Stamler work appeared before the Reformation began, but I think it hardly misleading to refer to it as Roman Catholic rather than Protestant.

133 Edw[ard] Brerewood, *Enquiries touching the diversity of languages, and religions through the chiefe parts of the world*, London, 1614; later editions, 1622, 1625, 1635, 1674; translations in French, 1640, 1662, 1663, in Latin 1650, 1659, 1679, 1687, 1701. This was followed in mid-century by the exceedingly influential work, Alexander Ross, ΠΑΝΣΕΒΕΙΑ: *or, a view of all religions in the world, [with the several Church-governments,] from the Creation, to these times. Together with a discovery of all known heresies, in all ages and places [throughout Asia, Africa, America, and Europe]*, London, 1653 (the words in parentheses are from the inner of the two title-pages). At least seven editions of this appeared before the century was out, and in addition translations in Dutch (1663), French (1666, 1669, . . .), and German (1667, 1701, 1717). In each case these translations or the Brerewood are the first titles with the plural in their respective languages that I have found (for Italian see just above, preceding note). Ten years after Ross, Lord Herbert of Cherbury published a comparable work but reverts to the singular: *De religione Gentilium, errorumque apud eos causis: Authore Edoardo Barone Herbert de Cherbury*, Amstelaedami, 1663; later editions, 1665, 1700; English translation also with the singular: *The Antient Religion of the Gentiles, and Causes of their Errors Consider'd: the Mistakes and Failures of the Heathen Priests and Wise-Men, in their Notions of the Deity, and Matters of Divine Worship, are Examin'd; with regard to their being altogether destitute of Divine Revelation . . .*, London, 1705.

The *Oxford English Dictionary*, s.v. 'Religion,' cites the first use (not in a title) of the plural in English in this sense (cf. above, note 51, 52) as 1594: 'The Church of Rome [. . .] did almost out of all religions take whatsoever had any fair and gorgeous show'—Richard Hooker, *Ecclesiastical Polity*, iv. xi. 2 (an echo of *religiones* meaning ritual practice is heard here?).

134 *Dyalogus*, etc., as above (note 132); the following subtitle is added on the first folio: *Dyalogus in modú Comici dramatis formatus: A Iohanne Stamler prespitero: succinte digestus: De Tartorum: Saracenorum: Turcorum: Iudeorum et Gentilium Sectis et Religionibus ac eorundé confutatione et cum nostre apostolice fidei historiarum figuratumque.* . . . It is to be noted, first, that the *religiones* so conceived are to be refuted (*confutatione*); second, that the phrase does not include the Christian, which is named not *religio* but *fides*.

It might be thought that I am making too much of a chance usage; but this is to underestimate the profundity of what is involved in these matters. We shall be examining the question at some length in our chap. 5, below.

135 In the title of the Ross work cited above (note 133), it may be noted that 'religions' is somewhat correlative with 'heresies'. Ross, however, one must remark further, has a basic ambivalence in his attitude, of appreciation and disparagement. This is reflected, actually, in his varying use of terminology, if one reads him carefully. In his 'Epistle Dedicatory' and his defensive 'Preface to the Reader', he on the one hand speaks of religion (in the singular, without the article) as a universal virtue (the Epistle), and on the other hand (the Preface) jeers at the 'false religions' *(sic)* of others ('the multitude of false Religions in the world, by which most men have been deluded; are not we so much the more bound to the goodness of Almighty God, who hath delivered us out of the darkness...'); yet he then uses these to argue from the *consensus gentium* that religion *(sic)* is something universal, good, and socially necessary. Similarly in the title: he has coined the term *pansebeia* ('pan-religiousness'—*sebeia* is a Greek term designating an inner sense of reverence or piety; see below, chap. 3, notes 4, 28) as a universalist personalist singular, and has followed it with the depersonalized or schematic plural.

I believe that I am not being fanciful in regarding it as not insignificant that the first Protestant uses of the plural are so late (a century to a century and a half after the Catholic) and not insignificant that it was Catholics who first formulated it. As we have already observed, Catholics were not much involved in the Protestant's sixteenth-century use of *religio* for piety, almost faith. They, following the non-Augustinian early Fathers in the designation of ritual practice and observance, and their own mediaeval usage in the monastic sense (both of which had plurals current), had a much more concrete, observable reference in mind. As we have seen, they were not hesitant to use it in the plural even for Christian sectarian practices. In fact, I doubt whether there was much difference at the time between the significance of Stamler's title, 1508 (above, note 132) and that of Ioannes Boemus, *Omnium gentium mores leges et ritus . . .*, Augustae Vindicorum, 1520 (new edd., 1536 bis, 1539, 1540, 1541, 1556, 1561 bis, 1570, 1571, 1576, 1596, 1604, 1610; translations into French, 1540, 1542 bis, 1545, 1547, 1558, 1570; Italian, 1549, 1558, 1560, 1566; Spanish, 1556; English, 1611. In none of these does the word 'religions' appear in the title). Protestants, on the other hand, had to wait more than a century until they had exchanged their use of *religio* as inner piety for an externalized systematic one, before they had a plural available that they could apply to the observables of other men's religious life.

136 To the end of the seventeenth century, the plural occurs almost equally to designate the 'strange and prodigious religions... of sundry nations' (from title of a London, 1683, work of 'R.D.', sc. Nathaniel Crouch) beyond the seas and of ancient times, on the one hand, and on the other hand in the phrase 'indifference to religions' (from title of a Geneva, 1692, work of Bénédict Pictet) or some counterpart. The latter usage, of course, refers to Christian sects, as the former did not; but it is still a usage by outsiders. The Pictet work (and others of similar phraseology) was written *against* this indifference, so that here we have a Christian using 'religions' in the plural in a sense that includes his own faith; but this is essentially a double negative, and illustrates my earlier point where a formulation of the attacker is accepted in apologetics. Against *l'indifférence des religions* the work, its title continues, would establish *la vraye religion* (true religion? the true religion?). The full title (taken from the Geneva, 1716, reissue) is: *Traité contre l'indifférence des religions où l'on établit les fondemens de la vraye religion et l'on répond aux principales objections des athées, des déistes ...* (from *Catalogue génerale de la B.N.*). Another similar title: D. Gottl. Wernsdorfii, *Comment. de indifferentismo religionum* (ref., without date or place, from Trinius, op. cit., p. 304).

137   As we have seen above, notes 111, 112. Similarly the term 'revealed religion' is used from 1714 (above, note 113) in an apologetic as correlative with 'natural religion' (which of course precedes it) and affirmatively from 1736, yet the dichotomy is stated earlier not in this way, which is in a sense an unwitting capitulation, but as between 'natural religion' and 'the Christian revelation'—in Samuel Clarke, *A Discourse concerning the Unchangeable Obligations of Natural Religion, and the Truth and Certainty of the Christian Revelation: Being eight sermons preach'd ... in the year 1705*, London, 1706. In the body of this work (that is, in the sermons) Clarke is fairly constant in using 'Christian revelation', though he does use 'natural and revealed religion' in the Preface, first page; his printer, however, puts the parallelism into the wording of the page titles across the top of every page in the book. Again, the point would seem almost too casual were it not typical of a great many instances no one of which is conclusive in itself but that all together seem illustrative of a general principle. Another subtle instance: in 1716 (i.e. two years after Halyburton; above, note 113) the above 1705 sermons were combined with the same author's work of the preceding year *A Demonstration of the Being and Attributes of God ...* to make a joint volume entitled *A Discourse concerning the Being and Attributes of God, the Obligations of Natural Religion, and the Truth and Certainty of the Christian Revelation. In answer to Mr. Hobbs, Spinoza, the author of the Oracles of Reason and other deniers of natural and revealed religion*. It may be observed that the phrase 'revealed religion' now does appear, but in a context of those who are deniers of it. The instance is, as we have said, minor, but it may be noted that these were highly influential writings (at least nine editions, a French translation, and a spate of literary repercussions and replies, followed within a generation).

It is not uninstructive to contrast with this the more precise thought of a writer (Catholic) who a generation earlier answered the naturalists without surrendering to their terms of reference: Vincentius Placcius, *Philosophiae moralis plenioris fructus praecipuus, qui est, agnoscere illius ope, philosophiam non sufficere beatati solidae ulli constituendae, nedum adquirendae; reuelationem· vero diuinam ei necessarium certisque signis, in sola religione christiana deprehendis, a falsa qualibet superstitione distinctam non posse non existare*, Helmstad., 1677.

138   Above, at note 126.

139   As indicated above (note 127), most of the titles that I have found with *religio* for this period are of this sort. As examples, apart from the Matthias and Tapper works cited above, note 124, we may instance the following as illustrative. [Martin Cromer] *De falsa nostri temporis, et vera Christi*

religione...Martino Cromero authore, Dilingae, 1559 and *De Falsa Luthera-norum sive evangelicorum nostri temporis et vera Christi religione...*, Parisiis, 1560. The third volume established the notion more succinctly: *Martini Cromeri de vera et falsa religione colloquiorum liber tertius ...*, Dilingae, 1561. These titles are the translator's, and are the first Catholic instance in modern times, I believe, of the concepts true and false *religio*—as with the Protestant Zwingli, both kinds here are Christians'. The Polish original of this has no concept *religio*, which was, I believe, not then yet available in Polish: Marcin Kromer, *Rozmowy Dworzanina z Mnichem*, 1551-1554. The 1560 German trans. from the Latin follows the Latin: *Von baiden der falschen ver-mainten auch warhafften Religion Christi jetzschwebender Zeiten*, Diligen. Another instance is [Diego Zunica] *Didaci Stunicae...De vera religione in omnes sui temporis haereticos libri tres, quibus haereses singulae his sexaginta annis in ecclesia natate, methodo ac ratione dispositae...*, Salmanticae, 1577. And so on; the anti-Protestant character of such works as I have found with this word in their title continues with surprising consistency, virtually to the end of the century and beyond.

140 Again there are many instances to choose among. Some examples (in addition to Pictet and Gottlieb, above, note 136): [Tomasso Campanella], *Ad divum Petrum, apostolorum principem, triumphantem; Atheismus trium-phatus, seu reductio ad religionem per scientiarum veritates, F. Thomae Campanellae contra anti-christianismum achitophellisticum*, Romae, 1631. *Traité de la religion contre les athées, les déistes et les nouveaux pyrrhoniens*, Paris, 1677 (also in German, but without our term: *Widerlegung der Atheis-ten, Deisten und neuen Zweifeler*, Prag., 1712, Francof., 1713); Io. Baptist. Rosemond, *Défense de la religion chrétienne et de l'écriture sainte contre les déistes*, Paris, 1681 (both these references from Walch, op. cit., I. 779, 780).

141 Especially in Catholic writing in Latin, the phrase *controversia* (or *controversiae*) *religionis* (*circa religionem; de religione*) abounds, from the late sixteenth century. An example: [Franciscus Costerus], *Enchiridion controuersiarum praecipuarum nostri temporis de religione, in gratiam Soda-litatis Beatiss. uirginis Mariae; nunc aliquot locis...emendatum*, Coloniae Agrippinae, 1589. As the title indicates, this is not the first edition, which I have not seen, but Walch, op. cit., p. 673, gives 1585 as its date, with virtually the same wording of title, and also from Köln; there was apparently a whole series of later editions also, 1591, 1599, 1608, 1612, 1621 'et praeterea saepius', and translations into German, French, and Flemish (ibid.). That *religio* here still meant more or less 'rite', is suggested by the fact that a 1605 *Augmentum enchiridii...* expands the first clause of the title to read...*controuersiarum nostri temporis de religione, praesertim de sacramento* (ibid.).

142 The former catechisms continued to be reissued, and new ones were added. Through the seventeenth century, so far as English is concerned, although there are exceptions, these usually employ the term 'Christian reli-gion'—for example the Baptist *A Brief Instruction in the Principles of Chris-tian Religion; agreeable to the Confession of Faith put forth by the Elders and Brethren of many congregations of Christians owning the doctrine of personal election and final perseverance*, 5th ed., London, 1695 (23 pp.). The British Museum general catalogue adds the note '[by William Collins]'; earlier edd.

are not entered. Subsequent editions (to an eighteenth and beyond) are listed through the following century; finally in 1794, however, a revised version title reads 'the Christian religion'.

143   As late as 1684, Richard Baxter published in London a 48-page posthumous booklet *The Judgment of the Late . . . Sir Matthew Hale, of the Nature of True Religion, the causes of its corruption, and the Churches Calamity, by mens Additions and Violences: with the desired Cure. In three discourses written by himself at several times . . . .* This takes up again Ficino's argument and irenic spirit. In the third discourse the author pleads vigorously for attention to what he regards as the pure heart of religion, bemoaning the consideration given to externals and telling the grief that concern for these has brought mankind. The final sentence is: 'The Conclusion therefore is, That men for their own sakes, and for the sake and honour of the Christian Religion, would use more Temperance, Prudence, and Moderation, in contests about Circumstantials' (p. 48). Also one may note *The life of God in the Soul of Man, Or, the nature and excellency of the Christian religion,* London, 1677, published anonymously but actually by Henry Scougal; eighteen editions in English in the next century and a half, and one French, are to be noted, and the fact that it influenced John Wesley, who published an abridgement in 1744. See also above, notes 119-120.

144   Immanuel Kant is another writer of major stature who has devoted a work specifically to *religion.* I have seen the second edition: *Die Religion innerhalb der Grenzen der blossen Vernunft,* Königsberg, 1794; the first ed. the preceding year was apparently hardly different. There is an English trans., with introduction and notes, by Theodore M. Greene and Hoyt H. Hudson, *Religion within the limits of reason alone,* Chicago and London, 1934; reprinted in revised form (revision chiefly by John R. Silber), New York, 1960.

Kant offers two definitions of *Religion.* In one, the term refers to a human quality or personal relationship to transcendence; in the other, to that transcendence itself. It is man's recognition of something; and he uses the same term also to designate what we recognize. 'Religion is (subjectively speaking) the recognition of all our duties as divine commands' ... 'True religion, the only true religion there is, consists of nothing but laws; that is, those practical principles of whose unconditioned necessity we can become aware, and which accordingly we recognize as revealed (not empirically but) through pure reason' (German, 1794 ed., pp. 229, 255; English trans., 1960, with somewhat different wording from mine, pp. 142, 156). In both his rationalism and his moralism he differs seriously, of course, at one level, from Schleiermacher; but the difference between these two men is a difference in what they see, more than in where they are looking. Like Schleiermacher, Kant discriminates strongly what he means by the term from the historical organized institutions. For these latter he uses the designations 'statutory religion' *(statutarische Religion)* and 'clericalism' *(Pfaffentum).* He does speak of 'a religion' but does not seem to use the plural *Religionen* at all. Indeed, the more he appreciates that which, for him, the generic singular signifies, the more he depreciates that to which, for others, the plural refers. He calls it a 'practical religious illusion' to confuse the two, and 'to deem ... statutory faith ... as essential to the service of God' (German, pp. 255-256, including footnote p. 256; English trans., p. 156, with footnote). Indeed this is close to his main thesis.

He uses the words *Christenthum* and *Judenthum* to name the historical developments (e.g., German, p. 253; English trans., p. 154); and speaks also of *die christliche Religion* and *der christliche Glaube*—'[the] Christian religion', '[the] Christian faith' (he distinguishes these two; for instance, p. 248, English trans., p. 151).

145 *Über die Religion. Reden an die Gebildeten unter ihren Verächtern*, Berlin, 1799 ('On religion: speeches to the cultured among its despisers'). It appeared anonymously. There have been numerous subsequent editions and translations, continuing until today.

146 From John Oman's translation, London, 1893, which is made from the later German edition, Gotha, 1888, which approximates the 2nd, Berlin, 1806; in the recent paperback reprint (*On Religion. Speeches to its cultured despisers.* Friedrich Schleiermacher, New York, 1958), p. 18 ('*Ich fordere also, dass Ihr, von allem sonst zur Religion Grechneten absehend, euer Augenmerk nur auf die inneren Erregungen und Stimmungen richtet'*—1888 ed., p. 84; the 1st ed. reads, '*Ich fordere also, dass Ihr von allem, was sonst Religion genannt wirt, absehend Euer Augenmerk nur auf diese einzelne Andeutungen und Stimmungen richtet'*—p. 30). In another place he writes: 'Ideas and principles are all foreign to religion' (ibid., 1958, p. 46) ('*Begriffe und Grundsätze, alle und jede, durchaus der Religion an sich fremd sind'*—1888 ed., p. 116. I do not find this sentence in the 1st edition).

Further, he throughout uses the term 'piety' (*Frommigkeit*) as almost interchangeable with 'religion', or at least as correlative with it. It is notable, too, that for his more mature exposition of what he himself called his 'philosophy of religion', he chose rather the term for 'faith': Friedrich Daniel Ernst Schleiermacher, *Der christliche Glaube, nach den Grundsätzen der evangelischen Kirche,* 2 Bde., Berlin, 1821–1822.

147 'Religion never appears quite pure' (English trans., 1958, p. 33) (*die Religion nie rein erscheint*—1st ed., p. 48; 1888 ed., p. 99).

148 'The different existing manifestations of religion you call positive religions. Under this name they have long been the object of a quite preeminent hate. . . . The positive religions are just the definite forms in which religion must exhibit itself' (English trans., pp. 214, 217) (*Positive Religionen nennt Ihr diese vorhandenen bestimmten religiösen Erscheinungen, und sie sind unter diesen Namen schon lange das Objekt eines ganz vorzüglichen Hasses gewesen*—1st ed., pp. 242-243; 1888 ed., p. 274 [reading *der Gegenstand* for *das Objekt*]; . . . *die positiven Religionen die bestimmten Gestalten sind, unter denen die Religion sich darstellen muss*—1888 ed., p. 278; the 1st ed. reads here rather, *die positiven Religionen diese bestimmten Gestalten sind, unter denen die unendliche Religion sich im Endlichen darstellt:* 'the positive Religions are these particular forms, under which infinite Religion represents itself within the finite').

149 1st ed., pp. 244ff.; 1888 ed., pp. 275ff.; Eng. trans., 1958, pp. 215f.

150 Ibid., pp. 242ff., 274ff., 217ff. respectively. The adjective that he uses is *verderben*.

151 Two examples: *Bibliotheea Historico-Sacra: or, an Historical library of the principal matters relating to religion, antient and modern . . . ,* 2 voll., London, 1737–1739 (anonymous, but actually by Thomas Broughton); reissued as *An Historical Dictionary of All Religions, from the Creation of the World to this Present Time,* 2 voll., 1742 (new ed., 1756) (the sequence of titles illustrates incidentally the transition from singular to plural); Paul Henri Thirty baron d'Holbach: *Examen impartial des principales religions du monde,* n.p., n.d. (*sc.* Amsterdam, *ca.* 1770?). Should one add also the certainly influential, but less certainly relevant, work of David Hume, 'The Natural History of Religion', first published in his *Four Dissertations,* London, 1757? Despite the title, this is (like his *Dialogues concerning natural religion,* London, 1779) more intellectualist than historical; Hume represents his ratiocinative age. His contribution in this realm would seem to me to have been more in the traditional concern of content than in our concern here, of form.

More significant, probably, in the evolution that we are tracing, than any of these works explicitly on the topic, was such a work as Johann Gottfried von Herder, *Ideen zur Philosophie der Geschichte der Menschheit,* 4 voll., Riga & Leipzig, 1784–1791, which includes religious phenomena in its purview of man's story as a development.

152 Georg Wilhelm Friedrich Hegel, *Vorlesungen über die Philosophie der Religion,* 1832. Published posthumously by his students and friends as the first instalment of their collected edition of his works. I have used the Stuttgart, 1928, edition, being voll. 15, 16 of his *Sämtliche Werke,* ed. Hermann Clockner.

153 Hegel does use the plural *Religionen* occasionally (e.g., *die Religionen, wie sie aufeinander gefolgt sind;* . . . [Die] *Folge der bestimmten Religionen,* vol. I, pp. 92, 97; *eine Religion* occurs I, 49) but rarely, and regularly not where one would most expect it. Thus he speaks in the singular of *die positive Religion* (e.g., I. 44), *die bestimmte Religion* (heading, I. 89 and the title of part II of the whole work, I, 269–II. 188), and *historische Religion, eine besondere Gestalt der Religion . . . eine Reihe von Gestaltungen, eine Geschichte der Religion* (I. 92, just preceding the first quotation given above). And, as his treatment in Part II indicates, particular religion for him is not primarily 'the religions' as conceptualized standardly, in recent times, one for each community, but the religion of nature, the religion of freedom, the religion of pain, and so on, in which the definite article in English is required perhaps only by the syntax, or even not at all?

154 *Passim;* cf. 'First of all, what we have before us is not religion in general but positive religion' (*Zunächst haben wir nicht Religion überhaupt als Gegenstand vor uns, sondern* positive *Religion,* I. 65). This is a notion that others have often repeated in a different sense. Other writers too, for instance Schleiermacher and for that matter Ficino and Augustine, had conceptualized religion as pre-existing its manifestations, but in their case it is man that externalizes it after it is in his heart; for Hegel it externalizes itself, which is radically different. The *religion* that he is hypostasizing is the religion of outward system, not of inner piety. For the first time, the conception is being launched of a 'religion in general' that is a generalization (or prototype) of the religions as socio-historical entities. This is quite a different matter from a

242

'religion in general' that generalizes or underlies the inner piety of personal life.

Until now, 'religion' in the singular had preceded 'religions' in the plural, logically. Hegel gave the former a new meaning, for him still transcendent. But it was one by which subsequent generations, more empiricist, could use the singular as comprehending, and logically following, the plural. Man in the past had been seen as the agent of a generic religion in the heavens; he now became in some sense the victim or product of a generic religion on the earth.

155 *Vorlesungen über das Wesen der Religion, nebst Zusätzen und Anmerkungen,* Leipzig, 1851 (*Ludwig Feuerbach's Sämmtliche Werke, 8er Band*). This substantial volume (comprising thirty lectures, delivered in Heidelberg during the winter 1848–1849) was preceded by a brief essay by him also entitled *Das Wesen der Religion,* apparently published in 1845 in a journal *Die Epigonen* (Stuttgart?), and reprinted in considerably expanded form but still retaining the same title in his *Sämmtliche Werke,* vol. I, Leipzig, 1846, pp. 410–486. Although his is the first book specifically on this matter, it is not the first time that such a phrase had been used, or the concept set forth that religion has a nature. It seems, however, the first time by a non-believer—that is, by one who is not conceiving religion to be something given by God, and therefore, since it has a nature, is implying that rather it exists in its own right as a definite entity. The earliest title that I have found is: *Io. Melchioris religio eiusque natura et principium; sive epistola, qua ad examen vocatur tractatus theologico-politicus,* Vltraiect, 1672, from a reference in Walch, op. cit., vol. I, p. 721, but I have not been able to locate a copy. In 1684 the words 'on the nature of true religion' occur in the title of the posthumous work of Matthew Hale (see above, note 143) (the wording is probably by Richard Baxter, the publisher, rather than Hale, to one judging from the title-page *in extenso* and the slightly different opening sentences of the text, Part I: 'Of religion'). However, the nature of religion is not the same thing as the nature of true religion. Herein lies the crux for subsequent writers. This is illustrated in the Christian writer Johann Jakob Breitinger, who published: *Liber de principiis in examinanda et definienda religionis essentia...,* Tiguri Helvetiorum, 1741, of which I have seen the French translation of the same year: *Examen des lettres sur la religion essentielle & dans lequel on discute les principes, qu'il faut employer, pour determiner l'essence de la religion. Traduit du latin de Mr. J. Jaques Breitinguer, . . . Avec des nôtes, & une préface du traducteur,* Zurich.

By the nature of religion such a writer means true religion in the Platonic sense that we have discussed (above, at notes 35, 45f) : to state the nature is to describe the ideal of which actual occurrences are more or less imperfect instances. The matter is quite different when one is not a Platonist or transcendentalist, so that the nature of a thing is fixed in this world. Moreover, 'religion' for Breitinger as 'faith' for John Cockburn, *An Enquiry into the Nature, Necessity, and Evidence of Christian Faith...,* London, 1696, refers to an inner quality of a person's heart, in relation to transcendence. Breitinger, who avers that religion is a relation between God and man (French ed., p. 3) finds the nature of it, then, in the nature of these two (*le fondement...se trouve tout à la fois dans la Nature de Dieu, & dans celle de l'Homme*—p. 2., quoting an anonymous writer) . Whether there be God or not has been disputed, but Western thought has long conceived that if He is, He has a nature, and also that man has a nature (this latter idea being a foundation of Western civilization). That to which I am calling attention here is the novelty of the notion of a fixed external or institutional quiddity in social history the nature of which is independent of the persons who are involved in it.

The title of another work of which I have not been able to locate a copy is *Das Wesentliche in der Religion vernunft und schriftmaesig untersucht*, Dresd., 1744 (Walch, *op. cit.*, I, p. 811, where it is attributed to Ioach. Gottlob Amenda or possibly Bern. Walth. Marpergerus. The British Museum and *Catalogue générale de la BN* enter Johann Joachim Gottlob am Ende, and Bernard Walther Marperger, without including this work under either). It is possible that the Enlightenment preceded Feuerbach in an essentialist formulation, though if so it would be of an intellectualist system rather than of an historical phenomenon.

One can see a transition towards Feuerbach's *Wesen* formulation in that same environment in the years leading up to the appearance of his two books. A friend of Schleiermacher's published the following: W. M. L. de Wette, *Ueber die Religion, ihr Wesen, ihre Erscheinungsformen und ihren Einfluss auf das Leben*, Berlin, 1827. A little later appeared: P. F. Stuhr, *Die Religions-Systeme der heidnischen Völker des Orients*, Berlin, 1836. In this, the presentation of the ways of Asian peoples is preceded by a brief foreword (*Vorrede*, pp. [iii]-[x]) and an extensive introduction, pp. i-lxiii; this introduction is listed in the Table of Contents as *Einleitung*, and has the title *Allgemeine Einleitung* at its head (p. i.), but it carries as running title on right-hand (odd-numbered) pages from vii to xix, *Das Wesen der Religion*. (The term *Systeme* in the work's general title may also be remarked.)

It may be noted that the English and French translations of Feuerbach rendered *Wesen* not by 'nature', which is perhaps a little more reified than the German, but by 'essence', which is still more so. The latter is a fully static term, to most minds. See next note.

156 *Das Wesen des Christenthums*, Leipzig, 1841; *Zweite vermehrte Auflage*, Leipzig, 1843. The latter ed. was translated into English by Marian Evans (*sc.* George Eliot): *The Essence of Christianity*, London, 1853, 1881, 1893, etc.; New York, 1855, 1857; Boston, 1881; etc.; New York (paperback), 1957. *Das Wesen der Religion* was rendered by Alexander Loos as *The Essence of Religion*, New York, 1873. Both appeared together in French as *L'essence du christianisme* and *L'essence de la religion* (this latter is the 1845 essay) in a collected translation by A. H. Ewerbeck, *Qu'est-ce que la religion, d'après la nouvelle philosophie allemande*, Paris, 1850.

157 Linked with the question of a nature of religion has been the question of its truth, which also I am bold enough finally to discard (below, chap. 7, note 14). 'The nature and truth of religion' became an established phrase: a recent example, Albert Lang, *Wesen und Wahrheit der Religion: Einführung in die Religionsphilosophie*, München, 1957 (I. Teil: *Das Wesen der Religion*, pp. 13-145; II. Teil, *Die Wahrheit der Religion*, pp. 147-end). Similarly for particular 'religions': in Georg Wobbermin, *Systematische Theologie, nach religionspsycholgischer Methode*, Leipzig, 3 voll., 1921-1925, the second volume was entitled *Das Wesen der Religion*, Leipzig, 1922 (2te *Auflage*, 1925; English trans. by Theophil Menzel and Daniel Sommer Robinson,

The Nature of Religion, New York, 1933), and the third, *Wesen und Wahrheit des Christentums,* Leipzig, 1925.

158 For 'the essence of Judaism' and others, see below, chap. 3, note 111.

159 In the latter part of the nineteenth century the Germans launched the term *Religionswissenschaft,* for which no English equivalent has yet been found. Its several branches, the History of Religion(s), Psychology of Religion, Sociology of Religion, Comparative Religion, and more recently Phenomenology of Religion, etc., indicate the range of study that has been vigorously pushed, with results of quite imposing dimensions. The most adequate history of the discipline is Henri Pinard de la Boullaye, *L'Étude comparée des religions,* 3 voll., Paris, 1920–1922.

160 In the European languages, the singular here may have an indefinite article. While *die Religion, la religion, la religióne, la religión,* etc., may express either English 'religion' or 'the religion' equally (and one has to be alert in translating to detect which is being meant), the phrases with *eine, une, una,* are unmistakably specific.

Notes for Chapter Three: Other Cultures. 'The Religions'

1 I have not made a systematic study of this, but a few illustrations at random might be: classical Hebrew *ḥāsîdh,* Greek *eusebēs, eulabēs, hosios,* Sanskrit *bhākta, vratin,* Chinese *ch'ien ch'êng,* ancient Egyptian *ḥfy (ḥfꜣ), ḥry.t.* I need hardly be reminded, of course, that there are in each case shades of characteristic meaning, which it would be gross to deny. It is interesting and instructive to note how divergent have been the emphases and how particular the interpretations in this realm. Yet such words have, each in its own selective way, referred to the same general order of personal life. Even within a given culture, of course, different persons and centuries have understood even the same term differently—apart from there often being more than one term, each with its characteristic orientation, as our illustrations concede. Across the world, both the similarities and the differences are sufficiently impressive that, rather than one more book on 'the religions of the world', it would be welcome if someone, by studying such concepts, or in any other way, would write a book on the religiousness of the world. Such a comparative and humanistic study would be most useful.

NOTES FOR CHAPTER THREE

1a   In some cases, as in Japanese *shinjin-bukai, shinkō-bukai* ('deep in faith'), the adjective is developed from a noun, rather than vice-versa.

2   See above, chap. 2, note 2. Modern anthropologists continue to use the word 'system', but may do so carefully and discriminatingly. For example, see William J. Goode, *Religion among the Primitives*, Glencoe, 1951, noting his last sentence of p. 55, and his heading of chap. 4; yet this author in his Conclusion and to some extent *passim* makes it evident that he uses this word to describe the empirical aspects of the religious life of the society, abstracted and structurally conceived. There is a more or less close parallel to my use of 'cumulative tradition' below, though of course without my concern for the historical dimension. Contrast also his title; cf. below, p. 132 at note 29.

3   H. J. Rose, s.v. 'Religion, Terms relating to', in *The Oxford Classical Dictionary*, M. Cary et al., edd., Oxford, 1949.

4   εὐσέβεια, θεοσέβεια, etc. Also εὐλάβεια, on which Karl Kerényi has devoted an article explicitly to show its equivalence to modern 'religion', I would say in its personalist sense. In the same article he goes on to note that the Greek term Θρησκεια signifies the outward observance of a cult. See his 'Εὐλάβεια. Über einen Bedeutungsverwandten des lat. Wortes *religio,*' in *Byzantinisch-Neugriechische Jahrbücher*, Athens, vol. 8 (1929–1930), pp. 306–116 [*sic; lege* 316].

5   *Il n'y a pas d'équivalent grec adéquat du latin* religio—E. Magnin, col. 2184 s.v. *Religion, le mot et la chose* in A. Vacant, E. Mangenot, É. Amann, edd., *Dictionnaire de théologie catholique*, vol. 13 (2e partie), Paris, 1937.

6   Paul Elmer More, *The Religion of Plato*, Princeton, 1921, p. 1 (2nd ed., 1928). This work is vol. I of the author's series *The Greek Tradition, from the death of Socrates to the Council of Chalcedon (399 B.C. to 451 A.D.)*. He goes on: 'No word, or combination of words, can be found in the language of Epicurus, or of Plato and St. Athanasius, to carry the exact equivalent of 'religion' in the tremendous line of the Epicurean poet of Rome: *Tantum religio potuit suadere malorum*'. It was the sentence that we have quoted here in our text that provoked Kerényi to write in response the article that we have cited in note 4 above. This is despite the fact that More explicitly stated, after the sentence to which Kerényi protested: 'The nearest approach to [the word 'religion', which we take from the Latin] perhaps is *eusebeia*, or *theosebeia*; but the meaning of these terms is rather 'piety', an aspect of religion, than religion in the more comprehensive sense' (p. 1). Kerényi's answer really illustrates the validity of this last sentence, also for his own term, rather than the falsity of the preceding one. One difficulty of all discussions of this kind is that writers, even careful scholars, tend to assume that the modern term 'religion' has some definite meaning, for an equivalent to which they search the alien texts, without realizing that they may and frequently do differ among themselves or from their readers as to what in fact the modern term conceptualizes.

7   *Ḥfy (ḥf3), ḥry.t* (Erman; Budge reads *ḥefi, ḥeri-t*, and also lists *àumi* in this sense, but this now seems hardly valid) referred to a personal religious sense, awe, piety, god-fearing-ness. But to no entry in, for instance,

Sir E. A. Wallis Budge, *An Egyptian Hieroglyphic Dictionary*, London, 2 voll., 1920, is the meaning 'religion' given as the English equivalent (see the 'Index of English words, names of gods and goddesses, etc.,' pp. 1067ff. [vol. 2]). The same is true of the incomplete Adolf Erman & Hermann Grapow, *Wörterbuch der aegyptischen Sprache, im Auftrage der deutschen Akademien*, 5 voll. and supplements, Leipzig, 1926-1931, according to the *Deutsch-aegyptisches Wörterver*, Berlin & Leipzig, 1950, published as the sixth volume to this. This absence of a concept 'religion' is despite 'an almost excessive richness of documentation' in the religious realm (see next note).

8 'No ancient Egyptian ever left to posterity, so far as we know, any account of the history, faith and rites of his cult'—Samuel A. B. Mercer, *The Religion of Ancient Egypt*, London, 1949, p. vii. This does not mean that they never left any reference to these! On the contrary: *La religion égyptienne de l'époque historique est connue par des témoignages innombrables, car il n'est guère de monument inscrit sur lequel quelque croyance relative au culte des dieux ou au culte des morts ne soit exprimée. Pourtant, malgré cette richesse presque excessive de documentation, il est impossible de l'exposer en une synthèse parfaitement cohérente. Cette difficulté tient au caractère même de cette religion*—Etienne Drioton & Jacques Vandier: *L'Egypte*, being *Les peuples de l'orient méditerranéen*, II, Paris, 1946 [1st ed., 1938], p. 63.

9 Mercer, op. cit., p. vii.

10 Alexandre Moret, *The Nile and Egyptian Civilization*, trans. by M. R. Dobie, London, 1927 (C. K. Ogden, ed., *The History of Civilization*), p. 353.

11 *Ibid*. This and the preceding quotation are from the 'Introduction' to Part III of his monograph, of which 'Religion' then constitutes Chapter 1 (pp. 355-410).

12 The opening paragraph of H. Frankfort, *Ancient Egyptian Religion*, New York, 1948, p. 3, sets forth the point that 'in the whole of the ancient world' the only instance of a religion similar to modern Western conceptions was the ephemeral cult of the sun introduced by the heretic Akhenaten. Actually among the matters by which this author is here characterizing 'religion as we Westerners know it' are not only 'teachings sufficiently coherent for exposition' as in the case of Jewish, Christian and Islamic scriptures but also monotheistic revelation and transmissibility. It is good to remind ourselves that what men mean (here, are expected to mean) by 'religion' is what *they* mean by it, which is coloured if not constituted in content and perhaps even in form by such knowledge of mankind's religious life as they are possessed of, which may be limited. What this scholar was doing in the lectures that compose this book is to endeavour to enlarge and modify his audience's concept of religion by presenting a people's religious life that does not fit their traditional concept. There emerges here then only by implication what is more explicit in other sources, though implicitly it 'is vivid enough here, that the concept itself is foreign. And even Akhenaten, though in his case the modern scholar may find the notion 'a religion' not so inapt as elsewhere, did not himself use such a concept.

13 Some rather than postulating 'a religion' of ancient Egypt write, instead, of 'Les religions égyptiennes' (e.g. C. Desroches-Noblecourt, in Maxime Gorce & Raoul Mortier, edd., *Histoire générale des religions*, vol. 1, Paris, 1948, pp. 204–327; note the opening sentence). One hesitates: 'The religion— or religions—of ancient Egypt' (Mercer, *op. cit.*, p. 3). Again, some writers resort to such phrases, rather, as *La vie religieuse dans l'ancienne Egypte* (Jean Sainte Fare Garnot, Paris, 1948). Cf. below, chap. 5, p. 132.

14 *Någon reflexion över de religiösa företeelserna såsom sådana finna vi icke här, följaktligen icke heller någon abstrakt idé 'religion'—detta ord saknar all motsvarighet pa iranskt område*—H. S. Nyberg, *Irans forntida religioner*, Stockholm/Uppsala, 1937, p. 126. The passage occurs in a discussion of the meaning of the word *daēnā*, sometimes translated so; Nyberg is arguing against such an interpretation. For a consideration of this Iranian term and its significance, and their development, see below, chap. 4, p. 99.

15 Here I am going on such statements as Frankfort's, quoted above, note 12, about 'the whole of the ancient world', and on the fact that to no word in Carl Bezold, *Babylonisch-assyrisches Glossar*, Heidelberg, 1926 is the meaning 'Religion' assigned, according to the 'Deutsches Wörterverzeichnis', pp. 297 ff. On the Akkadian word *dīnu, dēnu*, 'law', which subsequently got taken up into the stream out of which came eventually a later Middle Eastern concept for 'religion', see below, chap. 4, esp. at note 70.

16 Of many studies recently of 'the religion of' a particular people, the opening paragraph tends to set forth the point that the religion about to be presented is not (or, for instances in the past, was not) a unit. An example is Jacques Soustelle, 'La religion des Aztèques', in Gorce & Mortier, op. cit., I. 183. The most vivid and full study of this particular subject, which at the same time manifests that the Aztecs' 'religion' was no distinct entity, separable even conceptually from other facets of their life, is perhaps Alfonso Caso, *The Aztecs, people of the sun*, Norman, Oklahoma, 1958, 1959 (*El Pueblo del Sol*, México, 1954; earlier ed., *La religión de los Aztecas*, México, 1936, 1945, *The Religion of the Aztecs*, 1937). Through the kindness of Dr. Caso, his associate Angel Ma. Garibay has been good enough to supply me with a private communication elaborating the point that the Náhuatl language had neither any term corresponding to the modern Western concept 'religion' nor any name designating their specific 'religion'; but points out that of course they had no need for these.

17 One recent scholar puts it rather negatively: *Le dharma ou 'loi' hindoue (Radhakrishnan)—le sanskrit n'a pas d'autre terme pour désigner approximativement la religion*—Renou, in Louis Renou & Jean Filliozat, *L'Inde classique: manuel des études indiennes*, 2 voll., Paris, 1947–1953, I. 480 (para. 988). The laconic reference here to Radhakrishnan is presumably to the fact that this modern Western-educated and Western-oriented thinker uses *dharma* (like modern Hindi *dharam*) for the notion 'a religion'. (By *'la religion'* above Renou is referring not to 'religion' but to 'the religion', that is, Hinduism.) Contrast: 'Ancient India . . . had no word for "religion" '—from the opening sentence of Daniel H. H. Ingalls, 'Authority and Law in Ancient

India', *Journal of the American Oriental Society*, Baltimore, Supplement no. 17, 1954, p. 34.

18 'It has been constantly asserted that India is obsessed with religion. It might be equally well maintained that India takes no cognizance of religion, at least as an independent phenomenon'—Louis Renou, *Religions of Ancient India*, London, 1953, p. 48. Cf. Ingalls, preceding note.

19 The opening sentence of one of the most recent Western books on 'Buddhism' reads disarmingly as follows: 'Buddhism, in the sense of the field of thought which has grown up about the Buddha's name'; and that of the Introduction, 'Buddhism is a Western term . . .' (both these by the editor, in Christmas Humphreys, ed., *The Wisdom of Buddhism*, London, 1960, pp. 7, 13). Despite the former exceedingly broad reference and the latter disclaimer, this writer yet goes on in the latter case to give 'Buddhism' as the equivalent of the quite different and rather precise, transcendentalist, concept *dharma*. Within a paragraph or two, however, he modifies this again by stating that the term 'Buddhism' refers, not to that of which Gautama became aware in his Enlightenment, but rather to the path along which others may proceed 'to the same Enlightenment'. These are then combined in the reasonable 'Buddhism, then, is at once a body of doctrine and a way' (p. 13). Yet it is clear that he finds it difficult to be consistent.

Two other Buddhists, writing for a Western audience and casting about for a traditional term to parallel the Western one, choose differently, selecting a personalist Sanskrit word designating the discipline of the devotee, and giving it an emphatically subjective reference: 'The word used for religion in Buddhism is *brahma-cariya* which may be translated as "the ideal life" . . . any way of life which anyone may consider to be the ideal as a consequence of his holding a certain set of beliefs about the nature and destiny of man in the universe'—G. P. Malalasekera & K. N. Jayatilleke, *Buddhism and the Race Question*, (in the UNESCO series, *The Race Question and Modern Thought*), Paris, 1958, p. 14.

20 More strictly, it is constituted of taking refuge in three simultaneous refuges—that is, of man's relation to these things, rather than the things themselves. *Dharma* itself, in Buddhist conception (particularly for Thērāvādins), as the one absolute in an otherwise evanescent universe, corresponds in some ways more closely to 'God' in Christian conception than to 'religion'.

21 Such words are once again *dharma* ('orthodox' Hindus proudly oppose the Āryādharma or their inherited norms to deviations from it and to innovations and new-fangled proposals); *shāshana*, precept, rule; *mata*, doctrine, teaching. *Panthan, prasthāna, mārga, vāda*, indicate 'way', path. *Sampradāya* is tradition, transmission, rather like the Chinese *chiao* (see below). These have come in relatively recent centuries to be used for what a Westerner might call 'sect', though various terms of Muslim origin have, significantly, been taken over also for this purpose; and the use of *samāja*, community, group, is recent (cf. Renou & Filliozat, *op. cit.*, I. 620–621). *Āgama*, a particu-

lar text, is in process today of coming to serve as a translation of the Western concept 'religion' in Indonesian (cf. below, note 23). The Buddhist *yāna,* which Thomas translates 'career' (Edward J. Thomas, *The History of Buddhist Thought,* London, 1933, pp. 177ff.) , though originally personalist, came gradually to be institutionalized into almost 'sect', especially perhaps in the usage of one group when referring to the others of which they were not members. When Thomas uses the phraseology 'the conception of Buddhism as a religion', he is arguing that it was conceived or considered religiously rather than philosophically. That is, he is arguing for its *religiousness,* not for its conceptualized entity-ness, and his personalist implication appears in the succeeding clause ('as a religion, a career in which the destiny of the individual could be realized') , and he calls this conception (he clearly does not mean 'concept') a 'moving spirit' (p. 179) . All this is part of the sustained debate, to which we shall return, and one must remember that it is a Western debate, as to whether or not early Buddhism is 'a religion'. What Thomas is arguing, to use our terms strictly, is that it is religion, not that it is a religion. Anyway, the question itself illustrates that the Buddhists themselves did not verbalize their position in these or comparable terms. Had the Buddhists, or indeed the Hindus, a term or concept for 'religion', then their usage would have settled the question rather than leaving it for Westerners to formulate.

22 W. E. Soothill, *The Three Religions of China,* London, New York, &c, 1913, p. 6; 1923, 1929, pp. 14–15. That the author was professor of Chinese at Oxford is stated on the title-page of the second and third editions; but he did not hold the chair earlier—at the time of the first edition he was a missionary lecturing to missionaries. For further discussion, see below, pp. 62–63 and 67–71.

23 These questions are of considerable political importance as well as otherwise. For a subtle and illuminating analysis of how the modern Western political phrase 'freedom of religion', translated in Indonesian at a sophisticated level as *kemerdekaan agama,* is finally understood in Javanese villages unaccustomed to the conceptualizations involved, see C. A. O. van Nieuwenhuijze, *Aspects of Islam in post-colonial Indonesia.* The Hague and Bandung,́ 1958, chap. 2, section III (pp. 66–86) , especially pp. 80–83.
The title of Clifford Geertz, *The Religion of Java,* Glencoe, 1960, is a somewhat different usage. Its topic might be termed, rather, religion in Java: the religious behaviour of the populace of the island, analysed as constituted of three main strands, indigenous, Hindu, and Islamic. The second of these three, which Geertz calls 'the *prijaji* variant' of his general complex, is the particular strand to which the name *agama Djawa,* 'the religion of Java', is given in its more specific sense. This brilliant descriptive study might well be taken forcefully to document and to illustrate my general thesis of the unserviceability of an entity-concept of religions for an actually existing situation.

24 Of the Western religious tradition the Bible is the source of the content, not of the form; of Western religious ideas, but not of Western ideas about religion. The form of the Church as an organization, partly a novel construction of post-New-Testament Christians, was derived in part from the Roman Empire, and in part was one of a type of new religious organizations

arising at that time in the Middle East (cf. above, chap. 2 and below, chap. 4) ; the idea of 'religion', as we have seen, is Latin in origin; philosophical ideas about religious matters have developed in the West chiefly from the Greek tradition.

25 The word is Old-Persian *dāta, dātam,* 'law'. This term appears in the Old Testament (דת) after the 'return' of the community from the Persian empire, being used specifically for 'the law of the Medes and the Persians'; it becomes standard in later Persianized Aramaic. In the Old Testament it occurs a few times in Hebrew (once in Ezra, otherwise in the book of Esther, whose scene is set in the Persian court) , several times in Aramaic; chiefly referring to law. Some translators and commentators interpret it in the Aramaic of Daniel 6:6 as 'his religion'. For a full discussion of this particular concept see below, chap. 4, note 67. (For the impingement on Jewish religious life at this time of Iranian religious influences generally, and specifically in the direction of a closed and boundaried community with an *either/or* conceptual attitude, see below, chap. 4 *passim.*)

26 See especially the article πιστευω κτλ of Rudolph Bultmann and Artur Weiser in vol. 6 (1959) , pp. 174–230 of Gerhard Kittel, Gerhard Friedrich *et al.,* edd., *Theologisches Wörterbuch zum Neuen Testament,* in process, Stuttgart, 1933–   . [This article has now become available in an English translation, published separately: Rudolf Bultmann and Artur Weiser, *Faith,* trans. by Dorothea M. Barton, London, 1961, ed. P. R. Ackroyd in the series *Bible Key Words from Gerhard Kittel's Theologisches Wörterbuch zum Neuen Testament.*]

27 Calculated from Robert Morgenthaler, *Statistik des neutestamentlichen Wortschatzes,* Zurich/Frankfurt am Main, 1958, five entries under πιστ-, three under απιστ-, and two under 'ολιγοπιστ-.

28 The root σεβ- in many forms (θεοσεβης, θεοσεβεια, ευσεβης, ευσεβως, ευσεβεω, ευσεβεια, σεβομαι, σεβαζομαι, σεβαστος) and εὐλαβ- (εὐλαβης, εὐλαβεομαι, εὐλαβεια)—fifty times in all. See the concordances, and W. F. Arndt and F. W. Gingrich, *A Greek-English Lexicon of the New Testament and Other Early Christian Literature,* Cambridge and Chicago, 1957.

29 In Acts 26:5, St. Paul is reported as saying, ὅτι κατα την ἀκριβεστατην αἱρεσιν της ἡμετερας θρησκειας ἐζησα Φαρισαῖος—'I lived as a Pharisee according to the strictest school of our *thrēskeia'.* The past tense of the verb here would allow some to see his use of 'our' as referring back to an earlier time when he was still within the Jewish 'religion'; but two verses later he again uses 'our' in speaking in the present tense of the twelve tribes, so that apparently in addressing Agrippa he is thinking and speaking of 'us Jews'; this would seem to set the framework for his use of 'our *thrēskeia',* with some tinge of 'religious community'. Is *thrēskeia* here the Greek for Aramaic *dāth* (see just above, note 24, and below, chap. 4, note 67)?

30 Col. 2:18: θρησκεια των ἀγγελων—'worshipping angels'. The same noun is used twice, and the corresponding adjective *thrēskos* once, by St. James, all in one passage (his epistle, 1: 26, 27) . Here *thrēskos* has its usual sense of referring to a worshipper of God, a man fulfilling his practical reli-

NOTES FOR CHAPTER THREE

gious obligations, and the generic abstract noun designates as was customary ritual observance, the performance of one's due obligations, though the context forces a rather personalist interpretation of the standard meaning of outward act. These five are the only occurrences of this root in the New Testament. Kerényi (*loc. cit.*, note 4 above) discusses this term in classical Greek, and remarks also that it would have to do duty in modern Greek for the modern Western concept of 'religion' (except in the inner personal sense). I am not informed as to the history of this term in the intervening centuries; except that it is perhaps noteworthy that the sixteenth-century catechisms roughly paralleling the Latin and Western European *Institutio Christianae religionis* use Στοιχειωσις της Χριστιανων πιστεως (e.g., in a translation of Calvin by H. Estienne, Geneva, 1551; later edd. 1563, 1565, 1575, 1588, 1628). In 1655 the wording . . . τῆς Χριστιανίκης πιστέως is found (London: trans. revised by T. Berchetus).

31 The words *islām* and *muslim* occur in the Qur'ān itself. In most other cases names have been first given by outsiders, and are accepted only later and perhaps reluctantly by those involved. This was the case, for instance, with Christians, as we shall presently be exploring. This could indeed almost be constructed into a general rule for religious movements of all kinds, and particularly sects. A random example: 'The name of Pietists was given to the adherents of the movement by its enemies as a term of ridicule, like that of "Methodists" somewhat later in England'—(unsigned) article PIETISM in *Encyclopaedia Britannica*, 11th ed., 1910–11. This point is explored further below, chap. 4, note 2.

32 The first four are given s.vv. in *Oxford English Dictionary*. The other term here listed is from *Mémoire sur les trois plus fameuses sectes du Musulmanisme, les Wahabis, les Nosaïris et les Ismaélis. Par M. R. . . .*, Paris, 1818. The form 'Islamitic religion' occurs in 1843: *P.J.V. oratio de religionis Islamiticae ejusque historiae studio a theologis christianis minime negligendo*, Amsterdam. The initials are those of the author [Pieter Jan Veth]. The first usage of an abstract general term that I have found in a book-title is from 1676: *Hugo Grotius against Paganism, Judaism, Mahumetism. Translated by C.B.*, London. The translator was C. Barksdale; the work is a rendering of Books IV–VI of de Groot's *De Veritate* (see above, chap. 2, note 107). De Groot's Latin here is *Mahumetismus*, used in the heading of one of his sections.

33 Gibbon, in a famous passage: 'The faith which, under the name of *Islam*, he preached to his family and nation, is compounded of an eternal truth, and a necessary fiction, *That there is only one God, and that Mahomet is the apostle of God'*—Edward Gibbon, *The History of the Decline and Fall of the Roman Expire, volume the fifth*, London, 1788, p. 202—Chap. 50). Otherwise the first occurrence of this term as a name that Westerners themselves use seems to be in Shelley's poem 'The Revolt of Islam' (1818), a title that is otherwise curious. The first usage that I have found in a book-title is the revision in the second edition of John Muehleisen Arnold, *Ishmael; or, a Natural History of Islamism, and its relation to Christianity*, London, 1859, which appeared as *The Koran and the Bible, or Islam and Christianity, Second ed.*, London, 1866. The following year the term appears in a French title: Victor Imberdis: *Mahomet et l'Islam, étude historique*, Philippeville, 1867. In the third edition of the Arnold work, the word 'Islam' has moved up from

subtitle to title: *Islam: its history, character, and relation to Christianity* . . . *Third ed.*, London, 1874. A comparison of the wording of the three versions nicely illustrates the development that was going on in mid-nineteenth-century consciousness in these matters. 'Islam' was first used in English, curiously, for 'Muslim': See below, p. 83.

34 The form 'Manichisme' is given for 1626 s.v. 'Manichæism' in *Oxford English Dictionary*, 'Manicheism' for 1679 and in the eighteenth century, and 'Manichaeism' only from 1853. In Du Cange, *Glossarium mediae et infimae Latinitatis*, 8 voll., Paris, 1840–1857, the adjective and noun *Manichaeus*, 'Manichee', is given, but no abstract form; similarly in such other Latin and Greek dictionaries as I have consulted.

35 Of the prophet whom it called 'Zoroaster' Europe had heard, since Greek times; and as with *Manichaeus* (see preceding note) an adjective and noun for 'Zoroastrian' is found in Latin, but no abstract form (Du Cange, op. cit., has no entry on this, but Charlton T. Lewis and Charles Short, *A Latin Dictionary* . . . , Oxford, 1900 gives the adjective *Zoroastreus* but no abstract noun). The recent development of a term to designate a systematic 'religion' in this case is investigated below, chap. 4, note 27. The dates given in our text here for all these *-isms* are from *Oxford English Dictionary*, s.vv. So far as I have been able to ascertain, these English-language usages were earlier than corresponding occurrences in French, and even today German resists some of them (for instance, though other sources do use an abstract, *Muret-Sanders Encyclopaedic English-German and German-English Dictionary*, Unabridged edition, n.d. but recent, gives as the only equivalent for 'Confucianism' *Lehre des Konfutse*).

36 Isaac Jacob Schmidt, *Ueber die Verwandtschaft der gnostisch-theosophischen Lehren mit den Religionssystemen des Orients, vorzüglich dem Buddhaismus*, Leipzig, 1828. Cf. E. Upham, *The History and Doctrine of Buddhism, popularly illustrated with notices of the Kappooism, or Demon Worship, and of the Bali, or planetary incantations of Ceylon*, London, 1829. It is not merely the term that is new to Europe; the nineteenth century began with virtually no knowledge of the matter. The fourth edition of the *Encyclopaedia Britannica*, 1810, not only has no article on the Buddhist community or its tradition, but refers to what the end of the century called Chinese Buddhism as the 'sect . . . of the idol Fo', a pernicious superstition introduced from India contaminating the (deistic) 'purity' of 'the ancient religion of China' (article CHINA, vol. VI, pp. 26, 28–29; cf. also the article CONFUCIUS, vol. VI, pp. 496–498). There is an entry Fo, 'an idol of the Chinese' (vol. VIII, p. 781). In the 7th edition, 1842, there is an article BUDDHA, 'one of the two appearances of Vishnu' (vol. V, p. 636), who is said to have appeared thus in order to mislead the enemies of the gods, inducing them to take up false opinions and reject the Hindu religion and hence to be destroyed. This seems perhaps to reflect an Indian memory of a hated heresy? The 8th ed., 1853–1861, under JAPAN (vol. XII, p. 695) recognizes 'the religion of Buddha' as one of the religions of that country, and under CHINA (vol. VI, p. 568) there is mention of 'the follies and absurdities of the doctrine of Buddh'. It is the 9th ed., 1875, before one finds an article BUDDHISM (vol. IV, pp. 424–438).

NOTES FOR CHAPTER THREE

37 James Legge, *Confucianism in Relation to Christianity*, Shanghai 1877. The Rev. Dr. Legge was a missionary, and later first professor of Chinese at Oxford. He was very influential in spreading knowledge in the West, especially the English-speaking West, in the latter nineteenth century about Chinese religious matters, as well as popularizing the way in which for fifty years these were then thought of there. The full title of this particular book is instructive, illustrating as it does the obvious and yet important point that the concepts being fashioned to present the Chinese religious situation to the West were (naturally) fashioned 'in relation to' the concepts already in use for the Western situation.

38 Robert K. Douglas, *Confucianism and Taouism*, London, 1879 *(Non-Christian Religious Systems)*. In virtually all these cases, the terms are found in the titles of journal articles some years before they occur in titles of books. In this case, Joseph Edkins, another missionary, had read a paper before the China branch of the Royal Asiatic Society in 1855 under the title 'Tauism: phases in the development of Tauism'—published in the *Transactions* of the Branch, Part V, Art. IV, according to Henri Cordier, *Bibliotheca Sinica: dictionnaire bibliographique des ouvrages relatifs à l'empire chinois*, Paris, 1878, col. 302.

39 George A. Cobbold, *Religion in Japan: Shintoism, Buddhism, Christianity*, London, 1894 (London & New York, 1905). Three earlier titles than this are given in Genchi Kato, Karl Reitz, Wilhelm Schiffer, compp., *A Bibliography of Shinto in Western Languages from the oldest times till 1952*, Tokyo, 1953, but the only one that I have been able to identify proves to be a sixteen-page *extrait du compte-rendu sténographique du congrès international des sciences ethnographiques tenu à Paris du 15 au 17 juillet 1878*; it appeared as follows: Léon de Rosny, *La religion des Japonais: quelques renseignements sur le sintauïsme*, Paris, 1881. I suspect that 'Leon Metchnikoff, Notice sur la religion nationale des Japonais, le culte des Kami ou le Shintoisme, Lyon, 1878' (Kato et al., no. 638, p. 29) was also an article rather than a book (cf. preceding note) (the author but not this work is found in the catalogues of the British Museum, Bibliothèque Nationale, Library of Congress, etc.). About Kato et al., no. 606 (p. 27), 'R. S. Macaulay, Shintoism, New York, 1884' I have been unable to discover anything. Such an author is not entered in the catalogues mentioned; nor is this work in the New York Public Library. It may be, however, that my date for the first book with a word 'Shintoism' in the title will have to be set back by a decade.

40 For 'the religion of' individuals and groups, see above, p. 41; for the Islamic case, see below, p. 83; for 'Christianity' and 'Judaism', see below, pp. 71–79.
While I have investigated the development of specific names for oriental 'religions', which as we have seen is chiefly a nineteenth-century matter, I have observed how the traditions were referred to previously in only an incomplete way, except when the term 'religion' itself is used. It would appear that on the whole they were identified through the people concerned, plus a qualification designating one or more aspects of their religious life. These are 'customs, laws, and rites' in one of the earliest works, widely influential, Joannes Boemus, *Repertorium librorum trium Ioannis Boemi de omnium*

gentium ritibus. Item index rerum scitu digniorum in eosdem, Augustae Vindelicorum, 1520, whose inside title-page reads: *Omnium gentium mores leges et ritus . . .* (above, chap. 2, note 135). Alternatively the term 'sect' is still used as in [Henry Lord] *A display of two forraigne sects in the East Indies, viz: the sect of the Banians, the ancient natives of India, and the sect of the Persees the ancient inhabitants of Persia, together with the religion and maners of each. Collected by H. L.* 2 *pts.,* London, 1630 (later edd., 1732, 1744, 1752, 1808, etc.). A little later the word 'religion' is used, with the name of the people; an example is the French translation of this Lord work: *Histoire de la religion des Banians . . .,* Paris, 1667. The first independent title would appear to be Bernh. Varen, *Descriptio regni Japoniae et Siam. Item de Japoniorum religione et Siamesium. De diversibus omnium gentium religionibus . . .,* Cambridge, 1673 (being the 2nd ed. of a 1649 Amsterdam work with a different title) (I have not seen this book; the reference is from Gustav Mensching, *Geschichte der Religionswissenschaft,* Bonn, 1948, p. 41). A much more influential work, the foundation of the West's modern Iranian studies, was [Thomas Hyde] *Historia religionis veterum Persarum, eorumque Magorum . . .,* Oxonii, 1700. These usages continued into the nineteenth century. The phrases that I have used in the text are translations of the Varen work just cited, and of the following.

Sapientia Sinica is the title of the first (1662), and *Scientia Sinensis* the subtitle of the second (1687) work in a Western language on the Confucian tradition: see below, note 63. The other two I have taken from the writing of the first professor of Chinese at Paris, Abel Rémusat, in the early nineteenth century; in his *Mélanges asiatiques,* 2 tomes, Paris, 1825–1826, *La religion de Bouddha* is a chapter-title (vol. I, ch. vii), and in *Nouveaux mélanges asiatiques,* 2 tomes, Paris, Londres, Leipzig, 1829, *La philosophie des Hindoues* is so also (vol. II, chap. xl) (one may note in passing that for his own faith he uses a name: 'Le christianisme', title of 1829, vol. I, chap. xx).

41 Both 1911 articles are by Max Arthur Macauliffe; that of 1958 is by Horace Arthur Rose. How very tentative is another recent scholar, appears in the cautious statement in another currrent encyclopaedia: *Colliers,* s.v., article by John Clark Archer: 'On the whole, Sikhism, or the order of the Sikhs, may be considered vaguely something racial, religious, or communal, or sometimes merely as a movement'—1955 ed., 17:595b.

42 'CONFUCIANISM, a misleading general term for the teachings of the Chinese classics upon cosmology, the social order, government, morals and ethics'. The author, Lewis Hodous, calls it 'a system', and says, 'Confucianism was formulated in the Han dynasty (206 B.C.–A.D. 221)'.

43 Soothill, op. cit. at note 22 above. It should be remarked that the title was a rendering of the Chinese concept *San Chiao,* which I would translate rather 'the three traditions' (cf. below, pp. 67–70 and also chap. 6, where I develop the notion of traditions). The author did, of course, despite his title, inform his audience that the rendering by 'religions' was not close, as indicated above, p. 58 at note 22. A similar caveat had been entered by his forerunner who had proffered this particular phrase and who had done perhaps more than any other one person in the latter part of the nineteenth century to purvey in at least the English-speaking world an awareness of Chi-

nese religious thought, James Legge. He had written: 'For more than a thousand years "the Three Religions" has been a stereotyped phrase in China, meaning what we call Confucianism, Tâoism, and Buddhism. The phrase itself simply means "the Three Teachings," or systems of instruction, leaving the subject-matter of each "Teaching" to be learned by inquiry'—*The Sacred Books of the East*, ed. F. Max Müller, vol. 39 (James Legge, trans., *The Sacred Books of China. The Texts of Tâoism*, Part I), Oxford, 1891, p. 1. It is illuminating to recognize how much and yet how little these men were aware of divergence.

44 E. R. Hughes and K. Hughes, *Religion in China*, London, etc., (Hutchinson's University Library), 1950, p. 7, preface.

45 On this decline of usage cf. above, p. 55 at note 13, and see further below, chap. 5, section V, pp. 131–133.

46 The term *hindu*, and its dialectical alternative *sindhu*, are the Indo-Aryan word for 'river', and, as a proper noun, for the great river of the northwest of the subcontinent, still known locally as the Sindh and in the West through the Greek transliteration as Indus. As a designation for the territory around that river (that is, meaning roughly 'India') the word was used by foreigners but not internally, and indeed it (and the Persian counterpart 'Hindustan', introduced and used by Muslims) is still primarily an outsiders' name for the country. (The Indian word today for India is *Bhārat*.) 'India' is first found in two monument inscriptions of Darius in Iran, which date from 486 B.C. (*Hind'ush*. See Fr. Spiegel: *Die altpersische Keilinschriften, im Grundtexte mit Uebersetzung, Grammatik und Glossar*, 2te Auflage, Leipzig, 1881, I, lines 17–18, A, line 25, pp. 50, 54, 246). Half a century later Herodotus introduces it into Greek (*History*, iii. 98); and in the Aramaic of the book of Esther it is given as the name of one of the provinces of the Persian empire, 'Ahasuerus which reigned, from India even unto Ethiopia'—1.1; 'the provinces which are from India unto Ethiopia'—8.9. The use of *Hindu* in the meaning 'Indian' survived in popular English into the twentieth century; I can remember as a boy that in Canada we discriminated Red Indians from Hindu Indians; and I have heard the phrase a 'Hindu Muslim' as distinguished from an Arab or Turkish Muslim. Similarly in French: the only meaning given for *Hindou, Hindoue, adj. et n.*, in my *Nouveau Petit Larousse Illustré*, Paris, 130e éd., 1932, is *De l'Hindoustan*; and the article ART HINDOU explicitly includes the Muslim contribution to Indian art, not omitting mosques.

47 In the latter regard, however, as we have seen also in the case of Egypt (above, p. 55), the Aztecs (above, note 16), etc., he will encounter some considerable difficulty. The history of 'religion' will not be neatly discriminatable from that of metal-working, literature, sociology, or indeed economics.

48 In fact it has quite ceased to be standard to use the term 'Hinduism' for this period; modern students tend towards partial terms, 'Brahmanism', 'Vedism', 'Carvakism', and the like, if they use reifications at all. See below, chap. 5, note 25.

49 I have not ascertained whether it is used by the Muslims who came by sea to Sindh and the Malabar coast towards the end of the first millen-

nium. For the use after Mahmud of Ghaznah, who invaded in 1001 A.D. and after, see R. C. Majumdar and A. D. Pusalker, edd., *The History and Culture of the Indian People*, vol. 5, 'The Struggle for Empire', Bombay, 1957: R. C. Majumdar, pp. 398–399.

50 'For the first time in the history of India, the country was permanently divided, from a religious and social point of view, into two distinct entities'—Majumdar, *op. cit.*, p. 398. This Hindu writer goes on to say, completing that sentence, 'the gulf between which even seven centuries of peaceful existence side by side has not been able to bridge', which illustrates the fact that in his mind still today the entity-like-ness of a religious tradition is unnatural, and the implication is that his reader will agree that it is to be deplored. A Muslim writer would not have added such a clause, since he does not expect the gulf between 'two religions' to be bridged, religiously and socially. For him the distinctness, the self-conscious reality of a religious community or at least his own religious community is an accepted concept, and indeed a formulated dogma (the *ummah*, as the concept of his community, and *Islam* conceived as the name of his religion) —see our next chapter. A Westerner might expect the gulf to be bridged socially, but not religiously. A Muslim reader would understand Dr. Majumdar's remark as formulating the absorptive threat that the Hindus have all along, he feels, posed to his tradition.

51 In theory. In practice also, but not completely: in villages the line has at times been confused, as the census commissioners know.

52 That the Buddhist and Jain communities constituted separate religions outside, rather than particular movements within, the total complex of 'Hinduism' is, I would hold, impossible to maintain with either historical or logical consistency. One would hardly even attempt it except from purely arbitrary or anyway purely modern premises. By formulating this sentence on the basis of 'communities' I have taken sides on an important issue, but the same position would stand if one set it forth in terms of Buddhist and Jain doctrines. Let us suppose someone reasonably well informed about such movements as these and those of the Ajīvikas and others. Let us suppose him concerned to understand the rise of the Buddhist Sangha, the subsequent development of Buddhist separatism, the later intermingling of Buddhist and Shaiva motifs (for instance in the history of Indo-China and Indonesia as well as inside India) , the final dissolving of 'Buddhism' within 'Hinduism' in India, and emergence of 'Buddhism' without 'Hinduism' outside of India. I doubt that any such person could seriously maintain or would even wish seriously to maintain that the history of the fifteen hundred years preceding the Muslim invasion of India can best be conceptualized in terms of three separate religious entities labelled Hinduism, Buddhism, and Jainism— or indeed of any number of entities of which Hinduism was one.

For the unfeasibility even today of drawing a line to separate Hindus from animists in India, see our next note.

53 'M. W. M. Yeatts, C.I.E., I.C.S., Census Commissioner for India in 1941, after explaining the necessity for the change introduced in the Census

of 1941 of recording the tribal origin of persons as distinguished from the religion which they professed, goes on: "The fact is of course that while between Islam or Christianity and other religions there exists as it were a definite wall or fence over which or through which the convert must go, there is nothing between what is usually though vaguely described as animism and the equally vague and embracing concept of Hinduism but a very wide no man's land . . ." '—Rajendra Prasad, *India Divided*, Bombay, 3rd ed., 1947, p. 254.

54 The evidence of the census is supplemented at the theoretical level by the passing remark of the major French scholar Renou: *A vrai dire les Indiens ignorent à quel moment on sort de l'hindouisme* (in Louis Renou & Jean Filliozat, *L'Inde classique: manuel des études indiennes*, 2 tomes, Paris, 1947–1953, I. 621, para. 1270). At another point Renou recognizes, again virtually in passing and without pondering the matter, that the Western term is a catch-all for the plethora of Indian patterns in this realm: *L'ensemble des formes religieuses qui sont ici décrites d'après les sources littéraires constitue ce qu'on appelle d'ordinaire l'hindouisme'* (ibid., p. 480, para. 988).

55 The first part of this sentence would seem to conflict with the findings of the census, and perhaps logically with the second part. On the latter point, I shall later (chap. 8) deal with the important point that adjectives applicable to persons may derive their meaning not from some logically prior valid noun but indirectly and freely through the person from situations in which those persons may find themselves. So far as my retaining the term 'Hindu' is concerned even when it cannot with precision be operationally defined, I use it as a proper (rather than generic) noun connoting, in accord with its original usage, all indigenous religious traditions of India (I would not care to exclude Jains or Indian Buddhists). I would be willing to venture a prediction that before long it will be widely recognized that such a question as 'Is a Jain (*or*, a Sikh) a Hindu?' is not well put. By this I do not mean that the separation of these minority communities, at both the self-conscious and the sociological levels, may not be valid and may not remain and even grow. This is partly a political matter, and indeed the rise of conceptual separateness in modern times has been due not only to Western ideological influence but also very significantly to the development of modern (Western-derived, and in part of course British-imposed) political situations. It is rather that the term 'Hindu' will not adequately serve to designate those non-Jain non-Sikh non-Christian non-Muslim non-Scheduled-Caste non-animist persons in India whom it would have to cover if this particular development proceeded. 'Hindu' is a term without much serviceable function within India, at any level of precision (statistics, government, theology, etc.). Its chief usefulness, one might hazard, will be in the future what it originally was and has throughout primarily been, namely with a basically geographical orientation to refer in the worldwide conspectus of man's religiousness in a rough and ready way to those persons whose religious and social life is related to specifically Indian traditions. Where more precision is required, other terms will be necessary.

56 I have not succeeded in locating evidence for the earliest usages, and therefore not for the sense involved. A recent student states of the use of

'Hindu' 'in connection with a particular religion' that Dasgupta thinks that this 'may not date back more than three hundred years': but he gives no reference (A. C. Bouquet, *Hinduism*, London, n.d. [sc. 1949?], p. 9, I have not managed to find this in Surendranath Dasgupta, *A History of Indian Philosophy*, 4 voll., Cambridge, 1922–49, though it may be there). The phrase *Āryā dharma* is also given sometimes as an equivalent, and is certainly earlier than *Hindū dharma*, but apart from the limitations of *dharma*, there is a problem both of the inclusiveness of *Āryā* (for Buddhists and others) and its exclusiveness (for the Dravidian factors?). It was used relatively early, apparently, to oppose conceptually the Islamic intrusion.

57 Innumerable instances could be given. An illuminating one that ends up on my side, as it were, of the argument is Malcolm Pitt, *Introducing Hinduism*, New York, 1955. The opening sentence is 'Hinduism baffles definition' (p. 2). After playing with this for a little, the author writes on the next page, 'As Hinduism is the religion of the Hindus, let us begin with the Hindu himself' (p. 3). A paragraph that ensues fails to define Hindu, also—but cheerily. He then goes on to present actual Hindus: little vignettes of particular persons imaginary, perhaps, but also imaginative, and vivid. From this point on the effect is liberating. Apparently what has happened here is that the topic of this booklet and the title were presented to the author by the editors ('This book is one of a series of Popular Introductions to Living Religions, which includes the following titles: *Introducing Islam*, by J. Christy Wilson; *Introducing Hinduism*, by Malcolm Pitt; *Introducing Buddhism*, by Kenneth Scott Latourette . . .'—facing title-page), those editors being less sensitive, less *engagés*, less humane, and less informed in this realm than he. It takes him a page or two to recover, but he then does so, quite effectively. One may guess that a scholar with his personalist knowledge of and affection for India and its people would not spontaneously in this second half of the twentieth century devise so impersonalist, reified a title. And one may hope that the next time he will not even accept it, even for two pages, when it is proffered to him.

58 In the nineteenth century, in Western Europe; at the present time, also by Westernized Sikhs themselves: Trilochan Singh *et al.*, *Selections from the Sacred Writings of the Sikhs*, London 1960, p. 27. It is perhaps noteworthy that a sensitive Western commentator has by now become uneasy with the term: Arnold Toynbee, in his introduction to this work, speaks of Nanak as 'the founder of the Sikh religion', rather, and at once goes on to enter the caveat that Nanak would 'perhaps' not have seen it that way (ibid., p. 9). The Sikh editors also, of course, know well enough that the process of the emergence of the Sikh community was actually otherwise: they say in their next paragraph that 'the disciples that gathered round him—Shishyas—became the Sikhs' (p. 27), which is both historically much more accurate than, and radically different from, what is implied in the unreflecting phrase 'founder of Sikhism'. (A great deal turns on that always disarming term 'became', which here covers a highly intricate and long-extended process).

59 The actual date of the first launching of the Khalsah was Indian New Year's Day, 1699, but it then comprised only five persons, and the term

khālṣah or 'pure' was perhaps still at least in part an adjective. It is hardly farfetched to give the eighteenth century as the time when it became a norm and a technical term, and the organization became a structured membership community.

60 'It cannot be stated, nor written in innumerable writings'—the 28th Vār of Bhā'ī Gurdās (*ca.* 1560–1629), line 2: cf. next note. As in other cases, the term (*sikhī*) is not found in the community's Scripture (the *Granth Ṣāḥib*).

61 'The Guru's teaching, which is Sikhi' (*gurmat gur sikhī*)—ibid., line 6. The context shows the sense in which it is conceived:
'Smaller than a hair, it is said, sharper than the dagger's edge, we hear,
It cannot be stated, nor written in innumerable writings;
Wise people who know say it cannot be attained in one step;
People lick rock salt whereas this is sweeter than myriads of sugar cane;
Only a chosen few have got the fruit because the fruit of Bhakti grows rarely on trees.
With the love of the Satguru we find it, in the company of saintly men we comprehend the Guru's message which is Sikhi.'
(trans. S. Khushwant Singh)
The 'Satguru' here is Nanak. The Panjabi word for 'sugar cane' is *amrit*, of which the spiritual significance (and indeed the literal meaning) is immortality. The title of this Vār also indicates the transcendent and personalist quality of the conception: 'Sikhi is difficult but priceless' (*Sikhī aukhī par amolak hai*). (I have not been able to ascertain, however, whether the title is contemporary with the poem or a late addition). There are perhaps noteworthy and I think close parallels between the concept *sikhī* here and the idea of true discipleship in early Christian thought (below, notes 84, 86).

62 In part under Western influence. The third step, the organization of the community, took place under the massive outside pressure of a severely reificationist Islam. The tenth guru, Gobind Singh, was the son and great-grandson of men put to death by the Mughul emperor Awrangzeb. The development of the Sikh community historically cannot be understood except in the context of the attitude and behaviour of the Muslim community. For Islam in general, as representative of Near Eastern reificationist trends, see our next chapter; for the movement within Indian Islam at this time towards radically increased definiteness, particularity, communalism, see the present writer's forthcoming paper 'The 'ulamā' in Indian politics', to be published in a symposium by the School of Oriental and African Studies, University of London.

63 *Confucius Sinarum Philosophus, sive Scientia Sinensis Latinè exposita. Studio & opera Prosperi Intorcetta, Cristiani Herdtrich, Francisci Rougemont, Philippi Couplet...Adjecta est tabula chronologica sinicae monarchiae ab hujus exordio ad haec usque tempora, Parisiis,* in 4 parts, 1687. Twenty-five years earlier one of these missionaries and another member of his Jesuit order had obtained permission to publish in China a Latin exposition: *Sapientia Sinica, exponente P. Ignatio a Costa Lusitano Soc. Ies. à P. Prospero Intorcetta Siculo eiusd. Soc. Orbi Proposita, Kién Ch'āṁ in urbe Sinarū provinciae Kiāṁ Sī,* 1662—which is actually the first time that 'Con-

fucius' appears in a European language (*Cûm fū çù, seu Confucius*—opening sentence of the section *Vita Confucij Principis Sapientiae Sinicae* which follows the preliminary matter in Chinese and Latin and the *Ad Lectorem*). Copies of this book found their way to Europe, but I do not know how many. The 1687 Paris work was very influential.

64 Cited as occurring first in English in 1837, followed by 'Confucianist' in 1846. The former is twenty-five years earlier than the first cited use of 'Confucianism', above, p. 61.

65 My apologies to those of my readers who find this spelling perplexing or irritating, but I cannot happily help to perpetuate the practice of giving a Chinese name in a Latin form, Confucius. This is not purely a whim: one of the movements of our century, which I would rather encourage than resist, is that of the West's trying to see the Orient as it is rather than clothed in Western forms.

66 The Manichee was perhaps the most reified tradition with which the Chinese had to do (see our next chapter); and it is doubtless less illegitimate than in the other cases to say that we may call 'the Manichee religion' what the Chinese called *Ming Chiao*. Yet it does not follow that the Chinese saw it thus, or that except for converts one may set up therefore an equivalence of *chiao* = 'religion'. In other cases such an equation is seriously misleading.

67 See above, note 43.

68 *A ce moment* [that is, before the arrival of Chinese culture] *la religion nationale n'a pas de nom: c'est seulement après l'introduction du bouddhisme, au VIe siècle, qu'on jugera nécessaire de lui trouver un nom chinois, le Shinn-tô, c'est-à-dire la Voie des Dieux, pour la distinguer du Bout-Sou-dô, la Voie du Bouddha.* [Footnote:] *Le mot Shinntô n'eut pas besoin d'être forgé: il existait déjà, tout fait, en chinois* [there follows a quote from the Yih-king]. . . . *Quant à l'expression kami-no-mitchi, elle n'est que la traduction japonaise du mot chinois. . . . C'est d'ailleurs ce que reconnaissent très volontiers les théologiens du Shinntô* [ref. to Japanese sources]—Michel Revon, *Le Shinntoïsme. Tome premier: Les dieux du Shinntô*, Paris, 1907, p. 5.

69 Sokyo Ono, *The Kami Way: an introduction to Shrine Shinto*, Tokyo, 1959 (International Institute for the Study of Religions, Tokyo, Bulletin no. 8), p. 3.

70 It would be almost as feasible to analyse Japanese cultural history in terms of three streams ('Confucian', 'Buddhist', 'Shinto'—or more carefully, the Chinese classical norms, the Buddhist tradition, and indigenous Japanese mores) as Chinese. It so happens, however, that this has not usually been done. Rather, a two-fold analysis of the specifically 'religious' aspect of Japanese history has tended to prevail. Using Chinese terms the élite discriminated *Butsudo* (the Tao of the Buddha) and *Shinto* (the Tao of the gods, or

spirits). Yet although they honoured and practised in their social and particularly their governmental life and patterns the ethics of the Chinese *ju chiao,* this tradition in Japan seems not normally to have been conceptually reified in a way that would lead to its being correlated with the other two. This fact is to be related perhaps not only to its having crystallized less than in China into formal consciousness, but also to the other two having crystallized more.

Practice in these matters has not been rigid, however. Although it has become standard to think of Japan as a two-religion country and China as of three, I suggest in my next paragraph in our text that one might legitimately conceive four religions in China's culture, and there are writers who do, exceptionally, speak of three in Japan's. (All this is quite apart from possibly adding, for the twentieth century, also 'Christianity' and 'the new religions' as still others.) And I have found a Japanese writer who conceptualizes in terms (not explicitly) of four: Masaharu Anesaki, *Religious Life of the Japanese People: its present status and historical background,* Tokyo, 1938, has a chap. III entitled 'Chinese Culture: Confucianism and Taoism'. Evidently the entities are vaguer than will allow themselves to be clearly counted. (The phenomena are not in dispute; it is how they are conceptualized that varies.)

Linguistically, our point turns on the fact that in China, the classical (Confucian) , the Buddhist, and the Taoist traditions were each called by a common name *(chiao)* , while the animist tradition was not; in Japan, the Buddhist and the animist tradition were given one appellation *(tao,* Japanese *tô, dô),* the Confucian (also, Taoist) another *(chiao,* Japanese *kyo).*

Or, one may make the same point in another way, taking as a measuring standard the Buddhist tradition, which came into both Chinese and Japanese culture from the outside. The Chinese conceptualized it, and their own classical (Confucian) tradition, and the Taoist, all according to one concept *(chiao)* ; they did not conceptually correlate it with their animist tradition. The Japanese, on the other hand, conceptually paired the Buddhist tradition and their own autochthonous tradition *(tô)* , but conceived the Chinese classical (Confucian) tradition, also the Taoist, differently.

Certainly there were causes for this, on which it would be legitimate to elaborate; but there were also, I think, results from it, which it would be interesting to explore.

7¹ That there has been a 'living religion' of the Chinese masses different from the designated three traditions of the *San Chiao,* is sometimes observed. For instance: *Le Confucianisme . . . ne pénétra guère dans les masses populaires qui ne prirent de lui, comme des deux autres religions, que des éléments isolés, dans le curieux effort de syncrétisme qu'elles firent pour se créer aux temps modernes une religion vivante. . . . Le système confucianiste, système qui a contribué (et contribue encore) à la formation de la religion populaire, mais n'est pas plus celle-ci que le Bouddhisme ou le Taoïsme ne la sont* —Henri Maspero, *Mélanges posthumes sur les religions et l'histoire de la Chine,* 3 tomes, Paris, 1950; I, *Les Religions chinoises,* pp. 83, 115. One may note also the studies of J.J.M. DeGroot, summarized in his *The Religion of the Chinese,* New York, 1910, 1912.

7² This rather flat statement requires some modification. Above we added 'The way of the spirits' as an alternative for the Chinese form. As with other terms, the meaning has developed over the centuries; and as with other religious terms, the meaning has been different for different persons, especially for those within and those without. Nor, we venture to believe, have the connotations of the Chinese form (*shintô*) been always quite the same as that of the Japanese pronunciation of the same ideograms (*kami no michi*). Since the Japanese conception of *kami* is their own, and to understand the particularity of their religious life it is requisite that one understand how *they* see *kami*, what the term means to them, I think that there is some cogency in the recent suggestion that *shintô* should be translated into English (if at all) as 'the Kami way' (William P. Woodward, Preface to Sokyo Ono, op. cit., p. vi). On the other hand, the inadequacy of 'way' for *tao* (and perhaps, though to a less extent, of 'way' for *michi* and even, conceivably, of *michi* for *tao*?) is evident to those familiar with the Chinese usage.

73 'Shintoism' occurs in a book-title first in 1894 (above, note 39), and it (French, *le Shintoisme*; German, *der Shintoismus*) is the form used in all subsequent books that I have found for the nineteenth century. The first instance of 'Shinto' that I have found (except for learned journals) is 1905: W. G. Aston, *Shinto, or the Way of the Gods*, London. This form presently replaces the other in English in the present century, but in the other languages both forms continue.

74 One may note that the subtitle of the Revon study mentioned above (note 68), *Les dieux du Shinntô*, the gods of Shinto, could not be translated into Japanese.

75 There were, certainly, political considerations at work in this answer, and throughout the debate; but it seems not unfair to suggest that the two sides did not fully understand each other's positions (and indeed, if my general analysis of the concept 'religion' and *'tsung chiao'* has any validity, did not fully understand even their own).

The issue arose after the introduction, under Westernizing pressure, of a clause in the Meiji constitution, 1889, guaranteeing freedom of religion in Japan. The imperial government then took the position that ' (State) Shinto is not a religion' (to use the usual English phrasing; actually in Japanese the word *shin-tô* does not appear here, but *jinja*, shrine). This was in order that State-Shinto affairs should be on a different footing from what that government regarded as 'the religions', namely Buddhism, Christianity, and with some ambiguity, 'sectarian Shinto'. A great deal of confusion, controversy, and conflict ensued.

76 2.21: τοις ὑπερ του Ἰουδαϊσμου φιλωτιμως ἀνδραγαθησασιν ('those who were bravely and honourably fighting on behalf of *Iudaismos*). 8.1: μεμενηκοτας ἐν τῳ Ἰουδαϊσμῳ ('those that remained in *Iudaismos*'). It occurs also in 14:38 (bis), and again in the later work Fourth Maccabees.

77 The verb Ἑλλενιζω, a highly significant concept for the Greek-speaking Orient after Alexander's conquests, meant 'to adopt Greek ways'. The situation was remarkably parallel to that of Westernizing tendencies in the nineteenth- and twentieth-century Orient. Ἑλλενισμος, modern 'Hellenism', was originally then the process of 'going Greek'. Subsequently, and in

modern usage, it was used for the result of that process. Correspondingly, then, 'Ιουδαισμος too was a verbal noun, specifying the behaviour or orientation of those who rejected Europeanization and clung to or reverted to the traditional ways of their own community.

78 The Hebrew counterpart יהדות is recorded first in the second millennium A.D. (in the writings of Rashi, 1040–1105, and of Judah ben Barzillai, b. 1070); the alternative form יהודות (in *Midrash Esther*) may date from the latter half of the preceding millennium, but again may rather be even more recent than the other. See s.v. JUDAISM, article by Samuel S. Cohon, in *The Universal Jewish Encyclopedia*, 10 voll., New York, 1939–1942.

79 For the wider Middle Eastern context here, and especially the Iranian contribution, see below, our next chapter.

80 Galatians 1, 13-14: Ἠκούσατε γὰρ τὴν ἐμὴν ἀναστροφήν ποτε ἐν τῷ 'Ιουδαϊσμῷ, ὅτι καθ᾽ ὑπερβολὴν ἐδίωκον τὴν ἐκκλησίαν τοῦ Θεοῦ καὶ ἐπόρθουν αὐτήν, καὶ προέκοπτον ἐν τῷ 'Ιουδαϊσμῷ ὑπὲρ πολλοὺς συνηλικιώτας ἐν τῷ γένει μου, περισσοτέρως ζηλωτὴς ὑπάρχων τῶν πατρικῶν μου παραδόσεων. One might see in this: 'For you have heard of my formerly living in the deliberately and traditionally Jewish fashion, how I persecuted the church of God violently and tried to destroy it; and I went further than many of my own age among my people in practising Jewish ways, so extremely zealous was I for the traditions of my fathers'. Not uninteresting here is the indication of how far Saul, afterwards St. Paul, had even before becoming Christian been one of those Jews (a minority) who had opted for the *either/or* attitude in the religious life that was coming forward at that time. Cf. above, note 29, and below, next chapter.

81 Acts 11:26, in the King James version, 1611. The original reads, ἐγένετο . . . χρηματίσαι τε πρώτως ἐν 'Αντιοχείᾳ τοὺς μαθητὰς Χριστιανούς. Almost all translators in post-Reformation times seem to have taken the word in question as a noun rather than an adjective ('were called Christian'), which perhaps reflects the modern viewpoint more fully than it does the original meaning of the words?

82 'The name was orig. [-inally] applied to followers of Christ by outsiders. . . . Owing to its pagan origin the word was long avoided by Christian writers, except in reference to conflict with paganism'—article CHRISTIAN in *The Oxford Dictionary of the Christian Church*, F. L. Cross ed., London etc., 1957. This recent article is a good short statement of the matter and gives a bibliography of the scholarly literature. I would beg leave to differ, however, on the explanation of reluctance; this was 'owing to its pagan origin' less, it seems, than to the Christians' feeling that they did not deserve to be called, in effect, Messiah-ish or Christ-ish, of Christ. See next note.

83 The Empire used the term *Christianos* to designate those whom it would execute for this sedition. Ignatius says in effect, let us then accept the name, not as something of which we are worthy but as designating something to which we may aspire. They will put me to death, he writes, because they say I am 'Christian'; I hope that I may be found so—ἵνα μὴ μόνον λεγώμαι

Χριστιανος, ἀλλα και εὑρεθω (his letter to the Romans, chap. 3, verse 2). It is apparent that *Christianos* meant to these men something of the order of 'Christ-like', which explains their hesitation in using it of themselves and also their belief that by being martyred perhaps one could approximate to it.

84 Ἐαν γαρ ἡμας μιμησηται καθα πρασσομεν, οὑκ ἐτι ἐσμεν. Δια τουτο, μαθηται αὑτου γενομενοι, μαθωμεν κατα Χριστιανισμον ζην—Ignatius, letter to the Magnesians, Chap. 10, verse 1. 'If he [Christ] imitated us, in accordance with what we practice, we are no more! Therefore let us become his disciples (learners of him), and learn to live according to *Chris-tianismos*'—Kirsopp Lake translates 'let us learn to lead Christian lives' (*The Apostolic Fathers*, Loeb Classical Library, London and New York, vol. I, 1912, p. 207) ; since 'Christian' was a new word, one might explicate as 'learn to live Christ-centered (*or*, Christ-related, Christ-imitating) lives'. Roberts and Don-aldson render as 'live according to the principles of Christianity' (Alexander Roberts and James Donaldson, edd., *Ante-Nicene Christian Library*, vol. I, *The Apostolic Fathers*, Edinburgh, 1870, p. 182). This last is untenable, since 'Christianity' did not yet exist.

85 Ἀτοπον ἐστιν, Ἰησουν Χριστον λαλειν και ἰουδαϊζειν. Ὁ γαρ Χριστιανισμος οὑκ εἰς Ἰουδαϊσμον ἐπιστευσεν, ἀλλ᾽ Ἰουδαισμος εἰς Χριστιανισμον, εἰς ὁν πασα γλωσσα πιστευσασα εἰς θεον συνηχθη—Ignatius, Letter to the Magnesians, 10.3; which one might translate: 'It is quite out of place to speak of Jesus Christ and yet to Judaize (to adhere to Jewish ways, adopt Jewish norms, etc.—cf. ref. 77 above). For living according to Christ did not put faith in Jewish ways, but rather living according to Jewish ways [put faith—, led to or eventuated in putting faith] in living according to Christ—in which every tongue that has faith in God has been united'. Another reference for Ignatius's use of the term is his letters to the Philadelphians, 6.1. The date of these letters is nowadays taken as probably about 107–117 A.D.

86 In the verse cited above at note 84, the context makes clear that this is the idea. And indeed the *imitatio Christi* is one of Ignatius's great themes in all his exposition: μιμηται γινεσθε Ἰησου Χριστου, ὡς και αὑτος του πατρος αὑτου (to the Philadelphians, 7.2: 'become imitators of Jesus Christ, just as he is of his Father', etc.). He also writes insistently of living *in* Christ (ζην ἐν Ἰησου Χριστῳ—e.g. to the Ephesians, 20.2), and again of living 'accord-ing to Christ' (οὑ κατα ἀνθρωπον ζωντες, ἀλλα κατα Ἰησουν Χριστον —to the Trallians, 2.1). Both these last I would take as very closely parallel to what he has in mind for his new term *Christianismos*. (*La mystique de l'imitation et la mystique de l'unité ne s'opposent pas* for Ignatius, as Camelot writes in the introduction, p. 39, to his edition, which I have used for the Greek text here: *Ignace d'Antioche, Polycarpe de Smyrne, Lettres . . . texte grec, introduction, traduction et notes de P. Th. Camelot, 3e éd.*, Paris, 1958 [in H. de Lubac, J. Daniélou, C. Mondésert, edd., *Sources chrétiennes*, vol. 10]).

As this present book was being prepared for the press, there came to my hands the new work of Virginia Corwin, *St. Ignatius and Christianity in An-tioch*, New Haven, 1960. Part Three of that study, entitled 'Christian Life' (I liked the subtle absence of article), seems an excellent presentation of what the concept *Christianismos* meant to Ignatius. If the author were willing to accept the submission that this term did not (and could not) signify for that martyr what it has come in the last two or three centuries (see below) to signify in English, but can best be translated as 'living Christianly' (or by her own admirable and adequate 'Christian Life') , her difficulty with it on p. 234 would disappear.

87 First found in Tertullian; e.g., *Aduersus Marcionem,* bk. 4. chap. 6 (in *Quinti Septimi Florentis Tertulliani Opera, ex recensione Aemilii Kroymann, Pars III [Corpus Scriptorum Ecclesiasticorum Latinorum,* vol. 47], Vindobonae & Lipsiae, 1906, p. 433.) The context does not make the meaning manifest, but the parallel with such concepts as 'justice' should be noted.

88 First, it would seem, found in works of uncertain date wrongly attributed to the mid-third-century writer Cyprian: *De singularitate clericorum,* para. 7, and *Epistula* 4. These are found in *S. Thasci Caecili Cypriani Opera Omnia, rescensuit Guilelmus Hartel, Pars III, Opera Spuria (Corpus Scriptorum Ecclesiasticorum Latinorum,* vol. 3, pt. 3 Vindobonae, 1871), pp. 181, 277 respectively.

89 The word 'Christendom' (German, *das Christentum*) is simply a Germanic equivalent to the Greek *-ismos,* Latin *-itas* formation, and originally was used in the same ways. The community meaning has survived so unambiguously, however, that most modern English-speakers think of it as a different word. In German there is in modern times virtually no other form for 'Christianity'; curiously, what was once the alternative *die Christenheit* now means 'Christendom'. In modern French *la chrétienté* has this latter meaning, the Greek-derived word having become the abstract noun (*le christianisme =* 'Christianity') . This bifurcation is, however, recent. Though I have not traced the twin usage systematically, in early modern times when the concepts 'the Christian religion' and presently 'Christianity' were developing in Western Europe, both French terms and both German terms were used for it. To take one example, Calvin uses *la chrestienté* for *doctrina Christi (Catechismus ecclesiae Genevensis, hoc est, formula erudiendi pueros in doctrina Christi Authore Ioan. Calvino, Argentorati, 1545; Le Catéchisme de l'Eglise de Genève: c'est-à-dire, le Formulaire d'instruire les enfans en la Chrestienté . . . Par. I. Calvin,* 1545; both these titles were repeated in many subsequent editions. I have not seen the original of the French version here cited; the wording is taken from *Ioannis Calvini Opera quae supersunt omnia . . . edd. Guilielmus Baum, Eduardus Cunitz, Eduardus Reuss . . .,* vol. VI, p. x [=*Corpus Reformatorum,* vol. CXI].) For the German *Christenheit,* cf. below, note 93. Cf. further below, note 101.

90 Once again, negative statements are precarious, and this one may in the end not stand except as I have qualified it. The term does not occur in Ludwig Schütz, *Thomas-Lexikon. Sammlung, Übersetzung und Erklärung der in sämtlichen Werken des h. Thomas von Aquin vorkommenden Kunstausdrücke und wissenschaftlichen Aussprüche, zweite Auflage,* Paderborn, 1895 (New York reprint, 1957) ; nor in the index volume of *S. Thomae Aquinatis doctoris angelici Summa Theologica . . . de Rubeis, Billuart et al. . . .* vol. 6, Taurini, 17th imp., 1922 (reprinted as vol. IV of the Marietti ed., Torino/

Roma, 1948-1950), Roy J. Defarrari and M. Inviolata Barry, *A complete index of the Summa Theologica of St. Thomas Aquinas*, Washington, 1956, has as entry s.v. *Christianitas* '3.187.1.6', which I read as referring to articles 1 and 6 of Question 187 of *Secunda Partis Secundae*, but I am able to find it only in article 6, where it is not original with Aquinas but occurs in a quotation from Augustine (given above, chap. 2, note 36).

91 *Diuisiones decem nationum totius Christianitatis* (Rome, 1495? another edition, Rome, 1515?—British Museum general catalogue). This usage is found again in following centuries.

92 *Capita Christianismi, sive Catechismus fidei, expositus in scholae Tubingensis paedagogio. Cum praefatione Ioannis Brentij. Tubingae.* 1538. Again *The Summe of Christianitie, reduced unto eight propositions, briefly and plainly confirmed out of the holy worde of God.* (British Museum general catalogue adds: [London, 1560?] [By John Rogers]. Another ed., 1579).

93 *Catechismus ecclesiae Genevensis, hoc est, formula erudiendi pueros in doctrina Christi. Authore Ioan. Calvino, Argentorati,* 1545. This reappeared with the same wording in 1547, 1550, 1551. The Italian version of 1545 (anonymous) and the different Italian version of 1551 (bearing Calvin's name) both read . . . *la religione cristiana* . . .; the several English versions, from 1556, vacillate between 'the Christian religion' and 'Christian religion'; the Dutch, 1594, similarly *de christelijke religie*. Similarly the Spanish (*la Christiandad,* 1550); though the Spanish of 1559 reads *la religione de Dios.* The French version, however, of 1545, repeated in 1548, and again (substantially unchanged) in 1549, reads 'Chrestienté'; see above, note 89. I have not been able to see a copy of a German work of Calvin's of the following title: *Von dem Heiligthumb Joannis Calvini Vermanung in welcher angezeigt wirt, wie es zu gemeinem nutz gantzer Christenheit sogar dienstlich were dass der abgescheidnen Heiligen leychnam . . . Mülhusen,* which is entered *sub anno* 1559, p. 19, in A. Erichson, *Bibliographia Calviniana,* Berlin, 1900 (cf. vol. 58, col. 475 of Calvin *Opera* mentioned above, note 89). All translations and editions of Calvin's larger *Institutio* retain the phrase *religio Christiana* or its two-word equivalent, except one 1610 Latin abridgment by Jezler, which uses both *Christianismus* and *religio Christiana* in the title.

94 The Tübingen catechism above, note 92, calls itself in its preface *Christianae doctrinae epitome.* It also uses the phrase *religio Christianismi.*

95 Calvin, 1545: *doctrina Christi*—cf. note 89 above.

96 Eight hundred or one thousand copies of *Christianismi Restitutio* —anonymous; actually by Michael Servetus—were surreptitiously printed at Vienne, France, in 1553. The work was ordered destroyed; three copies only are known to have survived, and Servetus was executed by Calvin. The phrasing of the title was therefore presumably not influential, though the content of the ideas was perhaps not inconsequential. See: John F. Fulton, *Michael Servetus, humanist and martyr; with a bibliography of his works and census of known copies, by Madeline E. Stanton,* New York, 1953.

97 *Vier* (later *Fünff* . . ., 1684; . . . *Das sechste Buch,* 1693) *Bücher vom wahren Christenthum;* originally published apparently Magdeburg 1605–1609 (I have not seen the originals), and reissued through the seventeenth and eighteenth centuries. The first book appeared in English translation ('. . . true Christianity . . .') in London, 1646; another ed., 1660? and all four books 1712–1714, 1720, 1815. Latin version *(vero Christianismo),* London, 1708. It appeared also in Icelandic *(Sannur Christeñdomur), Kaupmannhøfn,* 1731–1732; in Lettish; etc.

98 Richard Baxter, London, 1667. Given thus, the wording may be a trifle misleading, for the term 'Godliness' is used in a sense different from that that it has in normal twentieth-century use; it seems to mean something such as a recognition and worship of God, and obedience to Him, a theoretical and practical-cum-spiritual activity to which he gives the name 'religion'. Thus far all this is 'revealed by Natural Light' (p. 189), that is, is 'natural religion' ('Part I. Of Natural Religion, or Godliness'—see 'Table of Contents'). The term *Christianity,* next, apparently refers to a theoretical recognition of, practical commitment to, and spiritual worship of, Christ; this also he calls religion, namely the *(sic)* Christian Religion (throughout Part II: this term rather than Christianity ·is actually dominant in the text). This he calls 'supernatural revelation' (see 'Table of Contents'). One may compare the same author's earlier *True Christianity; or, Christs absolute dominion and man's necessary selfe-resignation and subjection. In two Assize sermons preached at Worcester,* London, 1655 (another ed., 1666) where 'Christianity' evidently conceptualizes a personal relationship, perhaps even something that man does and Christ does (there are remnants here perhaps of a verbal noun).

The Baxter work of 1667 is thoroughly apologetic and comes at times very close to being impersonalist in its conceptions. The full title reads: *The Reasons of the Christian Religion. The first part, of Godliness: proving by natural evidence the being of God, the necessity of holiness, and a future life of retribution; the sinfulness of the world; the desert of Hell; and what hope of recovery mercies intimate. The second part, of Christianity: proving by evidence supernatural and natural, the certain truth of the Christian belief; and answering the objections of unbelievers.*

99 For instance, in the translations of Arndt (note 97 above), including an abridgement by John Wesley (1815), and in some other work of Wesley. His *Scriptural Christianity: a sermon preached August 24, 1744 at St. Mary's Church in Oxford, before the university* was distributed as a two-penny pamphlet in half-a-dozen and more editions; and it is striking that the mystic William Law's *A Practical Treatise upon Christian Perfection* was entitled in Wesley's abridgement *The Nature and Design of Christianity* (London, ca. 1760) —that is, of 'Christian living'; this is the name not of a religion but of a life. By this time, however, the term had become pretty widely established as designating a theoretical formulation of doctrines. The phrase 'practical Christianity', however, is worth cogitating—our minds have tended to become so benumbed by a multitude of uses that we seldom pause to reflect on what kind of thing is being named in such a context. Note, for instance, the title *Practical Christianity; or, an account of the holiness* [sic] *which the Gospel enjoyns* . . ., London, anonymous [actually, by Richard Lucas], 1681; 7th ed.,

1746. And the title of an anonymous French work *La practique de la religion chrestienne* was translated into Dutch as *De Oefening des waare Christendoms*, 1687.

100 Occurring constantly in titles of the eighteenth century, but there are plenty of examples already in the seventeenth. For instance, *Les solides raisons [sic] qui établissent les veritez du Christianisme*, anonymous, Paris, 1686. The word 'contain' in the following is also illuminating (the author was a Bishop, of Dromore): George Rust, *A Discourse of the use of reason in matters of religion, shewing that Christianity contains nothing repugnant to right reason*, London, 1683. When Arndt spoke of *Christenthum*, he did not have in mind anything that could *contain* something (for instance, a proposition).

101 *The reasonableness of Christianity, as delivered in the Scriptures*, published anonymously, London, 1695. The French translation the following year was apparently not yet ready for the noun; it appeared as *Que la religion chrétienne est très-raisonnable telle qu'elle nous est representée dans l'écriture sainte. . . . Traduit de l'anglois*, Amsterdam, 1696. Within a few decades, however, *le Christianisme* became quite current also in French. I believe that it was perhaps during the eighteenth century that the present-day discrimination between *christianisme* (English 'Christianity') and *chrétienté* (English 'Christendom') became established in French. Cf. above, note 89.

102 *Christianity as Old as the Creation; or, the Gospel a Republication of the Religion of Nature*, London, 1730. [Matthew Tindal, though it was first published anonymously.] This elicited some dozens of replies within three or four years; it itself went through a dozen editions within a few decades, and was still being republished late in the century.

103 *Christianity a Doctrine of the Cross; or, Passive obedience under any pretended invasion of legal rites and liberties*, London, 1691. British Museum general catalogue adds: [By John Kettlewell].

104 Among many examples: Benjamin Andrews Atkinson, *Christianity not older than the first Gospel-promise. In answer to a book entitled, Christianity as old as the Creation*, London, 1730. Again: *Christianity distinct from the Religion of Nature, in answer to a late book entitled, Christianity as Old as the Creation*, 3 pts., London, 1732 (by 'Phileleutherus Christianus', sc. Thomas Broughton). One may note also the considerable literature on the point than 'Christianity is' (or, again, is not) 'founded on argument': as in *Christianity not founded on Argument; and the true principle of Gospelevidence assigned: in a letter to a young gentleman at Oxford*, London, 1741 (anonymous; actually by Henry Dodwell the younger).

105 See above, note 40.

106 The entries under these three headings in the general catalogue of the British Museum, London, in June 1960. Of these there were 639 in all. (It is chiefly works first published anonymously that are so entered.) The items are arranged in alphabetical order; I rearranged them in chronological

order, and then counted them. Clearly the selection is not unweighted. It is biased in favour of English-language entries, being London (important works from all of Europe are included, but from England more unimportant ones as well). And other factors must be operating, for instance in the anonymity matter. Yet on the whole I wonder whether the distribution of forms within the selection is not probably typical. The figures at which I arrived and on which I have constructed my graph are as follows:

		15th cent.	16th	17th	18th	19th	20th to 1950
(a)	CHRISTIAN FAITH	2	19	5	3	20	3
(b)	CHRISTIAN RELIGION		17	42	76	38	5
(c)	CHRISTIANITY		4	15	159	186	45
(d)	TOTALS	2	40	62	238	244	53

Calculating (a) (b) and (c) as percentages of (d):

	15th cent.	16th	17th	18th	19th	20th to 1950
CHRISTIAN FAITH	100	47.5	8.1	1.3	8.2	5.7
CHRISTIAN RELIGION		42.5	67.7	31.9	15.6	9.4
CHRISTIANITY		10	24.2	66.8	76.2	84.9

The number for the fifteenth century is too small to be significant, except that it is so much in line with what one knows from other sources (cf. above, chap. 2) about the Middle Ages that there would seem little reason to reject it.

107 Of entries under 'Christian Religion', a little less than three-quarters, namely 131 out of 178, proved to be titles in the English language. Of these, the earliest is 1570. The last without the article is 1695. If one arranges these English titles, then, by half-centuries from 1550 to 1750, one gets the following:

	1551 to 1600	1600 to 1650	1651 to 1700	1701 to 1750
CHRISTIAN RELIGION	8	24	4	nil
THE CHRISTIAN RELIGION	1	nil	9	40

That is, this transition to impersonalism took place in the latter part of the seventeenth century.

108 My own collection of book-titles (cf. above, chap. 2, note 63), though it incorporates all the items in the above collection through the seventeenth century, includes many more entries for the early period (to 1700), fewer thereafter. An analysis of its contents on the same basis yields very much the same sort of result as that presented in the two preceding notes.

109 Karl Kautsky, *Foundations of Christianity: a study in Christian origins, authorized translation from the thirteenth German edition*, New York, 1925, pp. 21, 9. A similar historicist or empirical orientation is evident, and is explicit, in the following: 'In this essay I shall take Christianity such as it was, and still is, in the life of the Russian people, and not as it should have been according to the notion of some modern theologian or philosopher'—Julius F. Hecker, 'Christianity and Communism in the light of the Russian Revolution', in John Lewis, Karl Polanyi, Donald K. Kitchin, edd., *Christianity and the Social Revolution*, London, 1935, p. 297.

110 Curiously, however, the British resident in Katmandu, in writing home early last century to report to the Royal Asiatic Society in London his observations on the religious life around him, commented, 'In my note I have endeavoured carefully to separate Buddhism *as it is* (in Nipál) and Buddhism *as it ought to be*'—Brian Houghton Hodgson, 'Sketch of Buddhism, derived from the Bauddha Scriptures of Nipál', in *Transactions of the Royal Asiatic Society of Great Britain and Ireland*, vol. II, London, 1830, p. 231.

111 For the lack of information in Europe early last century on the Buddhist tradition, see above, note 36. On the history of the Christian tradition, of course, the West was much better informed; and the Buddhist world had some smattering of a knowledge of its own history. Yet neither East nor West had an informed and critical historical and developmental awareness, comparable to that at the present. Along with the new objective and dynamic (existential) sense, the notions 'Christianity', 'Buddhism' and the rest continued to have, for participants, an idealist meaning; the conceptual orientation can be observed spreading around the world at the end of the nineteenth century and the beginning of this. We noted above (chap. 2, note 156) Feuerbach's work *Das Wesen des Christenthums*, Leipzig, 1841. A half-century later a prominent Christian theologian took up this same phrase to entitle an outstandingly influential book: Adolf Harnack, *Das Wesen des Christentums*, Berlin, 1900. (This work went through fourteen editions in the next three decades; it has been translated into thirteen other languages, whose titles I have not examined, and by Thomas Bailey Saunders into English as *What is Christianity?*, London & New York, 1901, and often subsequently reissued; cf. below, chap. 5, note 36). Presently this was followed by Leo Bäck, *Das Wesen des Judentums*, Berlin, 1905 (6th German ed., Frankfurt, 1926. Leo Baeck, *The Essence of Judaism*, trans. by Victor Grubwieser and Leonard Pearl, London, 1936) and by such works as P. Lakshmi Narasu, *The Essence of Buddhism*, 1907 (I have seen only the 2nd. ed., 'revised and enlarged', Madras, 1912). (It is interesting that the author of this last, apart from writing in a European language, speaks also in his Preface of his 'expounding Buddhism in the light of modern knowledge', of the attention being given Buddhism in Europe and America, and of 'my Buddhist "modernism" '—pp. vii-viii, viii, x respectively). On an *Essence of Hinduism* by a Western-looking Hindu also see below, chap. 5, note 46.
[Since writing this I have found that in the Christian case these concepts did not go unquestioned by thinkers more deeply immersed in nineteenth-century historicism: Ernst Troeltsch, 'Was heisst "Wesen des Christentums"?', in *Die christliche Welt*, 1903, as reprinted in *Gesammelte Schriften von Ernst Troeltsch*, vol. II (1913), reprinted Tübingen, 1922, pp. 376-451 (cf. also other essays of this scholar in that volume). See also Heinrich Hoffmann, 'Die Frage nach dem Wesen des Christentums in der Aufklärungstheologie', in *Harnack-Ehrung: Beiträge zur Kirchengeschichte ihrem Lehrer Adolf von Harnack zu seinem siebzigsten Geburtstage (7. Mai 1921) dargebracht von einer Reihe seiner Schuler*, Leipzig, 1921, pp. 353-365; and William Adams Brown, *The Essence of Christianity: a study in the history of definition*, New York, 1902.]

Notes for Chapter Four: The Special Case of Islam

1   But see below, pp. 110-115, for a consideration of this.

2   We have noted above the cases of 'Hindu' (introduced in India by Muslims), 'Shinto' (introduced in Japan by Chinese), 'Christian' (introduced by the Roman Empire), and the modern names developed in Europe for the other traditions. The principle is of much wider application, covering a great many sects as well. In Christian history, we have seen that the Pietist and Methodist movements were both so called from nicknames first given by outsiders in mild derision, which stuck; again, the 'Quaker' community calls itself 'the Society of Friends'. The same holds also in the Islamic case: an example is the 'Wahhābī', a name given by its opponents in eighteenth-century Arabia, the adherents of this movement calling themselves rather *muwaḥḥidūn*, 'unitarians'. Similarly the Mu'tazilah called themselves *ahl al-tawḥīd wa al-'adl* ('people of unity and justice').

All this is not chance. The operating principle in each case is that a new movement that arises makes a claim for itself that people who do not become members of it do not accept (otherwise they would become members) : a claim to be true Christians, true unitarians, to be people of unity and justice, and so on. It is probably a widely applicable rule that sects, movements, or religious communities are conceded the name that they themselves claim chiefly in cases where the language in which they claim it is foreign and not understood: Westerners acquiescing in 'Islam' or 'Jodo Shin', for instance, orientals who are not Christians nonetheless referring to Jesus as 'Christ', or Muslims and Christians referring to Siddhartha Gautama as 'Buddha'. Such a rule operates less forcefully internally in India and China because of the principle, to be considered presently, that the traditions there are less exclusivist and more ready to accept other people's claims as in principle valid even when not applying them to oneself.

The reason for adherents of a movement resisting an appellation formulated from the proper name of the person that is their leader (e.g., 'Wahhābī' above) is that they hold whatever views they hold not on the grounds that the eponym promulgated them but on the grounds that those views are right. Thus even a Buddhist would resist being called a Gautamist, and Muslims resist the term 'Muhammadan'. Exceptions are in cases where a special metaphysical status is claimed for the leader; e.g., Aḥmadīyah. (Actually even in this case the leader's name was not, in fact, Aḥmad but Ghulām Aḥmad, which is profoundly different.)

For Wahhābī and Mu'tazilah, see *Encyclopaedia of Islām*, 4 voll. and supplement, Leyden, 1913–1938, s.vv.; for Aḥmadīyah, see *Encyclopaedia of Islam,* new ed. Leiden, vol. I, 1960, s.v. AḤMADIYYA. For Pietist, Methodist, Quaker, see above, chap. 3, note 31, and *Encyclopaedia Britannica,* s.vv. For Christian, see above, chap. 3, notes 82, 83.

3 . . . *wa raḍītu lakumu-l-islāma dīnan,* Qur'ān 5:3. When I say 'God is presented as announcing', I mean that my translation here given shows the way in which many Muslims understand this verse. As one example, see *The Holy Qur'ān: translated from the original Arabic with lexical, grammatical, historical, geographical and eschatological comments and explanations, and sidelights on Comparative Religion; by Abdul Mājid* [sc. Daryā'ābādī], several volumes, Lahore & Karachi, 1957–   , in process; vol I, p. 196. See also his various notes, esp. 170, 171 (p. 197); note 172, referring to number 290 (p. 102) and 608 (*lege* 609?) (p. 119). For an alternative translation of this verse, see below in this present chapter, at my note 102. That this translator is consciously aiming, in an apologist fashion, at countering universalist trends, presumably among Muslim youth, appears in his comment on 3:85 (cf. below, p. 113 with my notes 99, 100), his note 610: 'This repudiates the comfortable doctrine that all religions are equally good' (p. 119)—the word 'comfortable' here is revealing.

4 *Inna-d-dīna 'inda-llāhi-l-islām*—Qur'ān 3:19. The translation is my own, but represents a standard current reading. For example, the twice-a-month journal of the Holy Qur'an Society of Pakistan, Karachi, is called *Al-Islam* (1953–   ), and its masthead carries the legend, as a translation of this verse, 'Verily, the (only) Faith (acceptable) with Allah is AL-ISLAM'. Another example: the Daryā'ābādī translation (see preceding note), *ad. loc.*

5 The word *dīn* is unquestionably good Arabic from long before the appearance of Islam. What is in consideration here is rather whether these particular meanings are older than the Qur'ān, and if so how much older. See *The Shorter Encyclopaedia of Islam,* Leiden, 1953, s.v. (article by D. B. Macdonald); but a full investigation awaits a systematic study of the word in *jāhilī* poetry. This is becoming possible because of the complete concordance of that corpus of Arabic being compiled at the School of Oriental Studies, Hebrew University, Jerusalem. The authorities of that school were kind enough to send me a list of references in the summer of 1961, comprising in all 485 entries for *dīn* (and nine for the plural *adyān*). I have not investigated these as yet, and of course the problem of dating is delicate. Of entries under the corresponding verb *dāna,* the statistical report at the same date is as follows: form I, 125; other forms, 28. The topic will repay examination.

6 *Inna dīna Muḥammadin khayru-l-adyān.*

7 See above, chap. 2, note 21.

8 For Christian resistance to any idea that 'Christianity is one of the religions of the world', see below, chap. 5, at note 39; compare also chap. 5, p. 125 at notes 4 to 10. On the Church Fathers' use of *religio* for both the

pagans and the Christians, though not quite simultaneously (and perhaps in the sense of 'ritual observance'?), see above, chap. 2, notes 25, 26.

9 In the Qur'ān, the phrase *al-dīn kulluh*, 'religion altogether', occurs four times: 8:39—9:33=61:9—48:28. Recently, the following book appeared in Egypt: Muḥammad 'Abd Allāh Darāz, *al-Dīn: Buḥūth mumahhidah li-dirāsat ta'rīkh al-adyān*, Cairo, 1952 ('Religion: introductory studies in the history of religions'). One may note here that the author, who had studied in Paris, felt it good to explain in his Preface that the phrase *ta'rīkh al-adyān* is a translation into Arabic of the Western concept *histoire des religions*.

10 *Islām kā Niẓām-i Ḥayāt* ('Islam's system of life') is not only a current phrase but also the title of at least two books: one by 'Abdu-l-Wahhāb Ẓuhūrī, Ḥaydarābād-Dakkin, 1946 and one by Abū-l-A'lá Mawdūdī, Lahore [1948], 1953. The latter comprises five speeches: *Islām kā akhlāqī niẓām—Islām kā siyāsī niẓām*, and so on for ... *mu'āsharatī* ..., ... *iqtiṣādi* ..., and ... *rūḥānī* ...—'the moral (political, social, economic, spiritual) system of Islam'. Mawdūdī has published books also on Islam's educational (Lahore, n.d. [ca. 1942], and 1952) and other systems, and on the Islamic system absolutely (among others: *Islāmī niẓām: kis taraḥ qā'im hotā hay* ['the Islamic system: how it is established'], Rampur, n.d.). Despite his exceptional emphasis on this notion, however, and his unusual vigour in elaborating it, he is by no means the only representative of a modern trend towards systematization. The anti-traditionalist Ghulām Aḥmad Parwez also has a work entitled *Islāmī Niẓām: kis taraḥ qā'im ho-saktā hay*, Karachi, n.d. (ca. 1954). An instance of a rather meticulously reified concept is the following, published in the Nadwatu-l-Muṣannifīn series: Mawlānā Ḥāmid al-Anṣārī Ghāzī, *Islām kā niẓām-i ḥukūmat, ya'nī Islām kī riyāsat-i 'āmmah kā mukammal dastūr-i asāsī awr ẓābiṭah'-i ḥukūmat, jis meṇ Islām ke niẓām-i ḥukūmat ke tamām shu'boṇ, us ke naẓarīyah'-i siyāsat-o-siyādat ke tamām goshoṇ, riyāsat-o-mamlakat awr us ke muta'alliqāt awr 'āmm dastūrī ma'lūmāt ko ... nihāyat tafṣīl ke sāth wāẓiḥ kiyā gayā hay* ..., Delhi, 1362/1943.

11 The founder and president of the organization al-Ikhwān al-Muslimūn ('The Muslim Brotherhood'), writes that Muslims believe in Islam 'as a comprehensive system' (*niẓāman shāmilan*)—Hasan al-Bannā', *Ilá al-Shabāb*, Cairo, n.d., p. 13.

12 Often embroidered with pejoratives. Peter the Venerable (mid-twelfth-century), for instance, who was more concerned than most, writes two books *adversus nefandam sectam Saracenorum*; in an 1143 letter he speaks of the *sectam, sive haeresim Saracenorum;* and at another place writes of the heresies and sect of the devilish fraud of these people—*contra haereses et sectam diabolicae fraudis Saracenorum, sive Ismaelitarum*. See J. P. Migne, ed., *Patrologiae Cursus Completus ... series latina ...* 221 vols., Paris, 1844–1864, vol. 189, columns 659–720, 649-652, 651–658.

13 In the Stamler work, 1508, cited above, chap. 2, notes 132, 134.

14 The first occurrence that I have found: [Adrien Reland] *A. Relandi*

de Religione Mohammedica, libri duo, Ultrajecti, 1705 (and a rev. ed., 1717).
English and German translations preserved this sort of phrasing, the former adding also an *-ism: Of the Mahometan Religion, two books. . . . Done into English from the Latin . . . By A. Bobovius . . . with notes by T. Hyde. Historical and Critical Reflections upon Mahometanism and Socinianism*, 3 pts., London, 1712; *Hn. A. Reland's . . . zwey Bücher von der Türckischen oder Mohammedischen Religion . . .*, Hanover, 1717. A French version reverted to the more personalist *La religion des Mahometans*, La Haye, 1721.

15 Above, p. 60.

16 *Oxford English Dictionary*, s.v.

17 loc. cit.

18 'Mahometan', 'Mohametan', 'Mahomedan', etc.; 'Moosulman', etc.
(Anglo-Indian, from the Hindustani *musalmān*, colloquialism developed, perhaps in Iran, from *muslim*) ; 'Moslem' (this last is a misspelling, only now and very grudgingly being relinquished in favour of the correct form 'Muslim'),
etc.

19 'The rise of Islamism (so the Mahometans call their own religion)
. . .'—*Oxford English Dictionary*, s.v., citing 'Gentl. Mag.'

20 Also in other romance languages: e.g., Aldobrandino Malvezzi,
L'Islamismo e la cultura europea, Firenze, 1956.

21 An example: the *Encyclopaedia Britannica* had MAHOMMEDAN RE-
LIGION as the heading for its article in the 11th ed. (1911), the opening paragraph remarking that this phrase was presumably on the analogy of 'Christian Religion', for what is 'generally known as Islam'. The heading in the 1958 ed.
is ISLAM.

22 Since the point is one on which modern Muslims feel sensitive
(which is why I have felt the matter important), and since I am going to raise here certain questions about it, it is perhaps excusable to remark that I myself have taken a small but vigorous part in this. Not only have I never used any term but 'Islam' in my own writing (first publication in this realm, 1943), but also in my first published article in the West after my return from six years in the Muslim world, I inserted a prefatory note pleading for the use of 'Islam' and 'Muslim' in place of the older terms (*One Family*, Toronto, 1948, II, p. 27) ; I have written articles in the Montreal daily press specifically to push the same point; and have hardly given a public address or an introductory universary lecture without stressing it. I was unhappy, also, when my respected teacher Professor H. A. R. Gibb succumbed to his publishers' earlier-established practice and accepted the title *Mohammedanism* (Home University Library, London and New York, 1949, 1953, Mentor Books, New York, 1955) ; I found his little apology for this in his opening pages (p. 2; Mentor ed., pp. 11f.) at the time unconvincing. Only very recently have I come to see that

there are more facets to the question than I had at all appreciated, and that much deeper issues are at stake. As pled earlier, things that we have taken for granted and even those that we strongly believe are worth scrutiny occasionally and careful reconsideration.

23 With regard to the particular concept *sharī'ah*, however, I raise certain questions and adduce certain evidence suggesting that this has historically come to be true, perhaps relatively recently, rather than having been so more or less from the start; in a paper mentioned below, note 107.

24 Even though it exist transcendentally, Muslims would say, from the day of creation if not before.

25 Probably no outstanding figure has been so variously interpreted as Zarathushtra. I am not competent to enter upon or to assess the debates (even wrangles) among scholars in their reconstructions; although those who *are* competent, nonetheless diverge. It is reassuring that among them at least one, highly respectable, holds it legitimate to continue to regard 'the common opinion on Zoroaster . . . [as] not altogether absurd' (W. B. Henning, *Zoroaster: politician or witch-doctor?*, London, 1951, p. 51). In any case the precise historical reconstruction is not crucial to my argument, since I am concerned with the source, whoever he or whatever it was, of the mighty ideas that have been referred to him, and that concern us here.

26 The word here is *daēnā*, on which see below, p. 99.

27 Even for the nineteenth century I have found the term 'Zoroastrianism' as a title not actually of books but of offprints, pamphlets, etc., only: Mgr. Charles de Harlez, *Des Origines du Zoroastrianisme*, Paris, 1879, *extrait du Journal asiatique*, 8: 95–323 (1879); Nishikanta Chattopadhyaya, *Lecture on Zoroastrianism*, Bombay, 1894, 20 pp. (lecture delivered in 1893); Mauritz Kaufmann, *Some Modern Views of Zoroastrianism examined in the light of Christianity. Present Day Tracts, no. 81*, London, 1896, 64 pp. Earlier names are 'Parseeism' (J. M. Thoburn, a work of that title, London, 1884), and such phrases as 'the religion of the Parsis' and '. . . of the ancient Persians', which last goes back to the end of the seventeenth century: [Thomas Hyde], *Historia religionis veterum Persarum . . .*, Oxonii, 1700 (2nd ed., 1760). So much is involved from sources other than Zarathushtra, including even from the ancient traditions of Iran to which he was opposed, that modern scholars are beginning to have second, though mostly unconscious, thoughts on the appositeness of the name. R. C. Zaehner in the opening paragraph (p. 9) of a recent work writes: 'By "Zoroastrianism" I understand, arbitrarily, the dualist orthodoxy which seems to have been established under Shāpūr II in the fourth century A.D.', but chooses to entitle his book on this subject rather *The Teachings of the Magi*, London and New York, 1956; there is as subtitle 'A Compendium of Zoroastrian Beliefs'. Arthur Christensen, *L'Iran sous les Sassanides*, Paris, 2e ed., 1944, without actually saying so, would seem almost to be suggesting that 'Zurvanism' would be a more accurate name for the Sasani state religion; (cf. R. C. Zaehner, *Zurvan*, Oxford, 1955); and J. Duchesne-Guillemin, *Ormazd et Ahriman: l'aventure dualiste dans l'antiquité*,

Paris, 1953, chap. 10, pp. 135–153, calls it *le mazdéisme,* and uses this term even for its survival among the present Parsis of India (p. 151). (He also uses *le zoroastrisme* in passing, p. 149.) I doubt that anyone informed on the tradition would argue today against a proposition that a continued use of the term 'Zoroastrianism' (coined 1854—Oxford English Dictionary) is due to present Western practice rather than to the internal content of the historical tradition itself. This is apart from my objection to the '-ism' part of the name; both elements in the concept make it on the whole a misleading way of designating that to which it is applied.

Zarathushtra was an important religious reformer, but he was not exactly 'the founder of a religion'. The concept 'Zoroastrianism' underestimates the significance of his role for other traditions (such as the Christian, Muslim, Communist) at the same time as it overestimates it for the Parsi.

28 Some Westerners, especially those unfamiliar with the thought-patterns of India and China, may think it extravagant to discern here an historical continuity between ancient Iran and Marxism, mediated by the elements of ethical and cosmic dualism in the Judaeo-Christian tradition. I suggest, however, that the notions and attitudes developing from this early Persian source have influenced the whole of Western history to an extent so great that Westerners have failed to recognize it only because they have taken them so deeply for granted. From the perspective of a world history of ideas, it seems evident enough that a formulation of a Marxian ideology, with its pronounced conflict dualism, its chiliasm, etc., would have been altogether unlikely in, for instance, China with its *yin-yang* complement dualism, or in India with its polymorphic monism. The quip that for Communism 'There is no God, and Karl Marx is his prophet', rightly sets the movement in its Middle Eastern context. Moreover, not only the content of Marxian ideology, but the form of the Communist movement, are striking—a systematic membership group, with a strong *either/or* dichotomy. To it one clearly either does or does not belong, into it all are free to enter but through it only, and decisively, is man's final welfare to be found; those outside are doomed. This brand of organized community stands in direct historical continuity from the Middle Eastern development that we are here considering. Cf. below, note 33.

29 The messianic idea was contributed not only to the Semitic religious traditions from perhaps a source east of Palestine, but even, it may be, to the Mahayana Buddhist tradition also—if one may follow P. Masson-Oursel in seeing the Maitreya concept as of Iranian origin. He writes of its being injected in the Mahayana stream in Bactria as an important centre on the passage routes between India and China: *la notion d'un bouddha de l'avenir s'inspira [à Bactres] des Saoshyant avestiques et . . . son nom même, Maitreya, manifeste, si l'on peut dire, un avatar nouveau de Mithra*—in Gorce & Mortier, op. cit., vol. 3, p. 43.

30 Fractional parts of it have, sporadically, taken on such a form; and as a matter of fact the development of an explicit Manichee religious community with its conceptualized Manichee system of ideas constitutes a much larger chapter in human history for a thousand years than modern man's memory of them concedes. I am suggesting, however, that even if one left aside such developments there is still, within other traditions (the Christian, the

Islamic, etc.) a history, and a fundamentally important history, of ideas and attitudes here that is in principle observable but is not in principle reifiable.

3^1 The difference between the foreign policies of a John Foster Dulles and a Jawaharlal Nehru in mid-twentieth-century, I make bold to suggest, cannot be fully understood without recognizing that the one stands in an ideological tradition in which conflict dualism and a closed community have played a formative role, while the other's tradition has for two thousand years seen all religious forms as several personal and more or less valid but imperfect expressions of a formless ultimate. Dulles was a Calvinist, where the dichotomy between the saved and the damned is particularly sharp and emphatic; Nehru a Hindu, where all men are partly saved. Those Westerners most likely to make light of such a proffered interpretation are those most ineffective in formulating foreign policies able to reconcile rather than to antagonize the Eastern world.

3^2 To say that the Jewish community was 'a particular people' is in itself a subtle and intricate point. There is nothing unusual in the existence of a small society with clear boundaries, characterized by a distinctive religious and other life and very self-conscious in its 'we/they' attitudes, including often enough a derogatory attitude to outsiders. This phenomenon was once almost universal, and is as characteristic of India and China as of the Middle East and Europe. It is the giving of cosmic significance and metaphysical status to the discrimination that perhaps makes the difference.

33 See the chapter 'The Chinese' in my forthcoming *The Faith of Other Men.*

34 One consequence has been the problem of faith and reason, which has usually been considered in the West as in some sense a final problem and as primarily an intellectual or religious one; whereas I would see it as a local problem and as primarily an historical one, that of the relation between two traditions. See further below, chap. 7, note 9. Another consequence arising from this particular historical situation has been the problem in the West of the relation between Church and State, religion and secular society. For a contrast of this with the Islamic situation, set forth historically, see my *Islam in Modern History,* Princeton 1957, London 1958, pp. 30–31 (New York, 1959, pp. 38–39).

35 In fact, the term 'religion', from the Latin, designates only secondarily and derivedly what the Western world took from Palestine. Its original and fundamental designation is not that but rather those aspects of Graeco-Roman life that it did *not* take from Greece and Rome. In the encounter between Graeco-Roman life and the Christian Church, both these two survived and together produced the Western world; but in that encounter certain facets of Graeco-Roman life failed to survive, were explicitly superseded by the Christian tradition. Those facets have supplied both the word and the concept 'religion'. (This point may not be irrelevant to a Christian distrust of the concept religion, considered below, chap. 5, pp. 125, 139.)

3^6 See above, chap. 3, pp. 54-55.

37 On the use of the word 'church' here, and on other names for the community, see below, note 39.

38 If indeed Henning's (and the Parsis') image of him is to be accepted rather than that of more disparaging scholars (see above, note 25).

39 The word *church* used above (at note 37) is, of course, Christian and its use here is analogical (hence the quotation marks) but hardly extravagant. Its Greek original is ἐκκλησια. Mani's group used for itself the term Ἐκλογη, the unit of the ἐκλεκτοι or 'elect'. The members were called also the 'just', and the community postulated itself as Justice: in Greek, Δικαιοσυνη; Aramaic, *zaddīqūt* (later Arabic, *ṣiddīqūt*), Middle-Persian *ardāvīft*. See the Puech work mentioned just below (my note 41), p. 61 and notes 238 (pp. 143 f.) and 393 (p. 195). *Ekklēsia* itself is found in the Egyptian Manichee texts: see Carl Schmidt *und* H. J. Polotsky, *mit einem Beitrag von* . . . H. Ibschen, 'Ein Mani-Fund in Ägypten. Originalschriften des Mani und seiner Schüler', in *Sitzungsberichte der preussischen Akademie der Wissenschaften, 1933, phil.-hist. Klasse*, Berlin, 1933, pp. 4–90 (for an occurrence in the actual text, see p. 87).

40 See above, chap. 3, note 34.

41 Two of the most important presentations of modern scholarly knowledge of the movement are those of Polotsky and H. C. Puech. The former's chief contribution is to be found in his article 'Manichäismus' in *Paulys Real-Encyclopädie der classischen Altertumswissenschaft*, neue Bearbeitung: begonnen von Georg Wissowa . . . herausgegeben von Wilhelm Kroll; this appears not in its proper alphabetical place in the encyclopaedia but in Supplementband VI, coll. 240-271, Stuttgart, 1935. For the latter see esp. Henri-Charles Puech, *Le Manichéisme: son fondateur—sa doctrine*, Paris, 1949 (published in both annotated and unannotated editions; the former is immensely richer, and more than twice the size). Developments since 1949 are to be followed in the academic journals. (To these references should now be added the important 1960 article of C. Colpe, "Manichäismus", in *Die Religion in Geschichte und Gegenwart: Handwörterbuch für Theologie und Religionswissenschaft*, 3rd ed., Tübingen, 1957– , 4: 714–722.)

42 Finds from Central Asia are in Chinese, Uigur Turkish, and middle-Iranian dialects (Middle-Persian, Parthian, Sogdian); from the Fayyūm, in Subhamimi Coptic. Puech states in one place that the works are all translations (*nos textes, qui sont tous, ne l'oublions pas, des traductions*, op. cit., p. 29) but in another that this is so *en très grosse majorité* (p. 68). I have not had access, unfortunately, to any exception or exceptions.

43 In Middle Persian (southwestern Iran dialect), in the form *dēnān*, in a letter of Mani found in the Turfan region of Chinese Turkistan, where he contrasts 'my *dēn*' with 'former *dēn's*' דיד איד מך and פּישׁינ אן דינאך —fragment T II D 126, I R (1) and V (8), (17), as found in F. C. Andreas & Walter Henning, edd., *Mitteliranische Manichaica aus Chinesisch-Turkestan,*

II, pp. 4, 5—*Sonderausgabe aus den Sitzungsberichten der preussischen Akademie der Wissenschaften, phil.-hist. Klasse*, Berlin, 1933, VII, pp. 295–296. A parallel passage has been found in Coptic, in a recently discovered work, *Kephalaia*. In it, the same contrast is set forth, in much the same way, but it is in terms of '*my ecclēsia*' and former *ecclēsia*s. Earlier movements are presented as flowing into the new as rivers into a great river. He speaks also of 'all the prophets *(apostoloi)*, my brothers, who preceded me', and of their books, and their wisdom *(sophia)*, all now being superseded. For the Coptic text, see Schmidt-Polotsky, op. cit. (above, note 39), pp. 86, 87; trans., and the editors' remarks, e.g., ibid, pp. 40 ff. See further below; e.g., note 63. Kartīr (below, note 54) in his inscriptions, who does seem rather to think of *dēn* as religious system, does not use a plural.

44   For the form, see the preceding note. For a discussion of the meaning, see note 58 below.

45   Something a little like this had happened in India after the rise of a Buddhist community and a somewhat comparable Jain one. The particular situation in India, however, meant that no formalization ensued. Indeed in the end, although the teachings of the Buddha did not disappear in India, the phenomenon of a separated-off Buddhist community eventually did. There were many factors at work in this situation, too complex to go into here; and in any case why something did *not* happen in history is perhaps always a precarious question. The encounter of divergent communities in India was not on a world scale (radically different languages and cultural heritages were not involved, for instance), as was the case in the Sasani empire in Iran. And so on. Anyway, in the Iran case the results were different and momentous. Probably not irrelevant to this is the point that the basic orientation and metaphysical mood in India were different from the *either/or* outlook of which we have spoken in the Middle East. It is this outlook, I feel, that lies behind the fact that the Christian Church developed the way it did in the West while the Buddhist community—India's nearest approach to it organizationally—developed so much less systematically in China and Japan.

46   The Greek philosophic tradition did come nearer to this in the subsequent Islamic world than in, for instance, the West. It developed a name there (*al-Falsafah*, a foreign word which in classical Arabic partakes as much perhaps of the nature of a proper noun as of a common one, perhaps especially among certain groups in society). And the tradition was carried by a relatively small and almost identifiable group within the total community. Moreover it was a tradition, with an almost authoritative source (Aristotle and to a less extent Plato), rather than an attitude of mind; the meaning of the term *al-falsafah* is more adequately rendered from Arabic into English as 'the Greek philosophic tradition' than as 'philosophy' generically. I might suggest that formally there is perhaps a significant parallel between the role of *al-falsafah* in classical Islamic society and that which is implied in the concept *chiao* in Chinese. One may note, further, that it became a deep question in Islamic history whether it was feasible for a man to be both a *Faylasūf* (a member of the *Falsafah* tradition) and a Muslim (member of the Islamic Community), or whether he had to be one *or* the other.

47 I do not know with assurance that Mani was the first to discern it; this is essentially irrelevant to my argument. It may well be that more precise investigation will show that the processes that I am endeavouring to delineate here took place a little earlier, or that their details are different. To elucidate this is the task of scholars in this particular field. What I am concerned to establish, or rather to call attention to, is that the processes took place, and that this is of world importance. I am quite prepared to find that the details of how they took place may need some correction.

48 Or in the Buddha's case, the cosmic moral law *(dharma)*, which he did not call God but I do.

49 Although the reliable scholars in this field accept this designation by Mani of himself, I cannot feel confident about the authenticity of the wording since the authorities cited for it are post-Qur'ān, where the phrase again occurs (once) of Muḥammad (33:40—*kāna Muḥammad . . . rasūl Allāh wa-khātam al-nabīyīn*). The idea is certainly genuine: Mani unquestionably claimed to be supreme in a long line of 'sent ones' (Greek and Coptic, ἀπόστολοι; Middle Persian, *frystg*; cf. Arabic, *rasūl*) that began with Adam and included especially Zarathushtra, the Buddha, and Jesus. See Puech, op. cit. (1949), p. 61 and ref. 241, pp. 144-146. If Mani did use the designation of himself (with a word for 'seal'), this would seem to some of us a matter of immense significance for Islamic theology.

50 In the Old Testament there is a word and concept 'prophet' (נביא, cf. Arabic *nabī*), designating a role that some persons self-consciously filled. The meaning, however, in all its long and complex development, is different from that of the concept in the Manichee or the Islamic *Weltanschauung*. The alternative term for this latter *(rasūl)* does not trace back to the Old Testament; and the difference between the Islamic and the Hebrew notions is manifested in the failure of understanding today between the Islamic and the Judaeo-Christian communities in their interpretations.

51 Although the interpretation of Mani here given is my own, especially in the form-content dichotomy, yet the scholars have pointed out that Mani was unusually deliberate. Puech speaks of *un travail conscient et volontaire* (op. cit., p. 69—see also his ref. no. 266, p. 150) and of *ce syncrétisme conscient et délibéré* (in Gorce & Mortier, op. cit., III.90); Nyberg writes: *Dass er persönlich eine religiöse Natur mit besonders mit tiefem religionspsychologischem Blick ausgerüstet war, ist unleugbar, aber sein Werk trägt stark das Gepräge des Gemachten und Berechneten, ohne zu den tiefsten Quellen der Religion zu führen; er war von allem Religionspolitiker—Die Religionen des Alten Iran, Deutsch von H. H. Schaeder (Mitteilungen der vorderasiatisch-aegyptischen Gesellschaft [E.V.], 43. Band), Leipzig, 1938, p. 411.*

52 That it was complex is indicated by all scholars; emphatically, for instance, by Nyberg, who speaks of the 'unintegrated jumble' in which Semitic and Iranian (and one might add also, Indian) religion met and blended in the milieu into which Mani was born *(de gnostiska kretsarna i Mesopotamien,*

där semitisk och iransk religion möttes och blandades i ett outredlight virrvarr —*Irans forntida religioner*, Stockholm/Uppsala, 1937, p. 458; German trans. [cf. preceding note], p. 411). That it was fluid is also unanimously attested; as an example, Widengren writes of *den Prozess . . . wodurch eine . . . Religion . . . allmählich . . . hineinwächst und nach und nach, aber sehr zögernd, . . . übergeht* (Geo Widengren, 'Stand und Aufgaben der iranishcen Religionsgeschichte', *Numen*, Leiden, 1: 77 [1954]) ; and he uses the word 'process' many times in these pages.

53 Chiefly Nyberg, op. cit. (German trans., pp. 414–415) ; and Puech, though not committing himself, seems to accept the thesis as at least plausible (op. cit., p. 38 and note 137, pp. 119–121). That there was already something available at least to be written down, however, is quite evident; see, e.g., Widengren, op. cit., I. 75. [Since writing the above, I have found W. B. Henning, 'The Disintegration of the Avestic Studies', in *Transactions of the Philological Society, 1942*, London, 1944, p. 47, where a pre-Mani written text of the Avesta seems definitely proven.]

54 This is Kartīr (latter third century A.D.), who rose to a position of considerable power in the reign of the Sasani emperor Shapur I, and seems to have played a major role in establishing a state religious system for the subsequent centuries of that empire. Four inscriptions by him have recently been found in Iran and are being studied. See chiefly Martin Sprengling, *Third Century Iran: Sapor and Kartir*, Chicago, 1953 (also a preliminary and rather unsatisfactory editing in the same author's 'Kartīr, founder of Sasanian Zoroastrianism' in *The American Journal of Semitic Languages and Literatures*, Chicago, 57; 197–228, 330–340 [1940], 58: 169–176 [1941]). The inscription at what is today called the Naqsh-i Rajab includes the affirmation: 'There is a heaven, and there is a hell. And whoever is virtuous will go to heaven. And whoever is a sinner, will be cast into hell' (Middle-Persian text in Sprengling, 1953, p. 65). The persecuting activities launched by this fiery and virtually fanatic administrator suggest that he coupled this doctrine with an identifying of 'virtue' with the observance of one set of religious practices, 'sin' with observance of an alternative set—a combination that constitutes systematic and reified religion at its most rigid. (Note from another inscription his reference to those who 'within the magus-estate in matters of mazdayasnian religion and divine services did not observe orders'—ibid., text p. 47, trans. p. 52.)

R. C. Zaehner, in his *Zurvan, a Zoroastrian dilemma*, Oxford, 1955, after commenting on the former passage above, writes that Kartīr 'reconverted the amenable to Zoroastrian orthodoxy' (p. 25) ; but the concept 'orthodoxy' bears scrutiny (also the 're-' of 'reconverted'). Would it not be more historical to say that by the persecutions a Zoroastrian orthodoxy was brought into being? One creates an orthodoxy by defining and by giving weight, in some sociological form, to that definition.

Also, the word 'Zoroastrian' here is perhaps worth consideration. Kartīr, curiously, does not mention this figure. He does name the 'religion' that it was his self-appointed task to consolidate and institutionalize: the form *dyny mzdysn* (Mazdayasnian religion, the Mazdayasnian religion) is found six times in the inscriptions. A plural 'religions' (*dyn'n, dēnān*) does not occur.

55 Abstracting from out the tumultuous upsurge of developments, names have been given classically to two classes of phenomena in particular, two emergences: Gnostic and Mandaean. The latter continued to a sufficiently late period, and gradually became a sufficiently organized and cognizable movement, that a name for it seems eventually legitimate, as we shall see. (In fact, a Mandaean community, though tiny, still exists today in Iraq. One of its characteristics is that it practises a form of baptizing.) The Gnostic tradition, on the other hand, seems to me to have continued too disorganized for our intellectual apprehension of it to be aided by any systematic conceptualization. The modern term 'Gnosticism,' however, clings persistently. In a recent scholarly study, whose title sustains the notion, one reads: 'Defining Gnosticism is an extraordinarily difficult task, since modern writers use the term to cover a wide variety of speculative religious phenomena. These phenomena are encountered from Gaul in the West to Iran in the East, from the first century of our era to at least the ninth. . . . The systems include notions related to Zoroastrianism, Babylonian religion, Judaism, Hellenistic philosophy and religion, and Christianity. How are we to define Gnosticism as a whole?' (R. M. Grant, *Gnosticism and Early Christianity*, New York and London, 1959, p. 6; see also the whole section 'Origins', pp. 3–14). The author is nevertheless undaunted, and accepts (posits?) 'Gnosticism as a whole' as some sort of entity. In this case the adjective 'Gnostic' seems to me admissible in an evolving series of personalist-historical senses, whereas a noun Gnosticism is much more dubious. If a tradition must be conceived and apprehended, I would proffer the terms set forth in our next two chapters as solely adequate to such a task.

The Mandaean tradition, on the other hand, does eventually emerge (becoming perhaps distinct from the fifth century or later?—yet by then with a history) as that of a self-conscious and identifiable group. The fact of this gradual emergence is for our purposes of first-class importance.

Mandâ is Aramaic for that for which *gnōsis* is Greek (namely, 'knowledge'), and *Mandâyâ* (later, 'Mandaean') equals *gnōstikos*, 'knowing'). The early history of what later evolved to constitute the Mandaean tradition, therefore, is in part simply that history to which the word 'Gnostic', even as a gradually technical term, is relevant. Subsequently, one's task is to discern the process by which two streams came to be differentiated (one called by the Aramaic name, one by the Greek).

Turning to another facet of the evolving complex, one may remark that the ceremonial practice of baptism almost certainly has a continuous history at least from John the Baptist and doubtless a little earlier to the 'Mandaeans' of the seventh century (and since). In the third century, Mani's father was a baptist or was baptized, and brought his son up in some relation with such a group. Rather than asking, however, when 'Mandaeanism' arose, might we not better ask such questions as, was there a time when one could participate in these ceremonies without abjuring 'membership' in other communities? The answer here is obviously 'yes', since the crowds mentioned in the New Testament who went to the Jordan to hear John and to be baptized by him clearly had no conception that to do this was to choose it as an alternative to membership in the Jewish community. Further, since Roman soldiers were also involved, 'being a Jew' or not being one was also irrelevant. We may ask further, was there a time when this was no longer true. Apparently the answer here is again 'yes', since by the seventh century in Central Asia, it seems that a man might be *either* a Christian *or* a Mandaean, but not both—as in twentieth-century Baghdad one is either a Muslim or a Mandaean, but not both (though one can be both a Muslim and a Platonist, or both a Mandaean and a Platonist) . Then can one trace the process by which the one situation evolved into the other?

Again, by the seventh century, along with the baptismal ceremonies a complex of other rites and beliefs was apparently linked in a systematic pattern so that if a man chose one element in the pattern he was expected (or forced?) to choose all. At an earlier moment, however, these several elements are to be found in the area but they are not linked in this systematic way; so that some persons would observe some and others others. The process of this gradual systematization can presumably be historically traced. A concomitant process, related but not identical, is that of men's conceptualization of the systematization. At what point did anyone, and at what point did everyone, intellectualize the fact that the system was a coherent entity, so that in theory as well as (or instead of?) in practice the various elements were organized together?

It is in the conceptualization of the generic entity of religious system—that there exists a series of these, each one of which is of an abstractly comparable kind—that I see the role of Mani as significant, as either an original or an illustrative thinker and actor. This concept could not well arise in the West at this time, because it was not true in the West that there were several systems all of one generic kind. There was nothing really comparable to the Christian Church in the Mediterranean world—with due respects to the devotees of Mithra, Isis, and the others: it is in fact not really until the twentieth century that the Western Church is in a position, vis-à-vis the other major religious traditions of the world, like that of the Eastern Churches in the early centuries. One of its basic problems in this arises from the fact that it faces its twentieth-century problem with attitudes appropriate to, and largely derived from, its early confrontation with Roman paganism—which simply will not do.

The following story prettily illustrates the eighth (ninth?) -century situation with regard to conceptualizing religions as a series of entities, and can serve to measure the change that had taken place in the area over the preceding centuries. A Persian of considerable stature and culture at the court of the early 'Abbasis, by the name of Ibn al-Muqaffa', is reported to have been out to dinner the evening before he was to be formally admitted as a new convert to the Islamic community and faith. His host, a Muslim, under these circumstances expressed surprise at his guest's reciting Manichee prayers when the next morning he was to become a Muslim. Ibn al-Muqaffa' is said to have replied: 'I dislike the idea of passing a night without having a religion' (al-Balādhurī, *Ansāb al-Ashrāf*, manuscript quoted in S. D. Goitein, 'A Turning Point in the History of the Muslim State', *Islamic Culture*, Hyderabad, 23: 132 [1949]) .

56 After writing this paragraph, I find that Prof. Zaehner (despite the phraseology that I have ventured to criticize in note 54, just above) actually uses this very terminology in a more recent study in which he states that 'Zoroastrianism ... became crystallized into a dogmatic religion during the reign of Shāpūr II' [that is, 310–379 A.D.] (R. C. Zaehner, *The Teachings of the Magi*, London and New York, 1956, p. 11) .

57 The writings of virtually all modern scholars of this period in one

sense support this view, and yet their interpretations, or at least their phrasing, would have to be modified if this presentation were accepted. For almost all operate with a concept of systematic-religion in their minds, the product of the Western development that we traced in chap. 2 above. Since the concept holds reasonably well by the end of this period for the material being studied, it is not as misleading as in the study of some other cultures. Yet I hope that I may be forgiven for intruding where others are the specialists, with the suggestion that the developments being observed can more adequately be understood if one sees that this particular conceptualization is not *a priori* or in itself absolute, and that that to which it refers was in process of formulation in the lives and societies of the men whose history these centuries in this area constitute.

For example, we saw above (note 55) that Professor Grant feels that Gnosticism, despite the confusions, can be defined. He admits towards the end of his book, on the other hand, that Christianity in this area at this time cannot. In the West, where the alternatives to it were more radically different (polytheism, for instance), it was not long before one could say that oneself, or one's neighbour, either was a Christian (in the sense of being a member of the Church—we leave aside being a 'true Christian') or was something else (a worshipper of Jupiter, say). In the East this was less so. The *either/or* dichotomy would not operate in asking whether Marcion was a Christian or a Gnostic. (Christians in the West asked this, insistently, and pressed for an *either/or* answer; but in the East, as Grant implicitly recognizes, such a question could have had no meaning.) In Greek, *gnōstikos* means literally 'he who knows' (has transcendent knowledge, γνωσις; clearly this cannot be an *either/or* matter, since most even of the devotees will know in part. There was no doubt a tendency (as we saw also with 'Christian') towards the adjective's designating a relation not to *gnōsis* but to the human movement in search of it, in which case 'Gnostic' comes to mean not one who knows but one who wants to know. But even that need not be organized or systematic, and need not be *either/or*.

Again, a voluminous academic discussion has been devoted to the question of whether Mandaeanism precedes Manichaeanism or vice-versa (for a bibliography on the debate to 1949, see Puech, op. cit., pp. 40–41 and ref. 147, pp. 123–125; cf. also his ref. 154, p. 126). This way of framing the question presupposes, I think misleadingly, at least part of the answer. Again, since *mandâ* in Aramaic is originally equivalent to *gnōsis* in Greek, it is interesting that virtually all scholars discriminate between the concepts that they have constructed from the two terms. Surely one must use them, if at all, in reference to their use by the people concerned. And the people concerned were involved in the developing process of gradual conceptual reification about which we are speaking.

Puech is surely groping towards an analysis of this kind when he uses phrases such as the following: *une forme primitive du Mandéisme proprement dit, . . . ce Mandéisme primitif, ou ce 'Prémandéisme'*—op. cit., p. 41. And I hope that I am not being presumptuous when I suggest that his concluding section *Le Mandéisme, problème ouvert* in his admirable article *Le Mandéisme* in Gorce & Mortier, op. cit., vol. III, pp. 82–83, is in effect a description of just such a process towards self-conceptualization as I here propose—a process that cannot be said to have a dateable beginning but that culminates observably at the times that he mentions.

Similarly, of the Iranian tradition, Puech speaks of *le mazdéisme proprement dit*, in such a sentence as the following, which surely on analysis does not bear scrutiny: the early Sasani monarchs, he says, were thinking to *restaurer ou à instaurer une religion autre que le mazdéisme proprement dit, dont la forme officielle ne prévaudra que plus tard* (op. cit., p. 38). Widengren uses the phrase *der etwas Proteusartigen Zervanismus* (op. cit., *Numen*, I:76). We have seen other comparable statements on this period (e.g., above, note 52), and shall meet more (e.g., below, chap. 5, note 26). It is perhaps not illegitimate or presumptuous to generalize that the scholars of these developments have because of their studies almost but not quite shattered the traditional concepts by means of which men interpret religious history, but have not yet replaced them with alternative concepts adequate to reporting what they see.

58 This is a subject that will certainly repay thorough investigation. Unlike the situation with the term *religio* in the Western tradition, thus far it seems to have had only incidental study, careful though some of this has unquestionably been in detail. Several doctoral dissertations have been written on the development of *religio* (cf. above, chap. 2, note 4). Considerable further discussion, both at a more senior level than that and more incidentally, has been given to the problem. In the case of *dīn, daēnā, dēn*, on the other hand, I know of no systematic over-all discussion, let alone sustained research. One may hope that some aspiring doctoral candidate will be attracted to the subject, under the guidance of someone who combines philological and *religionswissenschaftliche* competence (cf. Widengren's foot-note, op. cit., *Numen*, I: 17). The dictionaries and glossaries are often content to give 'religion' as an equivalent, without specifying in what sense this Western word is to be understood. There is considerable room, for instance, to use my particular terms, for discriminating between such radically different matters as personal faith and objective system; between transcendent ideal and historical reality; between ideology and community; between static pattern of ideas and evolving sociological process. The translations are, of course, extremely helpful, and it would be churlish to criticize them. Yet one may perhaps remark that —as is not unexpected—most have been made by scholars not particularly interested in the questions of concern to us here, so that in the case of this particular word singulars are sometimes insouciantly rendered by plurals, or personal religion appears in English as 'the' or 'a' religion. We have seen that the same has been true even in the West in cases of modern translations from Latin, even by believers.

Almost every scholarly study of one or other of the Middle East traditions does, however, have a paragraph or so on the use of the word. These provide the place from which to start a full inquiry, of course, as they have provided me with some of what incipient insights I may have gleaned.

59 See above, note 54. I do not know whether the Kartīr inscriptions are the first time that this phrase is found.

60 In suggesting that the *dēn, dīn* tradition is comparable to the

religio one, which we have already considered, and that these two prove to be the channels for the conceptualization 'a religion', 'the religions of the world', and so on for the whole world today, I am concerned not primarily with language, which is a mere vehicle and at times almost incidental, but with the realm of metaphysical outlook. I do not mean to suggest that etymologies determine creeds, or that terminology altogether controls *Weltanschauung*. It does so to only a limited degree; while to a very marked degree it illustrates it. It is the influence and spread of ideas for which we are looking, and for which in this case the looking proves to be well worthwhile.

61   For a time (since the dictionary of Christian Bartholomae, *Altiranisches Wörterbuch*, Strassburg, 1904, s.v. *daēna*) two meanings were ascribed to this term, an inner, personal one (*inneres Wesen, geistiges Ich, Individualität*) and an outer, observable one (*Religion*). Only the former is now accepted as original. See Nyberg's discussion of the term, op. cit., pp. 126–132—in the German translation, pp. 114–120. His conclusion is that *daēnā* is the perceptivity that lies in every man, or his 'perceiving soul', understood as his religious faculty or organ; and also the collectivity of all those who perceive, or the cult community. This derivation from a root *dāy*, 'to see' (also in Paul Horn, *Grundriss der neupersischen Etymologie* [Sammlung indogermanischer Wörterbücher, iv], Strassburg, 1893, references under entry 413, p. 93 and entry 597, with fn., p. 133) is, however, challenged. Widengren has recently written that '*daēna* is the same word as Sanskrit *dhénā*, an old etymology that will be proved with new arguments by Dr. S. T. Hartman in a forthcoming work'—Geo Widengren, *Muḥammad, the Apostle of God, and his ascension*, Uppsala & Wiesbaden, 1955 (Widengren, *King and Saviour*, part V—*Uppsala Universitets Årsskrift*, 1955, no. 1), pp. 186–187; and the same author has further references on this point in his *Numen* article cited above, note 52, 1954, p. 33 and fn. 85. I have not seen the arguments in favour of this etymology, which would make *daēnā* signify 'nurture' rather than 'insight'. I suppose that the difference would be between religious faith's being thought of, from man's side, as something that we do, apprehending God in some sort of awareness, and from God's side, as His upholding us. I would still argue for 'faith' as the nearest equivalent in any case, thinking of the theological position that personal faith is a gift from God and not a human attainment—though no doubt we must await the philological explorations.

62   Nyberg cites one form of this myth in op. cit., pp. 131–132 (German, p. 119) where he tentatively argues, in a way that I do not find quite persuasive, that it represents rather the community; if valid, this would be an instance of our next sense. Duchesne-Guillemin chooses a deliberate ambiguity here and on the meaning of the term in general: *Il suffit de songer à un terme qui soit susceptible, selon le contexte, d'un sens soit abstrait, soit collectif, soit individuel. Le mot religion, en français, me paraît répondre à ce signalement, puisqu'il désigne tantôt une doctrine, tantôt l'ensemble des fidèles, tantôt enfin une caractéristique individuelle* (op. cit. above, note 27, pp. 67–68).

63   In the dictionaries and word-lists, Middle-Iranian *dēn* (orthographically *dyn*; or with the word-ending, *dyny*) is given as 'religion', some-

times with 'community, church', added (e.g., *Religion, Gemeinde, Kirche,* s.v. *dyn* in W. Henning, *Ein manichäisches Bet- und Beichtbuch,* Berlin, 1937 [*Einzelausgabe, Abhandlungen der preussischen Akademie der Wissenschaften, 1936, phil.-histor. Klasse, Nr.* 10], p. 110). The important thing is to see the contextual usages. Here the crucial occurrences are those where the Magi used it to name their own tradition, and Mani to name his new group. The two occur roughly contemporaneously. The two phrases are *dēn-i mazdayasn* as a designation of what is sometimes to-day called Mazdaeanism (*le Mazdéisme*), or Zoroastrianism, perhaps first found (*dyn-y mzdysn*) in the mid-third-century Kartīr inscriptions (above, notes 54 and 59); and *dēn-i man* (*dyn 'yg mn*) in the Middle-Persian version of a letter of Mani (see note 43 above). In this he is presented as speaking of 'my *dēn*', and contrasting it with earlier ones (in the plural)—either 'my religion' (systematic) and 'the earlier religions', could be meant, or 'my community' (my religious community, my church) and 'earlier communities'.

To decide whether the referent is a body of people or a pattern of ideas and practices—community, or system—or rather, to discern which came first and to reconstruct the process by which both are eventually conceptualized by the term, would require the careful study of more contextual occurrences than I have been able to examine, and perhaps more than have yet been published. This whole field is very much still in process of being explored. My tentative impression is that in Buddhist usage the term is not much employed, that in Zarathushtrian-Mazdean it is chiefly with a religious system in mind, and that in Manichee literature the word is used relatively more often for a community.

This last point would seem to have the implicit support of Prof. Henning's editions and translations of the Middle-Iranian Manichee material, which pretty consistently give *Gemeinde, Kirche* as an alternative to or explication of 'religion' (as we have seen one instance just above. On the other hand, in his *Sogdica* [Forlong Fund, vol. 21], London, 1940, p. 12, he translates the passage just cited as 'My religion is superior to former creeds', and one must reckon with the point that *dēn* is used a little later here as the object of a verb 'to teach'.) The community-hypothesis is strengthened by Coptic parallels (above, note 43) and by Manichee usage in some compounds, e.g., *dyn s'r'r* [*dēn sārār*] 'the leader of the *dēn*' as an ecclesiastical title (Andreas-Henning, op. cit. 1933 [note 43 above], s.v. *dyn* in Glossar, p. 51 [p. 342]) (cf. also our next note). That in the case of the *dēn-i Mazdayasn* the meaning is more systematic-ideal, I infer from such facts as that in Kartīr's time when he set up his inscription (mid-third century) there hardly was a Mazdaean community yet. The Christian Church had members, and Mani's community was hierarchically organized, with various classes of members, the 'elect', the 'catechumens', etc., but the Magian priesthood performed certain practices (e.g., fire-temple worship) and preached certain doctrines, but it was only considerably later that they and those who worshipped with them constituted a systematic membership community. Although it is true also that their doctrines and practices were not yet formulated into an independent coherent system either, nonetheless I personally find it easier to image Kartīr at this date conceptualizing this latter (probably practices more than doctrines) towards which he was moving, than conceptualizing the group; I may be wrong.

In a later text, *dēn-i Mazdayasnī* is equated with the law (*dāta*—below, note 67) of Ormazd; and the *dīn* is mentioned as an historical entity: 'at the beginning of the religion, Zarathushtra . . .' (text in *An Old Pahlavi-Pazand Glossary*, edited . . . by Destur Hoshangji Jamaspji Asa, . . . revised and enlarged . . . by Martin Haug, Bombay & London, 1870, pp. 22, 23 respectively [the second series of pagination]).

The Manichee observations would seem to hold for the cognate languages also. For Coptic, on the other hand, see above, note 43.

64 This is evinced in the compound adjectives, which occur with meanings such as 'devout', 'pious', religious in the sense of personal religion, inner faith (in the cognate languages equally): *dēndār, *dēnvar, etc. (Middle-Persian *dynd'r, dynwr,* Parthian *dyn'br,* Soghdian *δynδ'r*—see the Glossaries of Andreas-Henning, op. cit., 1933, p. 51; Mary Boyce, *The Manichaean Hymn-Cycles in Parthian*, London, New York, 1954, p. 187; Robert Gauthiot & E. Benveniste, *Essai de grammaire sogdienne*, Paris, 1914-23/1929, 2ème parti, p. 218 [*Mission Pelliot en Asie Centrale*, série petit, tome III.]) For compounds in which *dēn* signifies 'community', see the preceding note.

65 The form *dēnān* in the Mani letter just cited (above, note 63 and esp. note 43). It is tantalizing not to have evidence of what Aramaic concepts Mani used.

66 In the following century, the Edict of Milan, 313 A.D., of the Emperor Constantine, proclaiming freedom of worship for all religious groups, uses a plural also. The Greek term is Θρησκειαι; the Latin, *religiones*. These, however, denote 'rites', as is appropriate both for the previous meanings of these words and for the content of the edict, which recognized equal privileges for each system of observances in the empire. This was the point at issue: the state could control the performance of ritual, but its control of these externals had not, as it had found, suppressed the beliefs or the faith of the community —rather the contrary: the blood of the martyrs, in Tertullian's famous phrase, was the seed of the religious life of the Church. In strict accuracy there had been 'freedom of religions' all along: nothing that the state could do could prevent Christians from exercising their freedom to die for their faith. What the Edict of Milan proclaimed was freedom of worship, of ritual.

Similarly the Christian apologists, like the pagan Latins, used the plural *religiones*, as we have seen (above, chap. 2, note 47) to designate what the modern world might call 'a religion' in the singular, or its rites. Arnobius, the chief early example of this, is in any case later than Mani.

67 *Dāta* is an Old-Persian word, found in the Gathas, the rest of the Avesta, and subsequently. It meant Law—as a general ideal (*le droit, das Recht*), a system of law, and a particular law or regulation or legal decision (*la loi, das Gesetz*). It was used both for the law of God (i.e., of Ahura Mazda) and for that of the state (the law of the Medes and the Persians). In the former sense it is found with the adjective 'Zarathushtrian' as the moral law that Zarathushtra proclaimed. (See Christian Bartholomae, *Altiranische Wörterbuch*, Strassburg, 1904, s.v., col. 726). It was taken over by the Jews after their contact with the Achaemenid Persian empire, and is found

in the Hebrew of the late books of the Old Testament: once in Ezra, otherwise in Esther, in speaking of Persian law, ranging all the way from royal decrees to social conventions. In Biblical Aramaic it occurs fairly frequently, in the book of Daniel with its scene set, like that of Esther, in the Persian court, and again in Ezra; to designate the edicts of the King, and also (in the mouth of non-Jews) the law of the Jews' God (Dan. 6: 6 [Massoretic text; in the Authorized Version, 6: 5]; Ezra 7: 12, 14, 21, 25, 26). On *dāth* in the Old Testament see Francis Brown, S. R. Driver, Charles A. Briggs, edd., *A Hebrew and English Lexicon of the Old Testament,* Oxford, 1906, and Ludwig Koehler & Walter Baumgartner, edd., *Lexicon in Veteris Testamenti Libros,* 2 voll., Leiden, 1951-1953, in both cases s.v. in both the Hebrew and the Aramaic sections). (The same letters in the evidently faulty text of Deut. 33: 2 are recognized by scholars as not this word.)

The law presently became so distinctive a characteristic and so central an element of Jewish faith, that those who were adherents of what we might call one religious community could be discriminated from those adhering to another, by one's speaking of which law they observed. Thus some authorities would translate 'the *dāth* of his God [his god?]' in the Aramaic of Daniel 6:6 as 'his religion', which is all right provided one bears in mind that by 'religion' here one means 'law'. In later Aramaic it is used to designate the characteristics of various religious groups whether these were legal or not. (This was facilitated by the use of *dāth* to designate not only injunctions but social customs.) I have not ascertained when a plural in the sense of 'religions' was first used, though it presumably grew so naturally out of a plural for 'laws' that this would be difficult to trace. (D. Gustaf H. Dalman, *Aramäisch-neuhebräisches Handwörterbuch zu Targum, Talmud und Midrasch . . .* Zweite . . . Auflage, Frankfurt a. Main, 1922, s.v. דת for this period gives 1. *Gesetz, Gebrauch.* 2. *Religion*). Further inquiry in this field should bear in mind the possibility, which I have not investigated, that Mani and the subsequent Sasani developments, which I see as so crucial, may have been themselves influenced by previous developments in Jewish thought as well as in Jewish life: that the process of crystallization in conceptualization as well as sociologically had already gone further among the Jews (and Christians?) by the third century than I have recognized. Highly illuminating here would be to know whether in Mani's own mind the Aramaic equivalent of Pahlavi *dēn* was *dāth* or *dīn.* The latter does not appear to have been used in a religious sense in Jewish Aramaic (e.g. Dalman, op. cit., s.v.) ; was it in Manichee Aramaic? It was in Christian Aramaic (see below, note 69) , but whether before or after Mani I do not know. It would be helpful to know when the first Syriac plural for *dīn* occurs.

At the other end of the Iranian world and in another religious context, it is noteworthy that in the language of the Saka people *dāta* (documented from Tumšuq in the form *dāda*) was used by the Central Asian Buddhists as a translation for their concept *dharma* (Harold Walter Bailey, 'Languages of the Saka', in Karl Hoffman et al., *Iranistik—I. Linguistik,* Leiden, 1958 [B. Spuler & H. Kees, edd., *Der nahe und der mittlere Osten,* IV. Band, *in* B. Spuler et al., edd., *Handbuch der Orientalistik*], p. 149).

68 Against the word 'religion' in the *English-Hebrew Dictionary* by Israel Efros, Judah ibn-Shmuel Kaufman, Benjamin Silk, 18th printing, Tel Aviv, 1957 are given three entries: יראת שׁמים—אמונה—דת. These represent, respectively: law ('systematic religion'), faith, and awe or sense of the holy, religiousness (literally, 'fear of the heavens').

NOTES FOR CHAPTER FOUR

69 Carl Brockelmann, *Lexicon Syriacum*, 2nd ed., Halis Saxonum, 1928, s.v. (p. 151). There is a suggestion perhaps of personal religiousness for *dīn*, in the related *dīnī*, 'asceticism' (ibid.); though several other terms were used in Church Syriac for 'faith', personal religiousness—see ibid., s.v. *religio* in the 'Index Latinus', p. 905, and the references there given.

70 This is found as far back as Akkadian. The verb *diânu, dânu* is given as meaning *richten; ein Gericht abhalten; ein Urteil fällen; rechten; Recht schaffen; Recht behalten,* and the noun *dīnu, dênu* as *Recht; Gericht; Strafgericht; Prozess; Rechtsspruch; Entscheidung (des il Šamaš bei der Leberschau)* in Anton Deimel, ed., *Šumerisches Lexikon*, Rome, 1925–1937, III. Teil, Band 2: *Akkadisch-Šumerisches Glossar*, 1937, pp. 84, 84–85.

71 For example, in the universally memorized opening *sūrah*, in the phrase *mālik yawm al-dīn*; and a dozen other times. Note also *fī dīn al-malik* (12:76), 'according to the king's law'. The verb appears in the common Arabic proverb *kamā tadīnu tudān*, 'as you judge, so will you be judged' (I do not know how old this is, but it was proverbial already in the early Islamic centuries, and is presumably ancient). Expressing the same concept 'The Day of Judgement', the equivalent phrase *yawm dīnā* was found previously in Rabbinical Aramaic, Church Syriac, and Mandaean Aramaic, and *yawm ha-d-dīn* in Rabbinic Hebrew (Arthur Jeffery, *The Foreign Vocabulary of the Qur'ān*, Baroda, 1938, pp. 131–133). It is evident so soon as one pauses to reflect upon it that those Arabs who had not been in contact with these more advanced religious traditions did not conceptualize a 'day of judgement' and would not have understood this combination of words.

72 As in the Akkadian, above, note 70.

73 Before the technical meanings are discussed, such as 'religion' which are historically later, the literal (pre-Islamic) applications of the word *dīn* are listed as follows (*fī al-lughah yuṭlaqu 'alá* . . .): 'custom, way of personal life, accounting, coercion, sentence and judgement, obedience, condition, retribution [here the two instances cited also in our note 71 above are given as illustration], governing, opinion. Also [the verb *dāna* means] to disobey and to obey, to be contemptible and to be powerful [with reference to a commentary on this comprehending of opposites]'—in Mohammad Wajih *et al.*, Aloys Sprenger *et al.*, edd., [Muhammad 'Alī al-Ṭahānawī's] *Kashshāf iṣṭilāḥāt al-funūn: A Dictionary of the Technical Terms used in the Sciences of the Mussalmans*, [Calcutta] 1862, Part I, p. 503. I cite this not as conclusive (it is a rather late authority) but as illustrative: among later Arabs there was preserved a documented memory of the time when the word *dīn* in their language meant many other things but not yet systematic religion. See also s.v. in the traditional dictionaries.

74 Apart from the specific question of language, the Muslim is involved in a delicate issue in the whole area of the historical particularity of revelation. Yet faith does not alter, and must not and need not evade, the facts of particularist history. It sees the same facts in a different way, interprets the same situation differently. The historian must allow for variant interpretations, but his task of discerning the facts, and of uncovering the process by which relentlessly a situation develops, is uninterrupted.

75 This, indeed, is why there has been hesitation at allowing a translation of the Qur'ān, since any translation must at best express a human understanding of its meaning.

76 The one clear instance that has been noted of a use, in pre-Islamic Arabia, of the word *dīn* in the systematic-religion sense, is in a (rather depreciative) reference to the *dīn* of the Jews by a poet who was a Christian, one 'Urwah ibn al-Ward. Attention was called to this passage a century ago by Theodor Nöldeke, ed. & trans., *Die Gedichte des 'Urwa ibn Alward*, Göttingen, 1863, p. 42, where in a note (p. 79) to poem xiii, line 1, he says that this is the only indubitable pre-Islamic place where he finds *dīn* in the meaning 'religion'. Subsequent scholarship seems to have accepted this without either questioning the interpretation (actually from the context the word could be taken as referring to 'community' as well as to 'religious system') or expanding the instance. It is now becoming possible to make a full investigation of the matter, since a concordance of the vocabulary of pre-Qur'ān Arabic is currently being compiled at the Hebrew University, Jerusalem, and is available to students; a nice topic for a doctoral thesis is implicit here. See above, note 5. The compilation is still in process; additional entries will be available in future.

77 Muslims aver that the Jewish and Christian religious traditions stem from the preaching by Moses and Jesus respectively of revelations from God in the same transcendent series as, and (at least in part) ideally identical with, the revelation from God that, in its final, superseding, and universal form, was preached by Muhammad; but that the followers of the other two traditions have distorted and falsified these revelations. (See, for instance, my *Islam in Modern History*, chap. 1.) Many Muslims are genuinely pained when Christians and Jews do not accept this Muslim view of the three traditions. Once again the point is illustrated here that members of religious traditions have little awareness of how differently those inside and those outside interpret the same general facts—and how differently they *must* interpret them. See further below, pp. 107–108, especially at note 85.

78 Émil Durkheim, *Les formes élémentaires de la vie religieuse*, Paris, 1912. *The Elementary Forms of the Religious Life, a study in religious sociology*, trans. Joseph Ward Swain, London & New York, n.d. [1915]; New York, 1954.

79 Comparisons are delicate, and no doubt cannot be pushed far. In Christian doctrine the Church is the body of Christ, which means that it is given not only cosmic significance but ultimate ontological status. (With this has gone the difficulty that Christians, like Muslims, have had in giving any but a degraded metaphysical status to the rest of mankind.) My feeling that the Muslims carry their *ummah* concept in some ways further than this, at least sociologically, is due in part to the fact that this absolutizing of the Church has tended to become in practice if not in theory somewhat dis-

rupted since the Reformation; in part to the political-ecclesiastical dualism of Christian history and doctrine, whereby each Christian is a member of two communities of which the Church is but one; and in part to a distinction (cf. below, note 90) between the true Church and the visible Church. This distinction may obviate somewhat or divert the Christian's hypostasizing a sociological entity. The 'body of Christ' is explicitly a mystical concept, not quite a this-worldly one. By being a member of the Church the Christian participates (mystically) in a transcendent reality, and in a community that has a transcendent dimension (the communion of saints, the majority of whom are no longer alive on earth). The *ummah*, while making perhaps less arrogantly exclusivist pretensions metaphysically, is a more sociological concept than this, however much the two may otherwise approximate.

Cf. also below, chap. 7, note 4.

80　*Islam in Modern History*, chap. 1.

81　That is, in the present-day world. Mani is in part, in this as in many ways, a formal predecessor of Muhammad—though only in part, for Mani was brought up a gnostic of sorts, and even, those would say who use the term already for the third century, a Mandaean of sorts. Mani, like Muhammad, saw the religious community or system that he was preaching as superseding but embracing, perfecting, those that had come before (see especially the Turfan fragment and its Coptic counterpart cited above, note 43). The followers of previous 'prophets', Mani claimed, had falsified the preachings of those prophets (in his case, these were chiefly seen as Zarathushtra, Buddha, and Jesus), so that their religious tradition needed purifying. Essentially his mission was to reaffirm, though in more universalist fashion, what they had taught each to his own people. Mani, however, was not repudiating anything, as Muhammad repudiated the pagan religious tradition of his fellows. He rather accepted virtually all that he saw among those to whom he preached, to replace it with his new universal formulation. (In this he is followed by not a few twentieth-century universalists, who would establish a culminating global community!) Muhammad, on the other hand, rejected the religious heritage of those to whom primarily he preached (the pagan Arabs), accepting (for supersession) those of two in many ways *outside* communities. For some parallels between Mani and Muhammad, see the 1955 study of Widengren cited above, note 61. This is an area on which it would be extremely interesting to see scholarly studies by Muslims. They would interpret the facts no doubt very differently from a student whose faith is not *en jeu*; but whatever the interpretation, the facts are worthy of careful consideration.

82　And in the light of the recent finds one would now have to add, Manichee.

83　Above, note 77.

84　Jeffery, op. cit. above (note 71), p. 1.

85　I have nonetheless allowed myself to quote it, not as expressing my own formulations—which it certainly does not—but because it seems to me highly illuminating. It illustrates how an authoritative scholar views a situation, on the one hand; and, on the other, illustrates the point made above at the end of ref. 77 and at the end of this paragraph in my text, namely that there is an *inevitable* difference in how a believer and a non-believer view exactly the same facts—a difference that is not the result of perversity or malice. When I say 'inevitable' I mean that it must inevitably arise, and has always arisen in the past; I personally believe (cf. my article 'Comparative Religion—Whither and Why' in M. Eliade and J. Kitagawa, edd., *The History of Religions: essays in methodology*, Chicago, 1959, pp. 31–58; and our discussion below, chap. 5) that to deal with this situation constructively is one of the tasks to which mankind today is called, and I am not without hope that we can conceivably rise to it. Three of the greatest difficulties are for people to see that the problem exists, to believe that it can be solved, and to will to tackle it.

On the question of the Qur'ān as the word of God, the normal situation has been that men have been divided into two quite clear-cut groups on this issue. Muslims have believed that it is, others have believed that it is not. My own view is that the matter is not necessarily so simple; I hope to try an essay presently on 'Is the Qur'ān the word of God?' In any case, both Muslims and non-Muslims should recognize that any discussion that touches on the Qur'ān and that is not necessarily addressed exclusively to one or the other of these two separated groups, is in an exceedingly delicate position, and the form of any such argument is exceedingly delicate. In the past neither group has much recognized this. Indeed hardly any discussion on the subject has been put forward from either side that is in principle (though perhaps unwittingly) not partial, speaking only to one of the two groups.

86   There is even a second term in Qur'ān Arabic, *millah*, which was even more congruous, perhaps, with the Western concept 'religion' in its systematic sense. No evidence has yet been forthcoming, however, that Arabs had ever heard this word to designate a religious system before they heard it in the Qur'ān (Jeffery, op. cit., s.v. [p. 268–269]). It is used in the Qur'ān primarily for the religion of Abraham, which Muḥammad is presented as following. In fact one wonders if it is not the only word in any language or culture that designates a specific and transferable religion, one as distinct from others, and nothing else. It has never meant 'faith' in the intimately personal, non-transferable sense: one man's faith that is utterly his and no one else's. Nor could it be used of religion in general, a world-wide religiousness irrespective of the particular form. It seems to designate precisely the form, as an observable and even as it were abstractable, transferable something. In every case in which it is used in the Qur'ān, the reference is to someone following the *millah* of someone else. It is used of the 'religion' of the Pharaonic Egyptians and other such groups. There is even a passage *millat qawmin lā yu'minūn* (12:37). Chiefly, however, as we have said, it is the *millat Ibrāhīm*, the *millah* of Abraham, which Muḥammad is presented as following. And later lexicographers are cited as stating that the word 'can only be used for a religion that was proclaimed by a Prophet' (Jeffery, op. cit., p. 268, fn. 5); which perhaps illustrates the kind of impression that it increasingly made on the community. It is used only in the singular in the Qur'ān. A plural (*milal*) is found from the ninth century A.D. in the title of a work of Abū Ma'shar al-

Balkhī, and is popularized again in the tenth and eleventh (Ibn Ḥazm and Shahrastānī respectively) in what have been called the world's first treatises on comparative religion.

Curiously, however, this term did not become very common in Muslim culture. It is not found in Arabic in this meaning before the Qur'ān, and rather little after it. In later centuries it developed into meaning a particular religious community, the followers of one tradition as distinct from others and considered as a systematic group, rather than the tradition or faith that they followed—a sociological rather than an ideal system. This was formalized in the institutional Millet system of the Ottoman Empire. Today the word has come to mean 'nationality' in Turkish and Persian—at least in the language of the educated classes and for official purposes. In Urdu it is used rarely, and exclusively to designate the Muslim community (more or less equivalent to *ummah*). Otherwise it seems to have dropped out of current use.

Since it would seem to have played no considerable role in the history of ideas, I have allowed myself not to explore its use carefully.

87 Muhammad was neither a Christian nor a Jew, nor (in most cases) were those among whom he preached. Yet 'the religion' that he proffered, and that they accepted, was both in fact and in theory a reformulation of the Christian and Jewish.

88 This, and the further statistical statements in this and the next paragraph, are based on calculations that I have made from the admirable concordance of Muḥammad Fu'ād 'Abd al-Bāqī, *al-Mu'jam al-Mufahras li-Alfāz al-Qur'ān al-Karīm*, Cairo, 1364 [= 1945 A.D.]. The potential contribution of this splendid work to Qur'ān studies is beyond estimate. Citations from the Qur'ān, and verse numberings, I have given from the text of the Royal Egyptian edition.

89 *Mu'min* in its various inflexions is found 230 times, *muslim*, . . . 42.

90 Although I have not made a systematic investigation, I find some evidence to suggest that the practice of the members of this community calling themselves (and still later, their being called) 'Muslim' is an historical development that was preceded by a phase, lasting perhaps some centuries, in which it was more customary to use the term *mu'min* for this purpose. (Perhaps the adoption of *muslim* followed upon the theological-cum-political discussions as to the true nature of faith [*īmān*], originally the prime distinguishing characteristic. In these discussions there was a tendency for *islām* to come to mean outward conformity, *īmān* personal faith, so that gradually the distinction between the *mu'minīn* and the *muslimīn* came to be accepted in a sense roughly corresponding to the distinction in Christendom between the true and the visible Church? The theologians debated whether there was a difference; but I am referring to popular and largely unselfconscious usage.)

91 The verb *āmana* in this fourth form, but not counting the participle or the gerund, is listed 537 times; *aslama*, 22.

92 The figures here are 45, 8, 537. If one takes the two stems together

(*āmana* and *aslama*), the figures are: total occurrences, 884; of which verbal verb, 559 (63%); verbal adjective, 272 (31%); verbal noun, 53 (6%).

93   See below, chap. 7, for faith and belief. The Arabic verb *ẓanna*, which comes closer to 'believe' in one of its senses, occurs in the Qur'ān only to indicate a person's holding something that is in fact (according to the Qur'ān) false; *āmana* (of which *īmān* is the gerund) is used to indicate a person's 'recognizing', may we say, what is in fact true. An elaborate inquiry here into the concept *īmān* would be too technical and too vast; much has been written on it, and I propose perhaps to tackle it further eventually in a series of articles if not a monograph. A graduate seminar 'The concept of faith in Islam' at McGill University has proven rewarding. Specifically on the Qur'ān, see especially H. Ringgren, 'The Conception of Faith in the Koran', *Oriens*, Leiden, 4:1–20 (1951), and Toshihiko Izutsu, *The Structure of the Ethical Terms in the Koran, a study in semantics*, Tokyo, 1959, pp. 118–122, 173ff., and s.v. in index.

94   For an example, as a favourite of mine but also widely representative, even authoritative, see the section by Taftazani commenting on *īmān* in the doctrinal statement of Nasafī: *Sharḥ . . . Sa'd al-Dīn al-Taftāzānī 'alá al-'Aqā'id al-Nasafīyah . . .*; in the 'Isá al-Bābī al-Ḥalabī edition, Cairo, n.d., with supercommentaries, this section is pp. 124–132.
In the rather inadequate English translation by Earl E. Elder, *A Commentary on the Creed of Islam*, New York, 1950, *īmān* (the relevant section is chap. 13, pp. 116–126) is rendered as 'belief', which in my judgement obscures the very argument that it is endeavouring to reproduce. The term has regularly been translated so also in English versions of the Qur'ān, unfortunately.

95   Smith, op. cit., p. 17 (New York, p. 25).

96   Also some of its correlatives, such as *jaḥada;* also *kadhdhaba.* As with *āmana* (above, note 93), meaning to accept what the speaker regards as valid, so these verbs are used for rejecting what the speaker regards as right (hence also the standard 'to be ungrateful'). To reject what one should reject, to reject what is wrong or false or wicked, would involve another verb. One may note that the Qur'ān pattern of inflexion here is strikingly similar to that with *aslama* and *āmana*: of the total of 505 occurrences of *kafara*, 37 (7%) are the noun (*kufr*), 178 (35%) are adjectival or participial, 290 (58%) are strictly verbal.

97   More fully, 'And when there cometh to them what they know, they reject it'—*fa-lammā jā'ahum mā °arafū, kafarū bihi* (2:89). Another example with the alternative verb *jaḥada*: 'They rejected them [the signs of God], though in their hearts they knew very well that they were true'—*jaḥadū bihā, wa-stayqanat-hā anfusuhum* (27:14—*hā* is *āyātunā*, 27: 13). Throughout the Qur'ān there appears very little consideration of the point that those who did not accept the message that Muḥammad was proffering might not *believe* it, and were therefore genuine and sincere in not responding. Rather the attitude to such people is that what is obviously true has been presented to them, and out of perverse haughtiness (*ẓulman wa-°ulūwan*

—27:14 again) and ingratitude (k-f-r, passim) they stubbornly and wilfully refuse it. Both in this case and with the verb *āmana*, belief is taken for granted, is presupposed. Cf. also below, note 108.

98 Once so: *wa-kafarū ba°da islāmihim* (9:74). More usually: . . . *ba°da īmānihim* (3: 86, 90) and five other times with other personal pronouns, once (49:11) generally.

98a 49:17.

99 Above, p. 81, at note 4.

100 Abū Ja°far Muḥammad al-Ṭabarī interprets *dīn* here as *al-ṭā°ah wa al-dhallah*, and *islām* as *al-inqiyād bi-al-tadhallul wa-al-khushū°* (in the recent Shākir edition, vol. 6, pp. 273–274: Maḥmūd Muḥammad Shākir & Aḥmad Muḥammad Shākir, edd., *Tafsīr al-Ṭabarī*, Dār al-Ma°ārif, Cairo, several voll., in process, 1374 [=A.D. ca. 1954]-).

101 S.v. RELIGION in *The Catholic Encyclopedia: an international work of reference on the constitution, doctrine, discipline, and history of the Catholic Church*, ed. Charles G. Herbermann et al., 15 voll., New York, 1913. The article is by Charles F. Aiken; vol. XII, p. 739.

102 *Wa-man yabtaghi ghayr al-islāmi dīnan, fa-lan yuqbala minhu*— 3:85. Similarly 5:3 (above, note 3) may be, and has been, taken as meaning that God informs mankind that His pleasure is that their behaviour toward Him should be submission, obedience to His commands—so al-Ṭabarī, who states that in his view by *islām* here God means *al-istislām li-'amrī, wa-l-inqiyād li-ṭā°atī, °alā mā shara°tu lakum min ḥudūdihi wa-farā'iḍihi wa-ma°ālimih* (the pronominal suffix of the last three words here refers to *amr*?) and of *dīnan* he says that 'by that [God] means obedience from you to Me'— *ya°nī bi-dhālik ṭā°ah minkum lī* (op. cit., vol. 9, p. 522). Furthermore one may consider the modern interpretation of the passage earlier in this verse: *al-yawma akmaltu lakum dīnakum*. Nowadays this is usually taken as meaning, 'Today I have completed your religion for you', and as having been revealed, accordingly, at the very end of the Prophet's career, closing the exposition of Islām as a now completed system. This interpretation was apparently unknown in the third century to al-Ṭabarī and to those of the Companions whose views he reports, if one may argue *e silentio*. They did not know when this verse was revealed, and among their various suggestions did not proffer this one (ibid., vol. 9, pp. 517–531).

103 This is not a translation but a paraphrase of *Fa-man yuridi-llāhu an yahdiyahu, yashraḥ ṣadrahu li-l-islām*—6:125.

104 I am thinking of a passage such as the following, where not the gerund *islām* is used but another form of the same verb, and where one is precluded from taking it as a technical term because of its direct object: 'And they say, "No one shall enter Paradise except him who is a Jew, or a Chris-

tian". . . Nay! but whoever surrenders himself (*man aslama wajhahu*) to God, doing good deeds' (2: 111–112). Compare also 'Abraham was not a Jew, nor yet a Christian; but he was an upright man who had surrendered' (*kāna ḥanīfan musliman*) (3:67) (the translation in this latter case is that of the modern Muslim Pickthall, who adds in brackets at the end '[to Allah]'—Marmaduke Pickthall, *The Meaning of the Glorious Qur'ân, Text and Explanatory Translation*, Hyderabad-Deccan [India], 1938, I. 72).

105 There has been considerable study of this term and its use in the Qur'ān, both by Muslims traditionally and recently by Western scholars. The fullest and best inquiry among these latter is H. Ringgren, *Islam, 'aslama, and Muslim*, Uppsala, 1949. See also the abstract of an as yet unpublished paper, D. H. Baneth, 'The original meaning of *islām* as a religious term; a renewal of a medieval interpretation' in *Proceedings of the Twenty-Third International Congress of Orientalists, Cambridge 1954*, London, n.d. [sc. 1955?] pp. 305–306. Dr. Baneth was kind enough to let me see the manuscript of the whole. James Robson, '"Islām" as a Term', *The Muslim World*, Hartford, 44: 101–109 (1954) adds nothing to Ringgren for the classical period. Other references are: Mark Lidzbarski, 'Salâm und Islâm' in *Zeitschrift für Semitistik und verwandte Gebiete*, 1:85–96 (1922) (who traces Gnostic parallels), and David Künstlinger, ' "Islâm", "Muslim", "aslama" im Kurān', in *Rocznik Orjentalistyczny*, Lwów, 11: 128–137 (1935) (who takes Islam as primary among these three, yet as personalist rather than systematic). Of Muslim writing, unfortunately the 'résumé sommaire' is altogether too summary to be anything more than tantalizing, of M. Mustapha Abdel Razek, 'Le mot Islam, son sens primitif et son évolution' in *Actes du XVIIIe congrès international des orientalistes, Leiden, 7–12 septembre, 1931*, Leiden, 1932, pp. 225–226. I do not know of other modern Muslim inquiries. On classical Muslim study, see in part below, note 107.

106 I have been concerned here with the term *islām*. It would take us too far afield to analyse at all fully and systematically the usage of the word *dīn* in the Qur'ān. It occurs 92 times. Apart from Ṭabarī's interpretation of the word (see above, notes 100, 102) and our remarks above, pp. 101–102, it is interesting to note how often even the modern fairly representative Muslim Pickthall translates it not as 'the religion' but rather as 'religion' or even on several occasions as 'faith' (op. cit., *passim*).

107 The question is subtle, and the field vast. Greatly rewarding would be a full historical study of the use of the word *islām* over the centuries, to uncover the evolution of its connotations and the varieties of usage. Such a study would, for technical reasons, be more difficult to execute but surely no less illuminating than a study of 'religion' in the West, such as that of which we have given a preliminary sketch above in our second chapter. Another rewarding and more manageable task would be a history of the *tafsīr* of this word as used in the Qur'ān, or even of a single passage such as 3:19. I myself have made a systematic—and, within its limits, complete—study of one selected area, namely the occurrence of the term *islām* in approximately 25,000 book-titles in Arabic, from the 8th to the 20th centuries A.D. The results were presented to a conference at the University of London, School of Oriental and

African Studies, in 1958 and with other Proceedings will presently be published (unfortunately, in a somewhat abbreviated and modified form) by that School, under the title: 'The Historical Development in Islam of the Concept of Islam as an Historical Development'. The Proceedings will form one item in the series, *Historical Writings on the Peoples of Asia*. In that paper the general issues raised here are discussed, and the long-range historical trends considered; anyone who is interested in detailed evidence for the conclusions inferred here is referred to that forthcoming source. I have also made a study of the use of the term and concept *sharī'ah* (usually translated 'law') among the *mutakallimūn* (theologians), also of *shar'*, to the fifteenth century A.D. A preliminary report of results of this was read before the Arabic section, International Congress of Orientalists, Moscow, 1960, but the paper is not yet being published. However, it did present statistical and other evidence uncovering and documenting a gradual process of reification in that realm also, a process beginning quite surprisingly late.

108 Although I have not investigated its historical use systematically, I believe that the phrase *ghayr muslim*, current today in Arabic, Persian, Turkish, and Urdu (and perhaps other Muslim languages as well?), has long been standard to express what may be rendered in English quite straightforwardly as 'non-Muslim'. Normally no one pauses to reflect on such a usage; actually, however, it involves a very serious theological point, and possibly a very serious human misunderstanding. The implications may underlie Muslim attitudes to outsiders, giving metaphysical justification to a social and psychological rejection in a way that bears scrutiny. For in Arabic, and in the minds of Muslims, the designation suggests that the outsider rejects (even deliberately) a divine command, refuses (even wilfully) to submit to something sound that has been offered to him; instead of recognizing what is in fact the case in almost every instance, that the outsider does not believe (from the Muslim's point of view, does not see) that the command is indeed divine, that the scheme is indeed sound. He is not, therefore, a 'non-submitter'. He *does* submit, but to a different vision. He may be thought wrong; but it is illegitimate to think him recalcitrant. The term *ghayr muslim* involves within itself a misunderstanding of the religious position of those to whom it is applied.

Those who might suppose that I am exaggerating the significance of such a matter (I use it here illustratively only; the point is widely applicable in other communities as well) have forgotten the long and sorry history of interreligious misunderstanding and conflict and even of religious wars, in which mankind has until today been involved. For a plea to my fellow Christians to abandon even the inherently milder term 'non-Christian', see my article 'Christianity's Third Great Challenge' (the title was not the writer's own!) in *The Christian Century*, Chicago, vol. 77, no. 17 (April 27, 1960), pp. 505–508. To it I might now add the further point that, strictly speaking, no outsider can possibly reject Christ; he rejects only Jesus. What makes him an outsider is precisely that he has not seen that the latter is indeed the former. Cf. also above, note 97.

109 As indicated in note 107 just above, I have not investigated this matter historically in anything like a thorough fashion. Nor do I know of any scholarly investigation of it. Such evidence as I have examined tends to show

that both alternatives became current, but that on the whole the 'open' or personalist one tended to predominate for several centuries. Less pious, and secular, writers, as one should expect, are found on the side of reifying (this version of the term *islām* comes first, I think, in *adab*, and is first established there; secondly, in history, but perhaps chiefly after the fourteenth century), whereas the more pious or more theological writers are more unanimously personalist. (One must remember that it was not impossible to confuse the two meanings for someone who was persuaded that to obey God is synonymous with observing the prescriptions of a law that the Muslim community was in later centuries in gradual process of systematizing. At what date the law became and was felt to be a systematic entity is not quite clear.)

An important indication of the matter for religious thinkers up to his time (he died in the early fourth century *hijri* [tenth century A.D.]) is provided by the careful commentary of al-Ṭabarī, whom we have already considered. In addition to the references already given (above, notes 100 and 102), see the Shākir ed. there cited, vol. 6, pp. 273ff., and the references given there in fn. 1, p. 275: esp. vol. 4, pp. 251–255 (in these passages he reiterates, rather, his insistence that *islām* signifies the act of personal surrender); vol. 6, pp. 570–572 (one occurrence of *islām* where he takes it in a rather systematic sense, though perhaps not yet as a title—indeed here a transition towards its becoming a technical term can be discerned); vol. 12, pp. 98–103; etc. See also the index of words, under *aslama,* for the later volumes.

110 For the details, see my London paper just referred to (above, note 107). The figures are as follows: in Arabic book titles to the year 1300 *hijri* (ca. 1882 A.D.) I found *īmān* 56 times, *islām* 84. From that date forward, of a selected list equally open to either possibility, I found *īmān* 4 times, *islām* 52.

111 See above, p. 77.

112 See the London paper cited above, note 107, especially at its footnotes 30, 31. At the time of that writing the relation between apologetics and reification (see our present text, next sentence) had not yet become clear to me.

113 Above, pp. 42–44. The parallel seems to me both striking and important.

114 In Arabic of the classical and mediaeval periods I have not found it used in the modern sense of a religious system, or indeed any social system, in any book-title. As in the case of the term *islām* (above, note 107), this is based on the comprehensive index of Brockelmann, which lists some 25,000 titles.

115 See above, notes 10–11.

116 It might be objected to this that the law was a system even though it was not called by that name; and that its exponents in general, the *fuqahā'*, and a man like al-Ghazzālī in particular, looked at life in a way that

the modern age might interpret as coming closest to this. Yet (originally, at least) their conception was dynamic rather than static. Perhaps this is illustrated in their use of the activist word *madhhab* (from *dhahaba*, 'to go') even for the law, over against the congealed word *niẓām*. Even the word *sharīᶜah*, denoting the most systematic aspect of Muslim life, means originally a route to be followed, not a network or scheme to be imposed. And al-Ghazzālī's greatest endeavour was to give 'life' (*iḥyā'*) to religious theory, not to provide some inanimate pattern. In earlier times, so far as I can see, the 'Islam' by which the community aspired to live was a process, not an organization.

❧ Notes for Chapter Five: Is the Concept Adequate?

1 This point was made first, apparently, in nineteenth-century Germany; it has been developed recently in a serious and elaborate way by Karl Jaspers, who coins the appellation 'The Axial Period' (*Die Achsenzeit*). See his *Vom Ursprung und Ziel der Geschichte*, Zurich, 1949 (*The Origin and Goal of History*, translated by Michael Bullock, London, 1953). For his account of earlier observations on the period, see pp. 27f., 35f. (trans. pp. 8, 15).

2 By G. J. Holyoake. See Eric S. Waterhouse, article SECULARISM in James Hastings *et al.*, edd., *Encyclopaedia of Religion & Ethics*, Edinburgh, 1908–1921, voi. XI, p. 348b.

3 The two major matters that we have here considered are, in fact, interrelated. It was a radical innovation when man once learned to give his transcendent loyalty as participant in a community other than that of which he was a sociological member. This was involved in a Bactrian becoming a Buddhist, a Corinthian becoming a Christian, an Indian becoming a Muslim; or in a Jew leaving Palestine and settling in Elephantine or Rome without ceasing to be Jewish; or in some but not all Panjabis becoming Sikhs. Inherent in this socio-historical development, however, was another radical innovation, whereby the individual, by facing life as a member now of two communities, fragmented personal, and corporate, life into areas if not compartments. Before these two things had happened the concept 'a religion' and generic 'religion' could not arise, and they cannot retroactively apply. When and where they have happened such concepts are a first approximation to reporting the situation. Yet they remain only a first approximation, as we shall see. Modern man, of course, in his immensely complex life, is a member simultaneously

of a virtually unlimited series of communities, not only ranging in size from the nuclear family to the global community of mankind, but also crisscrossing and interpenetrating and often enough conflicting with each other. Loyalty to his religious community by no means exhausts his religious loyalty. And membership in a religious community decreasingly defines his religious life.

4 *Gottes Offenbarung als Aufhebung der Religion* ('The Revelation of God as the Abolition of Religion')—the title of section 17 (Part III) of Karl Barth, *Die Kirchliche Dogmatik, Erster Band, Prolegomena* . . . : *Die Lehre vom Wort Gottes,* 2er Halbband, 4te Auflage, Zurich, 1948, pp. 304–397; English trans. by G. T. Thomson, Harold Knight (G. W. Bromiley, T. F. Torrance. edd.), *Church Dogmatics,* vol. I; *Prolegomena* . . . : *The Doctrine of the Word of God,* 2nd half-volume, Edinburgh, 1956, pp. 280–361.

5 *Wir beginnen mit dem Satz: Religion ist Unglaube*—op. cit., p. 327. The official English translation reads: 'We begin by stating that religion is unbelief' (p. 299). *Religion als Unglaube* (in the English version, 'Religion as Unbelief') is the title of the second subsection of the section cited in the previous reference. I would prefer to translate *Unglaube* as 'nonfaith', or if it were tolerable, 'unfaith'.

6 *Hier, in der Geschichte des Christentums, gerade weil es die Offenbarungsreligion ist, sozusagen mit erhobener Hand gesündigt wird. Gesündigt! Denn die Widerspruch gegen die Gnade ist Unglaube, und Unglaube ist Sünde, d i e Sünde sogar* (p. 370). 'In the history of Christianity, just because it is the religion of revelation, the sin is, as it were, committed with a high hand. Yes, sin! For contradiction against grace is unbelief, and unbelief is sin, indeed it is *the* sin' (p. 337).

7 Emil Brunner, *Revelation and Reason: the Christian doctrine of faith and knowledge,* trans. by Olive Wyon, Philadelphia, 1946, pp. 272, 264. *(Diese Offenbarung sollte nicht Religion gennant werden* . . . ; *die Religion ist das Produkt der sündigen Verblendung des Menschen*—Emil Brunner, *Offenbarung und Vernunft: Die Lehre von der christlichen Glaubenserkenntnis,* 1941; 2te Auflage, Zurich & Stuttgart, 1961, pp. 299, 290.)

8 Paul Tillich, *Biblical religion and the search for ultimate reality,* Chicago, 1955, pp. 1–5 (section heading, 'The meaning of "Biblical religion" ').

9 In his Foreword to Joy Davidman, *Smoke on the Mountain: the ten commandments in terms of today,* London, 1955, p. 9. It may be noted that Lewis, whose sardonic protest is one of the mildest of those cited here, is the only one not a German; while Tillich, originally German, moved to an English-language environment (the United States) some twenty years before giving in English the lectures cited. We have remarked above on the point that the term (and concept?) 'religion' seems to have been accepted in German Christian circles less than in other Protestant countries of Europe. (Tillich, op. cit., p. 3, remarks that it is German readers who have 'strongly criticized' his using the word; 'they cannot understand that a modern theologian would use the word "religion" in a positive sense'.)

10 Also, 'religionless Christians'; and a 'complete religionlessness', for which the Western form of Christianity is a preparation (*ein religionsloses Christentum—religionslose Christen—Religionslosigkeit; also, nicht-religiös*). Dietrich Bonhoeffer, *Widerstand und Ergebung: Briefe und Aufzeichnungen aus der Haft*, herausgegeben von Eberhard Bethge, München, 1952, pp. 179, 182, 183. For his exposition of these notions see his letters dated 30.4.44 and 5.5.44. (English trans.: *Letters and papers from prison*, London, 1953, 1959, pp. 91, 93, 94.)

10a Milton Steinberg, *The Making of the Modern Jew*, Indianapolis, 1933, 1934, p. 290. Similarly: 'We must reject the assumption that Judaism is, or can be reduced to, a religion only'—Mordecai M. Kaplan, *Judaism as a Civilization: toward a re-construction of American-Jewish life*, New York, 1934, 1935, p. 304.

11 'I do not think it is correct to use [the word "Hinduism"—also "Hinduized", which has just been cited] . . . unless they are used in the widest sense of Indian culture. They are apt to mislead today when they are associated with a much narrower, and specifically religious, concept. . . . Hinduism, as a faith, is vague, amorphous, many-sided, all things to all men. It is hardly possible to define it, or indeed to say definitely whether it is a religion or not, in the usual sense of the word'—*The Discovery of India*, New York, 1946, pp. 63–64.

12 *Maha Thera* U Thittila, of Burma, in 'The Fundamental Principles of Theravada Buddhism', in Kenneth W. Morgan, ed., *The Path of the Buddha*, New York, 1956, p. 71.

13 Saïd Ramadan, *Islam, Doctrine and Way of Life*, Geneva, 1961, p. 11. Virtually the same wording, this time in Arabic, is found in Muḥammad al-Bahī, *al-Fikr al-Islāmī al-ḥadīth, wa ṣilatuhu bi-l-istiʿmār al-gharbī* [Cairo, 1376/1957], p. 222. Cf. also Abū-l-Aʿlá Mawdūdī, *Jamāʿat-i Islāmī: us-kā Maqṣad, tārīkh awr lāʾiḥah'-i ʿamal*, Lahore, n.d. (sc. 1951), pp. 9–10 [4th ed., Lahore, 1953, pp. 8ff.].

14 This is one of the themes of my *Islam in Modern History* (*passim*; as illustrative instances, see pp. 146, 240 and 307 of the Princeton 1957 and London 1958 edd., and pp. 151, 241, 307 of the New York 1959 ed.: 'A true Muslim, however, is not a man who believes in Islam . . .', 'A "Muslim" is one who submits not to Islam but to God', 'modern Muslims whose loyalty to Islam . . . seems greater than their faith in God'; and the arguments leading up to and flowing on from these remarks). However, at the time of writing that book I had myself not yet clarified the matter, had not recognized how this point can be seen as turning on the conceptualization of Islam. I had not yet asked myself the question, 'Is Islam the name of a religion?' (title of an address given at Princeton University, 1957), out of which this present inquiry has grown.

15 One may, perhaps, compare here the table set forth above, p. 77. Furthermore, I find the following statistics interesting (with them compare those on the occurrence of 'God', 'Faith', and 'Islam' in the Qur'ān, above,

chap. 4, p. 111, at notes 88–92): Aquinas in the *Summa Theologica* uses the word *Christus* 6,843 times, *Deus* more than twice that often, and *Christianitas* (as we have seen: above, chap. 3, note 90) either not at all or at most once or twice. Figures for Calvin's writing, though not quite so overwhelming in their ratio, are still impressive: *Christus*, about 700 times; *Deus*, about 450; *Christianismus*, 9. (These calculations are based on the entries s.vv. in Deferrari & Barry, op. cit. above, chap. 3, note 90, and in the *Index nominum et rerum*, vol. 58 of Calvin's *Opera . . . Omnia* cited above, chap. 2, note 92.)

16 Above, chap. 2, p. 41, at note 113 and the following paragraph.

17 Buddhists are an exception so far as the phrasing is concerned. Their formulation has diverged; but the spirit of their tradition is altogether in accord with the substance of the point that I am trying to establish. The Buddha did not preach a religion; he was quite emphatic about this, and scolded those of his disciples who were concerned with such matters, for giving attention to the wrong issues. He revealed (disclosed to men) not a religion but a transcendent, pre-existent, moral law (*dharma*). The 'religion of Buddhism' has been men's response. A particularly vivid illustration of the Buddha's attitude is found in his charming but powerful treatment, in a well-known passage, of questions of one Mālunkyā-putta. This disciple raised what we might call questions about religion. The Buddha compared man's condition to that of a person wounded by a poisoned arrow, and compared these questions to a fastidious and elaborate discussion about the arrow, which could go on in endless detail until the patient dies—whereas the important point, he insists, is not that but to pull the arrow out. The Buddha was concerned not with religion, but with men who were suffering. (Sutta 63 of the Majjhima Nikāya. This is the Cūla-Mālunkyasutta, no. 3 of Division II [*Bhikkhuvagga*] of Part II [*Majjhimapaṇṇāsa*]. Among several English translations, see the following: *The Collections of the Middle Length Sayings* [*Majjhima-Nikāya*]; translated from the Pali by I. B. Horner, 3 voll., London, 1954–1959 [Pali Text Society, Translation series, nos. 29–31], vol. 2, esp. pp. 99–100).

18 With the exception, perhaps, of K'ung?

19 One of the most outspoken recent Christians in his sensitivity to the utter inadequacy of Christianity as an expression of that which it ought to express, is again Karl Barth. For instance: 'We must insist, therefore, that at the beginning of a knowledge of the truth of the Christian religion, there stands the recognition that this religion, too, stands under the judgement that religion is unbelief. . . . Concretely this judgement affects the whole practice of our faith: our Christian conceptions of God and the things of God, our Christian theology, our Christian worship, our forms of Christian fellowship and order, our Christian morals, poetry and art, our attempts to give individual and social form to the Christian life, our Christian strategy and tactics in the interest of our Christian cause, in short our Christianity, to the extent that it is *our* Christianity, the human work which we undertake and adjust to all kinds of near and remote aims and which as such is seen to be on the same level as the human work in other religions. This judgement means that all this Christianity of ours, and all the details of it, are not as such what they

ought to be and pretend to be. . . . What we have here is in its own way—a different way from that of other religions, but no less seriously—unbelief, i.e., opposition to the divine revelation, and therefore active idolatry and self-righteousness' (op. cit., p. 327. The German original is op. cit., pp. 358–359).

20   The dichotomy between adherent and outsider, between those who do and those who do not 'believe' (have faith), has been much sharper in some cases than in others, both theoretically and sociologically; as we have been at pains to point out in our chap. 4 above. Some Hindus, for instance, have been on the whole much readier to recognize that Christians have in their tradition a transcendent reference than Christians have been for Hindus. This is of radical importance, and yet the Christian is quick to point out that the Hindu has not seen the *particular* transcendent reference of the Christian's faith, the unique and saving act of God in Christ. For the moment we are not concerned with the validity or otherwise of these varying positions, but simply with the fact that they do vary, and that the Christian Church and its cosmic role have been understood differently by Christians and by outsiders, even Hindus. The difference between the insider's and the outsider's view has been particularly radical in the case of those traditions historically related with Zarathushtra's conflict dualism—and especially in our day the Christian and the Islamic (followed, in reinvigorated fashion, by the Communist). It is not, however, in my judgement, final. It has been inevitable, but it may not, I believe, remain so. One of the exciting prospects before modern man is the new possibility of our learning to appreciate religious traditions other than our own.

21   Cf. above, chap. 4 note 2.

22   For convenience in simplifying the argument, we speak here of God. This is appropriate to many traditions, such as the Christian, Jewish, Islamic, Hindu (taking the term 'God' to render Brahman); but not to all, such as the Theravadin Buddhist, for which *Dhamma* (*Dharma*) or *Nirvana* would be more appropriate, and the less monotheistic traditions. The substance of our argument is not significantly modified by any modification in terminology here that might be useful for greater exactitude; not even in the case of those less sophisticated traditions where the transcendent element in the community's life may not be conceptualized denominatively at all. To phrase the point with perhaps more clarity or acceptability, but no more precision: the participant is concerned with what I, a Christian, term God.

23   We may give two examples, chosen somewhat at random though both are from significant scholars: The first is from the best recent general history of Japan: 'The use of the word Shintō ("The Way of the Gods") to describe the early beliefs of the Japanese is apt to be misleading in so far as it suggests an organized religion'—George Sansom, *A History of Japan to 1334*, London, 1958, pp. 24–25. The second is Robert N. Bellah, *Tokugawa Religion*, Glencoe, 1957, which title (note also the subtitle: 'The Values of pre-industrial Japan') departs from the traditional practice that designates at least two 'religions' (in the plural) in that country. This author expressly says in introducing his third chapter, called 'Japanese Religion: a general view', that that chapter-title is deliberately chosen to make the point that, at least from the seventeenth century 'there is some validity in speaking of Ja-

panese religion as an entity despite 'the various major religions . . . Confucianism . . . Shintō . . . Buddhism' (p. 59) in that country of whose common elements the abstraction (sic) is composed to which he proposes to give the single label. Both these authors exemplify (passim) a tendency back to speaking of 'religion' generically without the use of a definite article, in reporting as outsiders on a people and their culture. I find it significant also that Sansom should entitle a subsection in his work 'Buddhist Faith' (pp. 218–228) rather than 'The Buddhist Faith'.

24 In addition to the Hughes instance cited above, p. 63, at note 44, where the specific names are explicitly repudiated, one may find in recent literature a number of further illustrations of their supersession. An example: Karl Ludvig Reichelt, *Religion in Chinese Garment*, translated [from the Norwegian] by Joseph Tetlie, New York & London, 1951. One may note in passing that this last author writes, 'Nothing was more foreign to the purpose of Confucius than to be the founder of a religion' (p. 34).

25 At the theoretical level we have already observed some vague awareness among scholars of the ambiguity or inadequacy of 'Hinduism' as a term (see above, note 11 and chap. 3, notes 17, 53, 54; indeed virtually every discussion of the subject remarks on the point, though without conceding much to it). Similarly on 'Sikhism', see above, chap. 3, p. 62, at note 41. At the practical level, we will observe presently recent alternative headings: 'the religion of the Hindus' (below, note 28), and not 'Sikhism' but 'the Sikhs' (below, note 31).

It is time, however, to call attention to the serious divergence that actually prevails in usage. This divergence has occurred without any thoughtful attempt being made (or even need being felt?) to propose a way out of it, or to consider the implications of the fact that few observers of the 'religions of India' (a common title now for over fifty years) agree in how to count or to identify these. An interesting investigation would be to survey how many religions scholars have descried in the Indian situation, where they have drawn their boundaries, and what names they have applied. An example of lack of clarity in the area of terminology may be taken from a widely used textbook in modern America, John B. Noss, *Man's Religions*, New York, 1949, 1956. Note this author's discussion (pp. 113–114) of the phrase 'Early Hinduism', and of the difference of this from 'Later Hinduism'. (He capitalizes the adjectives as well as the nouns, suggesting that in his thinking Early Hinduism and Later Hinduism are in some degree names and not merely descriptive comments). He writes with some ambiguity, for he also speaks of a 'system' that he calls 'Hinduism proper', discriminated from the 'preparatory' Vedic and Brahmanistic developments (he calls the latter more reifiedly 'Brahmanism' in his section title, p. 126). It sounds as if he were adopting this terminology, yet actually without saying so he seems in practice to be equating this 'Hinduism proper' with his concept 'Later Hinduism', and the two earlier 'developments' with his 'Early Hinduism'. In his Foreword to what he calls 'The Religions of India', he seems to call 'philosophical Hinduism (Brahmanism)' (p. 112) one of the three chief religions with which he is concerned, along with Jainism and Buddhism (all page-references given here are to the 1956 edition). In addition he lists Jainism, Buddhism, and Sikhism (headings of chapters 4, 5-6, 8.)

Bouquet (as well as the editors, presumably, of Hutchinson's University Library, in which series his work appears) uses the one term 'Hinduism' to include all of these, with the partial exception of Buddhism. (A. C. Bouquet, *Hinduism*, London, n.d. [sc. ca. 1949]).

These are works of popularization, supplying the information and ideas of undergraduates and the general public. At the level of productive scholars, whom the others follow at a distance, the situation is not significantly different. Renou, in his recent Jordan Lectures (*Religions of Ancient India*, London, 1953—despite the adjective in the title, the coverage extends to Rabindranath Tagore and Sir S. Radhakrishnan) is willing to embrace 'all the religious manifestations of India, past and present' (p. vii) under four headings: Vedism, Hinduism, Jainism, and Buddhism (loc. cit., and his chapter titles). He explicitly rejects the proposal of dividing the second of these into an early period to be designated 'Brahmanism' and a later, 'Hinduism proper' (p. 46). Further, he admits casually that, for instance, the sect of 'the Vīraśaivas are in some respects less Hindu than the modern Jainas' (p. 90) and that currently 'Jainism . . . shows a tendency to return (*sic*) to the fold of Hinduism' (loc. cit.) . The Sikhs, he remarks in passing (whom I personally would regard as constituting as distinctive a group as do the Jains) , and other ' "reformed sects", to use Farquhar's phrase . . . are on the borderline of Hinduism, rather than outside it' (loc. cit.) . 'Hinduism', despite several caveats, he seems to take quite seriously as a cognizable something: 'The Vedic contribution to Hinduism . . . is not a large one' (p. 47) ; 'There are grounds for supposing that some form of Hinduism existed at the Vedic period, and probably even earlier. This is the prehistory of Hinduism; its history begins with the emergence of the great texts of Hindu *dharma*, and the first appearance of the Epic and of *Smṛti*. . . . The same period saw the origins of Buddhism and Jainism' (p. 99) . This hints at, but seems to underplay, a Dravidian origin for it.

A recent South Indian scholar, on the other hand, A. P. Karmarkar, whatever the merits of his particular reconstruction, legitimately challenges the literary tradition that begins India's religious history with the Vedas, by writing *The Religions of India. Vol. I: The Vrātya or Dravidian systems*, Lonavla (India), 1950. Except for the term 'Saivism', which he couples with 'Saiva Sects' (e.g., title of Part IV, pp. 216–251; he names partial Saivisms), he does not favour the '-ism' forms much, and despite the 'Vrātya systems' of his title he concludes with a singular, 'The Vrātya religion' (title of Part VI, pp. 316–320). And so on.

Tuxen, in one more work of the title *The Religions of India* (Copenhagen, 1949, by Sten Konow and Poul Tuxen) speaks of Nanak as 'the founder of Sikhism' (p. 178) , but treats this briefly and in passing, under the general subheading of *Bhakti*,—remarking, however, that 'The Sikh sect is, however, only loosely connected with bhakti religion' (p. 179) ; while in the next sentence we read of 'Northern Indian religion'.

Everyone seems agreed that there are religions in India, but scholars are not quite agreed as to which they are, and often enough a single observer seems not quite agreed with himself. I personally doubt that any scholar, if challenged, would reject the thesis that all classifications in this particular realm are to some degree arbitrary, are external conceptualizations rather than inherent categories. (See further above, pp. 63–64 at notes 46, 48, and chap. 4, note 45. Cf. also the final paragraph of our next note; on the whole it would seem that scholars in the ancient Middle Eastern religious field are further advanced in their current break away from the traditional entity-terms than are their counterparts dealing with India, though the two historical situations being studied are formally quite comparable. It is, of course, easier for the former because no present-day vested conceptual interests or emotions are involved.)

26 In addition to the instances remarked above in chap. 3, at notes 13, 14, 15, one may give the example of G. Contenau, in Gorce & Mortier, *Histoire générale des religions*, Paris, 5 tomes, 1944–1951, vol. I, pp. 339–340, where he complains of the custom, in treatments of ancient Mesopotamian peoples, of studying Assyro-Babylonian religion as a whole (*d'un bloc*). He asserts that from such a study one gets a picture of something that never really existed; that it was never a unity, on the one hand because of historical change and on the other hand because of its being a mixture of Assyrian and Babylonian, which latter itself in turn was based on a mixture of Akkadian and the prior and substantially different Sumerian. He therefore proposes to attempt to disengage the religion of this earliest community: *d'établir, au moins, dans ses grandes lignes, comme préface à l'étude de la religion assyro-babylonienne, les principaux traits particuliers de la religion sumérienne*—though he goes on to state that this also was itself not a unity. I would translate *la religion sumérienne* here, Contenau being primarily an historian and very conscious of historical change as well as of complexity, as 'Sumerian religion' and not as 'the Sumerian religion'.

Again, referring to Mesopotamia as late as the early third century A.D., a major scholar writes, as we have seen (above, chap. 4 note 52) that 'Semitic and Iranian religion met and blended in an unintegrated jumble'. Both what he says, and the way that he says it, are significant: the use of a generic singular is illustrative, though probably un-thought-out, rather than a concrete plural 'Semitic and Iranian religions'. This is from H. S. Nyberg, *Irans forntida religioner*, Stockholm/Uppsala, 1937, p. 458 (German trans., p. 411). The use of a plural in the title of this book ('Iran's ancient religions'), which comes in the category of usage considered just below, p. 132 at ref. 32, is also interesting. This does not contradict but reinforces my general point that the traditionally-conceived boundaries within the total history of man's religious life are, on closer scrutiny, dissolving. What had been conceptualized as a unit proves on careful study to be multiform while what had been conceptualized as two or more units can no longer on investigation be discriminated. In this connection note also Widengren's masterly recent survey of the religious history of pre-Islamic Iran (Geo Widengren, 'Stand und Aufgaben der iranischen Religionsgeschichte', in *Numen*, Leiden, 1: 16–83 [1954] and 2: 46–134 [1955]), where he discerns many strands in a developing complex, rather than a set of entities, distinct and independent. His vocabulary varies, but is constantly delicate and indefinite. To take one example from among many: he argues in favour of employing a concept 'folk-religion' in an analysis of the situation at a certain period, distinguishing this from 'state religion', and yet brings these together not in a plural as in Nyberg's title but in a comprehensive singular of 'Iranian religion', referring to the latter's various 'forms' (he contrasts *Staatsreligion* with *die anderen Formen* [sic] *iranischer Religion* [sic] —2:128). Another telling phrase is his '*der etwas Proteusartige Zervanismus*' (1: 76).

One could almost go so far as to say that the scholarly world has virtually abandoned, though rather unconsciously, any attempt to understand or portray the religious life of the ancient Middle East in terms of separate religious entities that can be counted, named, and visualized as boundaried.

27 As examples, one may see Pauw, and Goode, both cited below in note 29, and Howells, in note 31. The last-mentioned scholar, I find, has indeed expressed himself almost in my vein, without feeling impelled to follow through with it: 'As a matter of fact, I should prefer to abandon the word "religion" entirely, for my purposes, and substitute "religious behavior" throughout; but of course it is too clumsy'—Howells, op. cit., pp. 22-23; and, in almost the final paragraph of the book, 'Perhaps the difficulty has always been in trying to recognize religion as a thing by itself, instead of as a characteristic of man and his culture' (p. 292). We have earlier quoted him as stating, 'Primitive societies without religion have never been found' (above, chap. 2, note 2); he might have written, but significantly does not, 'without a religion'.

28 This is particularly common. One example among many: whereas recent generations of college students were offered textbooks on 'Hinduism', many of the present generation of them in America are presented rather with, for instance, Kenneth W. Morgan, ed., The Religion of the Hindus, New York, 1953. One may compare also two titles on the same topic: L. Austine Waddell, The Buddhism of Tibet, London, 1895, and a generation later Sir Charles Bell, The Religion of Tibet, Oxford, 1931. (The subtitle of the former was 'Or Lamaism, with its cults, symbolism and mythology, and in its relation to Indian Buddhism'.)

29 A recent scholarly example: William J. Goode, Religion among the Primitives, Glencoe, 1951. For 'religion in', in addition to examples such as Religion in China, above, chap. 3, p. 63 (and cf. just above, note 24), one may note a contemporary anthropological study, chosen at random: B. A. Pauw, Religion in a Tswana Chiefdom, London, New York, etc., 1960. The work's opening sentence reads, 'This book is a study of present-day religion in a rural Bantu society, viewed within the wider framework of their social structure and economy'; and the opening sentence on the publishers' dust-jacket, 'This book is a study of present-day religion among the Tihaping...'. This, of course, does not in itself prove anything, but it illustrates something; something that, according to my impression, is a wider trend. In each of the three cases the wording might have been 'the religion of...'; the alternative chosen (perhaps unconsciously?) suggests a delicate sense of less reification.

30 For example, Jean Sainte Fare Garnot, La vie religieuse dans l'ancienne Egypte, Paris, 1948 (above, chap. 3, note 13); Sir Flinders Petrie, Religious Life in Ancient Egypt, London &c., 1924. (Some while earlier this same author [at that time W. M. Flinders Petrie] had entitled a book on the same subject, published in the series 'Religions Ancient and Modern', The Religion of Ancient Egypt, London, 1908 [title proffered to him, perhaps, by the publishers of that series?], but his first book on the topic was rather Religion and Conscience in Ancient Egypt, London, 1898.)

31 Two examples: John Clark Archer, *The Sikhs*, Princeton 1946 (this carries the subtitle: 'in relation to Hindus, Moslems, Christians, and Ahmadiyyas. A study in comparative religion'); William Howells, *The Heathens*, New York, 1948 (subtitle: 'Primitive man and his religions'). Again, we have seen that the first edition of a work of Alfonso Caso was called *La religión de los aztecas*, Mexico, 1936, 1945, but the second edition had as title *El pueblo del Sol*, Mexico, 1954 (English versions: *The Religion of the Aztecs*, 1937, and *The Aztecs: people of the sun*, Norman, 1958, 1959). Lowell Dunham in an introduction to the last-mentioned version writes, 'Religion touched the daily life of every man, woman, and child in the Aztec world' and 'It was a profound knowledge of the Aztecs that prompted Alfonso Caso to entitle his first version of *El pueblo del Sol*, "*La religión de los aztecas*" ' (pp. xv–xvi, xv). I would suggest, rather, that it was a profound understanding of the religiousness of these people that prompted him to entitle the second version of his study of it simply by the (religious) name of the people themselves. This is an instance of a growing but as yet unselfconscious recognition that to study 'religion' is in fact to study people. Cf. below, concluding paragraph of this chapter (p. 153).

32 For a recent plural of 'Christianity', see below, next paragraph of our text (at note 37). For a plural 'Iran's ancient religions' (superseding a more traditional 'the ancient religion of Iran') see the Nyberg title in note 26 above, and our comment thereon. (The German translator, H. H. Schaeder, has rendered this rather *Die Religionen des alten Iran*, Leipzig, 1938). For other instances see above, chap. 3, note 13.

33 In my first book, *Modern Islam in India: a social analysis*, Lahore, 1943, London, '1946' (sc. 1947), I argued explicitly that 'modern Islam' is validly conceived as different from earlier phases of Islam, viewed as an historical development, and that the same applies to, for instance, Christianity (see, for example, pp. 44–45, 45–46, respectively of the two editions). Some Muslims took exception to the use of the qualifying adjective, arguing that Islam is timeless and that therefore one cannot speak of 'modern' or of 'classical' Islam—thereby illustrating my thesis presented earlier that 'a religion' is understood differently by those within and those without. No outsider observer was perplexed by or objected to the usage—indeed Muslims themselves have in fact fallen into the custom of using the term 'Islam' to designate the historical development that observers also see, and hence of writing of 'Islam in Ethiopia' and the like (Yūsuf Aḥmad, *al-Islām fī al-Ḥabashah*, Cairo, 1354 /1935). On 'Early Hinduism' cf. above, note 25. Many partial phrases have become standard, such as *Mahayana Buddhism* (e.g. title of a work by Beatrice Lane Suzuki [London, 1939], 2nd ed., London, 1948); *Japanese Buddhism* (e.g., title of work by Sir Charles Eliot, London, 1935); etc.

The process, however, continues on and on. 'Chinese Buddhism' was once accepted as legitimate and normal (even though it fractures some ideal of Buddhism, or even of Mahayana Buddhism). Now scholars, better informed, write that 'early Chinese Buddhism', rather, 'is a system *sui generis*' (E. Zürcher, *The Buddhist conquest of China: the spread and adaptation of Buddhism in early medieval China*, Leiden, 1959). They then go further to recognize that this, too, dissolves: 'One would be tempted to call this creed "early Chinese Buddhism" pure and simple, as is generally done. But ... this appellation, however convenient, appears to be a gross generalization (ibid., p. 2); and this author next discriminates off a type that he labels ('not without hesitation'!) ' "gentry Buddhism" ' (p. 4) . (Where can all this end?—except where in the next two chapters I propose that it should end: with persons, and an uninterruptedly evolving tradition.) I shall suggest later in this present chapter that it is far from easy to reassemble partial concepts into an integral simple concept. If 'Mahayana Buddhism' legitimately refers to something definite and intelligible, and so does 'Theravadin Buddhism', then one has considerable difficulty in saying to what the term 'Buddhism' refers, we shall see.

For partial uses in the Christian case, see below, notes 35–37; and such titles as F. J. Foakes-Jackson, *The Rise of Gentile Christianity*, New York, 1927.

34 Such as Bellah's 'Japanese Religion', note 23 above. His 'Tokugawa Religion' (ibid) is both partial and composite.

35 For instance: Otto Pfleiderer, *Das Urchristenthum*, Berlin, 1887 (of which the subtitle is significant: *Seine Schriften und Lehren, in geschichtlichem Zusammenhang beschrieben*). A little later: J. H. C. W. Beyschlag, *Neutestamentliche Theologie, oder geschichtliche Darstellung der Lehren Jesu und des Urchristenthums nach den neutestamentlichen Quellen*, 2 Bde., Halle, 1891–1892. In both cases the English translations (of the latter, by N. Buchanan, 2 voll., Edinburgh, [1894] 1895; of the former, by W. Montgomery, London and New York, 1906–1911) read 'primitive Christianity' for the compound. These terms continue until today. Rudolf Bultmann's important *Das Urchristentum im Rahmen der antiken Religionen*, Zurich, 1949, appeared in French as *Le Christianisme primitif*... trad. Pierre Jundt, Paris, 1950 and in English as *Primitive Christianity* ..., trans. R. H. Fuller, London and New York, 1956.

36 For example, John Dillenberger and Claude Welch, *Protestant Christianity: interpreted through its development*, New York, 1954. The authors give particular attention to Harnack's *Das Wesen des Christentums*—'(literally "The Essence of Christianity")' (p. 208) —as illustrative of liberalism, choosing its English title as title of a chapter section for their own book (' "What is Christianity?" ': X. 1, pp. 208 ff.). And they conclude their book with a chapter 'XIV. What is Protestantism?' (pp. 302–326), making it clear that they take Protestantism very seriously as an essence. They struggle with various attempts to define it (pp. 302ff.) but insist that nonetheless it is a real and important something. In fact, virtually they have written their book because they believe in Protestant Christianity. In choosing their title as illustrative, we have not chosen anything insignificant.

Symptomatic of the same point is that a series brought out by the New York publisher George Braziller on *Great Religions of Modern Man*, Richard A. Gard., ed., 1961, comprises six volumes, one each on *Judaism, Hinduism, Buddhism*, and *Islam* (so entitled) , but on Christianity not one volume but two, *Christianity: Catholicism* (George Brantl) and *Christianity: Protestantism* (J. Leslie Dunstan) . Similarly the large series currently announced by the Stuttgart publisher W. Kohlhammer, *Die Religionen der Menschheit*, in thirty-five big volumes, plus index, 1961–   , proposes seven of these on various partial Christianities.

I have even found that one man has written a book on German Protestantism and a book on American Protestantism; but they are not the same book—a fact that does not seem to have given people as much pause as it might well do: Andrew Landale Drummond, *Story of American Protestantism*, Edinburgh & London, 1949; *German Protestantism since Luther*, London, 1951.

37   Heading of a section (vol. 111, pp. 299–434) in Gorce & Mortier, op. cit.

38   I am not unaware of the considerable discussions among Muslim theologians as to whether *īmān* varies or not. Actually I have been gathering material for perhaps an eventual book on this subject.

39   A statement often heard. One authoritative reference is Emil Brunner: "The Christian faith, faith in the God revealed by Jesus Christ, is not '*one* of the religions of the world' " (op. cit. above, note 7; p. 258). (The original reads: *Der christliche Glaube, der Glaube an den in Jesus Christus geoffenbarten Gott, ist nicht 'eine der Religionen der Erde'*—op. cit., German original, p. 284. One may note that in the translation the English article is inserted in the first case ['the Christian faith'] out of habit, omitted in the second ['faith in the God . . .'] out of more careful regard for meaning; I would omit in both cases, reading, 'Christian faith . . . is not one of the religions of the world'—which makes much more sense. In fact, in this rendering it almost ceases to be controversial.) It is noteworthy that from the first time the phrase 'the religions of the world' was introduced into Europe it was contrasted not with the 'Christian religion' but with Christian 'faith': in the subtitle of the Stamler work, 1508, above, chap. 2, notes 132, 134 and in many, perhaps most subsequent works until today one finds this antithesis consciously or unconsciously maintained. This is true even of liberal writers: A. C. Bouquet, *The Christian Faith and non-Christian Religions*, London, 1958; and indeed is virtually standard for others. Some examples: Hendrik Kraemer, *Religion and the Christian Faith*, London, 1956; Walter Freytag, *The Gospel and the Religions: a Biblical enquiry*, London, 1957. (This last, the English translators have softened. The German original is different: *Das Rätsel der Religionen und die biblische Antwort*, Wuppertal-Barmen, 1956, the 'enigma' (*Rätsel*) stemming precisely 'from the fact that Christianity is one religion among many' [p. 14]. The title of chapter I concedes this: 'One Religion among many religions'; yet the title of the preliminary section is rather 'The Religions as a Challenge to our Faith' [p. 11].)

Brunner, later on in the same paragraph as that quoted above, is presented as saying, 'It [the Christian faith] cannot admit that its faith is one species of the genus 'religion,' or if it does so, only in the sense in which it regards itself as the true religion in contrast to the other false religions', expanded with the footnote, 'This is the Reformation idea of religion. Thus Zwingli entitles his main work *De vera religione;* thus Luther speaks of the Christian faith as the *vera et unica religio* (W. A., 25, 287) ; this is the meaning of Calvin in his *Institutio Christianae religionis'*. I take the liberty of questioning here the exactitude of Miss Olive Wyon's usually admirable translating, to wonder whether Brunner did not rather mean that Christian faith is not one of the religions of the world, that Christian faith 'regards itself as true religion' and 'Luther speaks of Christian faith as *vera et unica religio'*. Both are equally possible understandings of Brunner's actual German, in which language the discrimination is not verbally effected; but his own argument here seems to me to require the less reified translation, as well as Zwingli's, Luther's and Calvin's usage, which I doubt that Brunner has misunderstood. It might be argued that the use of the German article with the Latin noun in the footnote shifts some of the misunderstanding from Miss Wyon's shoulders back to Brunner's.

NOTES·FOR CHAPTER FIVE

40 P. 125.

41 Op. cit., p. 264 (English version).

42 And especially, the specific transcendent involvement that is the central significance of that religious life. The Muslim case *vis-à-vis* Christians is tricky, for with regard to the worship of God Muslims may regard Christians, Jews, and other *ahl al-kitāb* as, in a sense, errant members of the same 'religion' as themselves, so that in this respect they see Christian faith not altogether from the outside; and for this reason they have historically been more respectful of Christians' faith than Christians have of theirs. With regard to Christians' worship of Christ and doctrine of the Trinity, however, they look at this resolutely from the outside, in a burning repudiation.

43 The hymn is 'From Greenland's icy mountains', written in 1819 by Bishop Reginald Heber (1783–1826) (who also, by the way, wrote so major a hymn as 'Holy, Holy, Holy'). The second verse, as given in *The Methodist Hymn-Book, with tunes,* London, Wesleyan Conference Office, 1904, number 770, runs as follows:

> *What though the spicy breezes*
> *Blow soft o'er Ceylon's isle,*
> *Though every prospect pleases,*
> *And only man is vile;*
> *In vain with lavish kindness*
> *The gifts of God are strown,*
> *The heathen in his blindness*
> *Bows down to wood and stone.*

The hymn had extremely wide use in the English-speaking Protestant church for a time. Later, however, sentiment in the church changed. Some later versions amended the fourth line to read 'And only sin is vile'. It is interesting to note, however, that this verse is omitted entirely in the hymn as entered in *The Hymnary of the United Church of Canada, authorized by the General Council,* Toronto, 1930 ff., where the other three verses constitute number 256, and in *The Book of Common Praise (revised 1938), being the Hymn Book of the Church of England in Canada,* compiled by a Committee of the General Synod, Toronto, London, etc., n.d. (sc. ca. 1939?), where the other verses are number 275. One may perhaps recall that when this hymn was written, the West's first book on 'Buddhism' (above, chap. 3, note 36) had not yet been published. Nor was any information on the subject available in the then current edition of the *Encyclopaedia Britannica* (ibid.).

44 το γαρ μη ὸν οὐδεις οἰδεν ὁ τι ἐστιν, ἀλλα τι μεν σημαινει ὁ λογος ἠ το ὁνομα, ὁταν εἰπω τραγελαφος, τι δ' ἐστι τραγελαφος, ἀδυνατον εἰδεναι— 92ᵇ 5ff. I have used the edition of W. D. Ross, ΑΡΙΣΤΟΤΕΛΟΤΣ ΑΝΑΛΤΤΙΚΑ—*Aristotle's Prior and Posterior Analytics: a revised text with introduction and commentary,* Oxford, 1949. In addition to the above in particular, see his Book II and esp. chap. 7 in general.

45 I have taken the liberty of substituting the term 'unicorn', which only in modern times has come to be recognized as non-existent, for Aristotle's 'goat-stag'.

313

46 The phrase *Essence of Hinduism* has been used recently as the title of a book published in New York, 1946, by Swami Nikhilananda. 'The nature . . . of Hinduism', also, is a section by D. S. Sarma in the Morgan volume, 1953, cited above, note 28 ('The Nature and History of Hinduism' is chapter 1, pp. 3–47; the last twenty pages of this are 'The History of Hinduism' [p. 27], while the earlier section is devoted to considering what Hinduism 'essentially' [p. 3] is). Both of these are by highly Westernized Hindus writing in English for Western readers; they illustrate the influence of recent Western thought-patterns on the thinking of non-Westerners, and illustrate also the relevance of these concepts rather to outsiders, to whom these writings are addressed. In content, they do not dissuade me that the concept is illegitimate. If one thinks of the intellectually grander system of a Sankara, or of a Rāmānuja dissenting from it, one must recognize that these were proposing to describe (hardly to define) the universe, not Hinduism. An historian will take all four of these (along with much non-intellectualist data, no less important) as items within a total Hindu tradition, not as substitutes for it, nor even as synopses of it. We pass over here, as already sufficiently considered, the problem of the inadequacy of any intellectualization to one's own faith.

47 On this, one may refer to Harold Buschman, 'A critical survey of some recent theories of the origin and nature of religion', a Ph:D. thesis submitted to the University of Chicago in 1932. (Consulted in microfilm.)

48 Such as his insistence, relevant here, that in growing things, their nature (φυσις) can be known only in their final development.

49 It is still found currently today, perhaps more often tacitly assumed or quietly proffered in passing than critically argued; yet it is held by serious writers. Two illustrations that have by chance come to hand recently: 'If we are to know what religion is, we must also find something in common between the great religions of the world'—R. C. Zaehner, *At Sundry Times: an essay in the comparison of religions*, London, 1958, p. 15; again, the opening sentence of a 'Chapter One. Introductory. 1. What is Religion?': 'What is the common element which is present in all religions?'—J. H. Badley, *Form and Spirit: a study in religion*, London, 1951, p. 15 (though the latter author goes on at once to reword this so as to allow a shift of that common element from 'all religions' to all religious persons: 'Or, to put the question in another way, what is it that gives to a particular attitude to life its religious character?' —ibid.).

50 Were this chapter not long already, we ought perhaps to consider the device proposed by Max Weber to handle the difficulty of history's intractability to essence, namely the concept of 'ideal types'. Much is to be said in favour of this sort of intellectual postulate, to facilitate an observer's study of actuality. But against it this also must be said, perhaps decisively when the inquiry is of religious matters: that a concept of 'Christianity', 'Judaism', 'Islam', or the like that is explicitly and of set purpose a human product, a deliberate expedient, collides with an irrepressible characteristic of the life that is here being conceptualized. In other matters it is no doubt

useful to imagine a form, in order to deal intellectually with an actuality not inherently formal. To that imaginary form the real may be seen to approximate. But in religious affairs, what is going on is distorted if seen as tending, however asymptotically, towards a concept forged pragmatically in someone's mind. The conceptual process, when it operates in the opposite direction, I have argued, is misleading enough. Few Christians will wish to retain an idea of 'Christianity' that is a conscious fiction.

Notes for Chapter Six: The Cumulative Tradition

1 By this I do not mean that no one may legitimately approach the study of man's religious history with convictions. This was a conviction earlier of some academic minds; it is no longer persuasive. My point is rather that whatever a person's own faith, he must not approach the study of history with an assurance that he knows ahead of time the content or the validity of the faith of other men. A Muslim need not drop his conviction that the Qur'ān is the word of God, in order to understand human history (to ask this of him would be a foolish arrogance) ; but one may predict that he will fail in understanding if he couples with this a dogmatic conviction that other scriptures, or other nonscriptural modes, are necessarily *not* the word of God. Similarly, a Christian may and, indeed, surely must bring to the study his conviction that his own faith is valid; but he will proceed ineptly if he presupposes that therefore other men's faith is not. Again, the skeptic or objective historian is not asked to abandon his own skepticism or objectivity, but he will make little progress if he assumes that all those whom he studies who have a transcendentalist vision are fools (or even, wrong). On some aspects of this exceedingly important point, with its multiple implications, see my articles cited above, chap. 4, notes 85 and 108.

2 Some careful readers will protest that this wording indicates a collapse into the restrictedly humanistic notion of religious life as man's search for God or for the Truth rather than recognizing that rather it is God that takes the initiative to search out and to save mankind. It will be found that my analysis, I later contend, does not preclude this view, either for one's own tradition or, what is novel and important, for other people's. Yet even the most theocentric of believers (Christians, Muslims, Bhāktas, or whoever) will hardly challenge the statement that, even within the divinely founded community, Christians (Muslims, Bhāktas, . . .) have *wrestled* with the problem, at least on an intellectual level, of transcendence and its relation to the mundane—and have wrestled humanity; that is, fallibly and at times agonizingly.

3 X. 129. This is the hymn that begins, *Then was neither non-existence nor existence,* and ends,

The gods are later than this world's creation. Who then knows when first it came to being?
The source of this creation, and whether one formed it all or did not form it, He, who surveys from highest heaven, verily He knows. Or—perhaps—he does not know.

4 This is the famous question of the influence of one 'religion' upon another, or 'syncretism', etc. All such influence is through persons, is the influence of more than one tradition on the faith of some one individual or some individuals. In this case, the issue has long been moot whether the transition reflected in Sanskrit literature from a joyous swash-buckling life-affirming polytheism in the early Vedas to a later pessimistic monism—a transition for which this poem is the earliest literary evidence—was a curious development within the religion of the Aryans or a resurgence of the pre-Aryan religion of India. The only historically accurate way to ask or to answer such a question, I suggest, is in terms not of religions but of religious traditions and religious persons. In these terms the question becomes entirely manageable, and rather disarming.

5 Irrelevant to our argument is the (disputable) point of the degree to which any man's ideas, attitudes, orientations are to be understood in terms of individual or of social, economic, or other considerations. How a man's faith comes to be constituted does not mitigate the validity or serviceability of separating it in analysis from the overt religious tradition in which it takes place. See further our next chapter, on faith.

6 As I have earlier had occasion to indicate, I am not unconscious that some would dogmatically deny that man's spirit is open to anything that can legitimately or meaningfully be called transcendent. (Others would deny that this is so outside their own closed community.) We shall reconsider this matter in our next chapter. For the moment I merely remark that such a position if held at all is necessarily held on *a priori* grounds and against the evidence of mankind's religious history. (On some Christian aspects of this question, see my article cited below, chap. 7, note 4).

7 In the Muslim case, some of us witnessed something of this potential distress at the International Islamic Colloquium, Lahore, 1958, when a singularly bold Muslim outraged many of his fellows by raising, perhaps in somewhat provocative fashion, the question of an historical criticism of the Qur'ān. His paper read on that occasion is, significantly, not being included among the published proceedings of the Colloquium. (It has, however, appeared independently as Muhammad Daud Rahbar, 'The Challenge of Modern Ideas and Social Values to Muslim Society', in *The Muslim World*, Hartford, 48: 274–285 [1958].) In general, modern Muslims have not yet addressed

themselves to this question, but presumably will find it eventually intellectually challenging.

In the Christian case, the problem has been no less acute, and for many no less distressing, though it has been somewhat sooner and therefore more widely faced; conspicuously in recent times in, for instance, the widely discussed works of Rudolf Bultmann (e.g., above, chap. 5, note 35). More generally, the issue is one that has been perennial since a distinction was propounded between 'the Jesus of history and the Christ of experience' (see, for instance, the 1909 supplement *Jesus or Christ?* to the *Hibbert Journal*, London).

For all the burning particularity and the seriousness of this last question, it could be generalized in the observation that there is or will be a formally comparable problem for other religious men, which could be formulated as that between 'the Siddhartha Gautama of history and the Buddha of faith', 'the Qur'ān of history and the Holy Qur'ān of God', 'the history of Western Asia in the two millennia B.C. [E.] and God's election of, and law-giving and prophecy to, the Jews', and so on. (Cf. also below, chap. 7, note 20.)

8 One may note, for example, the *ḥadīth* text, extremely important both historically and theologically: 'My community will not concert in going astray' *(Inna ummatī lā tajtamiʻu ʻalā ḍalālah*—Ibn Mājah). It is an Islamic counterpart, in some sense, to the Christian doctrine of the Holy Spirit and its guidance of the Church. One may note also—as one illustration among many of a major attitude—an illuminating remark of a mediaeval Muslim about the eponymous leader of a school of thought which eventually (partly through the political expediencies of the Saljuq rulers) had become established as in some sense orthodox. 'The Muʻtazilah were holding high their heads, until God Most High brought al-Ashʻarī on the scene, and he made them shut up' (—cited in Abū Bakr Aḥmad ibn ʻAlī al-Khaṭīb al-Baghdādī, *Taʼrīkh Baghdād, aw madīnat al-salām*, ed. ʻAli Ajmal Shakl, 14 voll., Cairo & Baghdad, 1349/1931; XI. 347). This expresses the typical later view, formulated of course after the Ashʻarī tradition had in fact triumphed: namely, that that particular tradition, among the various alternatives, had all along been the *right* ('truly Islamic') one. An outside observer of the development of Islamic theological thought has no more reason to hold that God brought al-Ashʻarī on the scene than that He had brought the Muʻtazilah. He has no *a priori* reason to hold that the Ashʻarī interpretations would of course win the day. He has no reason to doubt that if some other viewpoint (e.g., the Muʻtazilah) had actually prevailed then *that* viewpoint would *ipso facto* have become recognized as proper. He may reasonably speculate that had this been the case, then some pious later writer would readily have opined: 'The Ashāʻirah tried to hold high their heads but God, who had sent the Muʻtazilah, brought Muʻtazilah supporters on the scene who made them shut up'.

All this is merely a rather elaborate way of saying that in the eyes of anyone except those who hold a certain version of an Islamic faith, Islamic history *including Islamic religious history* might have been different from what in fact it has been. The same, *mutatis mutandis*, applies to and is equally important for the historical development of the Buddhist religious tradition, the Christian (cf. above, the preceding note, and below, chap. 7, note 20), the Jewish, etc. (Muslim theory, of course, in answer to our above point, would rightly respond that, had the Muᶜtazilah triumphed, of course they would recognize it as the right Islamic view, since had it triumphed this would simply show that God wished it to triumph in Islamic development. Once again there is not disagreement on the facts; insiders and observers may interpret them differently. The same reasoning applies to any Roman Catholic interpretation of what the Church pronounces to be dogma. In general, however, it is perhaps legitimate and even relevant to point out the historical fact that doctrines of a divine ordinance of the course of history generally or of the history of one's own community were formulated and were widely held before knowledge of that history, in its modern scope, was available.)

9 In Muslim view a chief (but not the only) element in such a pattern is the Qur'ān, which God has injected into human history through the rather special intermediary of the person Muḥammad, who is given in Muslim faith what is called 'prophetic' rank, almost but not quite more than human. Yet even Christians, who give Christ a considerably more exalted rank, do not in their orthodox stream deny that He was also a fully human being.

On al- Shāfiᶜī here I am in broad outlines following the thesis of Schacht (Joseph Schacht, *The Origins of Muhammadan Jurisprudence*, Oxford, 1950, 1953). His interpretation is, perhaps, somewhat controversial; however, if al-Shāfiᶜī did not play the constructive role that Schacht discerns, in bringing into historical and explicated existence a consciously systematic formulation of Islamic *fiqh*, then someone else did. The system did not exist in the first century *hijrī*, and did in the fourth.

10 If every Christian theologian down the ages had said exactly the same thing, for twenty centuries, my religious situation would be seriously different from an early Christian's, just because in my case it would have been said over and over again, whereas he was hearing it for the first time.

11 The word 'innovation' is provocative here, since it comes close to a pejorative concept in Islamic thought. One must perhaps apologize, but one cannot retract. For I cannot but regard it as an innovation in history even to explicate in idea or in institution what may later be regarded as having been previously latent. In the strictest sense, indeed, for those who take human freedom seriously, it is an innovation even to choose, though unconsciously, to prolong what has already existed. To maintain in existence for a thousandth year what until now has existed for only nine hundred and ninety-nine, is to that extent to modify the *status quo*. Only the radical and profound quality of our freedom today, however, enables man to appreciate this subtle fact.

12 Therefore the strictures that, I urged, apply to the concept 'religion' or a particular religion are not applicable here. My concept can be defined, but not the reality to which it refers. And in explicitly abstracting away from the tradition its significance for him who is involved in it, I have avoided the error of those whose concept in fact omits that significance but who do not recognize this, or who feel that it does not crucially matter. Another difficulty that might be raised against my proffered concept is that of

discriminating in a given historical or social context between the religious cumulative tradition and a non-religious. This is in considerable part met by the indication that a cumulative tradition may be termed religious when it is the product and channel of men's faith. Admittedly, however, this latter personalist concept, as we shall see in our next chapter, is only in part logically prior to the present concept. For men's religious faith is continuous with their religious cumulative tradition as well as vice-versa, so that one may seem to be in part arguing here in a circle. This is less reprehensible than it would otherwise be in that a boundary between the religious and the non-religious not only may but must be tenuous and flexible if it is to be serviceable for interpreting human history. I shall suggest presently that an adjective religious has some legitimacy apart from any noun. In any case this problem is not generated by my analysis. On the contrary it stems from the traditional conceptualization and has proven unanswerable there, while my proposal goes perhaps some way, if not yet all the way, towards solving it.

Notes for Chapter Seven: Faith

1 It is a personal quality that differentiates *Gemeinschaft* from *Gesell-schaft*. Cf. Ferdinand Tönnies, *Gemeinschaft und Gesellschaft: Grundbegriffe der reinen Soziologie,* [1st ed., 1877] 6te & 7te Auflage, Berlin, 1926. A translation of this into English by Charles P. Loomis has been published under separate titles in the United States and Britain: *Fundamental Concepts of Sociology,* New York, (American Sociology Series), 1940; *Community and Association,* London (Karl Mannheim and W. J. H. Sprott, edd., International Library of Sociology and Social Reconstruction), 1955.

2 See above, chap. 4, note 78.

3 Above, p. 153.

4 The Christian Church and the Muslim *ummah* are, for instance, generally regarded by their members as metaphysically absolute entities, since in the respective doctrines these are divinely postulated communities, expressions of divine ideas. In so far as such doctrines are correlative to such matters as *Apartheid* policy in South Africa or the 1947 Panjab massacres, they will, one might humbly suggest, simply have to be modified. I personally tend to believe, and it is one possible interpretation, surely, of at least Christian revelation (and, if I may be allowed an opinion, I would suggest also of Islamic)

to believe, that the only human community ideal in the mind of God, the only human community there truly, ultimately is, is mankind as a whole.

Christians and Muslims, moreover, in strict theory, have discriminated between the true Church, or the truly Muslim section of mankind, and the observable community of historical actuality. This discrimination has some-times served more as a loophole of defence than as an avenue of brotherhood. Nonetheless, I recognize that there is an important and delicate problem here, for which I do not at the moment have an elaborated solution to proffer. In my defence I may urge that the problem does not stem from the concep-tual system that I am constructing. It arises within that system in a particular form but arises also, in some other form, in the traditional interpretations if only one is sensitive enough to fractured human relationships to see it. Fur-thermore, in my analysis the problem becomes one for the theologian of each exclusivist tradition, which is where, one may reasonably suggest, the problem rightly belongs. In the conceptual system of a Barth or a Mawdudi, the con-demnation of the outsider to an inferior status that infringes both human dignity and empirical observation, that shatters both human concord and his-torical continuity, are problems rather of God's making and for Him to solve or to leave unsolved. I believe that it is up to man to construct an intellectual position that will enable him to maintain loyalty to his own tradition and to the faith that he finds through it, without negating those of other men or disrupting empirical knowledge. For a preliminary discussion of some Chris-tian theological facets of this issue, see my review article 'A Presentation of Islam', in *The International Review of Missions*, London, 49: 220–226 (1960).

5 It is sometimes attractive but perhaps always precarious to hold that faith always has or must have some particular form of expression. Cer-tainly the practical has been a major form, and has received much attention.

6 James 2:26. In the Revised Standard Version: 'For as the body apart from the spirit is dead, so faith apart from works is dead'.

7 See, for instance, my article 'Some Similarities and Differences be-tween Christianity and Islam: an essay in comparative religion', in James Kritzeck and R. Bayly Winder, edd., *The World of Islam: Studies in honour of Philip K. Hitti*, London, 1959, pp. 47-59, and chapter 1 of my *Islam in Modern History*, Princeton 1957, London 1958, New York 1959.

8 Paul Tillich, *Systematic Theology*, Chicago, in process, 1951–

9 I use here my own terms 'tradition' and 'faith' deliberately. I do this partly to suggest that my analysis of human involvements in history has a potentially wider application than to the strictly religious field. (I rather imagine that finally all human activities—science, language, a university, and what not—could illuminatingly be conceptualized in terms of a dialectic be-tween a tangible tradition in process and something like faith of particular persons.) Equally, it is in order to suggest that this particular situation in Western civilization can be intelligently and helpfully viewed within a world context of man's religious traditions such as I am endeavouring to establish. To elaborate this point would require, however (and perhaps repay?), a book in itself. As indicated above (chap. 4, note 34), I see the famous Western prob-

lem of faith and reason (a problem partially shared by the Islamic world) as the problem of a person participant in two cumulative traditions, through each of which he is introduced to a transcendent that can be for him ultimately valuable and finally demanding. Formally, the problem is comparable to that of the Chinese who participates in more than one tradition; even though in content the Chinese has usually (not always) been spared the pain of conflict.

10   See the preceding note.

11   I say the 'later' Western situation, for this is not original. In the Greek New Testament there is a verb (πιστευω) as well as a noun (πιστις) for 'faith'. Presumably behind these in the Gospels lie the Aramaic and eventually Hebrew verb and noun pair, אמן—אמת. See above, chap. 3, note 26. It is also of considerable importance that the Latin verb *credo*, used in the Vulgate and in mediaeval liturgy etc., originally meant, not to 'believe', but (literally) to 'give credit to', hence to 'trust'; so that it was a valid correlative of the noun for 'faith'. A study of the historical transition to intellectualist 'belief' (perhaps eighteenth century?) would be rewarding.

12   One of the most weighty among such theologians was Archbishop Temple, for whom theology is to revelation as musical criticism is to music (p. 317). 'Revelation . . . neither is nor can be exhaustively represented in propositions' (p. 318). 'There is no such thing as revealed truth' [that is, truth of a conceptualist or intellectualist sort] (p. 317). 'Knowledge of God can be fully given to man only in a person, never in a doctrine' (p. 321; original in italics). The page references here are to William Temple, *Nature, Man and God: being the Gifford Lectures delivered in the University of Glasgow in the academical years 1932–33 and 1933–34*, London, 1934 (and frequently reprinted since).

13   Gustaf Aulén, *Den allmänneliga kristna tron*, Femte omarbetade upplagan, Stockholm/Lund, 1957. The original reads: *Den systematiska teologiens uppgift blir alltså att med alla till buds stående medel söka klarlägga den kristna trons innebörd och mening* (p. 11); *Den vill icke bestämma över tron men analysera den faktiskt förefintliga, levande kristna tron* (p. 12). I have considered at some length the question whether the words *den kristna tron(s)* here are more correctly represented by 'Christian faith' or by 'the Christian faith'. This is a matter of some delicacy and seriousness; but I have become persuaded that the former is inescapable—particularly for 'Christian faith as it actually exists', since 'the' Christian faith is an idealist concept, referring to something that does not 'actually exist'. (The Swedish is even more personalist here—is *levande* possibly a difference of editions?) Indeed, the whole thesis of Aulén throughout the book seems to me to be impaired if the article is inserted in English. It may at first seem presumptuous of me, and perhaps even tendentious, to give this rendering when the accepted English published version, which I have otherwise followed (it was done, admittedly, from the fourth Swedish edition, inaccessible to me, but it is apparent that on this particular point there is no critical difference) reads 'the Christian faith' in the two sentences that I have quoted—Gustaf Aulén, *The Faith of the Christian Church*, trans. Eric H. Wahlstrom and G. Everett Arden, Philadelphia, 1948, pp. 5, 6. I am undaunted, however, because apparently the translators, though seemingly unconscious of the problem, yet in fact

vacillate between the two but gradually adopt what I think is the correct interpretation as they go on—the course of Aulén's argument has led them, unconsciously it would seem, to adopt the existential rendering as they proceed. In the first few pages of their translation, including the sentences that we have quoted, they use the article fairly regularly, but on p. 7 they write 'Systematic theology seeks to investigate the significance of Christian faith' (the Swedish is once again *den kristna trons innebörd*, p. 14). Similarly, continuing, we find 'In the realm of Christian faith' (p. 8). On p. 43 'Christian faith' is used 4 times, 'the Christian faith' none, on the following page the former occurs 6 times, the latter once. Parts II, III, IV of the work they entitle 'The Content of Christian Faith'. I believe that most readers will agree that the book reads more cogently in English (as well as more consistently) if the article is dropped throughout.

14   Does this mean sheer relativism, making out that theology cannot be true or false? I would contend that the fundamental question is rather whether faith is true or false—the particular faith of a given person. This issue is tricky, and of course of ultimate significance. I rather imagine that a theological statement cannot be baldly true in itself, but rather can become true in the life of persons, when it is interiorized and lived. (But it can also become false, can be falsified?) Cf. below, note 16.

Further, I would contend that man's religious life is liberated, not devastated, when it is recognized that 'a religion' cannot in itself be true or false. The notion that a given religion may be true, or even more, that it may not be true, has caused untold mischief. Or again, that one religion is true while another is false; or, equally misleading, that all religions are equally true (which is, of course, nonsense). We must learn that this is not where truth and falsity lie, and especially not where religious truth and religious falsity lie. Religions, either singly or together, cannot be true or false—as one rejoices to recognize once one is emancipated from supposing that there are such things in our universe. What a deal of sorrow has flowed from asking a wrong question, and trying desperately but impossibly to answer it. Once men turn this particular corner, they can resume their ancient religious march, which has seemed bogged down of late.

15   Neither the truth nor the meaning of the verbalization 'I love you' is independent of the person who makes it. (Nor, indeed, of the person who hears it.) This point is not, I believe, silly: for the fact that natural science statements are always in the third person, while humanist statements are at least capable of the quite new dimensions of the first and second persons, is a fact of profound significance. All general statements about human affairs (for instance, this book's attempt to conceptualize religious life) are ultimately statements in the first person plural. To talk of man is, finally, to talk of 'us men'. Some social scientists' endeavours to get around this point are, I believe, misled. It is a fundamental error of modern 'behavioural sciences' to aim at purely *objective* knowledge as an ultimate goal. The humanities also, of course, must learn to become scientific, empirical—the social or behavioural scientist clings to 'objectivity', so long as the only alternatives that he sees to it are subjectivity and speculation. The revolution in this realm, which will undo the divorce between the social sciences and the humanities, will come, I be-

lieve, with the recognition that the ultimate goal of scientific knowledge in this area is a disciplined self-consciousness.

16 Interesting to note is that the truth of such a statement depends not only on the sincerity of the person who makes it, but also on his understanding. If one misapprehends what true love is (and which of us does not, in part?—yet some more than others), then one may believe that one loves, and may therefore sincerely say so, and yet one's statement will be to that extent not true. Here again the analogy with theology is not altogether remote.

17 W. C. Smith, 'Comparative Religion: whither—and why?' in M. Eliade and J. Kitagawa, edd., *The History of Religions: essays in methodology*, Chicago, 1959, p. 35.

18 For a fuller exploring of this point, see the essay noted in the immediately preceding reference. On the question of friendship and its relevance here, see particularly op. cit., p. 39, at fn. 18.

19 The cumulative tradition, we have seen, is the product of the personal faith of men in the past, and the avenue of faith for men in every present. One cannot then finally ask which comes first: the two continuously interact in the uninterrupted processes of history. Actually there are two ways in which it might be argued that the tradition precedes faith, rather than vice-versa. One is in human history generally, where our awareness of the cumulative tradition extends far further back into prehistoric times than can our awareness of men's personal faith. For obvious reasons, we know that Stone Age men buried their dead and elaborated other items that have been transmitted into the later religious tradition of mankind, for periods many thousands of years earlier than we can know or presumably ever shall know what these things meant to them. Secondly, in the life of the individual: the child is presented with an objective tradition that precedes him, and grows up among persons to whom that tradition is already meaningful, before his own faith comes to be expressed by that tradition, and certainly before he can, if a leader or genius or pervert, modify that tradition by constructive or damaging amendments out of his own personal creativity. Certainly there is no known religious figure, no matter how great, in the whole sweep of man's religious story whose religious life is not in some way a continuation, no matter how radically modified, of the tradition that he inherited.

Yet this is true of all human life, in every possible aspect; no man ever did anything that was utterly unrelated to what went before. (The problem, basically, is the same as that between, for instance, language and thought.) A tradition precedes all known faith; yet it would be false to conclude that it controls it, that faith is but a function of the tradition. Over against this the historian may point to innumerable specific items in the total cumulative religious tradition of mankind whose being introduced for the first time at particular moments by particular persons out of their particular capacities can be observed. Despite historical continuity, which it would be idle to deny or decry, there would seem legitimacy in seeing faith as at least logically prior to its concretizations. And no matter how much influence one may attribute to inherited traditions in moulding men's response to them, there would seem no avoiding the recognition that man appears to be constitutionally open to such responding, and also free to modify his response. He observably brings to the tradition an inherent capacity to respond, but also not to respond, and also to respond in new ways.

Fortunately, as with the chicken and the egg, there is perhaps no final need to solve this problem.

20   A Roman Catholic might perhaps be able to accept this phrasing; and yet it betrays, I suppose, a different orientation from his. Even in the Roman Church the formulating of theological expositions is a vigorous and recognizedly human activity. Neither has a full theology been pontificated *ex cathedra*, nor have theologians confused personal faith with verbal expressions of faith. Nonetheless, individual members of that Church accept, beyond theology, also dogma—by which is meant doctrines seen as revealed (rather like the Muslim view of truth revealed in the Qur'ān). These doctrines, then, as set forth in formal pronouncements of the Church, are for its members accordingly exempt from the mundane quality that I have here attributed to all verbalizations and conceptualizations.

I have not explored the question of language here: how a proposition in Latin is seen to escape the particularity of that historically produced and historically conditioned language. Nor indeed, at a more basic level, have I satisfactorily considered the deeper problem here involved, which in some ways is that of persons who do not have or feel the responsibility of individual decision. In all communities, of course, there are members who no doubt legitimately are content to follow their leaders—but suppose one is a leader? (Protestants, in addition, like Muslims, Hindus, Buddhists, and most others, can hardly evade nowadays the searching personal question, *which leader?*) One may leave (elect to leave) theological questions to theologians—but suppose one is a theologian? Ultimately, perhaps, the question for Roman Catholics is, suppose one is Pope? I hope that this question will not seem irreverent—it is meant to be serious. We are all, so far as I can see, human beings in this matter of religious living, and perhaps each person must decide for himself how far (and how) he sees the transcendent coming down into human life, and how far he sees it extending and ramifying in human life and society before it becomes limited or modified by the human agents through whom it acts (or by the products of human agents, such as the concepts of a language) .

Actually, the Roman Catholic situation is a particular instance of the general problem adumbrated above (chap. 6, notes 7, 8, 9; see also this present chapter, above, note 4, and below, note 21) of the transcendent-within-history. As indicated there, this poses a problem for the expositor of faith primarily, and only secondarily for the analytical theorist. Yet even for the latter it must not, I admit, be evaded.

On dogma, the following statements are revealing, from the *Enciclopedia Cattolica*, 12 voll., Città del Vaticano, 1948–1954, article DOGMA (by Cipriano Vagaggini): '*Una dottrina rivelata da Dio e proposta come tale dalla Chiesa con la garanzia dell 'infallibilità'* . . . '*D[ogma] e teologia non s'identificano, la teologia essendo in tutta la sua estensione un ulteriore studio umano scientifico dei d. e delle altre cose proposte dalla Chiesa, sebbene non come d.*'; and the intriguing historical comment, recalling our observations above, chap. 2

on intellectualization in the Enlightenment: *'Il termine d[ogma] per esprimere precisamenta questo concetto non prevalse in modo definitivo che a partire dal sec. xviii'* (vol. 4, pp. 1791, 1792, 1795).

21   Some readers might infer from this paragraph that I am asserting that Christians as a group have nothing distinctive in common; that what they have in common is simply what they have in common with all religious men, 'the transcendent itself'. The problem is one for the Christian theologian. I do assert, flatly, that God is not unknown outside the Christian community. It seems to me, as an observer, quite impossible to explain the religious history of mankind outside the Judeao-Christian tradition on any other hypothesis. Those Christian theologians who have postulated that that history has proceeded without contact with transcendence have done so without, in fact, knowing the history. Once it is recognized, as I claim that it must be, that God is known and is active in other communities, then it is a problem for the Christian theologian to formulate his conviction that He is known and is active in the Christian Church in a special way. What that special way is can be explicated, presumably; the explication will not, so far as I can see, conflict with the paragraph in my text.

It might perhaps be argued that I have purchased historical intelligibility and an almost mystical immediacy at the price of theological surrender: that by characterizing the cumulative tradition as something wholly within this world, I have rejected not the transcendent itself, which I have argued as integral to the analysis, but the transcendent-in-history, the word made flesh, the mystical body, the pre-existent Speech of God now between the two covers of the bound Qur'ān, and have thus left man without the stable support of an essential truth, in a world of flux and ambiguity. The analysis, however, rather leaves man where he has in fact always been, and where our analysis started: the citizen of two worlds, between history and eternity, the child of his time and place and the child of God. The analysis recognizes, but does not itself generate, the fact that people take their religious symbols from their fathers, but that every man must find out for himself what those symbols mean.

Notes for Chapter Eight: Conclusion

1   Another possibility is that through 'Departments of Religion' in universities, which are a growing fashion, the noun 'religion' will acquire a new and eventually legitimate signification, namely 'academic inquiry into religious matters'. It would thereby parallel terms like 'sociology' or 'optics'. 'Economics' also, as a noun (compare note 3 just below) refers not, strictly, to any entity in society—there is no such entity—but to the intellectual consideration of those aspects of society or of personal life to which the *adjective* 'economic' may apply.

2   Thus 'Greek religion' is a legitimate concept, 'the Greek religion' is not. (The former refers to the religiousness of the Greek people, obviously an amorphous actuality; there is nothing to which the latter can refer.) 'The religion of Greece' is sufficiently ambiguous to be both defensible and inadvisable. In French and German, ambiguity is built in: *la religion sumérienne* (above, chap. 5, ref. 26) ; *die Geschichte der griechischen Religion* (the meaning of this phrase in the mind of one scholar who knows more about the topic than most other men in modern times, is shown when he summarizes his two-volume work of that title [München, 1941–1950] under the phrase *Grekisk religiositet*: a Swedish title that one might render 'Greek religiousness'. The English translator considers 'religiosity' but rejects it; the summary appeared in English as Martin P. Nilsson, *Greek Piety*, trans. Herbert Jennings Rose, Oxford, 1948, 1951. In his 'Translator's Preface' Professor Rose remarks that *religiositet* occurs not only in the title but 'frequently in the text', and he renders it there by ' "religious feeling" generally, sometimes simply "religion" '.

3   The next great step in medicine will come when it is realized that diseases are adjectives, rather than nouns—if I may be allowed to build a positive personalist thesis on the basis of the negative position, against conceiving diseases as entities, that is set forth by F. G. Crookshank in C. K. Ogden and I. A. Richards, *The Meaning of Meaning*, London, 1923 (for purposes of checking I have consulted the New York and London 1956 impression of the 8th ed., where the Crookshank essay is Supplement II, pp. 337–355, and the relevant remarks of the two authors are found on pp. 43, 101) . To construct an appropriate theory of illness and its categories is, as Crookshank argues, the task of a science of medicine; but to see each patient as a person

afflicted with a given disease that is adjectival to him is the task of the practising doctor.

It has often been remarked that in the Semitic languages (apparently this is even more true of classical Japanese), the verb is primary, whereas in the Indo-European the noun has at least equal rank—and in Greek philosophy nouns were taken more seriously than verbs, so that ever since in Western thought reality has tended to be conceived in terms of entities, while in the Old Testament, for instance, it is conceived primarily in terms of events. I know of no major culture in which adjectives are given primacy, but I suggest that serious consideration deserves to be given to the notion that a truly personalist view of mankind's history and situation will require a recognition that in these realms, apart from proper names of persons, the only nouns that can stand up to final scrutiny are 'God' (or does this come under the heading of the proper name of a person?) and 'man' (ἄνθρωπος, homo). All else is either a conceptual abstraction and/or adjectival. (To note one minor implication: the apparent difficulty of discriminating between religion and economics [compare note 1 just above], religion and politics, or the like disappears once one realizes that adjectives such as 'economic', 'political', and 'religious' may readily and reasonably overlap, may readily and reasonably apply to the same person, action, or situation.) Even the nouns 'man' in the sense of ἀνήρ, vir, and 'woman' are in the final analysis misleading, and in this case even immoral. To think of a person whom one meets as fundamentally a woman, rather than as fundamentally a person with various attributes including the perhaps exceedingly important one of being feminine, is in the end disruptive of human relations.

The adjective 'religious' I have used also, by extension from the personalist meaning, to refer as well to the traditions that religious men produce, and to what is adjectival to those traditions. Cf. in part above, chap. 6, note 12.

4 Above, chap. 5, p. 132.

5 This was written with the case in mind of members of other religious communities. Also interesting would be the case where social scientists and other sceptics in the West might on this basis perhaps come to understand religious faith even when they had none of their own. Previous formulations have been an obstacle not only to men of faith in one tradition preventing them from understanding the faith of men in another, but an obstacle also to men without faith from understanding any faith at all. Such observers have tended to concentrate in fact only on the cumulative traditions, and not to recognize that they were thereby omitting from consideration a part of what they were attempting to handle.

6 In the first edition of my *Islam in Modern History*, Princeton, 1957, p. 104n., I corroborated Charles Malik's remark 'There isn't a single Moslem scholar in all history, so far as I know, who has written an authentic essay on Christianity', writing that I also knew no work by a Muslim 'showing any "feel" for the Christian position'. In more recent versions, on the other hand, I have been happy to amend this by reference to the striking work of two scholars. The first is Itrat Husain, *The Dogmatic and Mystical Theology of John Donne*, London, 1938 and *The Mystical Element in the Metaphysical*

Poets of the Seventeenth Century, London & Edinburgh, 1948. The other is the Cairo essayist and physician Muḥammad Kāmil Ḥusayn, whose extraordinary novel on the Crucifixion has attracted literary attention in Egypt and theological attention in Christendom (*Qaryah Ẓālimah*, Cairo, 1957; English translation by Kenneth Cragg, *City of Wrong: a Friday in Jerusalem*, Amsterdam, 1959). It is arresting to note that neither of these authors makes any attempt at all to deal with the distracting question, What is Christianity?—that issue does not arise. What these men have set out to do, and have succeeded brilliantly in doing, is to depict the actual faith of particular Christians—studying it in terms of what was the Christian cumulative tradition up to the time of those particular persons.

7 This applies also to the interestingly parallel case of conversations among representatives of diverse traditions *within* one community. Presbyterians and Methodists (also Sunnīs and Shīʿīs) used to revile, also to misunderstand, each other. They are now seeking concord and intelligibility, as yet with only partial success. Hendrik Kraemer is, I believe, right in contending that ecumenicity must compel radically new thinking. The supersession of notions like 'Anglicanism' and 'Presbyterianism' by notions of mundane historical traditions and concomitant personal faith transcendence-oriented, might well facilitate communication here also, though of course the various subcommunities may feel this too high a price to pay. In passing, one may note the illustration of my general thesis in the evident fact that the future of denominational development in Christendom is not given by the past of that development; and, in short, is not given, at all. It is rather something that must be historically continuous with that past and will be affected by its momentum, but otherwise is in the hands of present and coming generations, who have both the freedom and the inescapable responsibility of creating that future. We say 'creating' deliberately; there is nowhere in the universe a pattern for them to copy. (There are, however, to use their own terms—also mine—moral imperatives for them to obey, and divine indwelling for them to open themselves to.) (Cf. Hendrik Kraemer, *The Communication of the Christian Faith*, London, 1957, especially the opening pages.)

8 On both this and the preceding area, see my article, 'Comparative Religion: Whither—and Why?' in M. Eliade and J. Kitagawa, edd., *The History of Religions: essays in methodology*, Chicago, 1959, pp. 31–58.

9 Resistance at a certain level from Christians and Muslims will be particularly strong, since, in accord with the historical developments that we have studied, it is they who have most firmly reified their religious conceptions. This is related to a metaphysical *either/or* position which involves also a transcendently hypostasized community in each case. Dereifying may accordingly be expected to be reluctant. Nonetheless let no one imagine that the matter is simple; that there is only one level; or that my analysis of religious reality can be characterized unsophisticatedly, for instance as being Hindu or oriental rather than Christian, which would be absurd.

I have remarked negatively that from Hindus and Chinese I anticipate 'no major disquiet'. On the other hand it would seem historically probably that fewer among such readers will appreciate as deeply as Christendom either the scientific, historical, dynamic quality of the proffered analysis, or the global concern. One must recognize that whereas the Christian Church and the Muslim community have had perhaps the greatest theological stress on exclusivism, they have had also the immense drive of a profound sense of responsibility for the religious condition of the whole world, which has found expression in missions in the past and which may well provide in the future a basis for grappling with world interreligious problems and the establishment of fraternity, for which various other traditions have a less manifest ready counterpart.

Muslims and especially Christians, while theologically exclusivist, have been morally universalist (for Christians on this, see my article cited above, chap. 4, note 108). Hindus have on the whole more provision for interreligious comprehension on the theoretical level but less on the moral and practical, by far. Buddhists have on the whole combined metaphysical universalism with a strong missionary emphasis, though without a view of the final significance of a directional world history. It will be interesting to see what special contribution theirs will be in the coming world collaboration.

Another important consideration is that the proffered theory is based, I hope, on scientific method and, equally significant, is linked to the consciousness of a massive new dynamic of self-directed change with which science is providing mankind. Of all the world's major religious communities the Christian and the Jewish have had by far the most intimate experience of living with recent science, for good or ill. They are much the closest, for example, to the stupendously new moral orientation in which human society through scientific knowledge now can and knows that it can annihilate itself through nuclear fission. They are also closest to the distinctive experience in happier matters of remaking the social environment in accord with human deliberation, of in part controlling history. This element in the theory here propounded is, manifestly, strong.

The basic notion of process also, especially historical process, central to this thesis, is considerably more accessible to Christians and Jews, presumably, than to any other religious group. And so on.

It is perhaps neither fortuitous nor insignificant that this theory has been excogitated from within the Christian Church. The author is an ordained minister trying to be honest with himself and with the facts as modern knowledge sees them, and to be loyal to the vision of God and of human brotherhood to which the Christian tradition introduces him.

10 It may of course seem quite shocking that an outsider should venture an opinion in a matter of this kind—to those not yet adjusted to the newness and interpenetration of our one world, and whose conceptual framework does not yet allow room for understanding what is in fact, even in the religious realm, going on at the present time. Many more persons talk of religious 'dialogue', and presumably therefore concede its theoretical possibility, than have thought through its intellectual and theological implications. The degree to which mankind is already today religiously interdependent, let alone that to which we may become so tomorrow, transcends many men's present awareness.

11 Compare above, chap. 7, section vi (pp. 180–185).

12 It is not the business of the present essay to try to construct a
Christian theology in its terms; not even in part, for illustrative purposes.
Something may be gained, however, if I make it clear that in setting forth my
proposals I am not either unaware or insouciant of theological difficulties that
may seem to arise. My own conviction is that the position to which I have
come is compelled by the evidence and is intellectually valid, is nearer to the
truth than our more traditional positions—that is, is nearer to God; consequently I myself cannot but feel that the theological difficulties that seem to
arise are difficulties only in the human sense, and that a theory that has
solved them will be a truer theology than is one in which they do not yet
appear. To take the problem of authority as an example, many Christians
might at first feel that in depriving us of an essentialist concept of Christianity or of Christian faith, for instance, my view leaves us at a desperate loss in
the face of immediate present demand. 'Christian faith' has meant in the past
what historical inquiry and perceptive inference show us that it has in fact
meant in innumerable and various personal cases. But what, one may ask,
does it then mean for me today to be a Christian? If there is in principle no
fixed, essential meaning to the term, what am I to believe?

To begin with, one may point out that such a quandary is peculiar to the
personalist, existential view of Christian faith only in theory. In practice,
the same quandary confronts the essentialist: since in practice he is faced
with an ever growing multiplicity of interpretations as to what Christianity
really is. At the most oversimplified, the Roman Catholic says one thing, the
Baptist another; the liberal one thing, the fundamentalist another. Actually,
every theologian is busy elaborating one more interpretation. The older view
copes with such multiplicity by assuming that only one of these is right, or
more recently, that only one of them comes closest to being right; yet there
is in fact no way of telling which one it is. In effect, each man is free (is
forced into freedom) to choose an interpretation that seems to him best, or
even to produce a new one; which is why the essentialist is in no better case
than one who takes the historical, personalist view. In the past, each man has
perhaps tended to choose the interpretation in which he has been brought up;
but today this is hardly feasible any longer, with our broader knowledge and
our more rapid change. And in any case it would not alter the logic of the
situation. Even if men continued to follow their leaders, the leaders need
creative wisdom.

The difficulty is that both followers and leaders are being encouraged to
look for something that is perhaps not there.

The parallel to this situation in the Islamic case is today virtually exact.

The foregoing is basically a practical argument. It must and can be supplemented on the theological side. I said above that the concept 'faith' in my
analysis needed further elucidation. Let us look at it here in the light of this
particular predicament. I have rejected on principle any essentialist definition
of faith; also of Christian or of Muslim or of Buddhist faith. Yet suppose one
proffers an operational definition, such as that religious faith is what happens
to or in a man when he responds to the universe in a way that has been made
available to him by the or a cumulative tradition. This unquestionably makes
scholarship of the past possible and fruitful. Yet what of the theological im-

plications for the participant in the present? Does it liberate him beyond all guidance and throw him into blind confusion? It liberates him, certainly, but I would suggest, to theological advantage: to pursue not faith itself but truth, or God. If it is revolutionary, it is a revolution that is not a betrayal of religious values but a nearer loyalty to them.

For it is seriously misleading to suppose that the way to get religious faith is to find out what it is and then to go in pursuit of it. Rather, faith is the name that we give to the fact that one is in pursuit of something (or Someone) else.

This makes room for the theologians' conviction that that fact is at God's initiative, not one's own. The ability to recognize that there is something or Someone else worth pursuing is, they pertinently affirm, the greatest gift that man can receive. However that may be, it is a fact that man cannot choose to have faith. He discovers that he has it, when he has discovered or presumed that the transcendent is, in fact, there. Faith, therefore, is not an entity. It is, rather, the adjectival quality of a person's living in terms of transcendence.

That quality varies, of course, from person to person, situation to situation, as well as from tradition to tradition.

As for the participant, so for the observer. It is misleading to suppose that the way to study humanity's religious history is to find out first what faith is, and then to go out looking among the data for that particular thing. Rather, the scholar can report what faith has been, by observing whatever has in fact happened throughout man's development when he has been living in some modified contact with transcendence. Among his other limitations the scholar will of course always be precluded from telling what faith may become tomorrow.

The participant can learn then from historians (reporting on his own tradition or on that of others, nowadays at his free choice) what is possible (has been possible), but not what is necessary; not even what is good. The past is suggestive, but not binding. Religious authority lies not there, but is transcendent.

In the Christian case, doctrines of the sacraments, of the Church, and the like are relevant to the question of the transcendent's being truly encountered. With them it is possible to answer the problem of the moral responsibility of choice of the individual person, threatened otherwise with the existential terror of the decision that perhaps he cannot make. Once man has tasted the freedom that comes with having eaten the fruit of modern knowledge, he can no longer be cajoled by outwardly imposed authorities. His problem is indeed one that theology must answer, not evade. A theology in terms of our analysis, then, will speak to, not away from, the situation of modern man.

13 Cf. above chap. 4, note 79 and chap. 7, note 4.

14 The paragraph just above, pp. 197–198, beginning 'In the Christian case . . .' and ending '. . . not to both', was written as carefully and sincerely as possible by a Christian, about Christians, and in some ways for Christians. Considerably later it unexpectedly struck me that despite the opening eleven words the entire statement applies virtually without modification to the contemporary Islamic situation also. (One need only read 'Muslim' for 'Christian',

'Community' for 'Church', and 'thinkers' for 'theologians'. 'Inadequate' in this case would mean, of course: 'inadequate in the eyes of Muslims'.)

15 The persistence of what I call cumulative traditions has historically outlasted the 'religions' that others conceive, although the work of modern anthropologists has made it well known that the actual picture on earth today is much more confused than the conceptual one. Thus there are 'survivals' of 'parts' of 'Ancient Egyptian Religion' in villages of twentieth-century Egypt, and of ritual practices of 'the religion of ancient Greece' in villages of twentieth-century Greece. That is, the ongoing tradition that was in process in ancient Egypt is still alive for some Muslims (and of course is still changing); that from classical Greece is still alive for some Christians, and is still changing.

16 This crucial point, taken still more seriously just below as the chapter culminates, is elaborated somewhat in my *"The Faith of Other Men,* New York, (1963) 1972.

17 This perhaps odd-sounding phrase is no platitude; it is aimed not only against religious exclusivists but also against one current disruptive fashion in the social sciences whereby some writers express themselves as if they were, or ideally should be, standing outside the human situation that they describe. Modern scientific knowledge of human development is part of that development. I believe strongly (cf. above, chap. 7, note 15) that this truth must be recognized and its vast implications wrestled with. A little above, for instance (p. 201), I suggested modifying the phrasing of our 'applying' a test so as to read rather our exploratorily 'enacting' it, to take more explicit account of the difference between objective knowledge and the much more exciting matter of self-consciousness. If the present work, for example, at all achieves its objective of having the capacity of being simultaneously intelligible to, and even conceivably useable by, men of differing religious traditions and of none, then it will, so to speak, illustrate itself. It will itself be an emergence in the religio-historical process that it analyses; and it can be analysed as such. I have elsewhere written: 'Comparative religion may become the disciplined self-consciousness of man's variegated and-developing religious life' (in Eliade and Kitagawa, op. cit., p. 55). It will become so, if, and only if, we human beings can make it become so.

Index

INDEX

Istanbul, 173
'Itrat Ḥusayn, 327
iudaismos, 72, 73
Izutsu, Toshihiko, 296

Jains, 64, 257, 258, 280, 306, 307
Jalāl al-Dīn Rūmī, 149, 173
Janauschek, Leopold, 218
Jaspers, Karl, 301
Jayatilleke, K. N., 249
Jeffery, Arthur, 291, 293, 294, 295
Jerome, St., 28, 207, 210
Jesus, *see* Christ
Jezler, 267
Jñāna, 56
Jodo Shin, 147, 272
John the Baptist, 283
ju chiao, 69, 262
Judah ben Barzillai, 264
Jundt, Pierre, 311
Jupiter, 285

kāfir, 112, 296-297
Kagawa, Toyohiko, 167
kāma, 55
kami no michi, 70, 261, 263. Cf. *kami*, 254
Kant, Immanuel, 45, 240f.
Kaplan, Mordecai M., 303
karma, 56
Karmarkar, A. P., 307
Kartīr, 96-97, 176, 280, 282, 286, 288
Kato, Genchi, 254
Kätzler, J. B., 204, 205
Kaufmann, Judah ibn-Shmuel, 290
Kaufmann, Mauritz, 276
Kautsky, Karl, 78, 270
Kerényi, Karl, 246, 252
Kettlewell, John, 269
Khaṭīb al-Baghdādī, al-, *see under* Baghdādī
khālṣah, 67, 259-260

Khushwant Singh, 260
Kittel, Gerhard, 251
Knight, Harold, 302, [304-305]
Knox, John, 190
Kobbert, M., 204, 205
Koehler, Ludwig, 290
Koehler, Walther, 225
Konow, Sten, 307
Kraemer, Hendrik, 312, 328
Krishna, 128
Kristeller, Paul Oskar, 221, 222
Kromer, Marcin, 239
K'ung ("Confucius"), 69, 70, 93, 106, 122, 123, 253, 260-261, 304
Künstlinger, David, 298
kyo, 262

Lactantius Firmianus, 27-28, 204, 207, 208-210, 213, 218, 224
Lahore, 10
Lake, Kirsopp, 265
Lang, Albert, 244
Lao Tse, 69-70, 106
Latourette, Kenneth Scott, 259
latreia, latria, 214, 216
Law, William, 268
Leclerq, Jean, 218
Legge, James, 254, 256
Leonard, William Ellery, 206
Lewis, Clive Staples, 125, 302
Lidzbarski, Mark, 298
Livingstone, David, 167
Lloyd, W., 231
Locke, John, 75
logos, 158
London, 37, 63
Lord, Henry, 255
Lucas, Richard, 268
Lucretius Carus, Titus, 21-23, 28, 206, 209, [246]

Luther, Martin, 35, 128, 222-223, 224, 234, 312

Macaulay, R. S., 254
Macauliffe, Max Arthur, 255
Macdonald, Duncan Black, 273
Mackenzie, George, 232
Magdalene, Mary, 173
Magnin, E., 246
Mahāyāna, 148, 150, 168, 277, 310, 311
Maḥmūd, Sultān of Ghaznah, 257
Maitreya, 277
Majumdar, Ramesh Chandar, 257
Malalasekera, G. P., 249
Malik, Charles, 327
Mālunkyā-putta, 304
Malvezzi, Aldobrandino, 275
mandâ, 283, 285
Mandaeans, 89, 176, 283-284, 285, 293
Mani, 92-98, 100, 106, 128, 176, 279, 281, 282, 283, 284, 288, 289, 290, 293
Marcion, 285
mārga, 56, 249
Marperger, Bernard Walther, 244
Marx, Karl, 9, 89, 277
Mary Magdalene, 173
Maspero, Henri, 262
Masson-Oursel, P., 277
mata, 65, 249. Cf. *gurmat*, 260
Matthias von Zittart ("Matthias Aquensis"), 233, 238
Mattingly, Harold, 205
Mawdūdī, Abū-l-A'lá, 126, 274, 303, 320
māyā, 146
Mazdāh, 98. Cf. Ahura Mazda
Meiji Tenno, 263